Windows Script Host Programmer's Reference

Dino Esposito

Wrox Press Ltd. ®

Windows Script Host Programmer's Reference

First Published: June 1999
Reprinted: August 1999
Reprinted: April 2000

Published by Wrox Press Ltd,
Arden House, 1102 Warwick Road, Acocks Green, Birmingham B27 6BH, UK.
Printed in Canada

3 4 5 6 TRI 02 01 00

ISBN 1-861002-65-3

Trademark Acknowledgements

Credits

Author
Dino Esposito

Editors
Jon Hill
Robin Smith

Design/Layout
Mark Burdett

Index
Marilyn J. Rowland

Technical Reviewers
Andrew Clinick
Michael Corning
John Granade
Michael Harris
Eric Lippert

Cover
Andrew Guillaume
Image by Rita Ruban

About the Author

Dino Esposito is a trainer and consultant based in Rome, Italy. He specializes in web and Windows development, and works for Infomedia Communications, writing and teaching seminars on Win32 programming, VB, and ASP. He has extensive experience developing commercial Windows-based software, BackOffice solutions and system integration. Dino runs the *Cutting Edge* column in Microsoft Internet Developer, and contributes articles to several other magazines. He recently authored *Visual C++ Windows Shell Programming* for Wrox Press.

Dino married Silvia when Windows 95 was released, and they had their first son, Francesco, when Windows 98 arrived. He has no plans, though, for the upcoming release of Windows 2000. You can get in touch with Dino at desposito@infomedia.it or at http://www.programmers.net/artic/Esposito.

Acknowledgements

Let me say up front that while my name is the only one to appear on the front cover, my one-year old son Francesco contributed a lot! He broke three mice, stole a couple of mouse mats, and put countless keyboard buttons out of action. It was lucky that he concentrated his destructive attention on the keypad that I rarely use! My desktop was always surrounded by flying balloons, and the MSDN Universal Subscription CDs that he used to play Frisbee with. Again, it was lucky that he preferred the international CDs, as I have no interest in the Far East localized edition of Small Business Server!

Turning to the technical side of the matter, I was pleased to work again with Jon Hill as the lead technical editor, with Robin Smith assisting. A special, monumental "Thank You" goes to Mike Harris for his participation, programming wisdom, and strategic vision of the scripting world. The whole technical review team did a great job whose importance and dimension, as ever, you will never know! Ian Morrish and Michael Corning also contributed with ideas and suggestions, and they get another sincere "Thank You" from me.

What can I say about Andrew Clinick and Eric Lippert? They clarified a significant number of obscure points and answered many significant questions. And they did all this while they were actually writing WSH 2.0 that I was trying my best to cover. Thank you, guys!

I wrote this book in a remarkably short time, sacrificing other aspects of my daily activities. In particular, my activity at Computer Programming and Infomedia Communications was approaching zero, so thanks, therefore, to Natale Fino and Roberto Palumbo for cloning themselves in the name of WSH.

Who's ultimately responsible for this book? Certainly not me — I suspect Anthea Elston and Dominic Shakeshaft deserve that accolade.

Thanks to you all
—Dino

Table of Contents

Introduction 1
Windows Batch Files, At Last! 1
What Does this Book Cover? 2
What You Need to Use this Book 2
Conventions 4
Tell Us What You Think 5
Support 5

Chapter 1: What is the Windows Script Host? 7
Where WSH Fits in 8
A Neglected Category of Users 9
The Origins of WSH 9
Windows Batch Files 10
Batch Files from a Windows Perspective 10
WSH as a Host for Scripting Engines 11
The Windows Script Interfaces 11
Other Applications for Scripting Engines 11
Why WSH Should Interest You 12
The Features and Limitations of Windows Script Host 13
Some WSH Scenarios 13
Suites of (scriptable) Applications 14
System Administration 15
Bringing Separate Programs Together 15
Automating the Deployment of Applications 16
Writing Macros and Batch Files 16
Summary 16

Chapter 2: Windows Script Host Basics 19
The WSH Executables 19
Why Two Executables? 20
Win32 Console Applications 20

The "Hello World" Script 20
Message Boxes in JScript 21
The Echo Method 21
Solving the Problem with WSH 2.0 22
The Host's Command Line 23
Running a Script for a Predetermined Time 24
Suppressing (Some) Message Boxes 25
Changing the Default Host 25
Saving Per-user Command Line Settings 25
WSH Scripts 26
Changing the Script Extension 26
Script Execution 27
Shell Support for WSH Scripts 27
WSH Script Settings 28
A Quick COM Refresher 29
Summary 31

Chapter 3: The WSH Root Object 33
The Core Components of WSH 33
The Host Executable 34
What Does the Executable Do? 34
Windows Script Host Internals 35
The Object Model Implementation 36
A List of Objects 37
The WScript Object 38
The WScript Programmer's Reference 38
Getting Host Information 39
Adapting to the Host Executable 41
An Undocumented Property: Interactive 41
Terminating a Script 43
Specifying a Timeout 44
The WScript Object's Management Functions 46
Creating Objects 46
The Object's Local Name 47
Methods for Object Creation 48
Choosing the Right Method 48
A Word About Performance 49
Getting Objects 49
Objects from Files 50
Referencing Existing Objects 51
Releasing Objects 52
Handling Events 52

A Naming Convention for Handlers 53
Sinking Internet Explorer Events from WSH 54
Disconnecting Objects 55
The WshArguments Collection 56
The WshArguments Programmer's Reference 56
Enumerating the Command-line Arguments 57
Spaces and Long File Names 58
Summary 58

Chapter 4: The WSH Object Model 61
WSH Objects at a Glance 61
The WshShell Object 62
The WshShell Programmer's Reference 63
Showing Message Boxes 64
Popup vs. Echo 64
Using the Popup Method 64
Undocumented Features 67
Accessing the Registry 69
Backing up the Registry 70
Programming the Registry with WSH 71
Supported Types 71
Registry Paths 72
Reading from the Registry 72
Writing to the Registry 74
Deleting Entries and Values 79
Running External Programs 79
Styles of the Application Window 80
The Command Line 81
Opening Documents 82
Opening Folders 82
Working with Protocols 82
Synchronized Execution 85
Environment Variables 86
The WshShortcut Object 86
The WshShortcut Programmer's Reference 87
Creating a Shortcut 88
Resolving a Shortcut 89
Adding Icons to the Quick Launch Toolbar 90
Creating URL Shortcuts 91
The WshNetwork Object 92
The WshNetwork Programmer's Reference 92
Managing Network Connections 93
Managing Printers 94

Helper Objects 96
The WshEnvironment Object 96
The WshEnvironment Programmer's Reference 97
Enumerating Variables 98
The WshSpecialFolders Object 99
The WshSpecialFolders Programmer's Reference 99
The WshCollection Object 102
The WshCollection Programmer's Reference 102
Summary 103

Chapter 5: What's New in WSH 2.0 105
Windows Script Host 2.0 106
What Led to WSH 2.0? 106
Towards a New Script File 106
Windows Script Files 106
Running .ws Files 107
Using More Than One Scripting Language 107
Where's the Overhead? 108
XML and WSH 108
How the Elements Relate to Each Other 109
Working with .ws Files 109
XML Compliance 110
XML Run-time Options 111
Root Elements in .ws Files 112
The <job> Element 112
The <package> Element 112
Creating Global Objects 113
Identifying an Object by its ProgID 113
Identifying an Object by its CLSID 113
Referencing Type Libraries 114
The <reference> Element 114
Including External Files 115
The <script> Element 115
Other Supported Elements 118
New Features of the Object Model 119
A Sleep Method 119
New Scripting Engines 120
VBScript 5.0 121
Remote Automation 122
Regular Expressions 122
Classes 123
The With Statement 125
Run-time Code Evaluation 126

JScript 5.0 131
Remote Automation 131
Exception Handling 131
The instanceof Operator 134
Summary **135**

Chapter 6: Accessing the Windows File System **137**
The Scripting Run-time Library **137**
The File System Object 139
Manipulating Path Names 141
Copying Files and Folders 143
Moving Files and Folders 147
File and Folder Creation 148
Deleting Files and Folders 149
Checking the Existence of Drives, Folders and Files 150
Getting Objects Representing File System Entities 151
The Drive Object 151
Calculating Disk Space 152
Working with Very Large Disks 153
The Folder Object 153
Operations on Folders 156
Changing the Folder's Attributes 157
The Folders Collection 157
The File Object 158
Operations on Files 159
Changing the File's Attributes 160
The Files Collection 160
The TextStream Object 161
The File Pointer 163
Writing to a File 163
The Dictionary 164
A Word about Performance 165
Filtering the Files Collection 165
Does the File Match the Pattern? 166
Creating a Dictionary 167
Beyond the File System Objects **169**
Getting a Folder Object 169
The Shell's Folder Object 171
Enumerating the Content of a Special Folder 172
Copying and Moving Files 173
Installation Scripts **175**
Replacing Files in Use 175
Moving Files Until Reboot 176

The SRL vs. Shell Automation Objects 177
Summary 178

Chapter 7: Writing Reusable WSH Code 181

The WSH Handbook for Reusable Code 182
- An Example: Changing Folder View Properties 183
  - The Programming Interface 184
  - The Tools we Need 185

Writing General-Purpose VBScript Functions 186
- Identifying the Icon for the Folder 187
- Creating a desktop.ini File 187
- Get/Set Functions for Folder Options 188
  - Hiding Extensions for Known File Types 189
  - Toggling the 'Map Drive' Button 190
  - Adding an Attributes Column 190
- Some Points to Consider 191
  - Public and Private 191
  - Custom Icons in Windows 9x and Windows 2000 191
  - The ShowInfoTip Option 191
- A Full Demonstration using VBScript 5.0 192
  - A Rather Similar JScript Demonstration 193
- A Full Demonstration using WSH 2.0 194

Reusability Through Classes 195
- Writing VBScript Classes 195
  - The FolderOption VBScript Class 196
- A WSH 1.0 Demonstration 196
- A WSH 2.0 Demonstration 197
- Writing JScript Classes 198

Pros and Cons 198

COM Objects with Scripting Languages 199
- Script-based COM Objects 200
  - A Similar Case 200
  - The Scripting Runtime Engine 200
  - Creating a Windows Script Component 200
  - A Look at the Syntax 204
  - Implementing the Component 208
  - Generating a Type Library 212
  - Further Reading 214

Summary 214

Chapter 8: Dialog Boxes and the User Interface 217

A Better Input Box 217
A WSC Component for InputBox 218
Improving InputBox 219
Using the InputBox Object 220
Entering Multi-line Text 222
Advanced Features of InputBox 223
Putting it All Together 227
Towards More Structured Dialogs 231

Complex HTML-based Dialogs 231
A Flashback to Win32 232
Looking at Visual Basic Forms 232
A Flashback to Internet Explorer 233
The Definitive Solution 235
The Programming Interface of the DialogBox Object 235
Using the DialogBox Component 237
A Demonstration Dialog 238
Scripting Inside the Page 240
Displaying Help Text 241
Full Access to the Page 241
Implementation Details 242
Displaying the Form 244
Returning the Value 247
DHTML Events 247

Summary 248

Chapter 9: A WSH Component Gallery 251

Our List of WSH Components 252

Browsing for Files 252
Using the Browse Object 254
Multiple File Selection 255
Exploring for Files and Folders 257

A Whiteboard Component 259
A Modeless Dialog Component 260
The Programming Interface 260

Running Processes **267**
The List of Processes 270
Walking the List of Processes 271
Is This Process Running? 272
The Problem of Version Numbers 275
Summary **278**

Chapter 10: Windows Script Host Tidbits **281**
Creating Documents Dynamically **282**
What You Need to Get Started 282
Getting the Invoice Number 284
A Dialog Box for Data Entry 285
Preparing a Word Document 288
Using Document Bookmarks 288
Initializing the Word Object Model 289
Filling Out the Document 290
Saving the Document 290
Recording the Invoice 291
Filling Out the Record 291
Printing the Document 291
Documents as Folder Items 291
Sending the Invoice Through E-mail 293
The CDO for NT Server 294
A Very Simple COM Object for E-mail 294
Using Outlook to Send E-mail 294
Shell Facilities for WSH Scripts **296**
WS, VBS and JS in the New Menu 296
The New Menu 297
Providing a Template File 297
Registering a New File Type 297
Passing Arguments to Script Files 299
Running a Script File 299
Using the Command Line 300
Shell Drag-and-drop 301
Exploiting WSH Drag-and-drop 302
Towards a WSH IDE 303
Encoding WSH Scripts **304**
The Microsoft Script Encoder 304
How Encoding Works 305
Running Encoded Scripts 305
Tweaking the Registry for Encoded Scripts 305
Summary **309**

Appendix A: VBScript Reference 311

Array Handling 311
Assignments 312
Constants 312
Control Flow 315
Functions 317
Variable Declarations 323
Error Handling 323
Input/Output 323
Procedures 326
Other Keywords 326
Visual Basic Run-time Error Codes 327

Appendix B: JScript Reference 333

Values 333
Variables 334
Assignment Operators 334
Equality Operators 335
Other Operators 335
String Operators 336
Comments 336
Input/Output 336
alert 336
confirm 336
prompt 337
Control Flow 337
Conditional Statements 337
Loop Statements 338
Error Handling Statements 340
Built-in Functions 340
Built-in Objects 341
ActiveXObject Object 341
Array Object 341
Boolean Object 342
Date Object 343
Enumerator Object 345
Error Object 345
Function Object 345
Arguments Object 346
Math Object 346
Number Object 347
RegularExpression Object 348

RegExp Object 348
String Object 349
VBArray Object 351
Reserved Words 352

Index 355

Introduction

Welcome to *Windows Script Host Programmer's Reference*. The Windows Script Host (WSH) is a Win32 application that allows scripts to be run within the Windows environment. The possibilities this offers are numerous, and with this book you'll learn what the Windows Script Host can do, discover how to get the most out of its object model, and have a reference that you can come back to later on. You'll discover how to write your own objects that further enrich the capabilities of the environment, and find out about the latest developments that enable you to use XML as a tool for making your code reusable.

Windows Batch Files, At Last!

Windows owes its success to a number of factors, its graphical environment being one of the most significant. However, of equal importance are the user-friendly interface and the working metaphor that is a distant relation of the 'black-screen-of-death' you find on some other operating systems. In front of a black screen — on a Unix machine, for example — you type in complex commands with an endless sequence of switches, options and arguments, and have the system faithfully follow your instructions. Achieving the same result in Windows is often easier and is far more pleasant.

When it comes to automating some repetitive and boring tasks, however, Windows has had some significant limitations: it hasn't provided powerful command-line tools, and it hasn't made advanced features available to the user-administrator. Even MS-DOS provided a batch language that was suitable for controlling at least the range of applications you could develop on top of it.

These limitations have been around since the inception of Windows, and were only finally resolved with Windows 98. Starting with that version, and to be continued in Windows 2000, *any* Windows user — not just programmers — can use the Windows Script Host to write simple (and not-so-simple) scripts to perform some kind of batch processing. This scripting environment is fully COM-aware, and based on well-known and widely used scripting languages: VBScript and JScript.

What Does this Book Cover?

In this book, I shall begin by explaining the history of the Windows Script Host with a view to helping you understand where it 'fits' in the Windows hierarchy. I will then describe the different ways of using WSH, and provide full coverage of the facilities it offers by default. After that, I'll talk about some developments in scripting language technologies that affect what and how easily things can be done using WSH.

Then, in the last third of the book, I'll demonstrate how WSH script code can perform quite complex duties by using standard Windows objects and some custom objects that I've created. Samples of this will include administrative tasks and controlling the behavior of other applications on your machine that expose object models. Specifically, then, this book will:

- Provide annotated and accurate documentation for all the objects that form the Windows Script Host object model
- Demonstrate how to use the objects in the WSH object model and the applications to which they can be put
- Describe the latest versions (5.0) of VBScript and JScript, and the newly released version 2.0 of WSH
- Present a quick tutorial on Windows Script Components, a new way of writing COM objects with script code
- Show how to use any COM object you may have on your machine from within the Windows Script Host
- Give you a small library of versatile custom script components that I've developed, and explain how and why you might want to create your own

Each aspect of the Windows Script Host will be clearly explained with the help of numerous examples written using either VBScript or JScript. When discussing the creation of new objects, I'll make occasional use of Visual Basic. If you want to dissect the source code of my custom objects that's available from the Wrox web site, you'll need to understand Visual Basic and sometimes Visual C++ and ATL as well.

The examples I will present are designed to give you some ideas of ways in which WSH can be used in everyday tasks, but there are so many diverse application to which WSH can be put that I can really only scratch the surface. I hope, though, that my examples will give you the ideas and knowledge necessary to use WSH for *your* particular requirements.

What You Need to Use this Book

It goes almost without saying that in order to run the code contained in this book you need a PC running Windows 95, Windows 98 or Windows NT 4.0. The code has also been tested on a machine running the Beta 3 version of Windows 2000, and we have no reason to believe that it won't work on the release version of this product as well.

On machines running Windows 98 or above, being able to use WSH is just a matter of deciding to install it, and it's worth making sure that it has been set up on your machine before you begin. Head for the Windows Setup tab of the Add/Remove Programs Control Panel, and open the Accessories dialog:

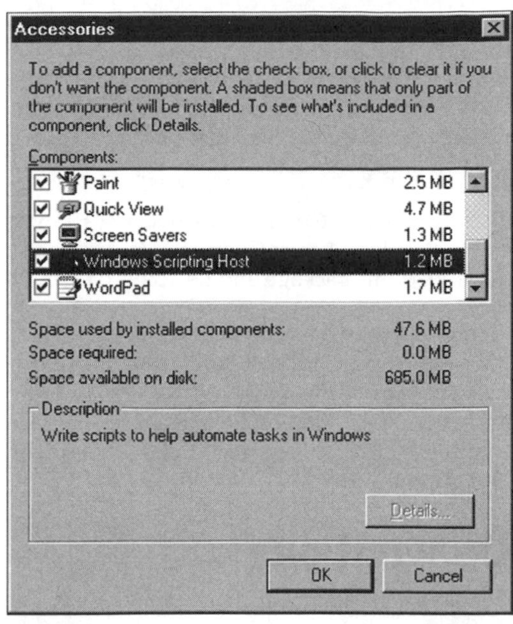

If you're using Windows 95 or Windows NT 4.0, however, you will need to download Windows Script Host from Microsoft at http://msdn.microsoft.com/scripting, and at this point another consideration emerges.

Microsoft has announced that it will release version 2.0 of WSH with Windows 2000, but in the meantime it has made a public beta version of WSH 2.0 available from its web site. I will examine the new facilities offered by this product at various (well-marked) points in the book, and if you want to experiment with them, you will need to download it — even if you're using Windows 98.

Of course, in terms of distributing your script code to clients, it's more likely at this point that they'll be using version 1.0 rather than 2.0, and you should certainly bear that in mind. Version 1.0 of WSH is what ships with Windows 98, and it's also available for Windows 95 and Windows NT 4.0. In summary, then, the situation is as follows:

	WSH 1.0	**WSH 2.0**
Windows 95	Available for download	Available for download
Windows NT 4.0	Available for download	Available for download
Windows 98	Available by default	Available for download
Windows 2000	N/A	Available by default

Also available for download are documentation and numerous sample scripts for both versions of WSH, and I heartily recommend getting hold of as much of this kind of information as you can.

The next things you need to use this book successfully are the latest versions (5.0) of the VBScript and JScript scripting engines. These shipped with the release version of Internet Explorer 5.0, so if you have that product, there is no further action you need to take. If you're tied to using version 4.0 of IE, you can download the version 5.0 scripting engines as a separate package, again from the Microsoft Windows Script Technologies web site.

Thirdly, Chapter 6 of the book discusses another new Microsoft scripting technology called Windows Script Components, and to use the examples there you'll need to download this package and its accompanying Wizard, again from the same location.

Finally, some of the code in the later chapters uses some custom components that I have developed, and these are available for download along with the rest of the source code for the book from the Wrox Press web site at http://www.wrox.com. As your last act before embarking on the pages ahead, I recommend that you run the executable (written for WSH, of course!) that will install and register all the necessary components on your machine.

Conventions

We have used a number of different styles of text and layout in the book to help differentiate between the different kinds of information. Here are examples of the styles we use, and an explanation of what they mean:

Advice, hints, and background information comes in this type of font.

Important pieces of information come in boxes like this.

Important Words are in a bold type font.

Words that appear on the screen in menus, like File or Window, are in a similar font to the one that you see on screen

Keys that you press on the keyboard, like *Ctrl* and *Enter*, are in italics.

Code comes in a number of different styles. If it's something we're talking about in the text — when we're discussing a `For...Next` loop, for example — it's in a fixed-width font. If it's a block of code from a program, then it's also in a gray box:

```
Select Case btnCode
   Case vbNo
      MsgBox "Clicked No"
   Case vbYes
      MsgBox "Clicked Yes"
   Case -1
     MsgBox "Timed Out"
End Select
```

Sometimes you'll see code in a mixture of styles, like this:

```
Select Case btnCode
   Case vbNo
      MsgBox "Clicked No"
   Case vbYes, -1                    ' Handle both Yes and timeout
      MsgBox "Clicked Yes"
End Select
```

The code with a white background is something that we've already looked at and don't wish to examine further.

These formats are designed to make sure that you know exactly what you're looking at. We hope they make life easier.

Tell Us What You Think

We've worked hard on this book to make it enjoyable and useful. Our best reward would be to hear from you that you liked it and that it was worth the money you paid for it. We've done our best to try to understand and match your expectations.

Please let us know what you think about it. Tell us what you liked best and what we could have done better. If you think this is just a marketing gimmick, then test us out — drop us a line! We'll answer, and we'll take whatever you say on board for future editions. The easiest way is to use e-mail: feedback@wrox.com

You can also find more details about Wrox Press on our web site. There you'll find the code from our latest books, sneak previews of forthcoming titles, and information about the authors and the editors. You can order Wrox titles directly from the site, or find out where your nearest local bookstore with Wrox titles is located. The address of our site is: http://www.wrox.com

Support

We've made every effort to make sure there are no errors in the text or the code. However, to err is human and as such we recognize the need to keep you, the reader, informed of any mistakes as they're spotted and corrected. The web site acts as a focus for providing the following information and support:

- Errata sheets
- Information about current and forthcoming titles
- Sample chapters
- Source code downloads
- An e-mail newsletter
- Developer's Journal subscription
- Articles and opinion on related topics

Errata sheets are available for all our books — please download them, or take part in the continuous improvement of our products and upload a 'fix' or a pointer to the solution.

Update

Since Dino wrote this book, Microsoft have released a newer beta version of the Script Host, so he's written an article which is up on the XML and Scripting section of http://www.wrox.com, which covers the new features which they have introduced.

1

What is the Windows Script Host?

The **Windows Script Host** (**WSH**) is a system-wide environment whose purpose is to help with the automation of tasks throughout 32-bit versions of the Windows operating system. It comes as a part of Windows 98 (and Windows 2000) by default, and it's also available as a separate component for Windows 95 and Windows NT 4.0.

> *If you're not sure that Windows Script Host is installed on your machine, or you want to discover how to get hold of the very latest versions of WSH and related technologies, take a look at the section of the Introduction entitled* What You Need to Use this Book.

Windows Script Host endows Windows with a simple but powerful tool for **batch processing**. It goes far beyond the batch (`.bat`) files you find in MS-DOS, but the assertion that the two are equivalent makes sense in general terms — it's certainly reasonable to say that in the same way `.bat` files are able to exploit the features of MS-DOS, Windows Script Host makes it possible to exploit the features of Windows. As Windows is the richer platform, WSH is the richer environment, and it can deal with the platform at all levels.

Before we start delving into code, however, I want to give you a little history, and a feel for the kinds of uses to which WSH can be put. In this first chapter, I'm going to cover:

- The ideas behind Windows Script Host, and the requirements that led to its creation
- What you need to know to use WSH
- Why WSH is useful
- Situations in which you should consider using WSH
- Some examples of the problems WSH addresses and helps to solve

Where WSH Fits in

I first came across Windows Script Host while looking at some early documentation about the features of what was then called Windows NT 5.0 (it's now called Windows 2000). Shortly afterwards, I ran into a Word document that described a mysterious-sounding object model, but I was still a long way from grasping the real scope of what that meant. Finally, when it became available, I downloaded the Windows 95 version of WSH, and started working with it.

The strongest impression I have about WSH is that it fills a hole. Windows Script Host is the missing link that makes the advanced features of Windows available to everyone. Previously, the needs of two contrasting kinds of Windows user had been fulfilled: those of the end user, and those of the low-level programmer. All the high-level facilities were for the former, and all the intricacies of a largely C-oriented API (Application Programming Interface) were reserved for the latter.

Windows did not cater well for people with needs in between those of the end user and the programmer, and so this is where most of its limitations were situated — characters like administrators and expert users were poorly served. This middle ground needed supporting by macro code, scripts, and automated means of accomplishing things quickly and repeatedly. There's an entire class of activities that can't be performed with the pure visual metaphor, but which by the same token shouldn't require you to write and compile a whole application.

Windows Script Host is a modern engine for batch processing that's easily capable of using the surrounding graphical infrastructure. To form a quick, but precise, idea of where WSH fits in the Windows jigsaw, have a look at the following figure:

This diagram represents the various layers of the overall Windows architecture. At the topmost level, the Windows shell provides an interactive interface based on the direct use of input devices such as the keyboard and the mouse. Everything that occurs at the shell level requires manual intervention from users that are not necessarily skilled.

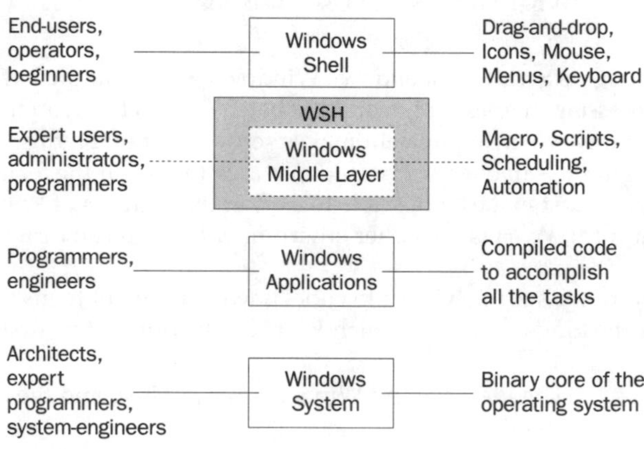

Before the introduction of WSH the next layer was that of the Windows applications — the third layer in the diagram. This includes all the task-specific programs that meet clear demands with a range of functionality. Writing applications requires advanced skills, regardless of which language or tool is chosen to do it.

The lowest layer of all, the Windows system layer, comprises the core system libraries that are the realm of expert engineers and developers.

The *real* Windows middle layer, with its own set of users and applications, and represented by the second box in the figure above, was missing until WSH came along.

A Neglected Category of Users

The figure above identifies the class of users and applications that the Windows Script Host was developed to serve. Into this category fall expert users, administrators and even programmers. The role of tools at this level is to provide an infrastructure that allows these users to write small, quick programs that create better ways of executing common tasks that are:

- Too specific and context-related to be addressed at the operating system level and hence part of the overall system design, or
- Too modest, too simple and sometimes too volatile to merit any investment in time for the planning and development of a custom application

The tasks that this middle layer should take care of simply can't be classified once and for all in a way that applies to all its potential users. One person may need to manipulate the registry, while another might dream of a tool to make Microsoft Word automatically print documents created on the fly. Another user may want a quick-and-dirty way to query a database, put the records in a spreadsheet, do some calculations and print out the results.

Switching networked printers on and off, sending e-mail messages automatically and executing file management operations without dropping down to the MS-DOS (command) prompt are all tasks that fit in this phantom Windows level. Until now however, all the users with such needs have been neglected, if not forgotten about completely!

The Origins of WSH

A complete understanding of the Windows Script Host must include an appreciation of its foundations, and for that we can return once again to the analogy with good old MS-DOS batch files. Wouldn't it be nice, went the argument, if you could open a MS-DOS (command) prompt and ask it to do more exciting things than copying from directory to directory, listing files and running programs?

With the introduction of Windows 95, the platform was enriched with countless items that attempt to present the system as a 'desktop', with all the tools and objects you may need to use in that context. You can manage these objects manually (using menus and drag-and-drop) and programmatically (from binary modules). However, the available programming environments don't all provide the same ease-of-use when it comes to managing things like shortcuts and the system registry. Think of what you can do (and what you cannot do), for example, with Visual Basic on the one hand and Visual C++ on the other.

While a compiled program will always offer superior power, it's often the case that you don't need it all. The extra potential for control can add unnecessary complexity, especially when all you want to accomplish is a logically simple and intuitive task. To create a shortcut, for example, or to enter a few lines in the registry, writing a compiled application is frankly overkill, but until now there haven't been many other options. What has been missing in Windows is a tool that lets you access *everything* in the system, without the need to resort to writing C++ or Visual Basic programs; a tool so simple that you can use Notepad to prepare the code, and then run it just by double clicking on a icon or typing its name at a command prompt.

Windows Batch Files

The Windows user interface is full of intuitive, high-level elements that have very little to do with the intricacies of file system tables and filenames. The idea of having a simple language that works at the level of the shell, pulling everything together, doesn't really correspond with this richness of graphical and 'metaphorical' objects.

MS-DOS, on the other hand, *does* support a simple language for arranging batch procedures that can execute tasks repeatedly and sequentially. These procedures are coded within `.bat` (or `.cmd`) files, which are also fully supported in Windows. They are considered to be a type of executable, and you can use them within a MS-DOS window. You might have thought, then, that Windows already had everything it needed to carry out task automation. Unfortunately, things don't quite turn out that way.

The MS-DOS batch file approach comes with several disadvantages. First and foremost, a `.bat` file may only contain simple sequences of MS-DOS commands. Looping is a tricky business, and branches and conditional statements can be used only in a simple manner. Dialogs and message boxes are not supported, and there's no notion of Windows-specific elements.

The problem is not only that some things are not possible with batch files (the Visual Studio build system is proof of how complicated and powerful a batch file can be), but that even when things *can* be done, they are so difficult to maintain, understand and debug that they are a real pain to use. WSH brings concepts like variables, subroutines and loops to the party, making the whole development process much more bearable.

Windows Script Host provides a coherent response to the need for a powerful and technologically up-to-date tool for automating tasks throughout the Windows shell. In other words, WSH was designed as a central console for executing any batch or administrative operation. It is capable of working on native Windows elements, and of providing more advanced programming logic including loops, conditional statements, variables, and a few other things as well.

Batch Files from a Windows Perspective

The structural limitations of MS-DOS batch files become more evident when you try to use them with Windows, because you're dealing with a far richer environment. The Windows counterpart of batch files needs to:

- Support a real, structured programming language
- Be able to access Windows-specific artifacts (the registry, shortcuts, folders, the recycle bin, etc.)
- Provide a way to communicate with users graphically
- Be able to communicate with other programs and components
- Provide programmatic access to a network
- Provide programmatic access to resources such as printers, faxes, e-mail and so on

In response to these needs, the programming languages used by WSH are modern scripting languages, and Windows resources are accessed through the methods and properties of objects that can be used from script code.

WSH as a Host for Scripting Engines

By default, Windows Script Host is compatible with scripts written in VBScript (`.vbs` files) and JScript (`.js` files), but it's possible to use other scripting languages too, as I'll be explaining in this section. One of the advantages this brings is that by its nature, almost all the users that may need to be directly involved in WSH development will already be fluent in at least one scripting language, so at least that aspect of learning to use it is unlikely to cause a problem.

Better still, being fluent with a scripting language is probably the *only* prerequisite for getting started with WSH, as the very act of using script should have given you the minimal knowledge you need about using ActiveX objects from script code, the other basic technique with which you need to be acquainted.

The Windows Script Interfaces

WSH is actually a fairly simple Win32 application that communicates with different scripting engines using the **Windows Script Interfaces**. In other words, it is capable of hosting library modules that take care of processing script files on its behalf. Scripting engines for VBScript and JScript are provided when WSH is installed.

Microsoft first introduced the Windows Script specification (it was then called **ActiveX Scripting**) in Internet Explorer 3.0, to allow independent software vendors (ISVs) to build scripting engines that would be hosted by the browser. The success of this policy has been such that third party engines now exist for (among others) Rexx, Python and Perl.

> *If you're interested in getting hold of a Perl (Practical Extraction and Report Language) scripting engine, look at* http://www.activestate.com/ActivePerl *or* http://www.mks.com.

When the host application (in our case, WSH) is required to execute some script code, it will use methods of the Windows Script Interfaces in order to instruct the appropriate scripting engine to do the actual processing. From the host's point of view, as long as an engine exists for the language in which the script is written, it isn't important what that language is.

Other Applications for Scripting Engines

The demand for instruments capable of automating the behavior of a collection of items has been around for a long time. It's one of the reasons for the success of tools like Visual Basic, while the introduction of the Visual Basic for Applications (VBA) programming language made Microsoft Office 97 even more successful. The point is that with only a few lines of code, the user is allowed to automate tasks using all the logic they need.

> *Because of this previous success, Office 2000 extends VBA support to all the components of the suite. Like Word and Excel, the new versions of Microsoft Outlook and Microsoft FrontPage will include the VBA IDE (Integrated Development Environment).*

Today's complex applications need a programming engine that allows their users to automate tasks and add new macro code to the native set of functionality. Win32 applications have two options in this area:

- Licensing the full VBA SDK from Microsoft
- Supporting the Windows Script Interfaces

The first solution is the more expensive, but it's also much more powerful. It uses the VBA language and provides a number of development tools, including an IDE, a debugger and an editor. The second, on which WSH is based, is free of charge, uses simpler languages such as VBScript or JScript, and has no accessory development tools other than the Microsoft Script Debugger.

> *When it comes to deciding which technology to employ in order to make your application scriptable, you shouldn't consider Windows Script and VBA as rivals, but as two levels of the same solution.*
>
> *To help application developers make their products scriptable, Microsoft has made available the* ***Script Control*** *as a free download from its Windows Script Technologies home page at* http://msdn.microsoft.com/scripting. *This is an ActiveX control without a user interface that (like WSH) links to the scripting engines you have installed and asks them to run script code on its behalf.*

Why WSH Should Interest You

Let's start to get down to specifics. The Windows Script Host has the potential to be of interest to a wide range of people working with computers. Seasoned and skilled users may use it to automate tasks involved with the programs they use daily — if a program exposes an object model, WSH makes it available. A large number of people are capable of working with scripting languages like VBScript or JScript, and so exactly the same number are capable of exploiting WSH for their own work.

Programmers can use WSH to test components, or to create a quick utility for recompiling, renaming and even rebuilding their projects that surpasses the capabilities of the specific development environment they use. I once searched desperately for something of this ilk, and eventually resorted to writing a little `.exe`!

There are countless possible ways of using Windows Script Host, as long as you know what its strengths and limitations are, and how to work with them. Most of these ways are going to be 'personal' to a particular user. You may want to exploit WSH to do something that doesn't sound exciting or useful to me, and vice versa. Put another way, WSH can be valuable to some extent to *everyone* who uses a Windows-based computer.

The Features and Limitations of Windows Script Host

From everything I've said so far in this chapter, you should now have a pretty good idea of what the characteristics of the WSH environment are, and why it was created that way. In summary:

- It's a script-based environment that can be called from Windows or the MS-DOS (command) prompt
- It supports any scripting language for which an engine compatible with the Windows Script specification exists
- It is available on 32-bit Windows platforms and is natively integrated into Windows 98 and Windows 2000
- It lets you access any object that supports Automation (formerly known as OLE Automation), anywhere in the system

As you may know, not all of the functionality of Windows is exposed through Automation interfaces — in fact, only a small portion of it is available in this way. To remedy this, WSH itself has an object model that encapsulates some Windows functionality and exposes it through Automation, and we'll be examining this over the next couple of chapters. Furthermore, WSH can access custom objects created with any COM-enabled development tool, including Visual Basic and Visual C++.

Despite this flexibility, however, there are still a few areas in which WSH isn't (or hasn't been) as helpful as it could be. Its object model and native facilities provide minimal support for things such as:

- Dialogs and user interface. There's no built-in way to create and display complex dialog boxes, so you have to rely on the tools made available by VBScript (such as `InputBox()`) or popup messages.
- Script code reusability. Before the advent of WSH 2.0, writing reusable code and mixing scripting languages was difficult or impossible to do.
- Management and execution of WSH scripts from the Windows GUI. `.vbs` and `.js` files are poorly served by drag-and-drop, context menu commands and property pages.

Throughout this book I'll be explaining in detail what WSH has to offer, how to work around its limitations, and how to extend its functionality.

Some WSH Scenarios

WSH programming increases the range of 'doable things' on the Windows platform. By this strange phrase, I'm referring to operations that are not provided natively by any program or system module, but which nevertheless are needed by some user. In most cases, these things have to do with automation, batch processing, or very tiny programs that serve to bind together the behavior of multiple applications.

The WSH programs you write can be considered as brand new, individual pieces of functionality. Of course, WSH is not magic, and everything you can do with it must also be possible by some other means. My point is that by writing scripts, you're providing a way of performing tasks that the system designers have not catered for in an atomic fashion.

Here are a few common scenarios in which WSH scripts may be of considerable help:

- Suites of (scriptable) applications
- System administration
- Bringing separate programs together
- Automating the deployment of applications, add-ons, and packages
- Writing macros and batch files

Suites of (scriptable) Applications

Microsoft Office is the typical example of a suite of applications. It is composed of a number of different programs with different missions, but they are all scriptable, and they all host a VBA engine to allow internal script processing. The thread that links all these different programs together from our point of view is that they all are Automation servers that expose an object model that can be scripted from the *outside*, using WSH.

If you're creating a product that is a collection of separate programs, then by making the programs scriptable, you're helping your users to write additional scripts that add new functionality. They could write their own code to implement an unsupported feature or facilitate a non-standard interaction.

> *Although hosting a VBA engine is mentioned in the above discussion, this is not directly relevant to the operation of WSH. You can control the behavior of an application using WSH only if it exposes an object model that's visible from the* outside. *In practice, however, it would be unusual for an application hosting VBA and supporting an object model not to make that same model available to external callers.*

Non-Automation Applications

An interesting case arises when the applications involved *don't* expose an object model. You can still make them available to and exploitable from WSH by writing and distributing (possibly as an add-on) an additional COM object that works as a proxy:

In the figure, the COM object communicates with the Windows Script Host through Automation, but uses other techniques under the hood to drive the applications (such as Windows messages or API calls).

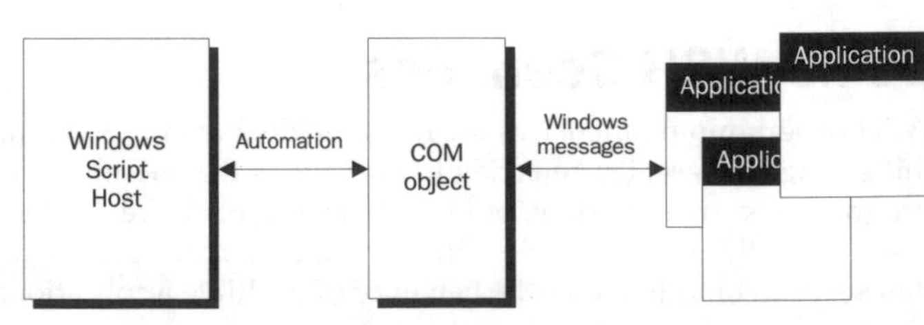

System Administration

Administrators are the people that have suffered most from the lack of a tool like WSH. They often need to edit the registry, manage policies, assign rights, monitor logged-on users, schedule tasks, and so forth. The administrator, however, is not a typical Windows 9x user, and this might have been an unconscious reason for Microsoft underestimating the importance of such a tool. Under Windows NT, a few specialized command-line routines, as well as a bunch of `.bat` files, allowed system administrators to do their jobs reasonably effectively.

The difference with WSH is the ease with which these operations can be performed. For example, let's consider the task of taking the rights to run the Registry Editor away from a user's account. This is an effect that's tied to the value of a certain registry key. Ultimately, modifying rights invariably means writing a value somewhere in the registry, and using a WSH script makes what you're doing much clearer than the alternative, which is to use a cryptic `.reg` file. I'll discuss this in detail in Chapter 4.

In addition, the WSH object model provides administrators with built-in collections of printers and network connections. It also allows access to **ADSI** (the Active Directory Service Interfaces), which makes available a rich object model for accessing objects across the network.

> *For an introduction to ADSI programming, have a look at* ADSI ASP Programmer's Reference *(Wrox Press, 1-861001-69-X).*

Bringing Separate Programs Together

Another situation in which WSH scripts can be valuable is when you need to arrange small applications that are simply a sequence of high-level operations involving different programs. Some people refer to this as the "WSH is glue" scenario. For example, a company may wish to:

1. Obtain customer information interactively
2. Prepare a Word document from a template and embed this information into it
3. Store the information into an Access database for reference
4. Print a copy of the information
5. Send an e-mail of the customer's details to the accounting department

This multi-stage procedure *could* be achieved using a custom Wizard built within Microsoft Word by using the VBA editor. Alternatively, it could be done using a function in a task-specific application, not to mention that it could even be performed manually! Probably the most direct way to accomplish it, however, is through WSH, using Automation to drive Word, to control Access, to send e-mails and so on. I'll present a demonstration of this in Chapter 10.

Automating the Deployment of Applications

Increasingly, we're moving towards multi-layered applications composed of modules that interact, integrate and combine to provide the overall behavior of the application. The core binaries are extended by a number of packages, add-ons, extensions, snap-ins, scripts, and almost anything else you can think of. In general, all of these things need some kind of installation and setup to be performed; classic examples of this state of affairs are **Microsoft Transaction Server** (MTS) packages.

The deployment of an MTS-based application requires you to register the various COM objects involved through specific containers called **packages**. You can arrange an 'ordinary' setup, using the classic installation tools, or you can try to come up with quicker solutions that are based on the native MTS administration tools being driven by a modest piece of VBScript or JScript code.

> *This technique is also demonstrated in the Microsoft Platform SDK. Check out the contents of the* `SAMPLES\COM\SERVICES\transaction\bank_administration` *folder.*

The MTS scenario is just one of the hottest around today; the same principle applies to anything that requires the creation of folder structures, the addition of a few entries to the registry, or a few COM calls in order to be properly installed and set to work. These are extremely tedious and time-consuming tasks if done by hand; WSH scripts are definitely a quick and powerful way to deploy applications.

Writing Macros and Batch Files

WSH is the candidate to replace MS-DOS batch files, and it has a number of significant features that justify this role. However, it would be no good if there were things that `.bat` files could do but WSH could not, and so it must provide at least the same features when it comes to running executables, manipulating files, making backups and so forth. Happily, moving to WSH doesn't limit your programming power in any way, as you'll discover in the chapters to come.

Summary

In this chapter, I have explained why you could be using WSH in the near future. The main reason for this is simply that it increases the range of things you can do across the system, but additional factors include:

- It is a superset of the old MS-DOS batch files
- It lets you use a high-level language (typically VBScript or JScript) for writing scripts
- It provides full support for COM, which means that you can access any existing Automation object, and create your own as well
- It gives you the possibility of controlling *everything* in the system from script code by means of additional COM components

Exactly how to use WSH to achieve the benefits I have outlined will begin to become clear starting with the next chapter, where I'll examine the nature of the host application itself.

2

Windows Script Host Basics

You've read that WSH is a Win32 application that hosts a scripting engine to process external script files. You've also discovered that it exposes its own object model to make some features of Windows available to these scripts. However, before dealing with the specifics of the WSH object model, which we'll begin to do in the next chapter, there are a few things to clarify and explore in more detail.

To start off with, I'll take a look at the executables that form the Windows Script Host and discuss their command line options. Then I'll move on to analyze some features of the script files run by WSH, the scripting engines that actually do the job of running them, and the relationship between WSH and the Component Object Model. Along the way, I'll be providing the ubiquitous "Hello World" application that will officially get you started with WSH programming.

The WSH Executables

The Windows Script Host itself is actually provided in *two* modules that have similar functionality, called `cscript.exe` and `wscript.exe`. Once you've installed WSH, you will find both of them in the `Windows` directory hierarchy. `cscript.exe` is a Win32 console application that runs inside a MS-DOS box and is stored in the `Command` subdirectory of `Windows`. `wscript.exe`, on the other hand, is targeted squarely at Windows itself. As you might have guessed, the "c" in the name stands for "console", while the "w" stands for "Windows".

> *To be precise, there's also a third module called* `wshom.ocx` *that contains a large part of the WSH object model. I'll say more about this in Chapters 3 and 4.*

In terms of their behavior, there are no significant differences between `cscript.exe` and `wscript.exe`. It's possible to run the former from the Windows GUI, and the latter from a console window. They can be considered as platform-specific implementations of the same core functionality.

Why Two Executables?

Given what I've said so far, a reasonable question to ask is, "Why does WSH need to have two executables?" To be honest, there doesn't seem to be any compelling reason for it. Instead, consider the situation as a kindly act on the part of Microsoft: there are two flavors of the same engine and no need for them, I suppose, to mix the Windows and console code.

Functionally speaking, `cscript.exe` and `wscript.exe` are nearly identical. The differences that exist are due to their different structure. `cscript.exe` is *intended* to work in an MS-DOS window, so its output (or 'echo') goes straight to the standard output channel. `wscript.exe`, on the other hand, has a different output engine that uses graphical message boxes — I'll have more to say about this later on.

You can execute your scripts with either engine and obtain the same results in the majority of cases. However, you might want to take advantage of the limited GUI capability of `wscript.exe` if you're working from the Windows shell, while, `cscript.exe` is probably a more natural choice if you decide to execute your script from the command prompt.

Win32 Console Applications

A Win32 console application is a character-mode program that doesn't generally produce its output using windows and controls. Instead, it defaults to taking input from (and sending output to) the standard I/O devices. Asking such an application to display a message results in that message being written in the console window, below the command prompt.

WSH console applications are an evolution of batch-mode, silent, non-graphical MS-DOS programs, but you should always remember that they *are* Win32 modules, so they can access any Windows feature if you need them to do so.

The "Hello World" Script

To open the floodgates of WSH programming, let's see what a "Hello World" script looks like. This also gives us an opportunity to see the slight differences between `cscript.exe` and `wscript.exe` in practice, and how the various command-line switches they support work.

The next listing contains a trivially simple VBScript program that defines a couple of variables and passes them to the `MsgBox()` function for display:

```
' HelloWorld.vbs

Dim strText1                    ' VBScript variables have no explicit type
Dim strText2

strText1 = "Hello, world!"
strText2 = "I'm the Windows Script Host."

MsgBox strText1 & vbCrLf & strText2
```

`MsgBox()` is a VBScript-specific function that displays a modal window. Save this code to a file called `HelloWorld.vbs` and double-click the icon in Explorer to execute it. The dialog opposite will appear:

However, attempting to rewrite the same piece of trivial code to use JScript presents us with our first problem: `MsgBox()` has no counterpart in JScript!

Message Boxes in JScript

Because the JScript language doesn't have a function for displaying dialog boxes, we have to look elsewhere for a solution. Conveniently, the WSH object model includes an object called `WScript`, and this object has a method called `Echo()` that's perfect for our requirements. The `WScript` object is always available from any script file being executed using WSH, and using `Echo()` is therefore as easy as this:

```
// HelloWorld.js

var strText1;                  // JScript variables have no explicit type
var strText2;

strText1 = "Hello, world!";
strText2 = "I'm the Windows Script Host.";

WScript.Echo(strText1 + "\n" + strText2);
```

The result is shown in this figure:

The different captions of the two dialog boxes illustrate their diverse origins. The source of the first was the VBScript engine; the source of the second was WSH itself.

> *Notice that the dialog's caption is actually* Windows Script*ing* Host. *At the time of writing, Microsoft has recently renamed a number of its script technologies in a standardization effort, and "Windows Script Host" is one of those amendments.*

The Echo Method

The `Echo()` method is intended to provide what its name might suggest: a way to output whatever text is passed to it. In other words, it writes on what we could consider to be the standard output channel: it just 'echoes' something. However, despite having the same programming interface, `Echo()` has different implementations in `wscript.exe` and `cscript.exe`. In `wscript.exe` — that is, in pure Windows code — it defaults to calling the `MessageBox()` API function. In console mode, on the other hand, it writes to the output device.

Even though you'll never find it described as the Windows standard output channel, `MessageBox()` *can realistically be considered as the standard way to display text in Windows.* `MessageBox()` *in Windows plays a not dissimilar role from that C programmer's old faithful,* `printf()`.

The following figure shows the output of the very same JScript code when launched from a console window with `cscript.exe`. The end result is quite different:

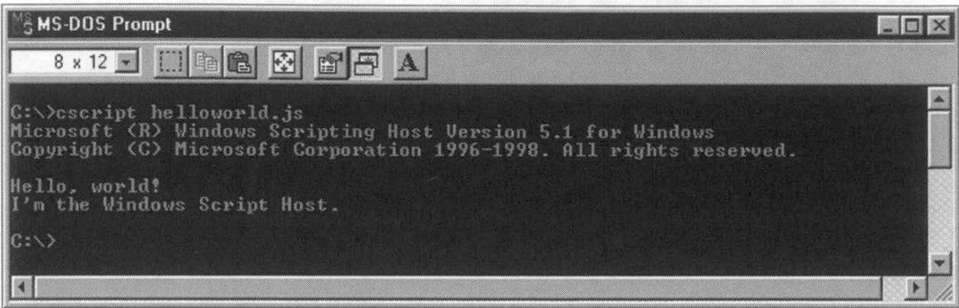

The `Echo()` method has again written its output to what it perceives as the 'standard' output channel, but this time it's the console window from which `cscript.exe` was executed.

Solving the Problem with WSH 2.0

Another way of solving problems due to language features that are available in VBScript but not in JScript (or vice versa) is to use one of the new facilities in WSH 2.0. As well as performing execution of VBScript and JScript files, WSH 2.0 adds support for 'Windows Script' (`.ws`) files, which are XML-based.

If you're contemplating the use of features that are specific to version 2.0 of WSH, bear in mind that as a new development, it is not guaranteed that your customers' machines will support it. In this book, I will try to provide "version 1" and "version 2" solutions whenever feasible, so that your options are left open.

Windows Script files allow you to mix VBScript and JScript in the same file, just like you can in HTML pages, so it's possible to write a VBScript wrapper for `MsgBox()` and call *that* from JScript code. I'll cover most of the features that are exclusive to WSH 2.0 in Chapter 5, but in the meantime this is how a `HelloWorld.ws` file might look:

```
<?xml version="1.0"?>
<!-- HelloWorld.ws -->

<job>
   <script language="VBScript">
      Function MessageBox(strText)
         MsgBox strText
      End Function
   </script>

   <script language="JScript">
      var strText1;
      var strText2;
```

```
        strText1 = "Hello, world!";
        strText2 = "I'm the Windows Script Host.";
        MessageBox(strText1 + "\n" + strText2);
    </script>
</job>
```

The Host's Command Line

`cscript.exe` and `wscript.exe` share the same command line, which looks like this:

```
wscript scriptfile [//options] [arguments]
cscript scriptfile [//options] [arguments]
```

Here, *`scriptfile`* is the name of the script to be executed, the `options` (which are listed in the table below) affect the behavior of the host, and the `arguments` are passed to the script to affect its actions. Note that you need to use a *double* slash to prefix each option, and that some documentation states incorrectly that each argument must be prefixed by a single slash.

The following, then, is a valid call that causes the `file.vbs` script to be executed, receiving `arg1` and `arg2` as its command line arguments:

```
wscript file.vbs arg1 arg2
```

Provided that options are prefixed by a double slash, their order and position in the command line is actually not important. Furthermore, the options available for `cscript.exe` and `wscript.exe` are almost identical; where there are differences they are pointed out in this table:

Option	Description
`B`	Runs the script in a 'batch', non-interactive mode. All message boxes, and anything else that requires the user to intervene, are suppressed.
`I`	Runs the script in interactive mode and prompts the user if necessary. Execution terminates at the end of the code, and there is no maximum execution time. This is the default option.
`Logo`	A banner is shown at startup. This option is valid only when you're using `cscript.exe`, for which it's the default. It is ignored by `wscript.exe`.
`Nologo`	No banner is shown at startup. This option is valid only for `cscript.exe`; it is ignored by `wscript.exe`.
`T:nn`	The script can only run for the specified time, expressed in seconds. By default, there is no time limit.
`S`	Saves the specified command line options, and makes them the default options for all scripts run by the current user.

Table Continued on Following Page

Option	Description
`H:wscript` or `H:cscript`	Sets the WSH executable that will run scripts by default. This setting affects the default item on the context menu for `.vbs`, `.js` and `.ws` files.
`?`	Displays the executable's usage.
`E:vbscript` or `E:jscript`	Sets the scripting engine to be used to run the specified script file. I'll say more on this later. (WSH 2.0 only)
`D`	Turns the debugger on. (WSH 2.0 only)
`X`	Launches the program in the debugger. (WSH 2.0 only)
`Job:ID`	Launches the specified job from the `.ws` file. (WSH 2.0 only)

As you can see, the command lines of `cscript.exe` and `wscript.exe` are *nearly* the same and only differ in the availability of the `Logo` and `Nologo` switches. Notice that the last four options are available only with WSH 2.0.

Command line switches can be concatenated with no limit by repeating the double slash (//) for each option. For example:

```
wscript file.vbs arg1 //B //logo arg2
```

Let's have a look at some examples of how to accomplish common tasks with the WSH executables.

Running a Script for a Predetermined Time

Some scripts can take a long time to complete. Imagine, for example, a script that needs to connect to a remote source and is therefore subject to the state of the underlying network. You can never know how much time will be necessary, or even whether the task will ultimately complete successfully. On the other hand, though, you can't leave the script's execution pending indefinitely.

WSH lets you define a maximum amount of time within which the script *must* complete execution. If the interval expires and the script is still working, then the scripting engine will terminate it. Since this is a feature included in the Windows Script specification, the engine will know how to handle a request to terminate the task abruptly without resulting in a loss of data. You should be aware, however, that the scripting engine can only stop itself at the *beginning* of a statement. If your script is set to time out after (say) 30 seconds, but the scripting engine has just called a method of an external object that takes a minute to execute, you're going to wait that minute until the timeout signal is processed.

The following line shows how to run a script file for a maximum of two seconds. Once this period has elapsed, the script terminates, regardless of whether all the statements in the program have actually completed:

```
wscript myfile.js //T:2
```

If you don't specify a timeout value, WSH will conform to its default behavior and run the script to completion.

Suppressing (Some) Message Boxes

If you want a WSH script to work without ever requiring user intervention, you can try using the `B` option to set it to work in batch mode. However, bear in mind that not all the output will be suppressed. Turning the interactive mode off actually only blocks the `WScript.Echo()` method, so `MsgBox()` and `InputBox()` (which are implemented by the VBScript engine) are unaffected by doing so. Similarly, any ActiveX control that has its own user interface will continue working as usual, regardless of batch mode being set.

The dialog boxes created by `Echo()` only have an OK button, and execution of scripts in batch mode always continues as if that button were being clicked by the user. Setting batch mode also suppresses all output using `Echo()` when the script is running in a console window.

Changing the Default Host

You can run WSH three ways: from the Start | Run... dialog box, from the command prompt, or from Explorer by double clicking on script file icons. Since there's no explicit mention of the host you want (`cscript.exe` or `wscript.exe`) in the first and last of these cases, the default one is started. When you install WSH, the default engine is `wscript.exe`, but this can be changed at any time with one of the following lines:

```
wscript //H:cscript
cscript //H:wscript
```

The `//H` option must be followed by the word `cscript` or `wscript` to denote the new default host.

Saving Per-user Command Line Settings

Using the `//S` option, you can to save all the other settings found on the same command line as new defaults for the current user. This just means that from that moment on, these settings will be 'assumed', as if they were always specified on any command line issued by the current user. These settings are stored in the system registry under this key:

```
HKEY_CURRENT_USER
   \Software
      \Microsoft
         \Windows Scripting Host
            \Settings
```

You can also change some of these settings manually by running `wscript.exe` with no arguments. In this case you'll displayed a dialog box like the following:

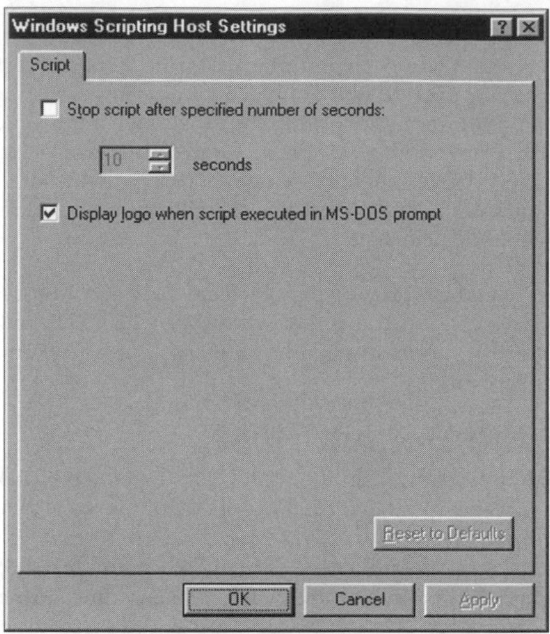

Alternatively, you can save settings on a per-file basis by creating a `.wsh` initialization file, as I'll show you in a moment.

WSH Scripts

By default, a WSH script is just a simple text file that can have one of three possible extensions: `.vbs`, `.js` and `.ws`. (In fact, the third of these was only added with the introduction of WSH 2.0.) You can consider them all to be new, legitimate kinds of executable file, no different from `.exe` or `.bat` files.

As you've seen (albeit briefly), `.vbs` and `.js` files contain a sequence of VBScript or JScript statements. WSH uses the file extension to distinguish which language the script is written in, and therefore which scripting engine to call. When and if you register a new engine, you can have other extensions (say, `.pl` for Perl files) supported by the system automatically.

`.ws` files are a little different. They are written following XML syntax, and can be seen as collections of various pieces of information, including blocks of script to be executed. A `.ws` file is not language-based, in the sense that it may include and mix blocks written in different languages, rather like HTML pages.

Changing the Script Extension

In general, a file with a `.vbs` extension is not necessarily a VBScript file. Although it would be rather silly, you could have a JScript file with a `.vbs` extension. This would confuse WSH, causing it to call the VBScript engine to work on a JScript file. It is a golden rule of Windows that the type of any file is determined by its extension.

In WSH 2.0, however, a new command line option has been added just in case of problems with this rigidity. Consider the following:

```
wscript //E:JScript myFile.txt
```

The `E` option can be used to force WSH to pass the contents of `myFile.txt` to the JScript scripting engine, despite the `.txt` extension of the file.

Script Execution

Execution of a script file begins at the first statement encountered by the engine, and while you can define subroutines throughout the body of the script, only WSH 2.0 and `.ws` files provide the native ability to reuse script code across different files. I'll be covering this subject thoroughly in Chapter 5.

By resorting to some tricky techniques, you *can* actually include a script file inside another one at runtime, provided that they're using the same language, and that you're using version 5.0 of the JScript and VBScript scripting engines. This is demonstrated in Chapter 7.

Shell Support for WSH Scripts

When you install Windows Script Host, you get some facilities for free. The setup program that comes with WSH 2.0 makes changes to the registry so that you can run `.vbs`, `.js` and `.ws` files just by double-clicking the filename anywhere in the Windows shell. Each time you activate them from Explorer, or type their names at the Run prompt, you cause `wscript.exe` to be launched in order to execute them.

The screenshot shows the context menu for a `.vbs` file, but it would be identical for `.js` or `.ws` files. The default item, Open, is linked to `wscript.exe`, causing the latter to run after a simple double click. The Open with MS-DOS Prompt item, on the other hand, is associated with `cscript.exe` and causes the item to run in a MS-DOS window. As I explained earlier, you can invert this setting by using the `//H` option on the host's command line.

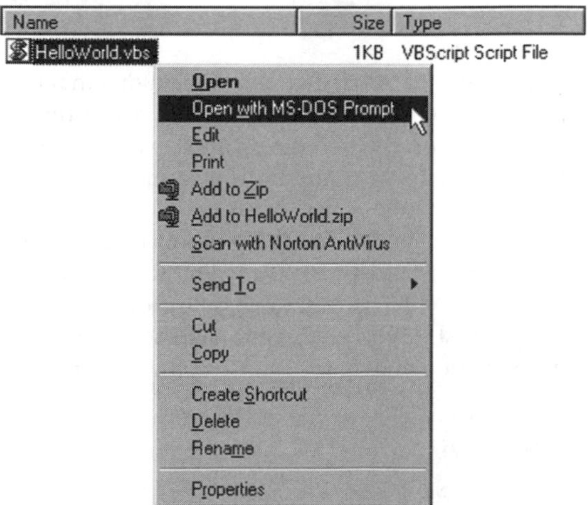

In the screenshot above, you can see an Edit command that *wasn't* added by WSH. (It was added by me!) If you select it, the source code of the highlighted file will be displayed using Notepad. In Chapter 10, you'll learn how to improve shell support for WSH files by adding specific commands like this one.

If you're interested in learning about the Windows shell, documents, context menus and the like, you should check out Visual C++ Windows Shell Programming *(Wrox Press, 1-861001-84-3). In particular, Chapter 13 is dedicated to the Windows Script Host.*

WSH Script Settings

When Windows Script Host is installed, `.vbs`, `.js` and `.ws` files acquire an additional property page entitled Script. It looks the same as the dialog box that you get when you run `wscript.exe` with no arguments, as you can see:

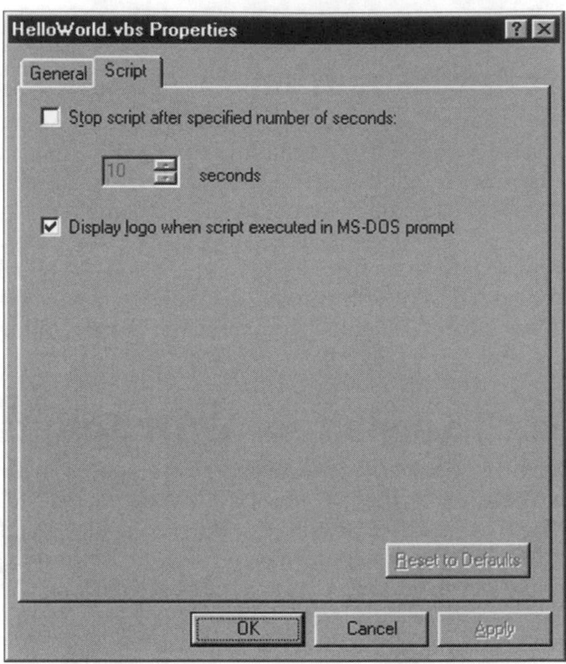

The page consists of a very few elements that control execution of the script file. In particular, you can set the maximum execution time in seconds, and whether or not the logo is required when the script is executed in an MS-DOS window (this feature relates to the `//nologo` command-line option that's supported only by `cscript.exe`).

When you change something in this page, you're changing the WSH settings only for the associated script file. Any alterations that alter the default settings are stored in a `.wsh` file, which is described by the documentation as a "settings" file for Windows Script Host. If you enable the Stop script after specified number of seconds check box in the dialog above, for example, the contents of the `.wsh` file will be as follows:

```
[ScriptFile]
Path=C:\WSH\HelloWorld.vbs

[Options]
Timeout=10
DisplayLogo=1
BatchMode=0
```

Unsurprisingly, the 'settings' file that gets created has the same name as the script file it refers to, albeit with the `.wsh` extension.

WSH "settings" files are important because they allow administrators to set different options for different users when they're executing the same script. For example, a user with lower privileges might be authorized to execute a certain operation for at most *n* seconds, while another may always be able to let it complete its work. This can be accomplished by copying different `.wsh` files to the users' machines. Each `.wsh` file defines specific options, but both point to the same script file to execute, as in the following sample files:

```
[ScriptFile]
Path=\\Server\Scripts\HelloWorld.vbs

[Options]
Timeout=10
DisplayLogo=1
BatchMode=0
```

```
[ScriptFile]
Path=\\Server\Scripts\HelloWorld.vbs

[Options]
DisplayLogo=1
BatchMode=0
```

In the case where you have files called `HelloWorld.vbs` and `HelloWorld.js` in the same folder,you *won't* have separate settings files, or an all-encompassing `HelloWorld.wsh` file. Unfortunately, the last change you make to the settings of either file overwrites any previous ones.

WSH Shortcuts

A `.wsh` file contains the link to its buddy script in the `Path` entry of the `ScriptFile` section. (You may have noticed that a `.wsh` file has syntax like a Windows `.ini` file.) From the shell's point of view, a `.wsh` file works like a shortcut to its linked script, so double-clicking a `.wsh` file causes the linked script file to execute with the settings stored in the `.wsh` document. Of course, before running a `.wsh` file you should make sure that the linked script really does exist; if it doesn't you'll get a message like this:

A Quick COM Refresher

I've now explained the reasons and history behind the development of Windows Script Host, and described the options that are available when you execute script files using it. Before we move on to discuss *how* to write scripts that perform useful functions, though, I want to make absolutely sure that we're talking the same language.

WSH is based on Microsoft's Component Object Model (COM), and it's extensible using it. So far, I've been using a few COM terms under the assumption that there has been nothing likely to be unfamiliar to a moderately experienced script author. Just in case you're unclear about some of the common concepts, however, and to prepare you for the material to come, here's a quick glossary of the terms that will crop up in this book.

Term	Description
Automation object (sometimes called an ActiveX control)	An object that is exposed to applications or programming tools through Automation. The properties and methods of such an object are programmable using script code, and it's also possible to sink their events (see below). An Automation object is simply a COM object that can be driven using Automation.
Interface	The term given to a group of methods and properties that an object makes available. It's the means by which you affect the behavior of an object.
ProgID	Abbreviation of "programmatic identifier"; a text string that is used to identify a COM object by name. Not all COM objects have a ProgID, but they all have a CLSID (see below).
CLSID	Abbreviation of "class identifier"; a 128-bit number that identifies a COM object uniquely.
Event sink	A function in your script that will be executed in response to something happening (an event) in a COM object.
Outgoing interface	An interface that groups together all the functions that an object allows a client to implement. These are the functions that get called when an event occurs.

The collection of objects that makes up the WSH object model, which we will start to look at in the next chapter, was never intended to make the whole of Windows' functionality available to the programmer. WSH just provides a way of running script files from the command line, and a few simple objects that encapsulate some common tasks. For all the tasks that it doesn't cover, other components are required.

These "other components" are Automation objects, and they are the link that ties WSH and COM together. You can access and use Automation objects that already exist elsewhere in the system, and you can create your own with COM-aware tools such as Visual C++ and Visual Basic. By using a new technology called Windows Script Components, which we'll discuss in Chapter 8, you can even create new Automation objects using script code!

Summary

In this chapter, I've covered some basic aspects of using the Windows Script Host. In particular, I've tried to delineate the potential of WSH and the key role that COM has in its overall architecture.

In addition, I demonstrated a trivial "Hello World" application written in VBScript and JScript, addressing some slight differences between the Windows and console mode WSH runtimes as I did so. I also provided a quick refresher of some COM terms.

The introduction of the `WScript` object and its `Echo()` method should have whetted your appetite for more information about the WSH object model, and it's this subject that we'll begin to pursue more tenaciously in the next chapter.

3

The WSH Root Object

Windows Script Host is composed of two core elements. There's the host itself (be it `cscript.exe` or `wscript.exe`) and a helper component that contains the larger portion of the WSH object model (`wshom.ocx`). In this chapter and the next one, I'll cover in detail all the standard objects you deal with when writing WSH scripts. My intention for this chapter is to show you:

- How to get information about the environment
- How to create an object from within a WSH script
- How to handle events in WSH
- How to retrieve the arguments passed to a WSH script

To begin, let's take a much closer look at the core components of Windows Script Host.

The Core Components of WSH

WSH is distributed in two main components:

- The host executable itself
- The object model implementation in `wshom.ocx`

The host executable is commonly perceived as being the 'whole' WSH, and as you saw in the last chapter, it has two flavors: a console mode engine (`cscript.exe`) and a pure Windows engine (`wscript.exe`). They provide the same functionality but keep console and Windows code neatly separate. The default engine is `wscript.exe`, but you can switch them at any time, as demonstrated in Chapter 2. From now on, unless indicated to the contrary, I'll be referring to `wscript.exe` as the WSH executable. When I mention `wscript.exe`, you can assume that I mean `cscript.exe` as well.

The Host Executable

The `wscript.exe` executable is stored in the `Windows` directory. It can be accessed from absolutely anywhere, as the `Windows` folder is in the standard Windows search path. Note that `cscript.exe`, on the other hand, is located in the `Command` subfolder of the `Windows` directory. However, this folder is also normally added to the `PATH` environment string in the `autoexec.bat` file, and thereby made available throughout the entire system as well.

What Does the Executable Do?

Whenever the WSH executable is loaded, it performs two basic operations:

- It initializes the Windows Script Interfaces that will take care of processing the script code
- It instantiates the WSH root object that scripts will call on to create other WSH objects, or indeed any other COM components

The WSH executable has a much smaller memory footprint than either Internet Explorer or Internet Information Server (IIS), but it provides the same kind of service: it interprets script code by using methods of the Windows Script Interfaces. IE performs this task on VBScript or JScript code embedded in the `<script>` blocks of HTML pages, while IIS, in conjunction with the ASP runtime, does the same thing for the `<% ... %>` blocks of ASP pages.

Preparing for Script Execution

When you're using WSH 1.0, the right engine for processing the script is determined by the extension of the script file. As mentioned in Chapter 2, however, this *doesn't* ensure that the right engine will always process a file if, for example, you consciously (or unconsciously) give a `.vbs` extension to a JScript file.

The system registry holds the links between different file extensions and the ProgIDs of the scripting engines used to process them.

Parsing a WS File

With WSH 2.0, things are a little different. As long as you use `.vbs` or `.js` files, things will remain unchanged, but WSH 2.0 introduces a new XML-based file format (`.ws`) that is processed by an XML parser. Its name is `scrobj.dll`, and it too is located in the `Windows` directory. The parser validates the format of the file and extracts the pieces of script code to be executed. These blocks are then processed by the script engine that the `language` attribute of the `<script>` tag indicates. If no such attribute is specified, JScript is assumed.

Calling a Specific Engine

As I mentioned earlier, using WSH 1.0 forces you to give your script a `.vbs` or a `.js` extension, and the content of the file must comply with that extension. WSH 2.0 relaxes this constraint by allowing you to require a specific (and properly registered) scripting engine to process a given file. The key to this is the `//E:`*`engine`* command line switch that we met in Chapter 2. By using it, you can assign a custom extension to your WSH scripts:

```
wscript.exe myfile.xyz //E:vbscript
```

The above command, for example, forces WSH to use the VBScript engine to process the code in the specified `.xyz` file.

Root Object Instantiation

The WSH object model has a hierarchical structure in which very few objects can be created publicly via their ProgIDs. I mentioned briefly in the last chapter that the root object is called `WScript`, and it's through this that you can create the other objects of the WSH object model. `WScript` is designated to be the root of the object model and doesn't need *any* preliminary action to be used safely. If you wish, you can use it in the very first instruction of your script file. For example, the following one-line script:

```
WScript.Echo("Hello, world!\nI'm the Windows Script Host.");
```

produces the same output as the examples in Chapter 2, proving beyond doubt that `WScript` can be used without prior initialization.

The other objects that can be created publicly are `WshShell` and `WshNetwork`, but they occupy a slightly lower level in the hierarchy and need instantiating before you can use them. The remaining objects in the model *can't* be created by using a ProgID; they can only be created with specific methods of `WScript`, `WshShell` and `WshNetwork`, as you'll soon discover.

A publicly creatable COM object is one that you can create from within any *process, provided that you know its ProgID or CLSID. Some objects, however, have a kind of centralized management policy that allows you to create them only by using the methods of other objects.*

Windows Script Host Internals

In this short section, I'll show you exactly why `WScript` doesn't need direct instantiation from script code. You might want to skip this if you know the subject already, or if you aren't interested in the nitty-gritty details for now.

You don't need to create an instance of `WScript` in a WSH script file simply because it gets initialized during the startup of the host executable. Once the script blocks to be executed have been identified, the host creates an instance of the `WScript` object. Next, it adds a reference to this object to the VBScript and/or JScript engine's internal collection of scriptable objects. This collection constitutes the set of objects that the scripting engine will be able to manage (that is, make calls to) successfully.

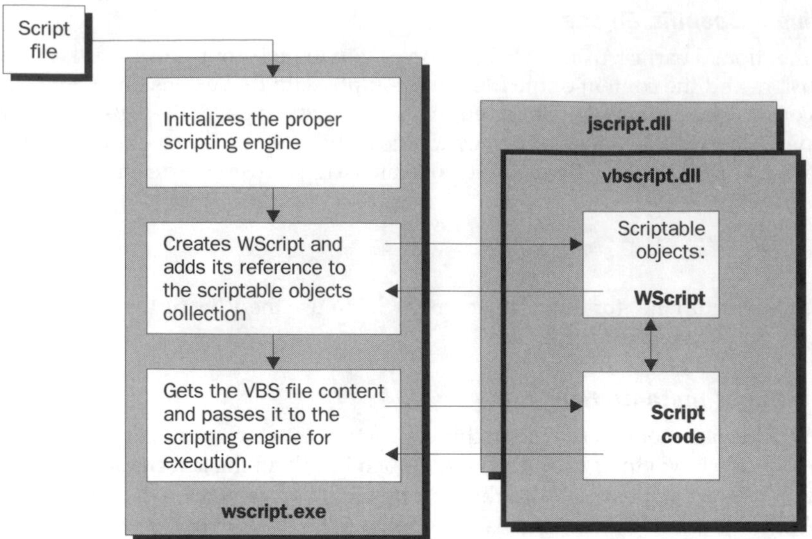

The figure above demonstrates this interaction in the case of a file with a VBScript code block, although the procedure is essentially identical with JScript code too. Each interaction between the two modules takes place through the interfaces defined by the Windows Script specification. Note that the script code can come from different sources in WSH 1.0 and WSH 2.0:

WSH 1.0	The entire content of a JScript `.js` file The entire content of a VBScript `.vbs` file
WSH 2.0	The entire content of a JScript `.js` file The entire content of a VBScript `.vbs` file The entire content of a file with any extension that contains VBScript or JScript code The content of a `<script>` block embedded in a `.ws` file

Of course, wherever you see VBScript or JScript here, you can substitute any other scripting engine compatible with the Windows Script specification.

A scripting engine will only be capable of making calls to the Automation objects whose references (actually, pointers to `IDispatch`) have previously been stored in its internal table. The `WScript` root object is created by the host executable, so any WSH script will find it already available when it begins to execute.

The Object Model Implementation

The `wscript.exe` program implements more than just the `WScript` object. It also includes the code for an object called `WshArguments` that contains the collection of command-line arguments that were passed to the script by the user. I'll have more to say about this later on.

The second core component of WSH — that is, the object model implementation — is a file called `wshom.ocx`. This is an ActiveX control that makes a number of additional WSH objects available through Automation. With the exception of `WScript` and `WshArguments`, the whole of the WSH object model is implemented by this `wshom.ocx` component.

A List of Objects

The following table summarizes the objects that `wshom.ocx` makes available, although I'll wait until the next chapter to cover them in detail:

Object	ProgID	Description
`WshShell`	`WScript.Shell`	Provides access to the registry and shortcuts. Also exposes some general-purpose methods to run programs and display messages.
`WshNetwork`	`WScript.Network`	Manages printers and network connections. Lets you map and 'un-map' a remote drive or a printer. Also returns information about the currently logged-on user.
`WshShortcut`	Not available	An object that completely encapsulates a shortcut.
`WshUrlShortcut`	Not available	An object that renders a shortcut to a URL.
`WshCollection`	Not available	A collection object that the `WshNetwork` object uses to return information about drives and printers.
`WshEnvironment`	Not available	A slightly specialized collection for managing environment variables.
`WshSpecialFolders`	Not available	A collection for managing Windows' special folders.

To complete the synopsis, here is a table containing the two objects exposed by `wscript.exe`:

Object	ProgID	Description
`WScript`	Not available	The WSH root object. Provides information about command-line arguments and manages the creation and destruction of objects.
`WshArguments`	Not available	A collection to manage the script's command-line arguments.

WScript has no ProgID, but as I explained above, there's no need for you to create an instance of it from within a WSH script.

The WScript Object

The WScript object is at the heart of any WSH script. It provides the spark for any significant activity that you can accomplish using Windows Script Host. The WScript programming interface is basically comprised of three types of function:

- Informational. This is the largest category, and includes properties and methods to find out about the command-line arguments, the name of the script file, the host filename, and the version information.
- Object Management. Functionally speaking, this is the most important category: it contains methods for creating, connecting to, and disconnecting from objects. It also lets you sink objects' events.
- Script Management. This category is limited to a method for stopping the script's execution programmatically, and the Echo() function we met in Chapter 2 that provides a means to output text on the default output device.

The WScript Programmer's Reference

The next table offers a synoptic view of the properties exposed by WScript:

Property	Description
Application	Returns a reference to the WScript object. Useful if you need to make copies of the WScript object, or to pass it as an argument.
Arguments	Retrieves the collection of the command-line arguments that the script file has been passed. Returns a reference to a WshArguments object.
BuildVersion	Retrieves the build version number of the WSH executable. This property is undocumented. (WSH 2.0 only)
FullName	Retrieves the fully qualified path of the WSH executable that's running the script. For example, c:\windows\wscript.exe. Useful if your script needs to know who's running it, with a view to altering its behavior.
Interactive	A read/write Boolean property that gets and sets the work mode (batch or interactive). This property is undocumented.
Name	Retrieves the descriptive name of the script host. This property evaluates to Windows Scripting Host.
Path	Retrieves the path name (drive and directory only, with no final backslash) of the WSH executable. For example, c:\windows.

Property	Description
`ScriptFullName`	Retrieves the fully qualified name of the script file currently running.
`ScriptName`	Retrieves the short name (file and extension only) of the script file currently running.
`Timeout`	Gets and sets the timeout setting on a per-script basis. If you set this property in a script file, the setting will apply only to that script. This property is undocumented. (WSH 2.0 only)
`Version`	Retrieves a string that contains the version number of the WSH executable. It's 5.1 if you're running the WSH 2.0 beta.

With the exceptions of `Interactive` and `Timeout`, all the properties shown above are read-only. Here are the methods of `WScript`:

Method	Description
`CreateObject()`	Creates and returns an instance of the COM object with the specified ProgID. It also lets you assign a name to the instance, in order to sink its events.
`DisconnectObject()`	Stops WSH from receiving events from an object. You pass it the script variable that holds your local object reference. Note that this method doesn't actually release the object — it just breaks the connection through which WSH manages the object's events (if any).
`GetObject()`	Retrieves a running object with the specified ProgID, or creates it from a file.
`Echo()`	Writes the parameters it receives in a popup window or a MS-DOS (console) window, according to the host in use at the time.
`Quit()`	Quits execution, returning the specified error code.
`Sleep()`	Suspends execution of the current script for a specified number of milliseconds. (WSH 2.0 only)

At this point, it's about time for us to try some test scripts that will demonstrate all these methods and properties in action.

Getting Host Information

Using the `WScript` object's properties is quite straightforward. Less trivial, however, is figuring out when a certain property might really be use*ful*. Let's start with a simple VBScript file that shows all the available information about the host and the file it's executing.

```
' HostInfo.vbs
' Displays all the information about the script file and the host engine
' --------------------------------------------------------------------------
Option Explicit

Dim strHostName                    ' VBScript variables have no explicit type
Dim strFrom
Dim strFile
Dim strScript

strHostName = WScript.Name & " ver. " & WScript.Version & vbCrLf
strFrom     = "The host is: " & WScript.FullName & " running"
strFile     = WScript.ScriptName & " from " & WScript.Path & vbCrLf
strScript   = "Script: " & WScript.ScriptFullName

MsgBox strHostName & vbCrLf & strFrom & vbCrLf & strFile & vbCrLf & strScript
```

Running this script on my Windows 98 machine causes the following dialog to appear:

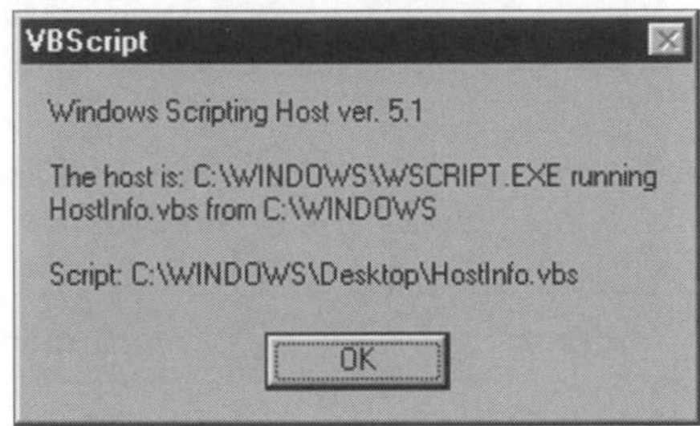

Of course, you might see differences in several of these values depending on the version of WSH you're running and the directories in which you store things.

As shown in the screenshot, the script has been executed with `wscript.exe`. Would the result have been different if I was using `cscript.exe` instead? On this occasion, there is only a small change: `cscript.exe` just causes the dialog to be displayed over a console window:

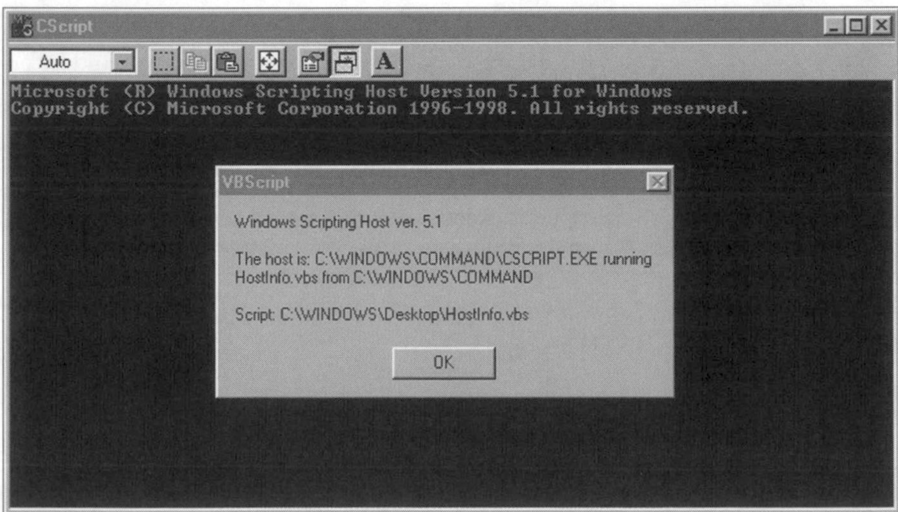

Of course, the information about the WSH executable is now different, as it reflects the path of `cscript.exe`.

Adapting to the Host Executable

`FullName` has the potential to be very useful if you need to adapt your script code to the underlying host. Consider the following scenario: you have a COM object that produces some output. Depending on the WSH executable, you might want it to use a normal message box or to write to the standard output device. To accomplish this, you could have the object expose two similar methods, or perhaps just one method with a switch argument. In both cases, you need to know which WSH executable is currently running from *inside* the script:

```
var strName;

strName = WScript.FullName;         // Get the script name
strName = strName.toLowerCase();    // Change to lower case

// If cscript.exe is included in the host path name...
if(strName.indexOf("cscript.exe") != -1)
{
   // Call the method that outputs to the standard output device
}
else
{
   // Call the method that uses message boxes
}
```

The code above uses `FullName` to detect which host is running and then invokes the appropriate method accordingly.

The Echo Method

As you saw in the previous chapter, `Echo()` is the standard WSH method for text output. Its syntax is the following:

```
WScript.Echo [argument_list]
```

It takes a variable-length list of arguments, and displays them one after another, separated by spaces. In console mode, the entire line is terminated with a pair of carriage-return (CR) and linefeed (LF) characters. An example call is therefore:

```
WScript.Echo "One", "Two", "Three"
```

An Undocumented Property: Interactive

When we looked at the host's command-line switches, we met an option for setting the mode of the script to 'batch' or 'interactive'. In interactive mode, the script is free to wait for the user to provide feedback; in batch mode, all the message boxes are automatically suppressed.

This is *more or less* what happens. However, the only method that actually seems to be affected by this property is `Echo()`. If you set `Interactive` to `False`, any call to `Echo()` is simply skipped. If you use VBScript's `MsgBox()` function to display messages, then nothing changes, regardless of the value you assign to `Interactive`.

Working Interactively

The initial value for the `Interactive` property depends upon the `//I` or `//B` option you send to the script on the command line. Remember that `//I` means "Be interactive", while `//B` stands for "Work in batch mode and don't be interactive". As the `Interactive` property is read/write, however, you can change its value at any time.

`Interactive` is not documented in the MSDN, but you can find information about it (including proof of its existence) by looking at the object model exposed by `wscript.exe` with an appropriate tool. One of my favorite tools for this task is the Visual Basic 6 Object Browser:

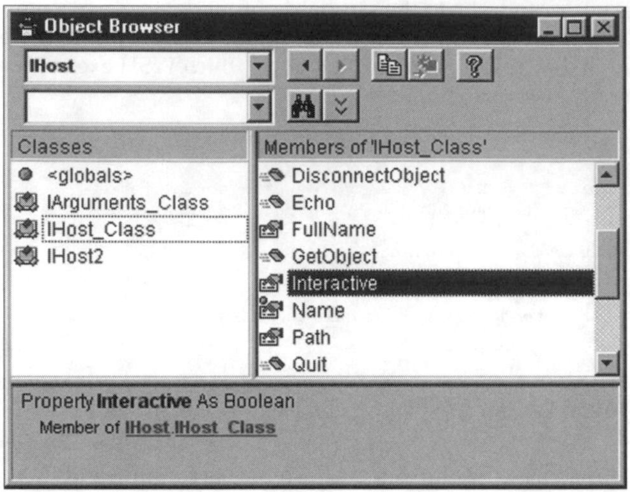

The following sample shows how to use the `Interactive` property (and indirectly demonstrates that it works in the way I've described). It makes use of the `Popup()` method of the `WshShell` object that we'll study in the next chapter; like `MsgBox()`, it is unaffected by `Interactive`:

```
// Interactive.js
// Demonstrates the undocumented Interactive property
//---------------------------------------------------------------

var oShell;
var yn;

// These constants come from the documentation of the WshShell
//  object we'll cover in Chapter 4. They map to the constants
//  used by the Win32 MessageBox() function.
MB_YESNO = 4;                    // Constant for Yes/No buttons
IDYES    = 6;                    // Returned when Yes is clicked

oShell = new ActiveXObject("WScript.Shell");

if(WScript.Interactive)
{
   yn = oShell.Popup("Running interactively. Change?",
                    0, "Interactive", MB_YESNO);
   if(yn == IDYES)
      WScript.Interactive = 0;
}
else
{
   oShell.Popup("Running in batch mode.");
}

// This line will be suppressed in batch mode
WScript.Echo("Hello, world!");
WScript.Quit();
```

When started in interactive mode, the code pops up a message asking whether to change to batch mode. It then sets the `Interactive` property accordingly. As a result, the final `Echo()` call may be skipped.

Terminating a Script

Execution of a script starts at the first executable line in the file, and terminates with the last one. Although this may sound obvious, it actually requires some explanation. The first *executable* line in a script is not necessarily the first non-empty and non-commented line. A script like this, for example:

```
function Init()
{
   return 0;
}
```

is not valid under WSH, even though it is formed by valid JScript code! The body of a *valid* script is composed of lines that don't belong to any procedure or function. Provided that is the case, a program begins with the first line and terminates *naturally* with the last line. For example, look at the following (not particularly useful) code:

```
MsgBox "First Line"

Function Foo1()
   A = 1
End Function

MsgBox "Second Line"

Function Foo2()
   A = 2
End Function

MsgBox "Third Line"
```

It is completely equivalent to this code:

```
MsgBox "First Line"
MsgBox "Second Line"
MsgBox "Third Line"

Function Foo1()
   A = 1
End Function

Function Foo2()
   A = 2
End Function
```

You can force execution to stop at any time by calling the `Quit()` method, which has the following simple syntax:

```
WScript.Quit [nErrorCode]
```

The argument is optional, and is meant to be the exit code to return to the caller. If you omit it, then a default value of 0 is returned. If `WScript.Quit` would be the final instruction in the script and you don't need to return a particular non-zero value, then you can omit it.

Specifying a Timeout

As mentioned in Chapter 2, you can make sure that a script always terminates after a fixed number of seconds. This time is just a maximum limit after which the host will ask the script engine to kill the script if it is still executing.

Timing a script out can be useful if you know that a given operation might be lengthy and subject to external conditions, such as the availability of a network connection or a phone line. For example, if you have an object that sends data through a modem, you might want to add a timeout to make sure that the line is hung up anyway after a certain period. It may even be necessary to determine that period dynamically, rather than fixing it statically by using a `.wsh` file.

As I mentioned in the table above, WSH 2.0 has introduced a brand new (though still undocumented) `Timeout` property that provides the ability to set a feature like this programmatically, but nothing similar was available in version 1.0. However, if you need this behavior when circumstances dictate that WSH 2.0 is unavailable, there are a couple of tricks you can use to simulate it.

The first "trick" is based on combined use of the `//T:n` and `//S` command-line options I described in Chapter 2:

```
wscript //T:8 //S
cscript //T:8 //S
```

Running either of the above sets a timeout of 8 seconds for *any* script executed by the currently logged-on user. To remove this setting and get back to the default (that is, no timeout), you just have to issue one of these commands:

```
wscript //S
cscript //S
```

To control the timeout value of a script programmatically, you can use the `WshShell` object's `Run()` method to run these commands from within *another* script, as shown below:

```
// Timeout.js
// Sets the script timeout to 5 seconds programmatically.

// This setting applies to ALL the scripts you run from now on!
// To reset, replace the last line with the commented one and run it again.
//-----------------------------------------------------------------------

// NB: At this point, THIS instance of WSH is loaded and already using the
//  previous settings. This instance will be unaffected by any changes.

var oSH;

// Get the WshShell object that's needed in order to run an external program
oSH = WScript.CreateObject("WScript.Shell");

// Run wscript.exe to save the command-line settings
oSH.Run("wscript //T:5 //S");

// Reset to no timeout for scripts
// oSH.Run("wscript //S");
```

Unfortunately, there are a couple of side effects with this approach: it turns out not to be the neat solution you might have hoped for. First and foremost, the new setting will only apply starting with the *next* script, although I suppose that's not surprising when you consider that you're running `wscript.exe` from within `wscript.exe` to change a specific behavior of `wscript.exe`! The running instance of `wscript.exe` has already read the settings you've just altered, and won't react to those changes.

As if that weren't enough, there's another drawback: a message box appears, as shown by the picture opposite:

This window pops up every time you run `wscript.exe` to save the command-line settings. The actual message shown may vary according to what you're actually doing, but a final window will always appear. When you return the settings to their default values, for example, the message is:

You're rather more likely to want a completely silent operation, but once again the `Interactive` property is of no help. The method responsible for the dialog is `WshShell.Popup()`, which you already know to be unaffected by the value of `Interactive`.

The definitive solution to this little problem with WSH 1.0 requires you to simulate what `wscript.exe` does under the hood when it manages the `//S` option. As mentioned in Chapter 2, these settings are stored in the registry, so what we need to do is update the entry in the sub-tree where this information is kept. To do this, however, we first need to be familiar with the registry manipulation methods of the `WshShell` object, and we'll be taking a look at those in Chapter 4.

> *It doesn't matter whether you use* `cscript.exe` *or* `wscript.exe` *to store user settings. The dialog box pops up in both cases.*

The WScript Object's Management Functions

In a COM-based environment, being able to create and manage objects is a fundamental task. Apart from a few of the very simple examples we've covered so far, everything that WSH can do requires the creation and utilization of one or more COM objects. `WScript` makes three methods available for this purpose:

- `CreateObject()`
- `GetObject()`
- `DisconnectObject()`

The first two of these both return a reference to an Automation object, although they obtain that reference in different ways. The third method disconnects any event handler that the script may have defined for the object's events.

> **`DisconnectObject()` *doesn't* release the object. For that to happen from VBScript code, you need to set the object to `Nothing` explicitly. From JScript, you should set it to `null`.**

Creating Objects

The syntax of `WScript.CreateObject()` is:

```
WScript.CreateObject(strProgID [,strPrefix])
```

The first argument is mandatory and must be a string containing the ProgID of the COM object to be created. The second argument, on the other hand, is optional but may be a string that assigns a local name to the object being created. I'll explain the role of this local name in a moment.

The method returns a reference to the object. (More precisely, it returns a pointer to the object's `IDispatch` interface.) If you're using `WScript.CreateObject()` from within VBScript, you must use the `Set` keyword to assign the result of the method to a variable:

```
Dim oSH
Set oSH = WScript.CreateObject("WScript.Shell")
```

With JScript, however, you simply assign the return value to a variable. Note that in JScript you can declare a variable and assign a value to it in the same instruction:

```
var oSH = WScript.CreateObject("WScript.Shell");
```

This technique is not permitted in VBScript.

The Object's Local Name

The optional `strPrefix` argument to `CreateObject()` serves a very particular purpose: it allows you to handle any events the object raises. I shall cover this subject in detail later in the chapter, but I'd like to give you some hints right now.

If you're familiar with Visual Basic or HTML scripting, you'll already know that in order to handle the events fired by an object, you need to define a local function with a predefined prototype and, more importantly, a predefined name. The prototype must respect the event declaration, and allows you to manage the parameters that the event passes back to you. The name helps the host environment to establish a link between the event it detects from the contained object and the procedure you defined to handle it. This technique is known as creating an **event sink**.

The point is that any object can raise its own events, and each event is instance-specific. This means that if you're hosting two objects of the same type, you should be able to distinguish the events fired by each one. In many high-level languages (particularly in scripting and Rapid Application Development environments) this is done by assigning a local name to the object and looking for a local procedure whose name matches the pattern `localname_eventname()`.

For example, to handle a click on a document window in a web page, you could write a JScript procedure with this name:

```
function document_onclick()
{
   // Do something
}
```

The equivalent method in VBScript would look like this:

```
Sub document_onclick()
   ' Do something
End Sub
```

The object's local name is the prefix that WSH will use to identify event handlers defined for that object. For example, suppose the object you're creating exposes an `onfinish` event:

```
var o1 = WScript.CreateObject("My.Object", "FirstObj_");
var o2 = WScript.CreateObject("My.Object", "SecondObj_");

function FirstObj_onfinish()
{
   // Do something
}

function SecondObj_onfinish()
{
   // Do something else
}
```

The above code is then a valid way to sink the event for both objects.

Methods for Object Creation

Using the WScript object's CreateObject() method is not the only means at your disposal for creating objects. Setting aside the facilities provided by WScript, you could use the scripting engine's native functions to create COM objects. Let's examine the pros and the cons of each approach.

Let me say up front that there's no approach that's head and shoulders above the rest. There are reasons to prefer WScript.CreateObject() — it lets you supply an additional parameter to allow event handling, for a start — but the script languages' native methods are more efficient. Let's analyze the various techniques and the circumstances under which each of them is preferable.

VBScript's CreateObject Method

This function has the following prototype:

```
Set obj = CreateObject(strProgID)
```

It takes the ProgID of a COM object as an argument, and returns an instance of that object. Although the function has been available since version 2.0 of the VBScript engine, the version 5.0 engine that comes with Internet Explorer 5 has a slightly different prototype that matches the one available from within Visual Basic or VBA-compliant applications, such as the Office 97 products:

```
Set obj = CreateObject(strProgID [,server])
```

It has an additional, optional parameter that lets you specify the remote, networked computer on which the object should be created.

> **This feature was broken in the VBScript engine that shipped with IE 5.0. The bug was fixed soon afterwards, and a working version of the engine is available for download from** http://msdn.microsoft.com/scripting.

JScript's ActiveXObject Object

In JScript 3.0, Microsoft introduced the ActiveXObject object as a specialization of JavaScript's native Object() function. To create a COM server, you use the following syntax:

```
var obj = new ActiveXObject(strProgID)
```

Note that ActiveXObject *is a JScript (that is, a non-ECMA) feature.*

Choosing the Right Method

The only reason to prefer WScript.CreateObject() over the scripting engines' native methods is its support for event handling. If the object you want to create doesn't fire events (or you just don't want to sink them) you should be using CreateObject() in VBScript code, and ActiveXObject in JScript code.

What if you're using a third-party language that doesn't provide a built-in function to support COM object creation? While plausible, this possibility appears to be rather unlikely. It's true that script languages such as Perl and Rexx were created in environments that had nothing to do with COM, but the people developing Windows Script compatible engines for these languages have (not unreasonably) tended to add support for COM objects. If you ever do come across an engine that lacks this facility, `WScript.CreateObject()` is a perfectly good, language-neutral replacement.

> *Speaking of techniques to create COM objects, there's a fourth approach you might find helpful. It is based on the capability of the Remote Data Service (RDS) component that comes with the Microsoft Data Access Components (MDAC), part of Visual Studio 98. RDS lets you create instances of remote COM objects using either DCOM or HTTP. For more information, see* http://www.ASPToday.com/default.asp?art=19990326.htm

A Word About Performance

As I've now told you about three distinct ways of creating a new object within WSH, you may wonder which is the fastest. (At least, that's what *I* wondered!) Fundamentally, the three techniques involve the same thing; they just call two COM functions in order to:

- Get the CLSID from the ProgID (`CLSIDFromProgID()`)
- Create an instance of the object (`CoCreateInstance()`)

I wrote some simple benchmark code to see whether calling each of the object creators repeatedly would lead to dramatically different results, but in the end I didn't notice any great variation. Creating objects through `WScript` was always slightly slower than using the native script engine methods, but for any realistic use the disparity was tiny. If you were ever to find yourself in a situation in which performance at this level *was* an issue, the question would not be which object creator to use, but whether you had chosen the right tool for your problem.

Getting Objects

Side by side with `WScript.CreateObject()`, there's an apparently similar method called `GetObject()`. It is mostly used to obtain a reference to an *existing* object, although you can also use it to return a reference to a *new* object. It has the following syntax:

```
WScript.GetObject(strPathname [,strProgID] [,strPrefix])
```

The `strPathname` argument can be the path to an existing file, or an empty string. However, it is a required argument, and it can't be omitted. If the string you supply *is* empty, then `strProgID` is required.

Specifying the path to an existing file causes `GetObject()` to return a reference to an object using the information stored in that file. If necessary, an instance of the server required to host the object is created. (For example, an instance of MS Word will be created to host a Word document.) Using an empty string for the `strPathName` argument causes `GetObject()` to create a new object of the specified class, just as `CreateObject()` would do.

Finally, the `strPrefix` parameter plays the same role it has in `CreateObject()` and lets you sink events for the referenced object.

Objects from Files

To load an Excel workbook from a specified file, for example, you could use the following code:

```
Set oWB = WScript.GetObject("d:\file.xls")
MsgBox TypeName(oWB)                  ' Displays the type of the object
```

When this code executes, the application associated with `file.xls` (usually, Microsoft Excel) is started, and the object in the specified file is activated. The `oWB` variable is of the type `Workbook` if you have installed Microsoft Excel correctly.

Note that if you run this code, you won't actually see a new Excel window open on your desktop. If necessary, the application is loaded in the background in order to make its object model available, and unloaded when the script completes execution.

When both a filename and a ProgID are specified, the function creates the object and 'loads' the file into it. The `strProgID` argument then denotes the *type* of the object you want to obtain. If you specify a ProgID, it must be that of an appropriate, registered object. The following code is incorrect, because it tries to bind a `Word.Application` object to a `.doc` document and fails:

```
Set obj = WScript.GetObject("c:\readme.doc", "Word.Application")
```

This code *will* work, however, because the `.doc` file just contains a `Word.Document` object:

```
Set obj = WScript.GetObject("c:\readme.doc", "Word.Document")
```

As a final demonstration of the behavior of the method under these circumstances, look at this example:

```
Set obj = WScript.GetObject("c:\readme.txt")
```

If there's no Automation object associated with `.txt` files (which is usually the case), this will fail and cause a run-time error.

When You May Need Objects from Files

`GetObject()` is a useful shortcut if you need to work with files that originate an object model when they're opened within their registered applications. Word, Excel and PowerPoint documents, Access databases and even HTML files all come into this category. Bitmaps are also callable through `GetObject()`, but unless you've registered a specialized application (as opposed to MS Paint) to handle them, they don't make an object model available, and there's nothing you can do with them from within script files. The following code snippet shows how you can get the source code for a HTML page by using `GetObject()`:

```
Set htmlPage = WScript.GetObject("d:\new.htm")
MsgBox TypeName(htmlPage)          ' Type is HTMLDocument
MsgBox htmlPage.body.outerHTML     ' Body of the page
```

Referencing Existing Objects

Unfortunately, `WScript.GetObject()` doesn't fulfill its second stated aim of letting you obtain a reference to an object that is already running. The intention of the following code, for example, is to obtain an existing instance of Microsoft Word:

```
Set wordApp = WScript.GetObject("", "Word.Application")
```

However, the result is somewhat surprising: a new instance of Word is created. This means that the first line is equivalent to calling `CreateObject()`.

VBScript's GetObject Function

Different behavior is provided by VBScript's native `GetObject()` function, which also accepts a filename and a ProgID. Each argument is optional in the presence of the other, but if *both* are omitted you'll get an error. If you specify a filename, the function behaves exactly like `WScript.GetObject()`, but the two lines of code below produce different results:

```
' Always returns a NEW instance of Word
Set wordApp1 = GetObject("", "Word.Application")

' Returns an existing instance of Word, if any. An error otherwise.
Set wordApp2 = GetObject(, "Word.Application")
```

In the first case, you're always returned a new instance of Word. In the second, you get a reference to an existing instance of Word — if none is running, you'll get an error. If there are multiple running instances of Word, which one you'll get is undefined, although the oldest was always returned in my experiments.

Detecting Whether an Application is Running

Given that the behavior of these methods can vary according to whether an object of the type you're requesting exists, it would be helpful to know whether a call is appropriate before you make it. There are several ways to accomplish this — some are more reliable than others — but almost all imply making calls to some Win32 API functions. Although calling API functions from within scripts is not impossible, it is rather difficult, and it requires the aid of specialized components that are beyond the scope of this book.

A simpler technique is to make the call, but to have a guard against it failing. Consider the following VBScript code:

```
On Error Resume Next
Set obj = GetObject(, "Word.Application")

If TypeName(obj) <> "Application" Then
   Set obj = CreateObject("Word.Application")     ' Create a new instance
End If
```

An attempt is made to get a reference to an existing instance of a `Word.Application` object, but if that fails a new object is created instead.

When You May Need Existing Objects

One reason for wanting to reference an existing object would be simply to preserve system resources and save memory. Another could be a situation in which the existing object has something you want — a document that's open in a running instance of Word, perhaps. Remember, though, that you can't request a *particular* object from a group of several existing ones — you'll always get the oldest of them.

Releasing Objects

An object instantiated by a WSH script *usually* dies when the instance of the WSH executable that's running the script terminates. To be a good citizen, and to accelerate the release of memory that you longer need, you can cause an object to be released by setting the variable that holds the object's reference to `Nothing` in VBScript, and to `null` if you're working with JScript:

```
Set obj = CreateObject("Scripting.FileSystemObject")

' Do something with the object

' Release it
Set obj = Nothing

' From now on the variable obj is unusable
```

Be aware, however, that if the object you're creating is a `.exe` application (Word or Excel, for example), then setting the object reference to `Nothing` or `null` only partially works:

```
Set obj = CreateObject("Word.Application")

' Do something with the object

' Releases the object variable but leaves the application running
Set obj = Nothing
```

This code makes the `obj` variable unusable within the script, but it doesn't affect the application, which continues to run. To stop it, you need to call the method it provides for doing so (in the case of Word, this is the `Word.Application.Quit()` method):

```
Set obj = CreateObject("Word.Application")

' Do something with the object

' Terminates the application and then releases the object
obj.Quit
Set obj = Nothing
```

Handling Events

When you create or retrieve an object with the methods provided by `WScript` for doing so, you're given the opportunity to assign it a prefix name to be used to sink events. Earlier in the chapter, I referred to this argument with the formal name of `strPrefix`. Specifying a non-empty value for `strPrefix` forces the `WScript` code to do some additional work that enables event handling.

If you pass the empty string or omit the parameter altogether, you won't be able to handle the object's events in your script code.

When the object fires an event, and assuming that you have enabled event handling, WSH calls a subroutine whose name is a concatenation of `strPrefix` and the event name. In other words, the contents of the `strPrefix` argument are used to generate the name of the procedure that will execute against an event dynamically.

Given the following code, for example, the `DownloadBegin` event of Internet Explorer will be handled by a procedure in your code called `Browser_DownloadBegin()`:

```
var IE;
IE = WScript.CreateObject("InternetExplorer.Application", "Browser_");
```

There are a couple of quick points that you should be aware of about this:

- The procedure that handles the event, also called an **event sink**, must have the appropriate prototype
- If you want an underscore (_) in the event sink's name, then you have to specify it explicitly

Any event that an object will fire has a well-defined prototype that is (or should be) fully described in the technical documentation for the object itself. `DownloadBegin`, which indicates that the browser is about to download pages from a URL, has the simplest possible declaration:

```
DownloadBegin()
```

As you can see, it doesn't take any arguments at all. By way of comparison, `DocumentComplete`, which notifies that a page has been completely downloaded, has a more complex prototype:

```
DocumentComplete(obj, URL)
```

The first parameter is an object that denotes the top-level or frame container for the page. In fact, this event is fired as many times as there are *frames* in your document. If you don't have multiple frames, it is fired only once. The `URL` parameter is a string containing the URL of the page in question.

When sinking these (and other) events, you *must* use procedures with exactly the same declarations; otherwise the event won't be handled. The following handler, which appears to be totally harmless, doesn't work because it violates the defined prototype of the `DownloadBegin` event.

```
Sub DownloadBegin(param)
   ' Actually, it doesn't make much sense to handle a parameter here...
End Sub
```

A Naming Convention for Handlers

A common convention states that the name of an event sink should be formed by concatenating the internal name of the object and the name of the event, and WSH conforms to this behavior.

An almost equally strong convention is that the resulting name should contain an underscore in the middle, between the object and event names. For example, if `DownloadBegin` is the event name and `MyIE` is the internal name of the object, the name of the event procedure will be `MyIE_DownloadBegin()`.

What needs some clarification (because the documentation is far from clear on this point) is that in WSH, the underscore is *not* automatically added. Thus, if you have a prefix like `MyIE`, WSH will be expecting an event handler called `MyIEDownloadBegin()`. If you want an underscore in the name, you must add it yourself as the final character of the prefix.

Sinking Internet Explorer Events from WSH

Let's take a look at an example of sinking events. The following WSH script creates an instance of the Internet Explorer application object and uses it to navigate to the Wrox Press web site. Along the way, the script detects events such as the beginning and the end of the download process for each frame, and the page becoming ready for you to access its object model:

```
' Events.vbs
' Navigates to a Web site and waits for some IE events.
'------------------------------------------------------------------------
Option Explicit

Dim IE

' Create the IE object
Set IE = WScript.CreateObject("InternetExplorer.Application", "Browser_")
IE.Visible = True
IE.Navigate "http://www.wrox.com"

' Loop until we close the browser...
While IE.Visible
Wend

' Here the browser is closed. Although technically unnecessary, let's tidy up
WScript.DisconnectObject IE
Set IE = Nothing

'------------------------------------------------------------------------
' Subroutines
'------------------------------------------------------------------------
Sub Browser_DownloadBegin()
   WScript.Echo "Download begins at " & Now
End Sub

Sub Browser_DownloadComplete()
   WScript.Echo "Download completed at " & Now
End Sub

Sub Browser_DocumentComplete(pDisp, URL)
   Dim doc
   Set doc = IE.Document
   WScript.Echo doc.Title
End Sub
```

In the `DocumentComplete` event handler, the script outputs the title of the page that has been downloaded.

Events are Always Asynchronous

The first time I tested the previous script, it was a bit simpler. In particular, it was missing the loop that keeps it alive until Internet Explorer is closed:

```
While IE.Visible
Wend
```

Try omitting those lines, and you'll find that you're only able to detect the `DownloadBegin` event! As you'll see in a moment, disconnecting an object is a much quicker operation than navigating to a web site, so if you terminate the script immediately after a call to `Navigate()`, the chances are that there won't be enough time to sink further events such as `DownloadComplete` or `DocumentComplete`. Events, on the other hand, are asynchronous.

In the light of my errors, I do really recommend that you remember this fact when you're dealing with events in WSH scripts. Each event you sink requires that the script is still running (and that the object has not been disconnected) when the object fires it.

Disconnecting Objects

After creation and retrieval, the third of `WScript`'s basic operations on server objects is **disconnection**. As opposed to *releasing* it, which I explained earlier, disconnecting an object means that your script is no longer called upon to handle the events it generates. The method that does this is called `DisconnectObject()`, and it's used like this:

```
WScript.DisconnectObject obj
```

All objects previously created or retrieved via any of the methods we've discussed so far can be subject to this method. If you call `DisconnectObject()` on an object that has already been disconnected (or which was never 'connected' in the first place), the method just does nothing.

Strangely, while you can decide the moment at which WSH disconnects from an object, there is no equivalent way of saying when you want to connect *to an object. At present, the latter can occur only when the object gets created.*

If you call `DisconnectObject()` from VBScript without also setting the object variable to `Nothing`, it doesn't prejudice your ability to use the object:

```
Set obj = WScript.CreateObject("Scripting.FileSystemObject", "FileSystem_")

' Do something with the object

WScript.DisconnectObject obj

' You're still capable of using methods and properties of obj
```

If you don't use the last argument of `CreateObject()` to sink events, then there's no need for you to call `DisconnectObject()`. Call it only if you're handling events and want this behavior to be stopped at a certain time. Bear in mind, though, that you can't reconnect to that instance of the object later on.

The WshArguments Collection

Having now discussed the methods, properties and capabilities of the WScript object, I want to end this chapter with a quick look at the other object exposed by the WSH executable. Its name is WshArguments.

This object is a collection that encompasses the command-line arguments passed to a script by its caller. When you run a WSH script by double-clicking its icon in Explorer, you're running it without arguments. When you start a script from the Run dialog or the command line, on the other hand, you *may* pass arguments. This is illustrated in the figure below, in which the arguments One, Two and Three are being passed to a script called args.js:

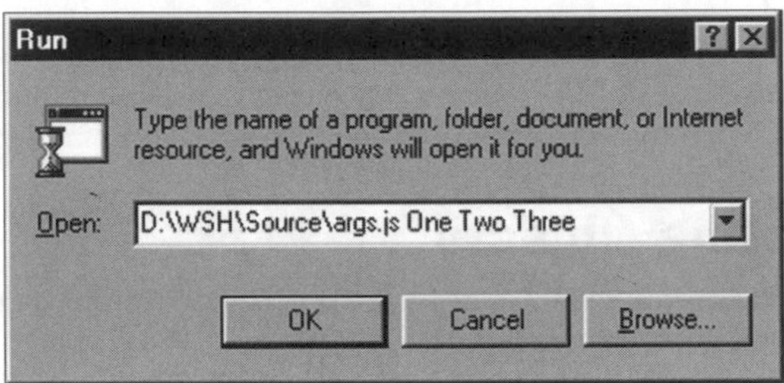

WSH handles the arguments by placing them in the WshArguments collection object. This isn't externally creatable, so in order to get a reference to it, you have to use a public method or property of another object. In this case, the WshArguments collection is returned by the Arguments property of the WScript object:

```
Dim args
Set args = WScript.Arguments
```

WshArguments is a perfectly ordinary collection object that lets you count and list the items it contains.

The WshArguments Programmer's Reference

The programming interface of WshArguments is very simple — for a start, it has no methods at all. The properties associated with it are listed in the following table:

Property	Description
Item	An array of strings containing the various command-line parameters. This is the default property of the object.
Count	Returns the number of command-line parameters.
length	This property provides the same functionality as the Count property, and is provided for JScript compatibility.

To address the *n*th argument on the command line, you need to add a 0-based index to `Item`:

```
WScript.Arguments.Item(0)
```

The above expression denotes the first argument in the collection. Since `Item` is also the default property, you can omit it altogether in VBScript. The following two `MsgBox` statements are both correct, and identify the first argument passed to the script:

```
Dim args
Set args = WScript.Arguments
MsgBox args(0)
MsgBox args.Item(0)
```

Enumerating the Command-line Arguments

If the index you specify is greater than the number of items present, you'll get a "Subscript out of range" error message. The best way to enumerate a collection is therefore by using a `For...Each` loop, like this:

```
For Each arg In WScript.Arguments
   MsgBox arg
Next
```

You can also use a `for` loop; the following JScript example shows how to enumerate and display all the arguments received by the script through the command line:

```
// Args.js
// Demonstrates how to manage the WshArguments collection and
// display the parameters received on the command line.
//-------------------------------------------------------------

var strArgs = "Arguments received:\n\n";

if(WScript.Arguments.length > 0)
{
   for(i = 1; i <= WScript.Arguments.Length; i++)
      strArgs += i + ") " + WScript.Arguments.Item(i - 1) + "\n";

   WScript.Echo(strArgs);
}
else
   WScript.Echo("No arguments specified.");
```

If you execute the command line shown in the previous figure against this script, you'll get this new window:

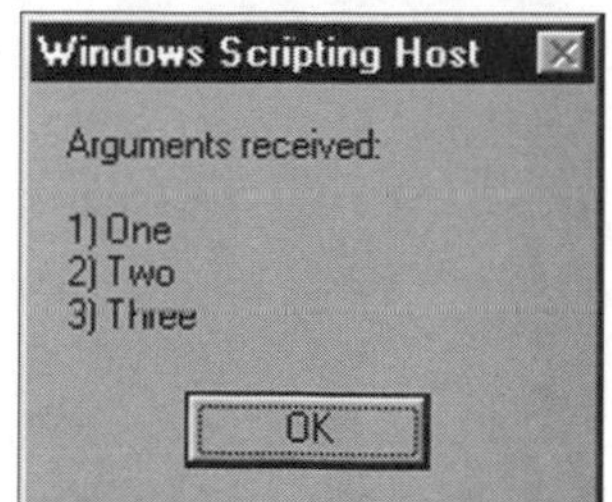

Spaces and Long File Names

Frequently, scripts are passed long filenames (LFNs) or complex strings that include spaces. To make sure that spaces don't confuse WSH, you should make certain that LFNs and strings with spaces are always surrounded by quotes. Spaces are considered to be the default delimiters in command lines, but a quoted string is always processed as a single entity, regardless of the number of spaces it contains.

Clearly, the use to which the `WshArguments` object has been put here isn't terribly exciting; it just demonstrates how to get access to the command-line arguments in your scripts. The arguments passed to a script on its command line can be used for anything from specifying the files it should work on, to the way it should present its results. A script that accepts arguments is generally more versatile and easy to use than one that does not.

Summary

In this chapter, we've begun our exploration of the WSH object model. We analyzed the `WScript` and `WshArguments` objects that are implemented in the host executable, `wscript.exe` (and of course in `cscript.exe` too). In particular, I covered the object management policy of `WScript`, and how you can detect and handle events. In short, this chapter demonstrated:

- How to create, retrieve and disconnect objects
- How to sink events
- How to access the command-line arguments of a running script

In the next chapter, we'll complete our survey of the WSH object model, covering in particular the objects for performing operations on the shell and the network.

4

The WSH Object Model

Like others of its kind, the WSH object model serves the purpose of making complex functions easily accessible from script. In the previous chapter, we examined the root object of this hierarchy — `WScript` — and its loyal companion `WshArguments`. They provided us with some basic functionality to create and manage Automation objects, display messages and retrieve command-line arguments. All of the system-specific features, though, have been left out of these objects — in particular, I'm thinking about the Windows shell, the registry, the network, and the global system environment.

The rest of the WSH object model supports this functionality. In this chapter, I'm going to cover that model in detail, providing an overall perspective as well as a programming reference for all of the objects. In addition, I'll focus on how to:

- Access the system registry
- Call shell functions and work with system folders
- Create shortcuts, including URL shortcuts
- Manage printer and network connections

With this chapter I'll finish my coverage of the core of WSH, and that's the point at which the book will *really* begin. Having acquired a working knowledge of the basic objects, you can start to exploit the real power of WSH by managing additional objects that extend and enrich the original model.

WSH Objects at a Glance

With the exceptions of `WScript` and `WshArguments`, the WSH object model is implemented in a separate module called `wshom.ocx`, which is located in your `Windows\System` directory. In Chapter 3, I presented a table of all the WSH objects that showed how only two of them expose a ProgID string: `WshShell` (`WScript.Shell`) and `WshNetwork` (`WScript.Network`). In all the remaining cases, you must rely on other means to create an instance of the required object. To get a running instance of the `WshShortcut` object, for example, you need to do this:

```
Set objShell = CreateObject("WScript.Shell")
Set objShortcut = objShell.CreateShortcut("shortcut.lnk")
```

In this case, the 'factory' is the `CreateShortcut()` method. Apart from `WScript`, which is automatically instantiated by the WSH executable, the only objects you can create directly using script are `WshShell` and `WshNetwork`. The diagram below shows the dependencies between the various standard WSH objects:

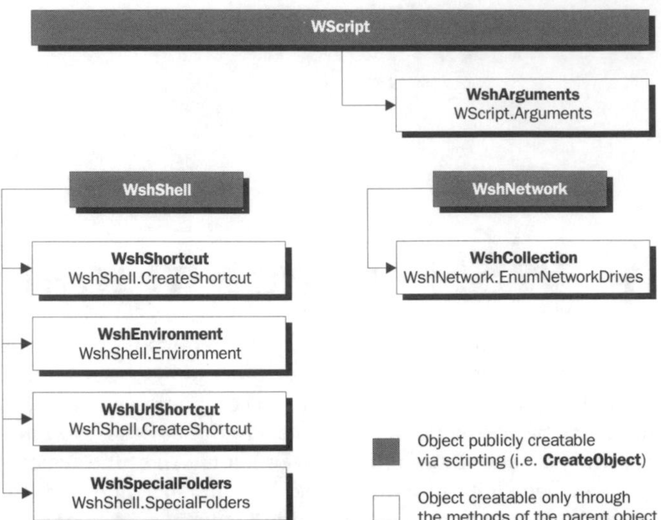

As you can see, they are divided into two main categories: those publicly creatable via calls to `CreateObject()` (and its language-specific counterparts), and those that can be instantiated only indirectly by calling a specific method of the parent object.

Any other object that you ever call from within WSH falls into the first category. It must be creatable through `CreateObject()` by specifying its ProgID.

The WshShell Object

`WshShell` is the component that gives you access to the native shell functionality provided by the Windows Script Host. Using it, you can run external programs, manipulate the contents of the registry, create shortcuts, and access system folders such as `Favorites`, `SendTo` and `StartMenu`.

The `WshShell` object wraps a certain amount of the shell's overall functionality, but not all of it. In Chapter 6 I'll discuss how to get more control of the shell by using the **Shell Automation Objects** *(formerly known as Shell Scriptable Objects).*

Let's have a look at the programming interface of `WshShell`. In VBScript, an instance of the `WshShell` object can be created in either of the following ways:

```
Set obj = WScript.CreateObject("WScript.Shell")
Set obj = CreateObject("WScript.Shell")
```

The same effect can be achieved in JScript like this:

```
obj = WScript.CreateObject("WScript.Shell");
obj = new ActiveXObject("WScript.Shell");
```

As I explained in the last chapter, though, you're encouraged to use the second form. The programmatic identifier of the object should be obvious from these examples: it is `WScript.Shell`.

> **Be aware that some old WSH documentation refers to this object with an incorrect ProgID: `WScript.WshShell`. If you try to use this, you'll get an error message because the scripting engine will be unable to create the object.**

The WshShell Programmer's Reference

The next table contains brief definitions of the properties that `WshShell` exports. There are only two of them, and they are both read-only:

Property	Description
`Environment`	Returns a reference to the `WshEnvironment` object that lets you access a number of environment variables.
`SpecialFolders`	Returns a reference to the `WshSpecialFolders` object that lets you enumerate the contents of some special folders, including `SendTo`, `StartMenu`, `Favorites` and a few others. However, not all of the special folders are accessible through this property. (See later in the chapter.)

The `WshShell` object also has seven methods, which are:

Method	Description
`CreateShortcut()`	Returns an empty `WshShortcut` or `WshUrlShorcut` object to be filled and saved later. The decision of which to create depends on whether a `.lnk` or a `.url` filename is passed as an argument.
`ExpandEnvironment Strings()`	If any sub-string of the string passed to this method is enclosed between a pair of `%` symbols, it is treated as an environment variable and expanded in place. If no such variable exists, the text is returned unchanged. For example, The %WINDIR% directory becomes The C:\Windows directory.
`Popup()`	Displays a message box regardless of which host executable is running (`cscript.exe` or `wscript.exe`).
`RegDelete()`	Deletes a key or a value from the registry.
`RegRead()`	Reads a key or a value from the registry.
`RegWrite()`	Writes a key or a value to the registry.
`Run()`	Launches an external program and offers the script the possibility of waiting for it to terminate.

As we did in the last chapter, let's try some test scripts that demonstrate these methods and properties in action.

Showing Message Boxes

You know that the `Popup()` method is not the only means you have for displaying popup messages with WSH. As I explained in Chapter 3, the `WScript.Echo()` method serves the same purpose in a more direct fashion (you don't have to create another object in order to use it). However, there are a number of significant differences between `WshShell.Popup()` and `WScript.Echo()`; their similarity doesn't really extend beyond their superficial basic functionality.

Popup vs. Echo

Let's compare the declarations of the two methods:

```
WScript.Echo [variable_list]
btnCode = WshShell.Popup(strText [,nSecsToWait] [,strTitle] [,nFlags])
```

`Echo()` is a wrapper for the standard output stream, while `Popup()` is built on the top of the `MessageBox()` API function. When a WSH script is running under `wscript.exe`, the standard output device is identified with a popup dialog box, and this causes the behaviors of the two methods to be similar. In console mode (when a script is running under `cscript.exe`), on the other hand, the two methods have completely different behaviors: `Popup()` still displays a graphical message box, while `Echo()` just dumps out the strings it receives to the console window.

But that's far from the end of the matter. As well as these presentational differences, `Popup()` sports a number of features that are far more Windows-oriented. It lets you specify:

- A title for the message box
- A maximum display time
- The icons and buttons that should appear on the message box

Furthermore, as I have indicated by including the `btnCode` variable in the declaration, `Popup()` returns an integer value denoting the button that was pressed to dismiss the message box.

Using the Popup Method

Let's have a look at the various arguments you can pass to `Popup()` in a bit more detail:

Parameter	Description

`strText`	The text to be displayed, which is subject to being wrapped automatically if it's too long. You can break it into multiple lines by concatenating the text with the newline character; this is `vbCrLf` in VBScript:
	`Obj.Popup "Hello" & vbCrLf & "world"`
	And `\n` in JScript:
	`obj.Popup("Hello" + "\n" + "world");`

`nSecsToWait`	An optional argument that specifies the maximum number of seconds for which the dialog will appear. If the user doesn't make any choice in this interval, the dialog is automatically destroyed. If this parameter is set to 0 (the default value), then the dialog will wait until the user closes it.
`strTitle`	An optional argument that specifies the string to be displayed in the dialog's caption bar. If this parameter is missing, the title defaults to Windows Scripting Host.
`nFlags`	An optional argument that lets you customize the appearance of the message box. This parameter is obtained by combining various groups of values that affect buttons and icons.

The dialog box created by `Popup()` can provide several predefined button combinations that address the most common scenarios. Each combination is assigned a number that you can use when specifying the `nFlags` parameter. They are:

Flag	VBScript constant	Buttons
0	`vbOKOnly`	Displays the OK button. The dialog can be canceled by pressing the *Esc* or *Alt-F4* keys.
1	`vbOKCancel`	Displays the OK and Cancel buttons. The dialog can be canceled by pressing the *Esc* or *Alt-F4* keys.
2	`vbAbortRetryIgnore`	Displays the Abort, Retry and Ignore buttons. The dialog can't be canceled from the keyboard.
3	`vbYesNoCancel`	Displays the Yes, No and Cancel buttons. The dialog can be canceled by pressing the *Esc* or *Alt-F4* keys.
4	`vbYesNo`	Displays the Yes and No buttons. The dialog can't be canceled from the keyboard.
5	`vbRetryCancel`	Displays the Retry and Cancel buttons. The dialog can be canceled by pressing the *Esc* or *Alt-F4* keys.

As you can see from the table, if the Cancel button is present (or if you have just the OK button), you can cancel the dialog by pressing *Esc* or *Alt-F4*. However, there is no special return value for this eventuality; `Popup()` will simply return the value that it would have returned had you clicked the button. There are a number of possible return values from `Popup()`, and they all depend on which button the user clicks to dismiss the dialog:

Return value	VBScript constant	Corresponding user action
1	vbOK	The OK button was clicked. This is also returned if you press *Esc* or *Alt-F4* to cancel a dialog that only has an OK button.
2	vbCancel	The Cancel button was clicked. This is also returned if you press *Esc* or *Alt-F4* to cancel a dialog that has a Cancel button.
3	vbAbort	The Abort button was clicked.
4	vbRetry	The Retry button was clicked.
5	vbIgnore	The Ignore button was clicked.
6	vbYes	The Yes button was clicked.
7	vbNo	The No button was clicked.
-1	-1	No button was clicked, but the timeout expired.

After that little digression about return values, let's go back to the flags that you can use to customize the appearance and operation of a message box. If you want the dialog to contain an icon as well as the buttons you've specified, just add one of the following values to `nFlags`:

Flag	Icon	VBScript constant	Icon displayed
16		vbCritical	The 'Stop' icon
32		vbQuestion	The 'Question Mark' icon
48		vbExclamation	The 'Exclamation Point' icon
64		vbInformation	The 'Information' icon

To display a message box with a question mark and a pair of Yes/No buttons, for example, you just have to combine the flag values. The (VBScript) code for doing this is shown on the next page:

```
Set obj = CreateObject("WScript.Shell")
btnCode = obj.Popup("Hello World!", 3, "3 seconds", vbQuestion + vbYesNo)
```

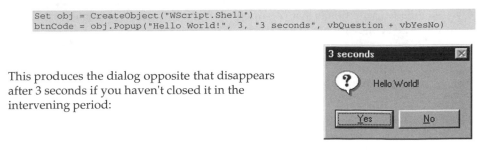

This produces the dialog opposite that disappears after 3 seconds if you haven't closed it in the intervening period:

Note that if you're using JScript, you'll need to define your own constants, as the language doesn't provide them by default. Alternatively, you can just use the numbers.

Timed-Out Message Boxes

If you specify a timeout value for a dialog box, you should be ready to handle this eventuality in your script, and it's easy enough to do. If `Popup()`'s return value is -1, you know that the user didn't choose any of the available options, and you may then want to take some default action in your code.

```
Set obj = CreateObject("WScript.Shell")
btnCode = obj.Popup("Hello World!", 3, "3 seconds", vbQuestion + vbYesNo)

Select Case btnCode
   Case vbNo
      MsgBox "Clicked No"
   Case vbYes
      MsgBox "Clicked Yes"
   Case -1
     MsgBox "Timed Out"
End Select
```

A typical way of handling timeouts is to use the same code as the button you have chosen to be the default action for the dialog. In the case below, this is the Yes button:

```
Set obj = CreateObject("WScript.Shell")
btnCode = obj.Popup("Hello World!", 3, "3 seconds", vbQuestion + vbYesNo)

Select Case btnCode
   Case vbNo
      MsgBox "Clicked No"
   Case vbYes, -1                   ' Handle both Yes and timeout
      MsgBox "Clicked Yes"
End Select
```

Undocumented Features

There are a number of things you can do with `Popup()` that the official documentation doesn't mention, and I'm going to demonstrate some of them here. If you're *really* interested in this kind of thing, however, I recommend that you delve into the Win32 SDK documentation for the `MessageBox()` API function to find out more. (As I mentioned earlier, `Popup()` is actually just a thin wrapper for `MessageBox()`.)

Experimentation with undocumented features can be hazardous, but on this occasion we're dealing with things that are *documented in the Win32 Software Developer's Kit, and you can proceed with confidence.*

Two potentially useful things that you can do quite easily using undocumented features of the `Popup()` method are:

- Setting the input focus to a particular dialog button
- Setting the 'topmost' flag

Choosing the Default Button

When you display a message box, the input focus goes to the leftmost button by default, but you can change this behavior by adding another value to the `nFlags` argument. This possibility is also described in the VBScript reference for `MsgBox()`.

Flag	VBScript constant	Default button
0	vbDefaultButton1	The first button
256	vbDefaultButton2	The second button
512	vbDefaultButton3	The third button

You can see the second of these values in action in the following code snippet:

```
Set obj = CreateObject("WScript.Shell")
obj.Popup "Hello World!", 3, "3 seconds", _
        vbQuestion + vbYesNo + vbDefaultButton2
```

Topmost Message Boxes

By default, a message box is modal with respect to the application that invoked it. This means that the user must respond to or close the dialog before they can continue working with the application. If you want to keep the window on the top of all the other windows in the system at all times, then add a value of 4096 to `nFlags`. The VBScript constant for this is `vbSystemModal`.

If another window also has the topmost flag set, both will continue to be 'topmost' with respect to all others. Between them, however, the topmost attribute is ignored. If you have WinZip on your machine, select the Always On Top item in its system menu, and then try running the following script:

```
Set obj = CreateObject("WScript.Shell")
obj.Popup "Hello World!", 0, "Topmost Window", _
        vbQuestion + vbYesNo + vbDefaultButton2 + vbSystemModal
```

You should find that the message box and WinZip windows can hide one another, but they will always be on top of all the other windows in the system.

Accessing the Registry

The registry is a kind of database where Windows stores all sorts of information: system and program settings, user preferences, installed software and hardware, and so forth. The registry has a hierarchical structure based on six **root nodes**, also known as **hives**. The next picture shows a view of the Windows 98 registry and its hives as seen in the Registry Editor, `regedit.exe`:

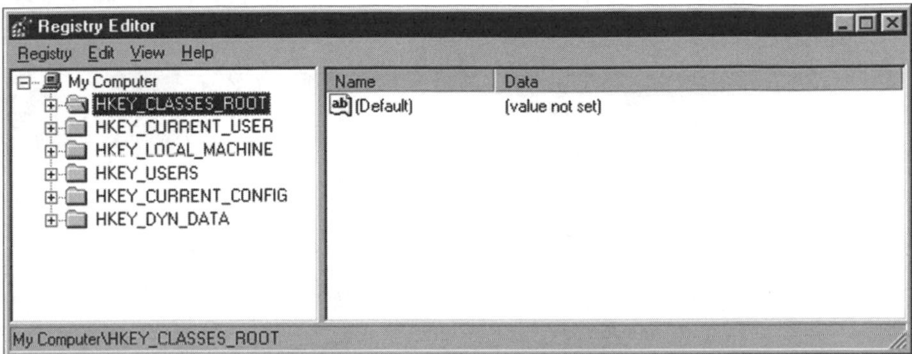

The following table explains the role of each of these root nodes by describing the kind of data it stores:

Root node	Shortcut	Information stored
`HKEY_CLASSES_ROOT`	`HKCR`	File types, associations, and COM objects.
`HKEY_CURRENT_USER`	`HKCU`	User-specific settings for software, hardware (keyboard layout, for example) and Internet connections. This node is actually an alias for a sub-node of `HKEY_USERS`.
`HKEY_LOCAL_MACHINE`	`HKLM`	Settings that apply to all users, but which are specific to this machine.
`HKEY_USERS`	----	Settings for the various registered users, including the current one. This is a 'physical' node in the sense that it occupies real space on disk, storing information. `HKCU`, by contrast, is a 'logical' node that the Registry Editor shows as stand-alone in order to provide a more user friendly interface.
`HKEY_CURRENT_CONFIG`	----	Current configuration of hardware and software.

The HKEY_DYN_DATA root node, which appears in the screenshot but not in the table, is used to store driver and performance information. It can't be accessed via WSH, so I didn't include it in the table. I don't think the lack of support is for any technical reason; rather it's because the need to grab this kind of information from script code is highly unlikely. If you do need to work with the registry, the chances are that you'll be using the first three nodes.

The following diagram shows how the registry is structured: there are **root nodes**, **keys**, and **values** (which can be named and unnamed):

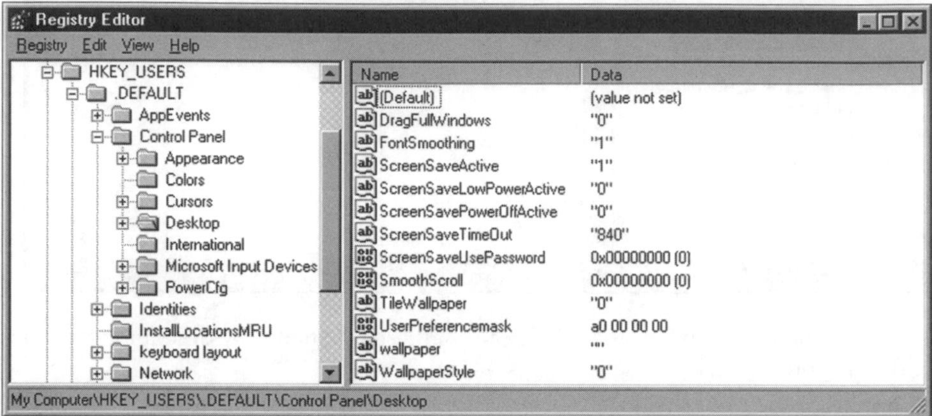

Root nodes (or hives) and **keys** are both types of node. To draw an analogy with the file system, keys are a bit like directories, while the root nodes are more akin to drives. Both can contain any number of values.

The **values** that each key contains are identified by name, with one exception. For reasons of compatibility with the Windows 3.x version of the registry, the default value of each key is unnamed; in the above screenshot, the label (Default) is used to represent it. If you try to read or write a value and omit its name, the action is performed on the default value.

The values in the registry are typed, but although the Win32 API supports a few more types than WSH, I think it's unlikely that you'll ever need anything that WSH doesn't provide you with.

Backing up the Registry

The registry is a very sensitive, very important part of the 32-bit Windows operating systems. For this reason, any modifications you make should be handled with the maximum of care.

I strongly advise that you never execute operations on the registry that you don't know how to undo, and that you only ever make modifications whose effects you understand completely.

It's sound practice to back up the registry on a regular basis. In Windows 98, there's a new utility called the Registry Checker that automatically backs up the registry every day. However, you can also run it yourself at any time. The program to run is `scanregw.exe`, which lives in the `Windows` directory.

All the backups made by this program can be found in the `SysBckup` folder of the `Windows` directory — they are `.cab` files named `rbXxx.cab`. To restore any of them, just double-click the one you want.

Programming the Registry with WSH

Windows Script Host provides you with the possibility of seamless access to the system registry. There are methods of the `WshShell` object that allow you to read and write keys and values, and even to delete them. The three `WshShell` methods that allow you to access the registry programmatically are:

- `RegRead()`
- `RegWrite()`
- `RegDelete()`

All three methods encapsulate three basic operations: they open the key you specify, do the job they're supposed to do, and then close the key again. After just a little more background information, we'll be in a position to put them to use.

Supported Types

As I mentioned earlier, the values in the registry are typed. WSH lets you read and write data of the following types:

Type	Example
REG_SZ	Strings
REG_DWORD	32-bit unsigned values
REG_BINARY	Binary data
REG_EXPAND_SZ	Strings that contain expandable macros, such as %WINDIR%

Knowing the type of a data item is important for the registry, but unfortunately scripting languages *aren't* strongly typed and support only a single data type: the `Variant`. This means that the `WshShell` object must also take care of conversions from `Variants` to native registry types, and vice versa.

When you're reading from the registry, you just need to specify the key; any necessary conversion is done silently by `RegRead()`. When you're writing a value through `RegWrite()`, on the other hand, you'll find that you have to specify the type involved using a string.

Registry Paths

I already mentioned that the registry can be considered to work a little like the file system, and that similarity extends to the way you identify a value or a key: you need to specify a path. A registry path is a string that looks just like a fully qualified file system path name. For example:

```
HKCU\
   Software\
      Microsoft\
         Windows\
            CurrentVersion\
               MSID
```

I've broken it into multiple lines for the sake of readability, but in reality it's a single string, like this: `HKCU\Software\Microsoft\Windows\CurrentVersion\MSID`.

Note that WSH uses a special, easy-to-remember notation for distinguishing between keys and values, which is slightly different from the Win32 API notation. If the string has a final slash, it refers to a key; otherwise, it addresses a value. The above string, for example, points to a value named `MSID` in the key called `HKCU\Software\Microsoft\Windows\CurrentVersion\`.

This approach, though, has an unpleasant side effect. Because the \ character is used exclusively to delimit nodes in a key's full name, you can't access named values whose names include a backslash. I don't think it's a problem you'll come across very often, but it's definitely a limitation, and you should be aware of it.

Note that in JScript you need to use a double backslash to delimit the various items in a registry path name.

Reading from the Registry

Now that we have sufficient theory, we can begin to analyze in detail the `WshShell` methods for working with the registry. The `RegRead()` method that's used to access registry data from a WSH script has the following prototype:

```
strData = WshShell.RegRead(strKeyOrValue)
```

If `strKeyOrValue` ends with a slash, it is meant to identify a key. Otherwise, it points to the value rendered by the final token of the path. However, although you can pass a key *or* a value to this method, you always end up reading values. Let's see why.

```
path = "HKLM\Software\Microsoft\Windows\CurrentVersion"
Set objShell = CreateObject("WScript.Shell")

Msgbox objShell.RegRead(path & "\")
Msgbox objShell.RegRead(path & "\CommonFilesDir")
```

Given the registry path shown in the figure below:

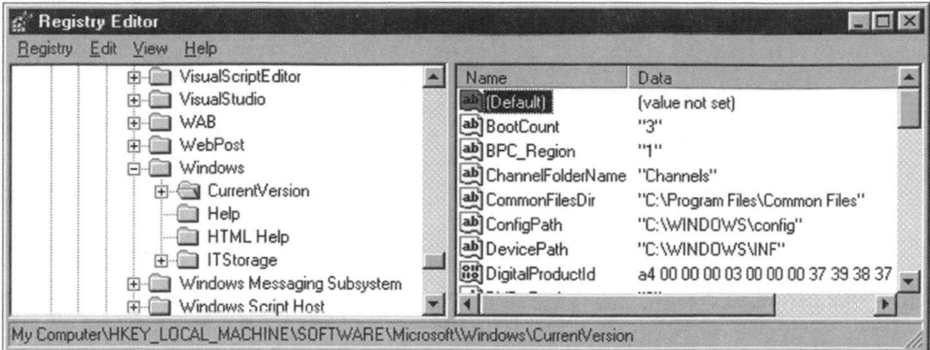

the first message box will contain nothing at all, which is what the `(Default)` unnamed value contains. The second message box, on the other hand, should hold the name of the common files directory, `C:\Program Files\Common Files`:

When it ends with a slash, `strKeyOrValue` is meant to identify the key, and 'reading the key' means reading its `(Default)` value. If `strKeyOrValue` addresses a value, `RegRead()` will return that value, as is the case for `CommonFilesDir` above.

If the method is unable to locate the path, you'll get an error; forgetting the final slash when you want to read the unnamed value is a common mistake. You don't need to specify the type of the data you want to read (just declare a variable to store it), but you'll get an error if the value is of a type that WSH doesn't support.

Detecting the Current Operating System

The registry path we visited a moment ago can provide us with more information that is sometimes important: which operating system the script is running on. The following script demonstrates a small VBScript function that returns the name of the current operating system:

```
Function GetOS
   REG_HKLM_WINDOWS = "HKLM\Software\Microsoft\Windows\CurrentVersion"
   Dim objShell
   Set objShell = CreateObject("WScript.Shell")

   GetOS = objShell.RegRead(REG_HKLM_WINDOWS & "\Version")
End Function
```

Accessing User Folders

To further test the Windows Script Host's registry-reading capability, let's try to figure out which folder contains the Internet Explorer cache. All these files are kept in a directory whose name is subject to change, but always stored under the HKCU node. The exact key is:

```
HKEY_CURRENT_USER\
   Software\
      Microsoft\
         Windows\
            CurrentVersion\
               Explorer\
                  Shell Folders\
```

The value is named Cache, and so the following code demonstrates how to get the name of the folder containing Internet Explorer's cache:

```
REG_HKCU_WINDOWS = "HKCU\Software\Microsoft\Windows\CurrentVersion\"
Set shell = CreateObject("WScript.Shell")
MsgBox shell.RegRead(REG_HKCU_WINDOWS & "Explorer\Shell Folders\Cache")
```

In the last two examples, I've defined a couple of strings that hold the names of often-visited areas of the registry. I frequently use strings like REG_HKCU_WINDOWS to address registry paths that are tedious to type (and to remember), and in the next chapter you'll discover how the new features of WSH 2.0 make it practical to maintain a single script file containing all the definitions you think you'll ever need.

Writing to the Registry

The RegWrite() method, with which you modify or write data in the registry, has the following prototype:

```
WshShell.RegWrite(strKeyOrValue, vValue [,strType])
```

Once again, the strKeyOrValue parameter denotes either a key or a specific value to update or create. As before, the final slash decides whether the path will be interpreted as a key or as a named value. If the parameter points to a key, the method will set its (Default) value.

If you pass one, the strType argument should be a string that will affect the way the value in vValue is interpreted by the method. The supported types (and therefore the valid strings to use) are REG_SZ, REG_EXPAND_SZ, REG_BINARY and REG_DWORD; let's see them in detail:

Type	Description
REG_SZ	A string to be stored in the registry. Any value you pass will be converted to a string by the RegWrite() method, so the number 123 (for example) becomes the string "123".
REG_EXPAND_SZ	An expandable string to be stored in the registry. Any sub-string enclosed between a pair of % characters will be taken to be an environment variable and properly expanded. If you store a string like %WINDIR%\notepad.exe, it will be written to the registry as is, but considered as c:\windows\notepad.exe.

Type	Description
REG_BINARY	A binary value. You need to pass a numeric value that is either decimal or hexadecimal. You can't pass a string because the conversion from the latter to the former will not be performed.
REG_DWORD	A numeric value. If you pass a string, then it will be converted to the corresponding numeric value. For example, "&HB" will be stored as the hexadecimal value B.

If you omit the strType argument, the method defaults to using the REG_SZ type (a string). If you try to use a type that is not legitimate, you'll get an 'invalid argument' error. If the key you specify already exists, the existing type is overwritten.

A New Context Menu Item for All Files

Our first example in this section will add a new item to the context menu of any file selected anywhere in Explorer that will open the specified file with Notepad. As well as demonstrating how to write to the registry, this is actually quite a useful facility in itself: the ability quickly to open text files such as .ini, .inf, and .asp, for which a default viewer is not registered, is a handy one.

This feature is planned to be a built-in facility of the new Windows 2000 shell.

To add a new item to the context menu of a file that's selected in Explorer, we need to add a node beneath the following path:

```
HKEY_CLASSES_ROOT\
    *\
        Shell\
```

You may not have a key called Shell *under* HKCR*\ *(it's not present by default, although some common applications add it), but that isn't a problem:* RegWrite() *will automatically create it for you if it's missing.*

What we have to add is a new node with a name that's unique with respect to the keys at the same level; I'm going to call mine Notepad. The name is used to identify the command, and it will also be used as the string that appears in the context menu unless we specify a different one as its (Default) entry. The advantage of setting a different string is that you can also specify an accelerator for the command.

The actual command to be executed is indicated by means of a sub-key named Command whose (Default) value contains the command line. The following script produces result shown in the subsequent figure:

```
' ContextMenu.vbs
' Adds a 'View with Notepad' menu item to any file's context menu
' -------------------------------------------------------------------------
Option Explicit

Dim shell
Dim REG_HKCR_ALL

' The registry path where our new entries should be added
' If your registry doesn't contain a Shell node, it'll be silently created
REG_HKCR_ALL = "HKCR\*\Shell"

' Adds a new key and a couple of entries. The item will have a underlined N
Set shell = CreateObject("WScript.Shell")
shell.RegWrite REG_HKCR_ALL & "\Notepad\", _
               "View with &Notepad", _
               "REG_SZ"
shell.RegWrite REG_HKCR_ALL & "\Notepad\Command\", _
               "%WINDIR%\notepad.exe %1", _
               "REG_EXPAND_SZ"
```

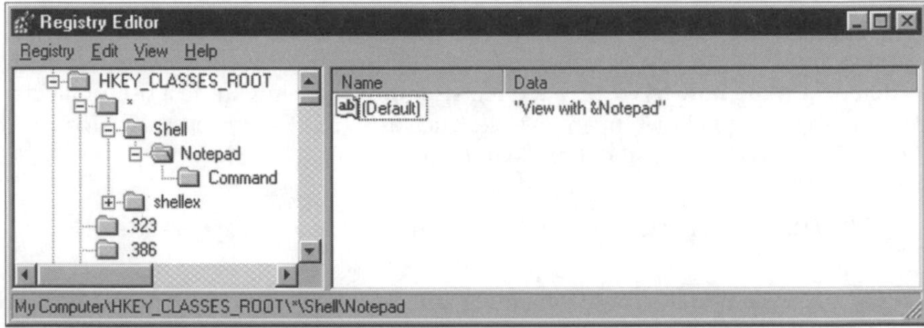

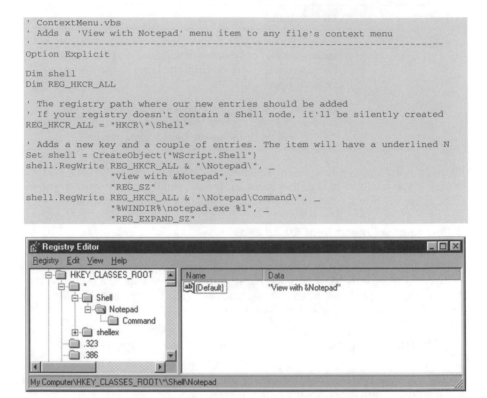

As you can see, any missing key is automatically created, and a path that ends with a slash causes the string to be written to the `(Default)` value. Now, as soon as you right-click on any file in the Windows Explorer, you'll see a brand new item:

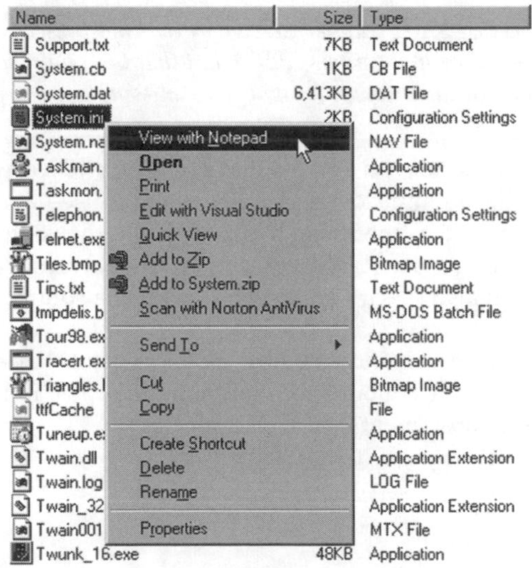

The default value of the Notepad key is stored as an ordinary string, so I could have omitted to specify the REG_SZ type in that case. The command to be executed, on the other hand, is stored as an *expandable* string. (The %1 in the command line string will contain the name of the selected file that is passed to Notepad.)

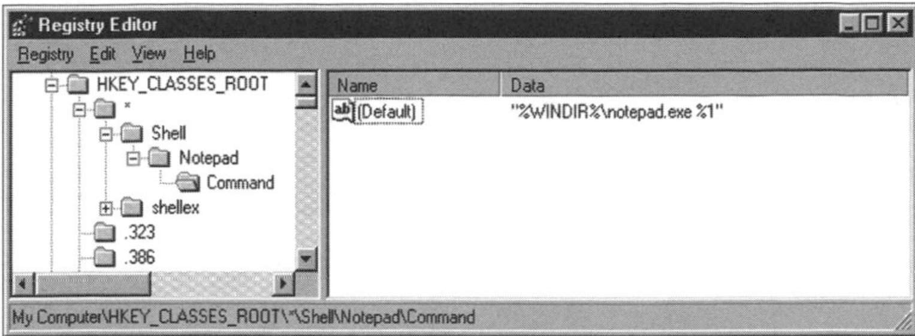

Judging purely by their appearance in the Registry Editor, there's no difference at all between a REG_SZ string and a REG_EXPAND_SZ string. This impression is further confirmed if you execute the following snippet that just reads back the value; the string it displays still contains %WINDIR% in its unexpanded form:

```
REG_HKCR_ALL = "HKCR\*\Shell"

Set shell = CreateObject("WScript.Shell")
str = shell.RegRead(REG_HKCR_ALL & "\Notepad\Command\")

MsgBox str
```

Despite this apparent similarity, however, there's a big difference between REG_SZ and REG_EXPAND_SZ. To prove it, try amending the ContextMenu.vbs program to use the following call that stores the string in the same place, but as type REG_SZ:

```
...

shell.RegWrite REG_HKCR_ALL & "\Notepad\Command\", _
               "%WINDIR%\notepad.exe %1", _
               "REG_SZ"
```

Run the program again, then right-click any file (say, system.ini) and select the View with Notepad item. You'll find that Explorer is no longer able to do as you request:

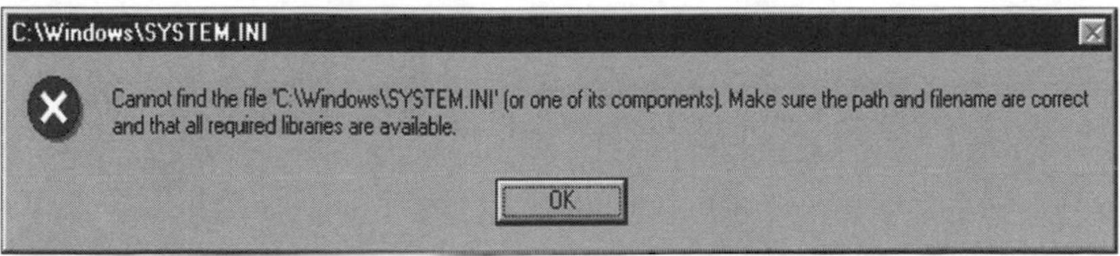

If you want to use the expanded version of a REG_EXPAND_SZ string in your scripts, you need to use the ExpandEnvironmentStrings() method of the WshShell object:

```
REG_HKCR_ALL = "HKCR\*\Shell"

Set shell = CreateObject("WScript.Shell")
str = shell.RegRead(REG_HKCR_ALL & "\Notepad\Command\")

MsgBox shell.ExpandEnvironmentStrings(str)
```

I'll cover `ExpandEnvironmentStrings()` in more detail later on in this chapter.

Writing Numeric Data

Let's see what happens when we try to write binary and numeric data to the registry. The following code will add two new (admittedly meaningless, but harmless) values to the same path as we created above:

```
REG_HKCR_ALL = "HKCR\*\Shell"

Set shell = CreateObject("WScript.Shell")
shell.RegWrite REG_HKCR_ALL & "\Notepad\Command\Binary", &HB, "REG_BINARY"
shell.RegWrite REG_HKCR_ALL & "\Notepad\Command\Dword", &HB, "REG_DWORD"
```

Looking at them in the Registry Editor, the binary and DWORD data appear to be slightly different:

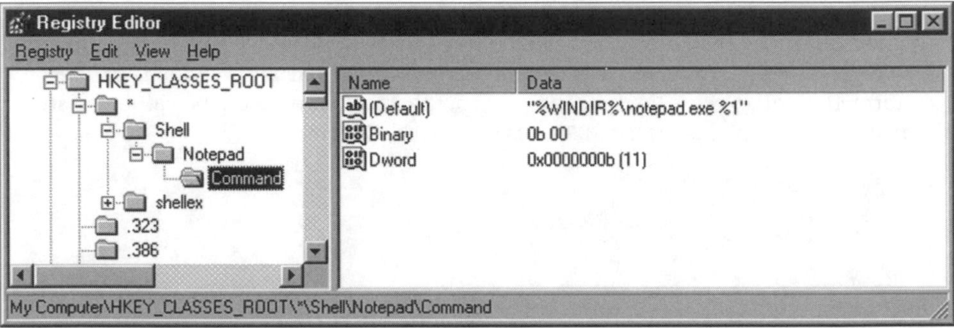

You can see that the `Dword` value (of type `REG_DWORD`) is represented as a number, while the `Binary` value (of type `REG_BINARY`) is a stream of data. If you double-click on the values in order to edit them, you'll be shown two different dialog boxes that reflect this difference.

It's possible to pass decimal or hexadecimal values as the `vValue` argument, provided that you use the correct language syntax to specify them. In the latter case, the letter `A` stands for a variable named `A`, while `&HA` represents the hexadecimal value that's equal to 10 in decimal notation.

Reading Back Numeric Data

Reading back a `REG_DWORD` value doesn't pose much of a problem — you can just store it in an ordinary 32-bit variable. Getting hold of binary data from the registry, on the other hand, is a bit trickier. As I mentioned earlier, binary data is considered simply to be a stream of bytes that you would normally specify using hexadecimal values. For example, you might use `&HFF00FF` to denote the RGB format of the color magenta:

```
shell.RegWrite REG_HKCR_ALL & "\Notepad\Command\Magenta", _
               &HFF00FF, _
               "REG_BINARY"
```

When you attempt to read it back, however, what you get is an array of `Variants`:

```
clrMag = shell.RegRead(REG_HKCR_ALL & "\Notepad\Command\Magenta")
```

The following code snippet demonstrates how to convert this array into a string by concatenating the individual bytes in a `For Each` loop:

```
clrMag = shell.RegRead(REG_HKCR_ALL & "\Notepad\Command\Magenta")
```

```
For Each char In clrMag
   datum = Right("00" & Hex(char), 2)
   str = datum & str                         ' Returns FF00FF
Next

MsgBox str
```

Binary values are stored 'backwards' in the registry, so the loop in the listing above reconstructs the stream in its original order by progressively adding each byte to the *front* of the string being assembled.

Deleting Entries and Values

The third (and most dangerous) of the `WshShell` object's registry manipulation methods is `RegDelete()`, which has the following simple syntax:

```
WshShell.RegDelete strKeyOrValue
```

Once again, the parameter can refer to a key as well as to a value; it all depends upon the presence of a final backslash.

Deleting under Windows NT and Windows 9x

Using `RegDelete()` under Windows NT and Windows 9x poses some problems, because the two operating systems follow different policies when it comes to deleting from the registry. Deleting a *value* is the same under Windows NT and Windows 9x, but things are slightly different for *key* deletion.

Windows 9x always provides automatic, recursive deletion. In other words, when a key is deleted, its entire sub-tree is removed as well, no matter how many sub-keys or values it contains. Under Windows NT, on the other hand, a key can be deleted only if it is empty. In this case, 'empty' means that it has no child keys; the number of values is not a factor in determining the 'emptiness' of a key.

In all likelihood, however, you will only be using `RegDelete()` to remove items from the registry that you have earlier added with `RegWrite()`. This being the case, you will know the exact locations of all the keys and values in question, so writing a routine that deletes them recursively (and therefore works on both Windows 9x and Windows NT) should not be a difficult task.

Running External Programs

The `WshShell` object exposes a method called `Run()` that allows you to create a new Windows process for running the external program of your choice. In addition to simply starting the process off, the method provides the following features:

- Control over the spawned program's window style (when the application supports this)
- The ability to take a document's name and start the program that handles it

- Synchronized execution, in which your script waits for the spawned program to terminate

The syntax of the method is:

```
nRetCode = WshShell.Run(strCommand [,nWindowtype] [,bWaitOnReturn])
```

Let's look at the role of each parameter:

Parameter	Description
strCommand	The command line to run. This may include any parameters you need to pass to the executable.
nWindowType	An optional argument for attempting to define the appearance of the window being created by the new process. Whether this attempt will be successful depends upon how the spawned program has been designed. There are programs (including calc.exe, the Windows calculator) that don't take the style you specify into account.
bWaitOnReturn	An optional argument with which you decide whether the call must wait for the program it spawns to terminate. Setting it to True results in this behavior, while False (which is the default setting) causes the method to return as soon as the program is launched.

If the script has to wait for the spawned program to terminate, then the return value is the return code of that spawned program. Otherwise, Run() returns 0.

Styles of the Application Window

The nWindowType argument specifies how a Windows-based application window is to be shown; the acceptable values are listed below. If you're an experienced Win32 programmer, these values will sound familiar, since they are the same as the SW_XXX flags supported by ShowWindow() and other window-specific API functions. To help you to identify the similarities and plan possible extensions, I've added references to the equivalent SW_XXX constants in the descriptions:

Constant	Description
0	Hides the window. (SW_HIDE)
1, 5	Displays the window and gives it the focus. This is the default setting. (SW_SHOWNORMAL)
2	Minimizes the window and gives it the focus. (SW_SHOWMINIMIZED)
3	Maximizes the window and gives it the focus. (SW_MAXIMIZE)
4	Displays the window without giving it the focus. (SW_SHOWNOACTIVATE)
6, 7	Minimizes the window without giving it the focus. (SW_MINIMIZE)

Note that these are not the only settings that can be applied to a window, but they are the only ones that make sense for an application that's just starting.

As I mentioned earlier, even if you set one of these styles, you can't guarantee that the program being spawned will pay any attention to it. The program receives the style as an argument to its startup procedure — the `WinMain()` function that any Windows program must have. A well-behaved Windows program is *supposed* to display its main window according to the specified style, but not all programs comply with this rule, and this has the potential to affect the outcome of the `Run()` method.

The Command Line

The command line passed to `Run()` should include the name of the executable to launch and any parameters you want to pass to that executable. If the command line contains any environment variables, they will be expanded automatically. To run Notepad, for example, you could do the following:

```
Set shell = CreateObject("WScript.Shell")
shell.Run "%WINDIR%\notepad.exe"
```

Because programs located in the `Windows` *directory are automatically in the system search path, running them doesn't* require *you to use the* `%WINDIR%` *environment variable. The technique demonstrated here is still valid, however.*

Paying Attention to Long Filenames

`Run()` is alert to the possibility of command-line parameters, and uses any whitespace it finds to isolate arguments. This may cause problems if you're using path names that contain spaces. For example:

```
shell.Run "c:\Program Files\Internet Explorer\IExplore.exe"
```

This will be interpreted as a request to run an executable called `c:\Program` with a couple of arguments: `Files\Internet` and `Explorer\IExplore.exe`. To work around this, you must make sure you embed the program name in quotes, ensuring that `Run()` will correctly distinguish between the name of the application and its arguments. Here are two valid examples of doing this in VBScript:

```
shell.Run Chr(34) & _
          "c:\Program Files\Internet Explorer\IExplore.exe" & Chr(34)

shell.Run """c:\Program Files\Internet Explorer\IExplore.exe"""
```

The first of these works because 34 is the ASCII code of the double-quote character (`"`). In JScript, on the other hand, you would just do this:

```
shell.Run("\"c:\\Program Files\\Internet Explorer\\IExplore.exe\"");
```

The quote character in JScript is given by `\"`, while the backslash is given by `\\`.

Opening Documents

The `Run()` method also lets you 'run' *documents*, provided that there is a program registered to handle them. For example, to open a document called `file.txt` in Notepad you have two options. There's the standard way:

```
Set shell = CreateObject("WScript.Shell")
shell.Run "notepad.exe file.txt"
```

But you can achieve the same result with a simpler command:

```
Set shell = CreateObject("WScript.Shell")
shell.Run "file.txt"
```

In the second case, it's up to the WSH executable to figure out what program is registered to handle `.txt` documents. If you want a different, unregistered program to work on the file, you must call the `Run()` method in the 'ordinary' way.

> *Note that you'll get different results from these two techniques if you try to open a document that doesn't exist. Trying to run such a document will produce an error, while the effect of attempting to pass it to an application will depend on the application in question*

Opening Folders

Along with applications and documents, the `WshShell.Run()` method also allows you to open a folder. The following code opens an Explorer window showing the contents of the C drive:

```
Set shell = CreateObject("WScript.Shell")
shell.Run "c:"
```

In Windows, there are folders that are part of the physical file system, and folders that aren't. To access and explore a folder that is tied directly to a file system directory, you can just pass its fully qualified name to `Run()`, as shown above.

When the actual path name is hidden behind a descriptive name, as is the case with `My Documents`, for example, the `WshShell` object makes available another object called `WshSpecialFolders` that lets you query for a physical path against a descriptive name. I'll describe this object in detail later in this chapter.

Working with Protocols

Yet another use of the `WshShell.Run()` method is in collaboration with **protocols**. When you see this term, you probably start thinking about HTTP and FTP (which are probably the most pervasive), but there are a few other protocols that we can use to execute useful actions in the context of WSH.

The protocols available on your machine are stored in the registry as sub-keys of `HKCR\Protocols\Handler\`. Of the list you'll see there (the size of which will depend on what version of what browser you have installed), `http`, `ftp`, `mailto` and `about` are particularly interesting and can turn out to be of practical value when used in conjunction with `Run()`:

Protocol	IE4+ only	Description
`http`		Lets you connect to a web site.
`ftp`		Lets you connect to a remote host via FTP.
`mailto`		Lets you send an e-mail message.
`about`	✓	Lets you display predefined pages with messages for the user. Only partially supported by Netscape browsers.

To use a protocol from the Windows Script Host, you build a URL and then ask your browser to navigate to it by passing it as an argument to `Run()`. Let's see some examples of this technique in action.

Sending an E-mail Message

In Windows, a protocol string like `mailto` is associated with a program and treated just like a kind of document. This makes it easy to use `Run()` for sending an e-mail message or navigating to a URL. The following code will allow you to send a message to the specified recipient, using your default e-mail program. If you're using Outlook or Outlook Express with the Send Later feature switched on, the message will go straight to your `Outbox` folder:

```
Set shell = CreateObject("WScript.Shell")
shell.Run "mailto:desposito@infomedia.it"
```

To specify more than one recipient at once, concatenate the addresses using semicolons:

```
Set shell = CreateObject("WScript.Shell")
shell.Run "mailto:desposito@infomedia.it;despos@tin.it"
```

If the recipient or recipients have entries in your address book, you could also use the display names in place of the e-mail addresses.

Navigating to a URL

The following syntax lets you navigate to the given URL; it supports all the registered URL protocols:

```
Set shell = CreateObject("WScript.Shell")
shell.Run "http://www.wrox.com"
```

By changing the URL, you can also connect to a FTP site should you wish to do so.

Sending HTML-based Messages to Users

The `about` protocol enables you to use HTML to format messages for your users. Its standard behavior (in that it is supported by Microsoft and Netscape browsers) is simply to output the text following the colon after its name. The next example shows how to format simple HTML messages on the fly:

```
HTML_THANKYOU = "<b>Thank you</b> for buying the book!"
HTML_ISBNMISSING = "You should enter the book's <i>ISBN</i>."

s = InputBox("Enter the ISBN")

If s <> "" Then
   Show(HTML_THANKYOU)
Else
   Show(HTML_ISBNMISSING)
End If

Function Show(s)
   Set shell = CreateObject("WScript.Shell")
   s = Chr(34) & "about:" & s & Chr(34)
   shell.Run s
End Function
```

Here's the output of this script on my machine, which has Internet Explorer installed as the default browser:

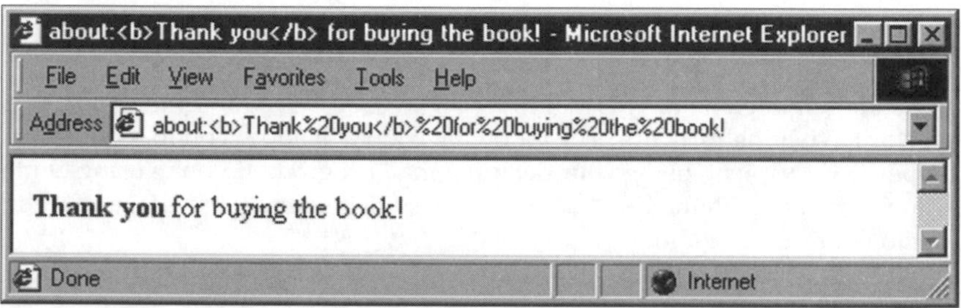

In case you need to show more specialized pages, IE lets you identify such things using an alias. Doing this also has the pleasant side effect of removing the raw text from the title and the address bar. The table that maps aliases with actual pages is kept in the registry, and this is also where Internet Explorer stores those nice pages that you see when navigation is canceled, or the page you want isn't available.

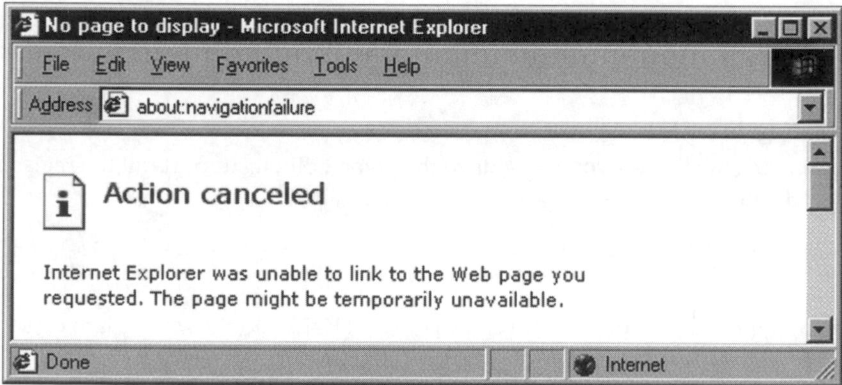

To register your own `about:` pages, just store them in a known location (say, `C:\About`), and add an entry like the following one to the registry:

```
REG_HKLM_ABOUT = "HKLM\Software\Microsoft\Internet Explorer\AboutURLs\"
Set shell = CreateObject("WScript.Shell")
shell.RegWrite REG_HKLM_ABOUT & "ThankYou", "c:\about\thankyou.htm"
```

Then, run this slightly modified code:

```
HTML_ISBNMISSING = "You should enter the book's <i>ISBN</i>."

s = InputBox("Enter the ISBN")

If s <> "" Then
   Show("ThankYou")
Else
   Show(HTML_ISBNMISSING)
End If

Function Show(s)
   Set shell = CreateObject("WScript.Shell")
   s = Chr(34) & "about:" & s & Chr(34)
   shell.Run s
End Function
```

I'm sure you'll agree that the output now has a much more professional look:

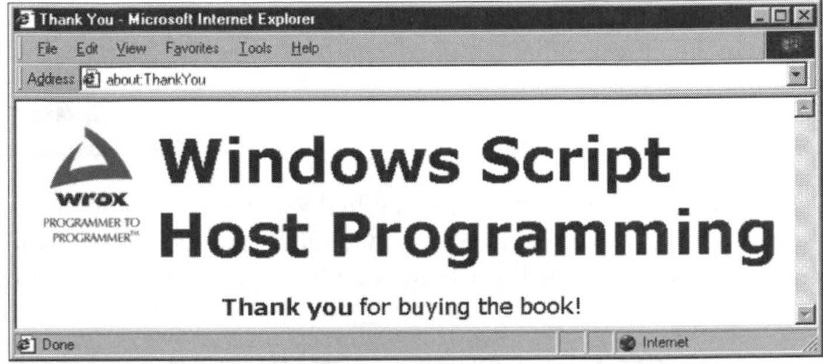

Synchronized Execution

The final aspect of the `Run()` method that we need to consider is its facility for synchronized execution. By setting its `bWaitOnReturn` argument to `True`, you can halt execution of the script until the spawned program terminates. This means that the time taken by the WSH script to complete is influenced by the time required by the external program to do its job. How can this be made to comply with any global WSH timeout settings?

Suppose that you set the maximum execution time for the WSH script to 8 seconds and then run a script like this:

```
' Set the timeout to 8 seconds
WScript.Timeout = 8                ' NB: this requires WSH 2.0

SW_SHOW = 1
Set shell = CreateObject("WScript.Shell")
MsgBox shell.Run("notepad.exe", SW_SHOW, True)
```

You might expect that after 8 seconds have elapsed, Notepad will be closed, but that turns out not to be the case: the synchronization takes precedence over the WSH timeout. If the WSH timeout expires while Notepad is still running, execution will continue as if you never set any timeout. However, if you close Notepad (thereby ending the synchronization) when the timeout period has not yet elapsed, the timeout *will* apply to the rest of the WSH code.

Beware of running a hidden program and waiting for it to finish. If you can't see a program that's waiting for user input, you will simply hang your script.

Environment Variables

To round off our discussion of the `WshShell` object, you may recall the brief mention I gave in the section about `RegWrite()` to a method capable of expanding environment variables that are embedded in strings. `ExpandEnvironmentStrings()` returns a correctly expanded version of the string it receives as input, in which any environment variables to be expanded must be enclosed between `%` symbols. Here's an example that retrieves the path to the Windows directory:

```
Set shell = CreateObject("WScript.Shell")
strText = shell.ExpandEnvironmentStrings("The Windows directory is %WINDIR%")
shell.Popup strText
```

On my PC, this is what happens:

If the specified environment variable doesn't exist, the method returns the original string that you passed in. If you have more than one environment variable, those that don't exist are returned unchanged, while the others are properly expanded:

```
Set shell = CreateObject("WScript.Shell")
strText = shell.ExpandEnvironmentStrings("%MYVAR% and %TEMP%")
shell.Popup strText
```

The environment variables that `ExpandEnvironmentStrings()` can retrieve include `PATH`, `WINDIR`, `COMSPEC` and `TEMP`. A complete list of these variables can be found in the Windows Script Host documentation.

The WshShortcut Object

The folders of the Windows file system are *full* of shortcuts. As well as their traditional role on the desktop, where they provide fast access to applications and documents located elsewhere, shortcuts make up the items in the Favorites folder and the targets in the Send To context menu. They're also used to define the items that appear at the top of the Start menu, and in the taskbar's Quick Launch toolbar.

As you'll see later in the book, WSH lends itself very well to the creation of scripts for the quick setup of software modules, and the generation of shortcuts for purposes such as those listed above is often an integral part of this process. Because shortcuts can reference files, programs and folders, they can be a great boon to users, and the ability to generate them programmatically during the installation procedure is a very useful one. This ability is exactly what the `WshShortcut` object provides.

In the next few sections, I'll be combining features of the WshShortcut and WshSpecialFolders objects to demonstrate how to add items to some particular system menus. Before moving any further, though, a proper look at the programming interface of the WshShortcut object is in order.

The WshShortcut Programmer's Reference

The programming interface of WshShortcut is made up of eight properties and a single method. The properties are:

Property	Description
Arguments	A string that contains the arguments to be passed to the executable pointed to by the shortcut.
Description	The shortcut's description string. (This is actually never used in the Windows Explorer.)
FullName	The full path name of the shortcut itself. This is an undocumented, read-only property.
Hotkey	A string containing the representation of a hotkey that launches the shortcut — *Ctrl+Alt+h*, for example. (Valid hotkeys always begin with *Ctrl+Alt*.) Be aware that this will be always processed *before* any identical hotkey you may have set in a user application (say, MS Word).
IconLocation	A string that contains the path and index of the icon for the shortcut. The path and the index are comma-separated, so a valid example would be c:\windows\system\shell32.dll,13. Here, 13 is the 0-based index of the icon in shell32.dll — in other words, the icon required is the 14th stored in the given file.
TargetPath	The target of a shortcut can be a folder, an executable, or a file to be run.
WindowStyle	This takes the same values as the constants listed in the earlier section entitled *Styles of the Application Window*. Note once again that some programs may ignore this style.
WorkingDirectory	The directory from which to start the executable.

The only method exposed by WshShortcut is:

Method	Description
Save()	Saves the shortcut object to the location specified by the FullName property

Creating a Shortcut

An object of type `WshShortcut` is returned by the `WshShell.CreateShortcut()` method when you pass it an argument containing the name of the shortcut to be created, like this:

```
shell = CreateObject("WScript.Shell")
objShortcut = shell.CreateShortcut(strLnkFile)
```

However, simply calling the `CreateShortcut()` method doesn't result in the creation of a shortcut. The object will only be made persistent to file later on by a call to its `Save()` method. Creating a shortcut is therefore a three-step process:

- Getting an instance of the `WshShortcut` object
- Setting the properties of the object to choose the shortcut's look and behavior
- Saving the object to a file

The string you pass to `CreateShortcut()` will be stored in the object's `FullName` property; it's the filename that will be used later in actually creating the shortcut. It may have one of two extensions (`.url` or `.lnk`), and attempting to specify any other extension will cause an error. If the extension is `.lnk`, the object will prepare to create a traditional, Windows-based shortcut. Otherwise, it will be an Internet shortcut linked to a web page.

> *URL shortcuts have a different object model and are managed through an object called* `WshUrlShortcut` *that I'll discuss in more depth later on.*

In order to create a shortcut, then, we must first obtain a reference to a `WshShortcut` object by specifying the name of the file we want to create. After that, the object can be tailored to your needs by setting its properties. At the very least, you need to set the `TargetPath` property that denotes the file object that the shortcut points to. When you've done, just call `Save()` to make it persistent to disk.

The following JScript code snippet shows how to create a shortcut to the `Favorites` folder in the current directory. `SpecialFolders` is a property of the `WshShell` object that can provide the exact path of the `Favorites` folder, and I'll have more to say about it later in the chapter.

```
shell = new ActiveXObject("WScript.Shell");
lnk = shell.CreateShortcut("Favorites.lnk");
lnk.TargetPath = shell.SpecialFolders("Favorites");
lnk.Save();
```

You can address pretty much anything through a shortcut: drives, directories, single files, and of course executable programs. The only drawback is that the WSH support for shortcuts doesn't allow you to manage non file-system objects, such as printer links or scheduled tasks.

Resolving a Shortcut

The process of "resolving" a shortcut involves the system attempting to locate whatever it is the shortcut refers to. When you're managing shortcuts in Windows applications, you can resolve them by calling a function that attempts to find something at the path stored in the `TargetPath` field.

Unfortunately, the `WshShortcut` object doesn't expose a method for resolving shortcuts in this way. When you call `CreateShortcut()` on an existing shortcut file, you're returned a reference to a `WshShortcut` object whose properties have been initialized with the content of the shortcut file, but this *doesn't* mean that the shortcut is resolved. If the `.lnk` file points to a missing file, you won't receive an error.

Given this information, though, it's fairly easy to check whether the shortcut points to an existing file. This code uses an object called `Scripting.FileSystemObject` that I won't describe in detail until Chapter 6, but it should be fairly obvious what it's doing here: its `FileExists()` and `FolderExists()` methods simply check for the presence of a file or a folder at the path you specify. The object will be present on your machine by default, and this script should work out of the box.

```
// Resolve.js
// Resolves a shortcut or creates a new one to c:\
// --------------------------------------------------------------

STR_POINTSTO = "The shortcut points to "
STR_MISSING  = "The shortcut points to a missing file or folder: "
STR_CREATE   = "The shortcut doesn't exist. Create one?"

YES = 6                      // See the documentation for Popup()
BTN_YESNO = 4                // See the documentation for Popup()

// Create the necessary objects
shell = new ActiveXObject("WScript.Shell");
fso = new ActiveXObject("Scripting.FileSystemObject");

// Access the LNK file
lnk = shell.CreateShortcut("myShortcut.lnk");

// Checks the target path
if(lnk.TargetPath != "")
{
   b = fso.FileExists(lnk.TargetPath);
   if(b)
      shell.Popup(STR_POINTSTO + lnk.TargetPath);      // OK, resolved
   else
   {
      // The target path isn't empty and it isn't a file. Is it a folder?
      b = fso.FolderExists(lnk.TargetPath);
      if(b)
         shell.Popup(STR_POINTSTO + lnk.TargetPath);
      else
         shell.Popup(STR_MISSING + lnk.TargetPath);
   }
}
else
{
   // Create a new shortcut? If so, make it point to c:\
   rc = shell.Popup(STR_CREATE, 0, "Shortcut", BTN_YESNO);
   if(rc == YES)
   {
      lnk.TargetPath = "c:\\";
      lnk.Save();
   }
}
```

Once you have successfully opened an existing shortcut, you can change any of its properties, with the exception of `FullName`. In particular, you can change the `TargetPath` property and the icon. If you assign a `.lnk` file to be the target path of a shortcut, it will be automatically resolved to the target file. To see what this means more clearly, create a shortcut to the Notepad called `Notepad.lnk` on your desktop and then run this code:

```
// Creates a new shortcut on the Windows desktop
shell = new ActiveXObject("WScript.Shell");
desktopDir = shell.SpecialFolders("Desktop");

lnk = shell.CreateShortcut(desktopDir + "\\Shortcut to notepad.lnk");
lnk.TargetPath = desktopDir + "\\notepad.lnk";
lnk.Save();
```

If you now examine the properties of this new shortcut, you'll find that its target is `Notepad.exe`, which is also the target of `Notepad.lnk`:

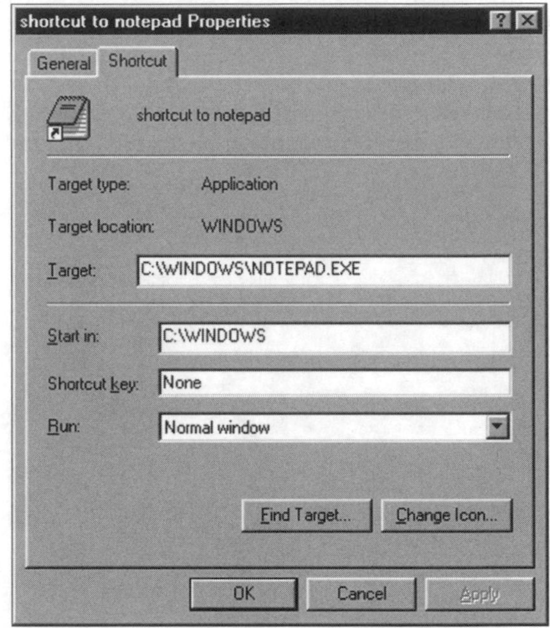

Adding Icons to the Quick Launch Toolbar

The Quick Launch toolbar is a part of the Active Desktop Windows interface, a standard part of the Windows 98 user interface that's available under Windows 95 and Windows NT 4.0 through Internet Explorer 4.0.

> *Note that Active Desktop* doesn't *ship with Internet Explorer 5.0, so if you're running Windows 95 or Windows NT 4.0, you must install IE 4.0 with Active Desktop first, and then upgrade to IE 5.0.*

As shown below, the Quick Launch toolbar is a good place to put shortcuts to programs that you run frequently. By default, the Active Desktop setup program places shortcuts to IE, Outlook Express, the desktop and the channels in the toolbar, but most people customize it to their own needs using drag-and-drop.

However, it's also possible to customize the toolbar using a simple WSH script, which you might want to include as part of an installation procedure. The following script, for example, adds a shortcut to Notepad to the toolbar:

```
// QuickLaunch.js
// Add Notepad to the Quick Launch toolbar
// ------------------------------------------------------------

shell = new ActiveXObject("WScript.Shell");

// Prepares the path to the Quick Launch folder
appDataDir = shell.SpecialFolders("AppData");
lnkPath = appDataDir + "\\Microsoft\\Internet Explorer\\Quick Launch"

// Creates the shortcut
lnk = shell.CreateShortcut(lnkPath + "\\notepad.lnk");
lnk.TargetPath = "notepad.exe";
lnk.Save();
```

The new shortcut appears immediately after execution of the script, with no need to perform any kind of 'refresh' operation.

Creating URL Shortcuts

URL shortcuts differ from traditional shortcuts in three ways:

- They have a different file extension (`.url`)
- They are far simpler and support fewer properties
- They always point to a URL

A URL shortcut (that is, a `WshUrlShortcut` object) is created and managed in exactly the same way as a `WshShortcut` object. However, its programming interface is made up only of the `Save()` method and these two properties:

Property	Description
`FullName`	Retrieves the full path name of the `.url` file
`TargetPath`	The target can be a web page, a folder, or a file

If `TargetPath` doesn't contain a protocol as specified, then `file://` will be added as a default. A file with the extension `.url` is of type Internet Shortcut — that is, a URL pointing to something that can be a web page, a folder or a file.

The following code snippet demonstrates how to create a URL shortcut to a web site and place it in the Quick Launch toolbar:

```
// Url.js
// Add a link to Wrox's site to the Quick Launch toolbar
// ---------------------------------------------------------------

shell = new ActiveXObject("WScript.Shell");

// Prepares the path to the Quick Launch folder
appDataDir = shell.SpecialFolders("AppData");
urlPath = appDataDir + "\\Microsoft\\Internet Explorer\\Quick Launch"

// Creates the shortcut
url = shell.CreateShortcut(urlPath + "\\Wrox.url");
url.TargetPath = "http://www.wrox.com";
url.Save();
```

There isn't much difference between the creation processes of the two kinds of shortcut, but they are quite different objects. A file system shortcut is stored in a binary format whose details are undocumented, while a URL shortcut is a plain ASCII file. The `wrox.url` shortcut created above, for example, looks like this:

```
[InternetShortcut]
URL=http://www.wrox.com/
```

However, even though it would be quite easy to create a URL shortcut as a raw text file, it is strongly recommended that you pass through the official `WshUrlShortcut` interface for future compatibility.

The WshNetwork Object

The `WshNetwork` object does a good job of aggregating some tasks that relate to remote printer and network connections. You can create an instance of it either by going through `WScript`, or by using the usual VBScript and JScript object creators:

```
Set nw = CreateObject("WScript.Network")
```

As with the `WshShell` object, note that some old documentation gives the ProgID of the `WshNetwork` object as `WScript.WshNetwork`. This is simply not the case.

The WshNetwork Programmer's Reference

The following tables provide descriptions of the methods and properties of `WshNetwork`, which I've divided into two categories: network connections and printers. Let's start with the former:

Method	Description
`EnumNetworkDrives()`	Allows you to enumerate the network drives. Any drives it finds are returned through a `WshCollection` object.
`MapNetworkDrive()`	Establishes a connection and maps a network drive.
`RemoveNetworkDrive()`	Removes a connection with a network drive.

`WshNetwork` also exposes three properties whose roles are quite self-explanatory. They are:

Property	Description
`ComputerName`	String representation of the computer's name
`UserDomain`	String representation of the user's domain name
`UserName`	String representation of the user's name

The methods for working with printers are:

Method	Description
`AddPrinterConnection()`	Establishes a connection and maps the specified remote printer.
`RemovePrinterConnection()`	Removes the connection to the specified remote printer.
`EnumPrinterConnections()`	Allows you to enumerate the remote printers. Any printers it finds are returned through a `WshCollection` object.
`SetDefaultPrinter()`	Sets the default printer. If it's a remote printer, you need to specify its full UNC (Universal Naming Convention) name (say, `\\Server\My Printer`).

Managing Network Connections

`WshNetwork` provides two explicit methods to map and un-map a network drive to a local name. To establish a link with a network drive, you should call `MapNetworkDrive()`, whose prototype is as follows:

```
WshNetwork.MapNetworkDrive(strLocalName, strRemoteName
                          [,bUpdateProfile] [,strUser] [,strPassword])
```

Parameter	Description
`strLocalName`	Name by which the drive will be available on the local computer (`G:`, for example).
`strRemoteName`	UNC path of the remote drive to be mapped. If the path can't be located, you'll get an error message box.
`bUpdateProfile`	Optional Boolean argument. If set to `True`, the connection will be saved in the user's profile. Set to `False` by default.

Parameter	Description
strUser	Optional argument you can use if you're mapping a remote drive using someone else's credentials. This is for the user name.
strPassword	Optional argument you can use if you're mapping a remote drive using someone else's credentials. This is for the password.

You can un-map a remote drive by calling RemoveNetworkDrive(), which in simple operation just takes the local name assigned to the drive as an argument:

```
WshNetwork.RemoveNetworkDrive(strName [,bForce] [,bUpdateProfile])
```

Here's a table that describes the arguments of the RemoveNetworkDrive() method in more detail:

Parameter	Description
strName	Name that identifies the network drive on the local machine.
bForce	Optional Boolean argument. If set to True, the mapping is removed whether the drive is being used or not. Set to False by default.
bUpdateProfile	Optional Boolean argument. If set to True, the user's profile will be updated. Set to False by default.

You can loop over all the network drives that are mapped at a certain moment in time by using the EnumNetworkDrives() method. This returns a WshCollection object for you to parse; the following code therefore displays all the mapped drives:

```
net = new ActiveXObject("WScript.Network");
oDrives = net.EnumNetworkDrives();

if(oDrives.length == 0)
   WScript.Echo("No network drives found.");
else
   for(i = 0; i < oDrives.length; i++)
      WScript.Echo(oDrives(i));
```

Managing Printers

Managing printers is much the same as managing network drives; the method names and prototypes are very similar. To establish a link with a network printer, you call AddPrinterConnection(), whose prototype is as follows:

```
AddPrinterConnection(strLocalName, strRemoteName
                     [,bUpdateProfile] [,strUser] [,strPassword])
```

Parameter	Description
strLocalName	Name by which the printer will be available on the local computer.
strRemoteName	UNC path of the remote printer to be mapped. If the path can't be located, you'll get an error message box.
bUpdateProfile	Optional Boolean argument. If set to True, the connection will be saved in the user's profile. Set to False by default.
strUser	Optional argument you can use if you're mapping a remote printer using someone else's credentials. This is for the user name.
strPassword	Optional argument you can use if you're mapping a remote printer using someone else's credentials. This is for the password.

As you can see, it's akin to the MapNetworkDrive() method we met above. To connect to a network printer, use code like this:

```
net = new ActiveXObject("WScript.Network");
net.AddPrinterConnection("Printer 1", "\\Server\Print1");
```

Removing a Connected Printer

To remove a link, use RemovePrinterConnection(), which is declared as follows:

```
WshNetwork.RemovePrinterConnection(strName [,bForce] [,bUpdateProfile])
```

Parameter	Description
strName	Name that identifies the printer. If the printer has been connected using AddPrinterConnection(), you must use the local name here. Otherwise, the UNC name is fine.
bForce	Optional Boolean argument. If set to True, the connection will be removed whether or not any user is connected. Set to False by default.
bUpdateProfile	Optional Boolean argument. If set to True, the change will be saved in the user's profile. Set to False by default.

Setting the Default Printer

WshNetwork provides a means for setting the default printer via the SetDefaultPrinter() function. Unfortunately, though, it isn't of any help when it comes to *getting* the name of the *current* default printer:

```
WshNetwork.SetDefaultPrinter(strName)
```

In addition, some documentation claims that strName must be the name of a *remote* printer, but this is untrue; the method is also capable of switching to a local printer.

Getting the Default Printer

To work around this little failing of the WshNetwork object, it's useful to know that the name of the current default printer is held in the registry, at the following location:

```
HKEY_CURRENT_CONFIG\
    System\
        CurrentControlSet\
            Control\
                Print\
                    Printers\
                        Default
```

The following VBScript code snippet shows how to read the name of the default printer for the machine:

```
HKCC = "HKEY_CURRENT_CONFIG\"
HKCC_PRINTER = HKCC & "System\CurrentControlSet\Control\Print\Printers\"
Set shell = CreateObject("WScript.Shell")
MsgBox shell.RegRead(HKCC_PRINTER & "Default")
```

With a little invention, it's possible to work your way around all kinds of small problems like these!

Helper Objects

In this final major section of the chapter, I'll discuss the programming interfaces of the helper objects that have been touched upon elsewhere. In particular, I'm going to look at:

- WshEnvironment
- WshSpecialFolders
- WshCollection

Though the functionality these objects provide is important, they play a minor role in comparison with WshShell or WshNetwork. In general, they are specialized, 0-based collections, and similar in their respective properties and methods.

The WshEnvironment Object

The WshShell.Environment property instantiates and returns an object called WshEnvironment that is meant to work as a kind of dictionary for groups of environment variables. The exact syntax is the following:

```
WshShell.Environment([strType])
```

The strType argument is an optional, case-insensitive string that lets you define the type of environment variables you want to work with. The options available are:

Type	Description
`Process`	A collection of all the environment variables that are available to any process. This is the default option under Windows 9x, and in fact it's the only way to access environment variables on that platform. You can remove or replace any of the variables in the collection for the duration of the current process.
`System`	These variables are always set no matter who logs on, and no user can change them. Because they are always present, they may be used in logon scripts. They are also visible through the Control Panel. *This collection is empty under Windows 9x.*
`User`	The variables defined for this specific user. They can be viewed, added, deleted or modified from the Control Panel, and they take precedence over `System` environment variables. *This collection is empty under Windows 9x.*
`Volatile`	The variables that have been added on the fly and which don't survive the end of the current process.

Under Windows 9x, you can forget about the existence of the various types and always take the default — the `Process` type. `WshShell.ExpandEnvironmentStrings()` only expands variables that are defined in the `Process` space.

The WshEnvironment Programmer's Reference

The programming interface of `WshEnvironment` is made up of three properties and just one method. The properties are:

Property	Description

`Item`	Sets or returns the value of the specified environment variable. This is the default property, which means that you don't need to specify it in VBScript. The following expressions are both valid:
	`env.Item("WINDIR")`
	`env("WINDIR")`

`Count`	Returns the number of environment variables found.
`length`	This property provides the same functionality as the `Count` property, and is provided for JScript compatibility.

The only method is:

Method	Description

`Remove()`	Does just what its name suggests: it removes an existing variable by name. Here's how to proceed:
	`Set shell = CreateObject("WScript.Shell")`
	`Set env = shell.Environment()`
	`env.Remove("PATH")`

Properties and methods work on the set of variables belonging to the specified type of environment (process, user, volatile, system).

Enumerating Variables

`WshEnvironment` is a collection object, so you can easily enumerate its items in VBScript by using a `For...Each` construct:

```
Set shell = CreateObject("WScript.Shell")
For Each strName In shell.Environment
   shell.Popup strName
Next
```

For JScript programmers, this translates to:

```
var shell = new ActiveXObject("WScript.Shell");
var e = new Enumerator(shell.Environment);
for(; !e.atEnd(); e.moveNext())
   shell.Popup(e.item());
```

The variables returned in the above code snippets are in the form "`var=value`", as the following screenshot demonstrates:

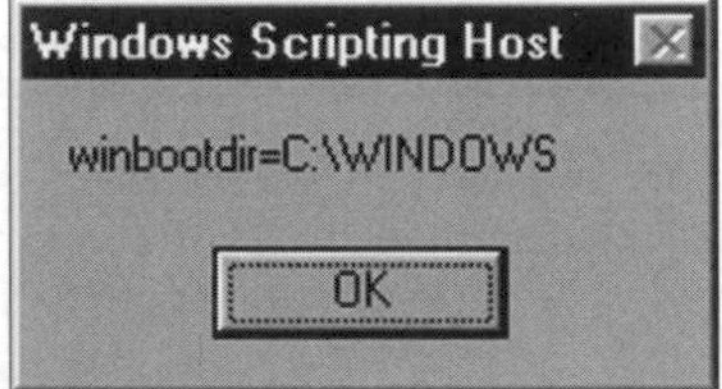

To verify how `Volatile` variables are managed, try this VBScript code:

```
' EnvVars.vbs
' Demonstrates environmental variables
' ----------------------------------------------------------
Option Explicit

Dim shell
Dim env
Dim strName

Set shell = CreateObject("WScript.Shell")
Set env = shell.Environment("Volatile")
env("THISFILE") = "EnvVars.vbs"

' Remove the %PATH% variable and scan the list
shell.Environment.Remove("PATH")
Msgbox "Scan the Process space without %PATH%..."
For Each strName In shell.Environment("Process")
   shell.Popup strName
Next

' This includes %THISFILE%
Msgbox "Scan the Volatile space..."
For Each strName In shell.Environment("Volatile")
   shell.Popup strName
Next
```

Even if the `%THISFILE%` variable has never been removed explicitly, running the script again (without the lines that add it) will show an empty list of volatile variables.

The WshSpecialFolders Object

As I've mentioned on a few occasions, Windows defines a number of **special folders** that differ from the others (called **file folders**) in terms of their content. There are two flavors of special folders:

- Folders that are tied to a physical directory and contain files, but which are considered 'special' because their files have a particular meaning to the system. Examples of these are the `StartMenu` and the `Favorites` folders.
- Folders that aren't tied to a physical directory and don't contain files, but do contain information about objects in the system. Examples of this type are `My Computer`, `Printers` and `Dial-up Networking`. To access this kind of 'special' folder, you need to use the Shell Automation objects that I'll cover in Chapter 6.

The `WshShell` object has a property that can provide you with an object for accessing a few of the Windows special folders. The name of the object is `WshSpecialFolders`, and it is returned by the `SpecialFolders` property:

```
objFolder = WshShell.SpecialFolders
```

Through the programming interface of this object, you can ask for the path names of some system folders, identified by descriptive names. However, you *can't* access the *contents* of these folders. To do that, you have to employ some other objects too.

The WshSpecialFolders Programmer's Reference

The programming interface of `WshSpecialFolders` is made up three properties and *no* methods. Its properties are:

Property	Description

`Item`	Returns the path of the specified special folder. The folders are recognized via their descriptive names, which are listed later. `Item` is the default property, so you don't need to specify it in VBScript; the following expressions are both valid:
	`objFolder.Item("Desktop")`
	`objFolder("Desktop")`

`Count`	Returns the number of folders found. This number might be different under Windows 9x and Windows NT, because not all the folders the collection manages are defined under Windows 9x.
`length`	This property provides the same functionality as the `Count` property, and is provided for JScript compatibility.

Accessing special folders is particularly useful in the context of installing applications. In fact, it's helpful whenever you want to make the overall working environment more comfortable by adding objects like files, applications and printers to system containers such as folders and menus. The folders whose paths `WshSpecialFolders.Item` is capable of retrieving are:

Name	Folder
AllUsersDesktop	Contains shortcuts that appear on the desktop for all users. A typical path is: C:\WINNT\Profiles\All Users\Desktop *Unsupported under Windows 9x.*
AllUsersStartMenu	Contains shortcuts that appear on the Start menu for all users. A typical path is: C:\WINNT\Profiles\All Users\Start Menu *Unsupported under Windows 9x.*
AllUsersPrograms	Contains shortcuts that appear on the Start menu's Programs menu for all users. A typical path is: C:\..\All Users\Start Menu\Programs *Unsupported under Windows 9x.*
AllUsersStartup	Contains shortcuts that appear in the Start | Programs | Startup menu for all users. A typical path is: C:\..\All Users\Start Menu\Programs\Startup *Unsupported under Windows 9x.*
AppData	User-specific folder that is supposed to contain application-specific data. It points to the Application Data directory.
Desktop	Physically contains desktop folders and shortcuts. This is the Desktop directory in the Windows folder. Under NT it is usually: C:\WINNT\Profiles\<username>\Desktop
Favorites	User-specific folder to store the shortcuts that appear in the Favorites menu. It usually points to the Favorites directory, but the actual location of this folder is stored in the registry, and you may change it at your leisure.
Fonts	Contains fonts — this is the Fonts directory in the Windows folder.
MyDocuments	User-specific folder to store the user's documents. A link to this folder appears as a separate node in the left pane of an Explorer view. The actual location of this folder is stored in the registry, and you may change it at your leisure.
NetHood	User-specific file system directory that serves as a common repository for network connections. It points to the NetHood directory.

Name	Folder
PrintHood	User-specific file system directory that serves as a common repository for printer links. It points to the PrintHood directory.
Programs	User-specific folder to store the shortcuts that appear in the Start | Programs menu. It points to the Start Menu\Programs directory.
Recent	User-specific folder to store the shortcuts that appear in the Start | Documents menu. It points to the Recent directory.
SendTo	User-specific folder to store the shortcuts that appear in the Send To menu. It points to the SendTo directory.
StartMenu	User-specific folder to store the shortcuts that appear in the Start menu. It points to the Start Menu directory.
Startup	User-specific folder to store the shortcuts that appear in the StartUp folder of the Start | Programs menu. It points to the Start Menu\Programs\Startup directory.
Templates	User-specific folder to store the document templates used to arrange the New menu. It points to the ShellNew directory.

Note that the descriptive names for the folders must be passed as string values, and are all case-insensitive.

Under Windows NT, a user-specific folder is usually located under C:\WINNT\Profiles*username*, where *username* is the name of the user. Under Windows 9x, on the other hand, they are always located under the Windows folder.

Locating User Shell Folders

The above list doesn't include all the folders that play a special role in the Windows system, but they are the only ones for which WshSpecialFolders provides a name. The Active Desktop added new folders such as Cookies, History and Cache that relate to the activity of browsing with Internet Explorer, and the actual paths of these folders for the current user are stored in the registry at the following position:

```
HKEY_CURRENT_USER\
   Software\
      Microsoft\
         Windows\
            CurrentVersion\
               Explorer\
                  User Shell Folders
```

By using the registry functions mentioned earlier, it's possible to read and change the settings of these new folders as well. I demonstrated this technique in the section called *Reading from the Registry*.

Enumerating Special Folders

Since WshSpecialFolders is a collection, you can navigate its items using code like this:

```
Set shell = CreateObject("WScript.Shell")
For i = 0 To shell.SpecialFolders.Count - 1
   MsgBox shell.SpecialFolders.Item(i)
Next
```

Adding a SendTo Menu Item

When you right-click on a file in Explorer, one of the items in the context menu that gets displayed is the Send To popup menu. It lists a series of places to which the selected file can be sent. When you click on one of the items in this list, an associated program gets executed with the name of the selected file on its command line.

To add a new item (say, Notepad) to this menu, you just need to create a shortcut in the `SendTo` special folder:

```
// SendTo.js
// Add Notepad to the SendTo menu
// ------------------------------------------------------------

shell = new ActiveXObject("WScript.Shell");

// Prepares the path to the SendTo folder
sendtoPath = shell.SpecialFolders("SendTo");

// Creates the shortcut
lnk = shell.CreateShortcut(sendtoPath + "\\notepad.lnk");
lnk.TargetPath = "notepad.exe";
lnk.Save();
```

Adding to Favorites and the Start Menu

With a slight modification, you can use the above code to add items to the `Favorites` folder and the Start menu as well. Apart from the detail of the actual shortcut to insert, you need just to change the identifier of the special folder: `Favorites` for the `Favorites` folder, and `StartMenu` for the Start menu.

The WshCollection Object

A `WshCollection` object is a simple collection that the `WshNetwork` object returns when you ask it to enumerate the available printers or network connections. This object just returns strings identifying the name of the resource (whatever that resource may be), so functionally speaking there's no real difference between managing connections and managing printers.

The WshCollection Programmer's Reference

The programming interface of `WshCollection` is made up of the three typical properties of a collection object. Once again, they are:

Property	Description
`Item`	Takes an index for input, and returns the associated string that identifies a network or a printer connection
`Count`	Returns the total number of printers or network connections found
`length`	This property provides the same functionality as the `Count` property, and is provided for JScript compatibility

Enumerating Network Connections and Printers

You can navigate the items of a collection in the same way regardless of whether it holds network drive mappings or printer names. Using VBScript's For...Each construct, the code looks like this:

```
Set network = CreateObject("WScript.Network")
For Each strConn In network.EnumNetworkDrives
   MsgBox strConn
Next
For Each strConn In network.EnumPrinterConnections
   MsgBox strConn
Next
```

The collection returned by EnumPrinterConnections() only includes remote printers, while returned drive names might be like G:, or in the UNC form \\server\sharename.

Summary

The standard WSH object model is very much the starting point for learning about the Windows Script Host. It's sensible and necessary to find out how to use it and what it's capable of, but in most real-world situations you'll need to go further than the standard objects. In my opinion, the real power of WSH lies in its extensibility and its position in the overall Windows architecture. WSH is customizable by design and by nature.

Finding out about WScript and WshShell should have provided you with a firm foundation and whetted your appetite for the challenges of the chapters to come. In this chapter, I've covered:

- The shell functions that WSH provides
- Methods to access the system registry
- How to link and unlink to network printers and drives
- Managing environment variables and special folders
- The collection objects of WSH

WSH has actually been around for quite a while, but as its scripting technologies and operating systems evolve, Microsoft has to continue working on it so that it keeps pace with developments. What I've covered so far represents the core of WSH, but there is more to look at than this, and it comes from two distinct directions.

- New features in the VBScript and JScript engines that shipped with Internet Explorer 5.0
- New features in version 2.0 of the WSH executable

None of this will affect what you've read so far; rather, it will bring forward many new features and open up new development opportunities. It will also be my subject for the next chapter.

5

What's New in WSH 2.0

The WSH environment lets you write scripts using any Windows Script compliant scripting engine, and when you install the WSH executables, scripting engines are installed on your machine too. However, while they have a considerable effect on the way you work with WSH, scripting engines are very definitely separate components that you can update or replace at any time.

Internet Explorer and other hosts *also* come with scripting engines, and any time an upgraded engine is installed on your machine, the hosts can exploit the new features that come with it. The release of Internet Explorer 5.0, for example, brought with it significant enhancements to the VBScript and JScript engines that weren't available in earlier versions. While this might seem to have little to do with WSH at first, it actually influences the way you write your scripts.

The downside to this burgeoning innovation is that the dream of a consolidated, 'standard' Windows 98 platform is finished: depending on what it does, your code may need to check whether the latest version of Internet Explorer is installed, whether the latest SDK (Software Development Kit) and run-time engine are available, and so forth. In this chapter, I'm going to cover all the latest technologies, as well as changes to existing technologies, that may affect WSH. In particular, you'll find out about:

- The newest WSH script file format (`.ws`)
- The `job`, `reference`, and `object` keywords
- Minor changes and extensions to the WSH object model
- What's new in VBScript and JScript 5.0

In order to run the code in this chapter successfully, you'll need to have installed the release version of Internet Explorer 5.0 (for the newest scripting engines) and beta 1 of WSH 2.0 (for the new features of WSH). The place to look for the very latest news on these technologies is http://msdn.microsoft.com/scripting/windowshost.

Windows Script Host 2.0

WSH has achieved considerable success since its first release more than a year ago, and like any successful piece of software, there's a great deal of interest in its new version. While WSH 1.0 is useful and well produced, it still has some minor (and not-so-minor) drawbacks:

- It lacks a mechanism for importing constants from type libraries
- It lacks a standard mechanism for including external files
- It lacks a standard mechanism for providing user-defined dialogs
- It lacks a dedicated editor with proper, time-saving features

What Led to WSH 2.0?

Some of the weak points identified in the previous section are relatively minor, as their resolution just requires an additional, made-to-measure component. This is certainly true for dialogs and editing. The other points, though, begin to turn your attention to architectural issues: *why* doesn't a WSH script provide a way of including or referencing external files and type libraries? To find the answer, let's look at what a WSH 1.0 script actually is. It's a pure ASCII file whose contents evaluate to an executable VBScript or JScript string. In other words, a WSH script has no structure other than the one provided by the native language, and the language doesn't provide any of the mechanisms we want.

Towards a New Script File

WSH scripts are tightly linked to the language in which they're written, whatever that language may be. This peculiarity has a further downside: when you design your WSH applets, you tend to start thinking in terms of the language, and end up losing sight of the overall application.

Windows Script Host version 2.0 is designed to remedy this situation. It introduces a new type of script file and gives you a new, fresher way to think about your WSH applications. With WSH 2.0, you can write two types of files for running scripts:

- The traditional VBScript or JScript files
- The new `.ws` files (Windows script files)

Interestingly, `.ws` files are not pure ASCII documents — or rather, they are not *just* pure ASCII documents. Windows script files are *XML files* whose structure is very similar to that of **Windows Script Components** (**WSC**s), which I'll be covering in Chapter 7.

Windows Script Files

Windows script (`.ws`) files were designed to introduce new features with the intention of working around the limitations of VBScript and JScript files. By employing a `.ws` file, you can get the following benefits:

- Incorporate functions from existing VBScript or JScript files
- Use more than one scripting language per file
- Reference type libraries and add named constants to your code
- Write and edit WSH scripts with any XML editor

These features radically affect the way you look at WSH scripts. They are no longer the simple ASCII files you wrote in VBScript or JScript, but evolve towards the position of being fully-fledged script objects that run within the Windows shell.

Running .ws Files

A `.ws` file can be run using the ordinary `cscript.exe` or `wscript.exe` programs. The file type is registered in the system registry in the normal fashion by the WSH 2.0 installation program, and enjoys shell support that's identical to that of `.vbs` and `.js` files. You can execute a `.ws` file by double-clicking its icon within the Windows shell, by starting it from the Run dialog box, or by typing its name at a command prompt.

As I'll show you in a moment, a `.ws` file is composed of a sequence of script blocks that execute in the same order they are declared. Each script block can use a different language, which means, for example, that you could have a piece of JScript code, then some VBScript, and finally JScript again. At that, you might be concerned about creating overheads for WSH and reducing its performance, but there's actually nothing to worry about.

Using More Than One Scripting Language

Different hosts handle things in different ways. If you try to put VBScript and JScript code blocks into an *ASP* page, for example, you'll find that all the VBScript blocks run first, followed by all the JScript blocks. (The converse occurs if you set JScript as the default language.) This unfortunate fact is due to the characteristics of the ASP cache, which doesn't keep track of the order in which the blocks appear on the page.

Happily, this problem doesn't arise with Windows Script Host code, where each block executes sequentially. This doesn't mean, however, that each block of code will produce its *result* in a sequential manner. Don't fret about the ins and outs of the syntax at the moment, but if you have a `.ws` file that contains code like this:

```
<job>
   <script language="JScript">
      shellApp = new ActiveXObject("Shell.Application")
      shellApp.FindFiles();        // Displays the Find Folders dialog
   </script>

   <script language="VBScript">
      MsgBox "Hello, I'm WSH 2.0"
   </script>
</job>
```

the chances are that VBScript's `MsgBox()` function will show its effect before the Find dialog box appears. However, this is just due to asynchronous processing and the different execution times that the two code snippets require; the first block will always *commence* execution before the second.

In addition to using more than one scripting language in a single `.ws` file, it is also possible to mix languages — that is, to have VBScript procedures invoking JScript functions and vice versa. I will deal with this subject later on in the chapter.

Where's the Overhead?

The need to use more than one scripting engine doesn't often arise, but it can happen. I can think of two particularly strong reasons for wanting to do it:

- Reusing some existing code that was written in another language
- Exploiting some features that another language doesn't provide

Clearly, using two engines instead of one is going to introduce some overhead costs, and if you use three, you'll cause even more! The question is, do these overheads significantly affect performance?

For a start, overall execution time is going to increase, because two script engines must be loaded instead of one. Having multiple engines also increases the number of namespaces to search in order to resolve global names, and increases the memory footprint of WSH.

Consider, though, that the code for a script is parsed only once and then kept in memory in its 'compiled' state. In addition, WSH scripts run locally, and usually in a context where you don't have very tight time constraints; if that *doesn't* describe your situation, it may be that you should think about using a different tool anyway.

XML and WSH

`.ws` files are XML files, and the use of this language helps you to build scripts that can be considered more as 'objects' than simply as files, by which I mean that they are structured and well-organized, with a series of identifiable blocks of information.

In the context of WSH, there are five XML tags that you should know about. They are:

- `<package>`
- `<job>`
- `<object>`
- `<reference>`
- `<script>`

As you probably know, XML is actually a *meta*-language, in the sense that it can be used as a basis for defining more specialized languages. An XML-based language differs from pure XML in that it has a finite vocabulary of legal element names, and a set of syntax rules that apply to those elements. These features exist on top of all the general XML compliance rules defined in the XML 1.0 standard document.

To define a custom XML language, you need to provide a specification of the elements that you want to recognize. For each element, you also have to specify the attributes that it takes. This information is commonly stored in a **Document Type Definition** (DTD) file. In practice, the DTD defines the grammar of the XML-based language.

If you're interested in learning more about XML and XML-based languages, have a look at XML in IE5 Programmer's Reference *(Wrox Press, 1-861001-57-6). For a very quick approach, check out my article entitled* XML Languages *that appeared in the June 1999 issue of MIND (Microsoft Internet Developer) magazine.*

A generic XML file can accept any tag, provided that the overall syntax of the document is compliant with the XML standard. The same is not true for `.ws` files, which only support the tags listed above. In other words, `.ws` files behave as if they are documents of a specific XML-based language, even though there's no physical evidence of a DTD.

How the Elements Relate to Each Other

The most important element in a `.ws` file is `<job>`, which identifies a task that can be performed by the code in the file. Each job can be composed of any number of `<script>`, `<object>` and `<reference>` tags.

If the `.ws` file contains just one job, then `<job>` must be the root element of the file. However, it's possible for a `.ws` file to contain more than one job, in which case all the jobs must be enclosed in a `<package>` element:

```
<package>

   <job>
      <script />
      <object />
      <reference />
   </job>

   <job>
      <script />
      <object />
      <reference />
   </job>

</package>
```

A `.ws` file can contain at most one `<package>` element, but its inclusion is optional if there's only one job in the file.

Working with .ws Files

Let's start to examine the roles and the syntax of the elements you can employ in a `.ws` file. A "Hello World" script written as a `.ws` file might look something like this:

```
<?xml version="1.0"?>

<job>
   <script language="VBScript">
      MsgBox "Hello, world!"
   </script>
</job>
```

More typically, though, you'll end up dealing with a file that looks like this:

```
<?xml version="1.0"?>
<?job error="true" debug="true"?>

<!-- WS demo file: Demo1.ws -->

<job>

   <object progid="Shell.Application" id="shellApplication" />
   <reference object="ADODB.Recordset" />

   <script language="JScript">
      shellApplication.FindFiles();
   </script>

   <script language="VBScript">
      MsgBox "adOpenStatic = " + CStr(adOpenStatic)
   </script>

</job>
```

This doesn't do anything particularly significant, but it does demonstrate all the new tags in action. Run it, and you'll see the Find: All Files window and a message box displaying the value of a constant called `adOpenStatic`. As you can see, it's very different from any `.vbs` or `.js` file you may have written or used before.

XML Compliance

Not all of the above code is strictly inherent to it being a Windows script file. For example, consider the first line:

```
<?xml version="1.0"?>
```

This is the **XML declaration**, and it identifies 1.0 as the version of the language that the file conforms to. The module that parses the XML code requires this information, and the line that contains it can only be placed at the top of the file. Put it anywhere else, and you'll get an error.

If you don't put this line in a `.ws` file, you are authorizing the parser to accept a looser syntax that's almost identical to the one you use with HTML pages. This mode was introduced to help people deal with some of the stricter rules of 'pure' XML; it makes using XML easier for experienced HTML programmers.

> *Comments* `<!-- ... -->` *in the script file must always appear after any XML declaration you've used.*

Using CDATA to Wrap Scripts

Be aware that once you've decided to be XML-compliant, you can run into some very odd errors in your script code. Consider the following lines:

```
<script language="VBScript">
   num = 1
   MsgBox "The result is = " & num
</script>
```

If you insert these into a file that declares itself to be XML-compliant, they provoke a message box that looks something like this:

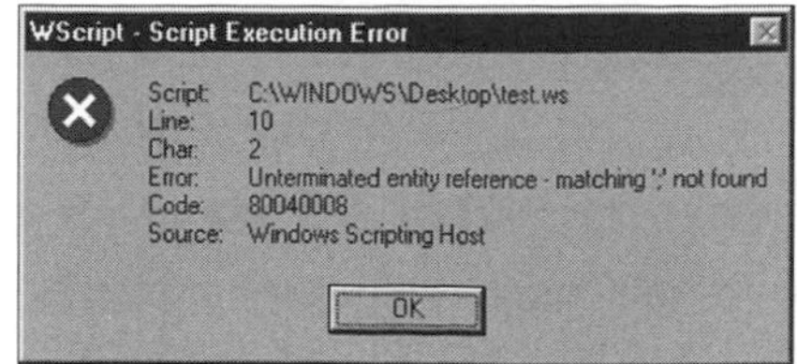

The cause of this error is that you're using a **reserved character** — in this case, an ampersand. When the XML parser encounters this character, it assumes the presence of an **XML entity**, which is always followed by a semicolon. It doesn't find one, and so the parser complains. Similar errors with different descriptions will arise if you use < to make numeric comparisons. However, using > is fine.

To work around this problem, and to assign `&` its intended, original role in VBScript, you can wrap all of your script code in **character data delimiters**:

```
<![CDATA[ ... ]]>
```

The presence of a `CDATA` delimiter tells the XML parser that the embedded code does not need parsing. The `CDATA` operator must only enclose the script code itself, and not the `<script>` tags, so the XML-compliant way to write the code you saw above is therefore:

```
<script language="VBScript">
   <![CDATA[
      num = 1
      MsgBox "The result is = " & num
   ]]>
</script>
```

In this specific case, you could also have used the + operator to concatenate strings, and the `CStr()` *function to convert the number into a string. (This is what I did in the example earlier in the chapter.)*

XML Run-time Options

The `.ws` file you saw above also included a `<?job?>` XML element, like this:

```
<?job error="true" debug="true"?>
```

This is an XML **processing instruction** that specifies attributes for error handling and debugging. The complete syntax for the instruction is:

```
<?job error="flag" debug="flag"?>
```

Here, *`flag`* is a placeholder for a Boolean string value: `true` or `false`. Let's examine the role of each attribute in a bit more detail:

Attribute	Description
`error`	If set to `true`, this causes the scripting engine to display messages for syntax and runtime errors.
`debug`	If set to `true`, this enables debugging. If it's set to `false`, there's no way for you to run the script debugger.

When you're ready to deploy the file, you might want to turn off the debugging attribute.

Root Elements in .ws Files

As I mentioned earlier, a .ws file can have two possible root elements: one is <job> and the other is <package>. Both of these are elements that can enclose and thereby 'glue together' a number of constituent elements. The <job> element encloses a task that you want your script to execute, while the <package> element groups multiple jobs defined in a single file.

The <job> Element

The syntax for a job is:

```
<job id="JobID">
   ...
</job>
```

The id attribute is optional, but when it's present *JobID* is the identifier of the job and must be unique throughout the file. When you have several jobs in the same file, you should always give each job an ID. By default, the first job in a file is run, but you can get different behavior by specifying the ID of the job you want to execute.

The <package> Element

You can specify a package with the following notation:

```
<package id="PackageID">
   ...
</package>
```

A package must contain at least one job, but can contain more, as shown below:

```
<package id="main">

   <job id="job1">
   </job>

   <job id="job2">
   </job>

</package>
```

The above code is perfectly valid, even though it does nothing at all. Anything you put within the <package> tag is ignored *unless* it is a <job> element. If you have multiple jobs in a single package, only the first one executes automatically.

Multiple Jobs in One File

The main goal of the <package> and <job> elements is to allow multiple jobs to be gathered in a single .ws file. When you run a .ws file, the first job executes unless you specify the ID of a different one on the command line by using the //job switch:

```
wscript.exe package.ws //job:jobID
```

Here *jobID* must be the ID of a job defined in the package.ws file. If no job exists with that ID, you'll get an error.

Creating Global Objects

Creating and using objects from within a WSH script are very common actions. As we've seen, it's possible to create objects with either the instructions made available by the language you're using, or the `WScript` object's `CreateObject()` method. With `.ws` files, however, there's no need to resort to script code in order to create an instance of a given object. Instead, the `<object>` tag allows you to associate a job with one or more objects. This technique has two basic advantages:

- The object is global to all the `<script>` blocks you may have in the job
- The object can be identified and created via its CLSID or its ProgID

Also, the object is bound earlier than it would be with the usual `CreateObject()` instantiation, providing the potential for specialized editing tools to supply IntelliSense support. The downside, however, is that you can't create objects on a remote server or sink events.

The syntax of the `<object>` tag is:

```
<object id="objID" [classid="clsid:GUID" | progid="progID"]/>
```

The *`objID`* value is a placeholder for the string identifier that will distinguish the object throughout the script. This ID must begin with a letter, and can contain numbers as well as underscores. Sadly, attempting to use the ID to create an event sink (the way you would with `WScript.CreateObject()`) doesn't work.

Although they look similar, this tag has nothing whatever to do with HTML's `<object>` tag.

As I've mentioned already, you have two ways to identify the COM object to be created: by CLSID and by ProgID. These two approaches are mutually exclusive, and one of them must be always specified.

Identifying an Object by its ProgID

If you know the ProgID of an object (and you usually will), you can use that to create an instance:

```
<object id="shell" progid="Shell.Application" />
```

This creates an instance of the `Shell.Application` object, the COM server that provides Automation services for the Windows shell, which we'll look at in more detail in the next chapter.

Identifying an Object by its CLSID

If you only know the CLSID of the COM object you're interested in (or if it simply doesn't have a ProgID), `.ws` files let you link to an object using that instead. The syntax used is similar to when you refer to ActiveX controls on HTML pages. For example:

```
<object id="shell" classid="clsid:13709620-C279-11CE-A49E-444553540000" />
```

The following example demonstrates a small .ws file that declares and uses objects:

```
<?xml version="1.0"?>
<?job error="true" debug="true"?>

<!-- WS demo file: demo2.ws -->

<job>
   <object id="shell1" progid="Shell.Application"/>
   <object id="shell2" classid="clsid:13709620-C279-11CE-A49E-444553540000"/>

   <script language="JScript">
      <![CDATA[
         shell1.FindFiles();
      ]]>
   </script>

   <script language="VBScript">
      <![CDATA[
         shell2.FileRun
      ]]>
   </script>
</job>
```

In this code, two instances of the same object are being created by different means. The first instance is created via its ProgID, and the second using its CLSID.

Referencing Type Libraries

When you create an instance of an object, you end up just holding a reference to the object in memory. You can call methods and pass arguments, but you can't use any constants that are part of the object's type library. In most cases, these constants are enumerated types of some kind, and to understand their importance, consider the following Visual Basic example:

```
Dim rs As Object
Set rs = CreateObject("ADODB.Recordset")
rs.CursorType = adOpenStatic
rs.Open "select * from author", "Biblio"
```

In Visual Basic, you can use the mnemonic constant adOpenStatic as long as you've referenced the type library of the ADO (ActiveX Data Object) recordset. When porting this Visual Basic snippet to VBScript (to be used across the Web, or in Windows Script Host code), however, you discover that you can't use the constant — you have to resort to using its explicit value instead. Broadly speaking, referencing a type library is like extending your namespace with all the public symbols exposed by that library.

Unless you somehow link the ADO library with the .ws file, there's no way to know that adOpenStatic is a constant equal to 3; it's just treated as a undeclared variable. Having to choose between using mnemonic constants or literal values wouldn't be a problem were it not for the fact that in almost all cases, remembering what a literal value means is quite impossible. The number 3 means very little, while a name like adOpenStatic is much more evocative for ADO programmers.

The <reference> Element

To address this problem, which lots of programmers are very sensitive to, a <reference> element has been added to the syntax of .ws files. It looks like this:

```
<reference [object="progID" | guid="typelibGUID"] [version="version"] />
```

You can identify which object's type library should be referenced in two ways: via the *object's* ProgID, or via the *type library's* CLSID. Only one of the `object` and `guid` attributes can be used at a time. Here are some examples:

```
<reference object="ADODB.Recordset" />
<reference guid="13709620-C279-11CE-A49E-444553540000" />
```

The ProgID is the program identifier of the object, from which the type library can be derived, and it can also include a version number. A type library can be embedded in the same module (`.dll` or `.exe`) as the object, or in a separate file, often with a `.tlb` extension. The `guid` attribute, on the other hand, is *always* the CLSID of the type library.

The `version` attribute refers to the version number of the type library. It is optional, defaults to version 1.0 when not specified, and must be in the form `major[.minor]`.

If the `object` attribute is used to specify the type library and the version is not specified, the version is derived from the registry key for the specified ProgID. If none can be found, the default is again 1.0.

If a `<reference>` element appears in a `.ws` file with multiple jobs, it only applies to the job that contains it.

Including External Files

Another common problem for WSH developers that version 2.0 is intended to solve is that of linking to external files. When you're writing script code to be used on web pages, you can use the `src` attribute of the `<script>` tag to reference external files full of useful VBScript or JScript routines. This gives you a clear advantage, because it means you can isolate all the general-purpose routines you may wish to use across several different projects into separate files.

Unfortunately, the feature isn't available in version 1.0 of WSH, and there's no obvious support for it in the VBScript and JScript scripting engines either. As I'll show you later, however, it's possible to provide an acceptable mechanism by writing a specialized function in any version of JScript and version 5.0 of VBScript. In the meantime, let's look at how to link to external files from a `.ws` file.

The <script> Element

The key to the proceedings is the `<script>` element, which looks a lot like its HTML counterpart. Its syntax is the following:

```
<script language="language" [src="file"]>
   ...
</script>
```

`language` and *`file`* are placeholders for the name of the scripting engine to be used, and the script file to be imported. When you import a file, consider that its content will be embedded in a `<script>` section, so just write `functions` or `subs`. More importantly, the `<script>` section that will receive the imported file must be of the same language as the imported file, so you can't have this:

```
<script language="VBScript" src="file.js">
```

All of the following declarations, however, are perfectly acceptable:

```
<script language="VBScript" src="file.vbs" />
<script language="JScript" src="file.js" />
<script src="file.js" />
```

If you don't specify a scripting language, the WSH runtime will assume JScript as the default language. This behavior is identical to the script blocks in HTML pages.

Script Execution

You can use the `<script>` element to specify lines of code to be executed as the body of a job *and* to import external files *at the same time*. The following code is quite legal:

```
<?xml version="1.0" ?>
<?job error="true" debug="true"?>

<!--
   IEDemo.ws
   A WS file that navigates the Web and imports external functions.
-->

<job>
   <script language="VBscript" src="one.vbs">
      <![CDATA[

         Set IE = CreateObject("InternetExplorer.Application")
         IE.Visible = True
         IE.Navigate "http://www.wrox.com"

         ' Loop until we close the browser...
         While IE.Visible
         Wend

         ' Clean-up
         WScript.DisconnectObject IE
         Set IE = Nothing

         ' Call an external function from one.vbs
         One_SayHello

      ]]>
   </script>
</job>
```

In the same `<script>` block, we're defining the code to be executed *and* importing the contents of `one.vbs`:

```
' one.vbs

Function One_SayHello
   MsgBox "Hello from VBScript"
End Function
```

When you're defining script files to be imported by other modules, make a habit of prefixing the name of any function or subroutine with a string that identifies the file it comes from. In the above case, I'm using `One` followed by a underscore. By doing so, you should avoid (or at least significantly reduce) naming conflicts. Furthermore, you'll make code maintenance easier, and simplify the process of locating the module that actually contains a given routine.

> **Note the use of `CDATA` to delimit the script code and keep it compliant with the XML 1.0 specification.**

Mixing Languages

The <script> element allows you to inject script code anywhere in your .ws file, and the really great thing is that these 'injections' can be written in any language for which there's a Windows Script engine. You can call JScript routines from within a VBScript block, and vice versa. This has two practical advantages:

- You can reuse script code without the need to translate it into another language
- You can choose the best language available to perform a particular operation

While the trend is towards programming languages of equal power and versatility, each still retains a number of things that it can do better, or that are easier and more familiar to you. Given the choice, I'd never be without VBScript's For...Each construct, or the overall syntax of JScript that's more attuned to my C/C++ origins.

The following code demonstrates the combined use of VBScript and JScript routines in a single .ws file. It is adapted from the IEDemo.ws file shown above:

```
<?xml version="1.0" ?>
<?job error="true" debug="true" ?>

<!--
   IEDemo.ws
   A WS file that navigates the Web and imports external functions.
-->

<job>
   <script language="JScript" src="one.js">
      function JS_Echo(str)
      {
         WScript.Echo(str);
      }
   </script>

   <script language="VBScript" src="one.vbs">
      <![CDATA[

         Set IE = CreateObject("InternetExplorer.Application")
         IE.Visible = True
         IE.Navigate "http://www.wrox.com"

         ' Loop until we close the browser...
         While IE.Visible
         Wend

         ' Clean-up
         WScript.DisconnectObject IE
         Set IE = Nothing

         ' Call an external function from one.vbs
         One_SayHello

         ' Call an external function from one.js
         OneJS_WaveGoodbye

         ' Call a JScript function defined earlier
         JS_Echo "Done"

      ]]>
   </script>
</job>
```

The JScript function JS_Echo() is defined in the file above and called from within a VBScript block. The OneJS_WaveGoodbye() routine, on the other hand, comes from the imported script one.js:

```
// one.js
function OneJS_WaveGoodbye()
{
   WScript.Echo("Goodbye from JScript");
}
```

Other Supported Elements

In addition to the elements we've looked at so far, there are two others that you can use despite the fact that they're not (yet) documented as being valid .ws file syntax:

- <comment>
- <resource>

These elements appear in the documentation for Windows Script Components (which is available for download from http://msdn.microsoft.com/scripting), and the reason why WSH 2.0 scripts support them is simple: the same module that parses .ws files is used to work with Windows Script Components!

The <comment> Element

This element is meant to enclose raw text that the parser will ignore, and which you can therefore use for, say, documentation purposes.

```
<comment> Place text here... </comment>
```

The <comment> element plays the same role as the <!-- and --> delimiters. You can place it anywhere in the .ws file.

The <resource> Element

More interesting is the <resource> element that lets you isolate things in your code that are constant, and which you don't want to hard-code repeatedly in the script. All of these resources are referenced by identifiers:

```
<resource id="hello">Hello, world!</resource>
<resource id="version">1.02</resource>
```

The ID must then be passed to a global function called getResource() to obtain the stored data.

Typical information that you might want to manage through the <resource> element is data that might be subject to localization or frequent change. Functionally speaking there's no difference between using the <resource> element and using a group of language constants, although the former does look more elegant, and it's language-neutral. A <resource> element must be a child of a <job> block, and its scope is limited to that job.

The following example shows how to use the <resource> and <comment> elements:

```
<?xml version="1.0"?>
<?job error="true" debug="true"?>

<job>
   <comment>
      The resource element is documented as part of the WSC kit,
      but you can use it in .ws files as well.
   </comment>
```

```
   <resource id="hello">Hello, world!</resource>

   <script language="VBScript">
      MsgBox getResource("hello")
   </script>
</job>
```

New Features of the Object Model

In Chapters 3 and 4, I described the various objects that form the WSH object model. The greatest innovation with WSH 2.0 is undoubtedly the introduction of `.ws` files, but there are also some (relatively minor) changes to the object model. There are two things worthy of our attention:

- A new `Sleep()` method for the `WScript` object
- Internal restructuring of the `WshNetwork` object

The second point sounds like it could have a serious impact, but it shouldn't affect the operation of any existing code: the external interface is supposed to have remained intact. The internal code on which `WshNetwork` is based, however, has been optimized and should work faster, especially on Windows 9x platforms, where it was a bit slow before.

A Sleep Method

`Sleep()` is a new method of `WScript` that suspends execution of the current script for a specified interval in milliseconds:

```
WScript.Sleep(nMilliseconds)
```

This method is built on the top of the `Sleep()` SDK function, which introduces a delay in thread execution without affecting the CPU. The thread running the script is suspended, its execution to be resumed as soon as the interval expires. Note that *when* execution resumes, it will only be for the remainder of the previous time slice. In other words, resuming execution doesn't mean assigning the thread a new time slice.

A time slice is the number of milliseconds (about 50ms) assigned to each thread by the CPU. After this time, the thread is suspended and a new one executes. This schedule is governed by the operating system, and is affected by thread priorities.

If you specify an interval of 0 milliseconds then the thread relinquishes the remainder of its time slice and is suspended as if it had completed it. Here's a simple example of calling `Sleep()`:

```
MsgBox "Before"

' 1000 is 1 second
WScript.Sleep 1000

' This instruction executes one second later
MsgBox "After"
```

Unfortunately, `Sleep()` is not a means of synchronizing the script with other running applications. You can't use it to wait for a condition to occur, such as receiving a message or signaling one of the Win32 synchronization objects. `Sleep()` just puts the script to sleep and wakes it up when the specified interval has expired.

> *The Win32 SDK provides a* `SleepEx()` *API function that supports an additional Boolean parameter called* `bAlertable`*. Set it to* `True`*, and the thread will be awoken by events other than the timeout occurring. (See the MSDN documentation for more details.) This feature is not provided by the current version of the* `WScript.Sleep()` *method, but who knows what the future may hold?*

The ability to pause execution of your script is probably not something for which you can see an immediate application, but the need to do it may arise if you have to cope with asynchronous operations and multiple processes. Delaying one such process by introducing a sleep interval could help obtain the combined result you want. In this situation, using `Sleep()` is far more efficient than dummy loops because it actually suspends the thread and stops the CPU from working.

The following code just delays the script for 1 second with a dummy loop:

```
d1 = Now                                ' What time is now

' Waits for 1 seconds
While DateDiff("s", d1, Now) < 1        ' Returns the difference in seconds
Wend

d2 = Now                                ' What time is now
MsgBox DateDiff("s", d1, d2)
```

The effect it has on your script is exactly the same as the one produced by this code, which has the considerable benefit of not hogging the CPU while it sleeps:

```
d1 = Now                                ' What time is now

' Waits for 1 second
WScript.Sleep(1000)                     ' Uses milliseconds

d2 = Now                                ' What time is now
MsgBox DateDiff("s", d1, d2)
```

New Scripting Engines

Many developers noticed a quick jump of the scripting engines' version numbers from 3.1 to version 5.0, and wondered what had happened in between. In fact, there *are* version 4.0 variants of VBScript and JScript, but they added no new language features; they were created for inclusion in the Visual Studio 98 suite to provide IntelliSense support.

Versions 5.0 certainly *are* major releases, since they introduce significant enhancements to both JScript and VBScript. Moreover, they not only address the expressiveness of the languages, but also improve performance and add the possibility of encoding your scripts.

An overall consideration of the changes made to VBScript and JScript leads me to think that Microsoft is trying to make the languages functionally equivalent. Yes, each language still has its native features and offers advantages over the other in certain situations, but in general Microsoft seems committed to filling in the gaps between the languages.

To see what I mean, consider that one limitation of VBScript was the lack of a means to evaluate run-time expressions, when JScript had the `eval()` function. On the other hand, JScript was still missing a mechanism to catch run-time errors. With versions 5.0 these limitations have been fixed, and even overturned! VBScript is now *more* powerful than JScript when it comes to evaluating expressions at runtime, and JScript provides far *better* error handling than VBScript.

Before we go any further, I want to show you a pair of very short routines (one in VBScript, the other in JScript) for building up strings containing the version numbers of the scripting engines that are installed on the machine running them. With this knowledge, you can avoid using features in your code that are unsupported by the machine on which it finds itself.

```
' Version.vbs

s = ScriptEngine & " "
s = s & ScriptEngineMajorVersion & "."
s = s & ScriptEngineMinorVersion & "."
s = s & ScriptEngineBuildVersion
MsgBox s
```

```
// Version.js

s = "";
s += ScriptEngine() + " ";
s += ScriptEngineMajorVersion() + ".";
s += ScriptEngineMinorVersion() + ".";
s += ScriptEngineBuildVersion();
WScript.Echo(s);
```

VBScript 5.0

The new language features of VBScript 5.0 can be summarized as follows:

- Remote automation
- Regular expressions
- Classes
- The `With` statement
- Run-time code evaluation

I'm not going to cover the syntax in detail here. Instead, I'll try to highlight what's new and turn your attention to what's particularly interesting from the WSH perspective. For more information, refer to Appendix A, or consult the documentation available at http://msdn.microsoft.com/scripting.

Remote Automation

Distributed COM (DCOM) provides a mechanism for calling COM objects remotely, and support for it was added to the Visual Basic 6.0 `CreateObject()` function. Similar support had been missing from scripting languages, but the VBScript 5.0 `CreateObject()` function now takes an additional parameter that is interpreted as the name of the remote machine on which to create the object. The syntax is identical to the function of the same name in Visual Basic 6.0:

```
CreateObject(progID [,location])
```

Here, `progID` denotes the program identifier of the COM server being created, and the optional argument `location` is the name of the remote computer on which to create it.

```
Set rObj = CreateObject("Object.Application", "\\notebook")
```

The above snippet will create in `rObj` a local reference to an object that is found and instantiated on the specified machine.

Regular Expressions

VBScript's **regular expressions** (RE) have been created to match their JScript counterparts closely. By using RE, you can manipulate strings easily, especially when they follow a set pattern (like e-mail addresses and URLs). This feature takes VBScript closer to JScript and Perl:

```
' VB5RegExp.vbs
' Demonstrates Regular Expressions with VBScript 5.0
' ---------------------------------------------------
Option Explicit

Dim re
Dim str

Set re = New RegExp

' Check for a pattern given by "word@word"
re.pattern = "\w+\@[.\w]+"
str = InputBox("E-mail Address")

' Test the e-mail address entered
If re.Test(str) Then
   MsgBox "Your e-mail address is correct."
Else
   MsgBox "Re-enter your e-mail address."
End if
```

The `RegExp` object has a property called `pattern`, in which you define the structure of the strings you're interested in. Arranging this pattern can be tricky, since you have to deal with a number of special characters and conventions, as the following (actually quite simple) pattern demonstrates:

```
re.pattern = "\w+\@[.\w]+"
```

In the above string, `\w` stands for any numeric or alphabetical character, including an underscore. The + symbol means, "one or more of the previous character," so `\w+` is the way to denote a word, *any* word. The backslash symbol can also be used to indicate a special character, so (for example) `\@` just denotes the @ character, and `\"` denotes the " character.

That just leaves the `[.\w]+` string. To understand this, you need to know that everything enclosed in square brackets is a possible character that can appear at that point. This means that `[.\w]` is the union of all numeric, alphabetical characters plus the underscore and the dot. The final + signifies that the string can contain any non-zero number of such characters. In other words, `[.\w]+` is any string, including any number of dots.

In the listing above, you'll probably have noticed the presence of the `New` *operator, which is pretty unusual for VBScript code. In fact, this is related to the introduction of classes, which we'll look at in the next section. Note, however, that it would also have been possible to use* `CreateObject()` *to generate an instance of the* `VBScript.RegExp` *object. Note also that in some older documentation, the ProgID of this object is erroneously given as* `Scripting.RegExp`.

Because the thing that allows you to make use of regular expressions in VBScript is a COM object, this means that you can exploit regular expressions from within Visual Basic (and any other COM-aware client) as well.

Classes

Version 5.0 has also provided VBScript with the ability to create **classes**, which its parent language, Visual Basic, has been able to do for some time. The difference between Visual Basic and VBScript is that VBScript doesn't rely on external `.cls` files, but instead uses a different syntax. Unfortunately, this also means that porting your existing Visual Basic classes to VBScript is not necessarily a trivial task.

VBScript 5.0 introduces the `Class` keyword, which allows the definition of a language-specific component with properties and methods. Here's an example of a simple class that works as a timer, counting the seconds elapsed between two blocks of instructions.

```
' ClassDemo.vbs
' Demonstrates the Class statement in VBScript 5.0
'--------------------------------------------------------------
Option Explicit

Class TickCounter

   Public IntervalType

   Private m_started          ' Whether the timer is started
   Private m_startedAt        ' Time when the timer started

   ' Initializes the counter
   Public Sub Start()
      m_started = True
      m_startedAt = Now
   End Sub

   ' Stops the counter and returns time elapsed since Start() was last called
   Public Function StopIt()
      If m_started = False Then
          StopIt = -1          ' Returns -1 if the timer wasn't started earlier
      End If
```

Continued on Following Page

```
      Dim stoppedAt
      stoppedAt = Now
      m_started = False

      ' Return the time elapsed; IntervalType supports the same
      '  flags as DateDiff. Set to "s" (seconds) by default.
      StopIt = DateDiff(IntervalType, m_startedAt, stoppedAt)
   End Function

   ' Class "constructor"
   Private Sub Class_Initialize()
      IntervalType = "s"
   End Sub

End Class


' Uses the above class
Dim t
Set t = New TickCounter

t.Start
WScript.Sleep(1000)
MsgBox t.StopIt()
```

The class defines a timer with two methods (`Start()` and `StopIt()`), and a public property called `IntervalType`. In this case, the property is exposed directly and is read/write — there are no `Get/Set` methods to validate the values you assign. To employ read-only or write-only properties, or to define `Get/Set` methods to manage properties, use `Property Get` or `Property Set` statements, like this:

```
Private strEmailName          ' Internal variable to store the property

Property Get EmailName
   EmailName = strEmailName
End Property
```

You can use the `Private` and `Public` keywords to expose or hide your methods and properties, but remember that all elements are public by default.

Note that the `classdemo.vbs` file contains both the class declaration and the code that uses it. I'll have more to say about this in a moment.

The New Operator

Once you've created a VBScript class, you can instantiate it with the `New` operator:

```
Dim t
Set t = New TickCounter
```

Note that you *can't* declare and create a class on the same line, as you would in Visual Basic. Code like this is incorrect.

```
Dim t = New TickCounter                  ' Don't do this!
```

When a class is instantiated, the `Initialize()` event is fired. This lets you execute some code that initializes some internal variables to default values. In the example above, I used it to assign a default value to the `IntervalType` member variable.

The documentation claims that the `Initialize` *event should be handle using a subroutine called* `classname_Initialize()`, *where* `classname` *stands for the name of the class. In truth, however, this handler has a fixed name (just like in Visual Basic):* `Class_Initialize()`.

In addition to the initialization notification, a class also receives a notification event when it is about to be unloaded. In this case, the handler subroutine to write within the class code should be called `Class_Terminate()`.

Importing Classes with WSH 2.0

WSH 2.0 lets you import external files through the `src` attribute of the `<script>` tag, providing you with the ability to isolate the class implementation into a separate file and then import it into a `.ws` script, resulting in quite elegant code:

```
<?xml version="1.0"?>
<!-- UserCounter.ws, demonstrates using the TickCounter class -->

<job>
   <script language="VBScript" src="TickCounter.vbs" />

   <script language="VBScript">
      Dim t
      Set t = new TickCounter

      t.Start
      WScript.Sleep(1000)
      MsgBox t.StopIt
   </script>
</job>
```

I'll be returning to the subject of writing reusable script code in Chapter 7.

The With Statement

The `With` statement is another piece of Visual Basic that has been brought to VBScript. Its role is quite straightforward: it serves the purpose of saving you from too much typing! When you're working with an object (as in this sample code), you need to use its name to address methods and properties:

```
Dim counter
Set counter = new TickCounter
counter.IntervalType = "n"
counter.Start
MsgBox counter.StopIt
```

In some circumstances, when you're dealing with complex objects, you'll find yourself writing lines of code that repeat the name of the same object over and over again. Quite apart from being boring for you, it's a nuisance for VBScript too, because every time it comes across the name it has to figure out which object you're referencing. The `With` statement is a smart shortcut for this tedious procedure:

```
Dim counter
Set counter = new TickCounter
With counter
   .IntervalType = "n"   ' The With statement here saves you from specifying
   .Start                '  the name of the object (counter) again
   MsgBox .StopIt
End With
```

Because the VBScript engine is able to keep hold of the reference to the `TickCounter` object for the duration of all three calls, this is a more efficient way of accessing a set of methods and properties.

Run-time Code Evaluation

VBScript developers have long been waiting for a tool that can evaluate code at runtime. Such a tool allows you to consider source code as a kind of new data type to be created and processed during execution, something that's particularly exciting in light of the fresh support for classes in VBScript.

If the features of WSH 2.0 are not available to you, importing external code in VBScript files is still a problem because the language doesn't provide any native constructs to help with the task. As I mentioned at the time, testing my `TickCounter` class with pure VBScript code required me to include the complete source code for it in `classdemo.vbs`, together with the code that used it.

The run-time code evaluation facilities built into VBScript 5.0 make it possible for you to *import* the code for a class into any VBScript file, separating the implementation of a class from the code that actually utilizes it. In addition, they let you treat code as a data type to be passed between procedures, allowing callbacks and even a kind of 'event sinking' for VBScript classes. I'll demonstrate this in action later in the chapter.

The Eval Function

Run-time code evaluation is a feature that *JScript* has supported for some time, thanks to the `eval()` function. This takes a code string as input, evaluates it and executes it. Porting this simple schema to VBScript, however, poses a non-trivial problem: the syntax of VBScript allows for ambiguity between the comparison operator and the assignment operator. For example:

```
a = b
```

In typing the above code, you may intend the result of a comparison (which implies a Boolean return value), or a simple assignment. In JScript (and in C/C++), you have to use different operators (= and ==), making your intentions completely clear.

As the syntax of VBScript doesn't provide distinct operators, VBScript 5.0 introduces two different categories of run-time code processors. You have one function to *evaluate* the code (`Eval()`) and two other functions to *execute* code (`Execute()` and `ExecuteGlobal()`).

Apart from resolving the ambiguity over the = symbol, `Eval()` and `Execute()` do broadly similar things. The only significant difference is if there's a return value, `Eval()` will return it. `Execute()` is implemented as a procedure, and never returns anything. The `Eval()` function has the following prototype:

```
[result = ]Eval(expression)
```

Returning a result is not mandatory.

Execute and ExecuteGlobal

Both of these functions provide the ability to execute VBScript code that you've specified through a string. Multiple instructions can be issued as long as you separate them with colons. The syntax is quite straightforward:

```
Execute statements
ExecuteGlobal statements
```

The difference between the two is that `Execute()` works in the local namespace, while `ExecuteGlobal()` affects the global namespace. To understand what this means, take a look at the following code:

```
' Exec.vbs
' Demonstrates the Execute() function
'--------------------------------------------------------------

' Call the main function (this is the GLOBAL scope)
Main


' First function that gets called
Function Main
   Dim strCode
   strCode = "Dim a: a = 1"

   ' Declares the variable 'a' and initializes it to 1
   Execute strCode

   ' The value HERE is 1
   MsgBox a

   ' Call another function
   AnotherFunc
End Function


Function AnotherFunc
   ' HERE the value of 'a' is the empty string
   MsgBox a
End Function
```

The body of the script calls a `Main()` function that declares and initializes a variable using `Execute()`. The scope of the variable (and therefore the namespace affected) is limited to the body of the function. It isn't visible from within another function, such as `AnotherFunc()`.

It's clear that `Execute()` doesn't add the new symbols to the global namespace, but `ExecuteGlobal()` certainly does. The following script is a very slightly modified version of the previous one:

```
' ExecGlob.vbs
' Demonstrates the ExecuteGlobal() function
'--------------------------------------------------------------

' Call the main function (this is the GLOBAL scope)
Main


' First function that gets called
Function Main
   Dim strCode
   strCode = "Dim a: a = 1"

   ' Declares the variable 'a' and initializes it to 1
   ExecuteGlobal strCode

   ' The value HERE is 1
   MsgBox a

   ' Call another function
   AnotherFunc
End Function


Function AnotherFunc
   ' The value of 'a' is 1 HERE as well
   MsgBox a
End Function
```

Using ExecuteGlobal() instead of Execute() adds the new variable (in this case, a) to the global scope and makes it visible to all the functions in the script. The effect produced by ExecuteGlobal() is the same as would be achieved by adding the variable declaration at the beginning of the script, outside any Function or Sub.

Importing Routines at Runtime

ExecuteGlobal() lends itself very well to creating and adding classes at runtime, and also to importing external files in the current script. The idea behind this is quite simple: you read the file you want to import (which contains routines and/or constants) into a string, and then execute that string 'globally'. Then, any other function will be able to call the new routines and use the new constants:

```
' Include.vbs
' Simulates an "include" statement using ExecuteGlobal
'-----------------------------------------------------------
Option Explicit

Include "one.vbs"
One_SayHello

' You need to add this short piece of code to any WSH script that needs it
Sub Include(file)
   Dim fso
   Dim f
   Dim str

   Set fso = CreateObject("Scripting.FileSystemObject")
   Set f = fso.OpenTextFile(file, 1)
   str = f.ReadAll
   f.Close

   ExecuteGlobal str
End Sub
```

The Include() routine exploits the features of the FileSystemObject object (more on this in Chapter 6) to read the contents of a text file into a single string. Then, it simply passes this string to ExecuteGlobal(). Had we used Execute(), the only routine to benefit from the inclusion would have been the Include() subroutine itself!

If you plan to use this technique in your own scripts, remember that the Include() procedure must be duplicated in every file in which you use it. Of course, if you can utilize WSH 2.0 and its .ws files, you don't need Include() or ExecuteGlobal() to import external files — you can just use the src attribute of the <script> tag.

Note that JScript's eval() *function works in the same way as VBScript's* Execute(). *It doesn't add new symbols to the global scope unless you call it from the global code — that is, outside of any function. If you call* eval() *from within a function, it adds new symbols only to the scope of the function it is being called from.*

Passing Code Among Procedures

Since you can evaluate code at runtime, a string of code (a sequence of statements, or the name of a function) becomes a kind of data type that you can pass from procedure to procedure.

When you pass code to another procedure or function to be executed, you're actually using a **callback**. A first, very simple example of using a callback is the following:

```
' Repeat.vbs
' Demonstrates callbacks with VBScript 5.0
' ---------------------------------------------------------------------------
Option Explicit

Dim count
RepeatCode "Test", 4                ' Code that causes the callback

Function Test()                     ' The function that will be called back
   MsgBox "Call number " & count
End Function

Function RepeatCode(strCode, nTimes)
   For count = 1 To nTimes
      Execute strCode               ' Executes code received as an argument
   Next
End Function
```

The script calls a function named `RepeatCode()` that takes a piece of code and a number as input, and then executes the code the specified number of times. In this case, the code to execute is the name of a function, but it could equally have been a sequence of colon-separated statements.

Adding Support for Events to VBScript Classes

VBScript classes can expose methods and properties, but they can't fire events. As I'll show you in a moment, however, you can use the run-time code evaluation features to provide a class with code that should be executed when certain events occur. From the class's point of view, there's no event to fire; from the client's standpoint, there's no event to sink (at least, not in the traditional way).

In this scheme, the class will expose properties such as `OnInit` and `OnClick` that can be set to contain code blocks. These blocks will then be called internally in lieu of firing events. (You find a similar approach used in Dynamic HTML pages.) If that's not quite clear, try the following example.

What changes do we need to make to the `TickCounter` class in order for it to expose an `OnFormatString` pseudo-event? Well, `OnFormatString` will be a property containing a code block, and the code you assign to `OnFormatString` will be called back when the count has terminated. By default, the `StopIt()` method returns a number denoting seconds, but you can change the format of the returned value by 'sinking' the `OnFormatString` event:

```
' TickCounter2.vbs
' A counter class in VBScript 5.0
'------------------------------------------------------------

Class TickCounter2

   Public IntervalType
   Public OnFormatString        ' Code to execute from within StopIt()

   Private m_started            ' Whether the timer is started
   Private m_startedAt          ' Time when the timer started

   ' Initializes the counter
   Public Sub Start()
      m_started = True
      m_startedAt = Now
   End Sub
```

Continued on Following Page

```
    ' Stops the counter and returns time elapsed since Start() was last called
    Public Function StopIt()
       If m_started = False Then
          StopIt = -1         ' Returns -1 if the timer wasn't started earlier
       End If

       Dim stoppedAt
       stoppedAt = Now
       m_started = False

       ' Return the time elapsed; IntervalType supports the same
       '  flags as DateDiff. Set to "s" (seconds) by default.
       Dim retc
       retc = DateDiff(IntervalType, m_startedAt, stoppedAt)

       ' Execute the code
       StopIt = retc
       On Error Resume Next   ' In case OnFormatString isn't specified
       StopIt = Eval(OnFormatString & "(" & retc & ")")
    End Function

    ' Class "constructor"
    Private Sub Class_Initialize()
       IntervalType = "s"
    End Sub

 End Class
```

`StopIt()` now evaluates the content of `OnFormatString` after stopping the counter. The class assumes that the callback code has a precise structure — in this case, that it contains the name of a VBScript function that accepts just one argument.

> *Notice that a return value is needed from the code that* `OnFormatString` *contains. For this reason we must use* `Eval()` *rather than* `Execute()`.

To see how this works, suppose that `OnFormatString` refers a to function called `Hello`. In that case, the code being evaluated has the form `Hello(`*n*`)`, where *n* is the result returned by the `DateDiff()` function. Here's a VBScript program that utilizes the class:

```
<?xml version="1.0"?>
<!-- UserCounter2.ws, demonstrates using the TickCounter2 class -->

<job>
   <script language="VBScript" src="TickCounter2.vbs" />

   <script language="VBScript">
      <![CDATA[
         Dim t
         Set t = new TickCounter2

         t.OnFormatString = "ElapsedTime"    ' No trailing parentheses
         t.Start
         WScript.Sleep(1000)
         MsgBox t.StopIt

         ' Callback function
         Function ElapsedTime(n)
            ElapsedTime = n & " second(s) elapsed."
         End Function
      ]]>
   </script>
</job>
```

Run this code and you'll see a message box informing you that about a second has elapsed since you started it!

JScript 5.0

The changes in JScript 5.0 are less evident and less numerous than the ones made to VBScript. Apart from the addition of DCOM support to `ActiveXObject()`, there's been just one major enhancement: support for an exception handling mechanism. To summarize what's new in JScript 5.0, we have:

- Remote automation
- Exception handling
- The `instanceof` operator

Remote Automation

DCOM support has been added to JScript 5.0, and it affects the language's means of creating objects. In VBScript, this was `CreateObject()`; in JScript, it's `ActiveXObject()`:

```
var newObject = new ActiveXObject(progID [,location])
```

Again, `progID` denotes the program identifier of the server being created, and the optional argument `location` is the name of the network machine where the object is to be created.

Exception Handling

Until JScript 5.0, there was no powerful way of intercepting error conditions in your JScript code. For example, to check whether or not an object had been properly created, you needed code like this:

```
if(typeof(obj) == "undefined")
{
   ...
}
```

As if that weren't enough, you also had to pepper your programs with `else` branches in order to test return codes.

The mechanism used in JScript 5.0 is more modern and powerful. It is based on exceptions, which will be familiar to you if you've done some C++ programming. If that doesn't describe you, it's enough for now to say that an exception is an error situation that is somehow "brought to your code's attention". Conceptually, handling an exception is rather like sinking an event. You associate some code with an action, and that code executes only if the JScript runtime environment detects an error while performing that action.

The syntax employed is borrowed from C++'s `try...catch` construct:

```
try
   tryStatement
catch(exception)
   catchStatement
```

The *tryStatement* placeholder stands for any sequence of commands that you want to check for errors. The *catchStatement* block, on the other hand, gathers all the instructions to be executed when an error occurs in the `try` block. The *exception* element is a piece of information that describes the error. Usually, that element evaluates to an **Error object**, which is another new entry in the JScript 5.0 arena. Let's look at an example:

```
try
{
   var obj = new ActiveXObject("Object.Hello");
   obj.DoSomething();
}
catch(err)
{
   WScript.Echo("Got an error: " + err.description);
}
```

The `err` in the code is a new JScript object that is akin to Visual Basic's `Err` object. If you try to run this code, it's likely that it won't be able to find an object called `Object.Hello`. This will result in the generation of an error, and control will be passed to the `catch` block.

It's impossible to write code like this in VBScript. There, the error handling capabilities are limited to the `On Error Resume Next` statement, which just causes execution to resume with the next instruction. In fact, it has more in common with the following Visual Basic code:

```
On Error Goto ErrCreateObject
Set obj = CreateObject("Object.Hello")

...

ErrCreateObject:
MsgBox "Got an error : & Err.Description
```

The Error Object

`Error` is a new JScript object that has just two properties: `number` and `description`. By default, an instance of this object is created every time an error is trapped within a `try` block. The object is 'filled' with the error number and its description, and passed automatically to the matching `catch` block. You can also create and fill an `Error` object yourself:

```
e = new Error;
e.number = 1;
e.description = "Unspecified error";
```

You might want to do something like this if you have detected an error yourself, and you explicitly want to raise an exception.

Exception handling is a layered mechanism, in which the system takes the lowest position. When your code tries to execute an action that the system can't accomplish, the system creates its own `Error` object and raises an exception. During execution, though, there might be situations that are unacceptable for your code but perfectly legitimate for the scripting engine — a variable with the wrong value perhaps, or input received in the wrong format. In this case, it's up to you to detect and handle the error condition:

```
bufferSize = 100;

try
{
   if(bufferSize < 10000)
   {
      e = new Error;
      e.number = -1;
      e.description = "Buffer too small";
      throw(e);
   }
}
catch(e)
{
   WScript.Echo("Got an error: " + e.description);
}
```

The example above demonstrates how to raise an exception from JScript code. You set the number and the description yourself, and then use the `throw` statement.

The throw Statement

The `throw` statement has the following syntax:

```
throw(exception)
```

Here, *`exception`* can be any expression at all, but usually it will be either an instance of the `Error` object or a string. The `throw` statement causes an exception to be thrown, while the block that catches it receives the content of *`exception`* via the parameter to `catch`. If you need to check the type of the expression being sent dynamically, you can exploit the `instanceof` operator:

```
catch(e)
{
   if(e instanceof Error)
      WScript.Echo("Got an error: " + e.description);
}
```

`try...catch` blocks can be nested, and the act of catching an exception only applies to a single level of the nested structure. You can throw the exception again in order to let external blocks handle it, as shown in the figure opposite:

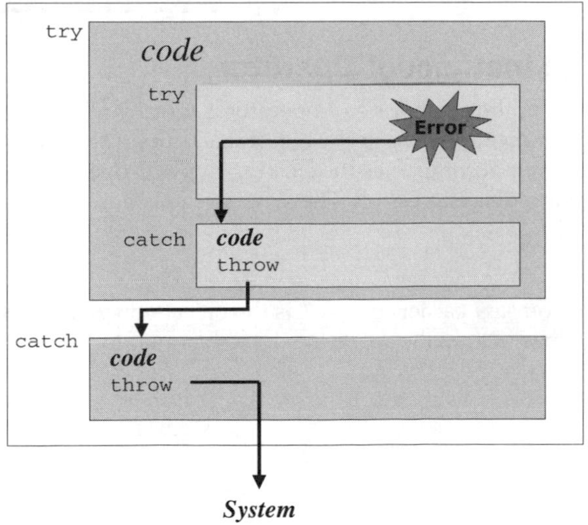

To do this, just call `throw` again from within the `catch` block. For example, if you're trying to create an object:

```
try
{
   var obj = new ActiveXObject("Object.Hello");
   obj.DoSomething();
}
catch(err)
{
   WScript.Echo("Got an error: " + err.description);
   throw(err)
}
```

and the object isn't registered, the first thing you'll see is a message like this:

This message is caused by the first-level catch block, the one you're providing personally. If you re-throw the exception, it gets handled by the JScript runtime and originates another dialog box:

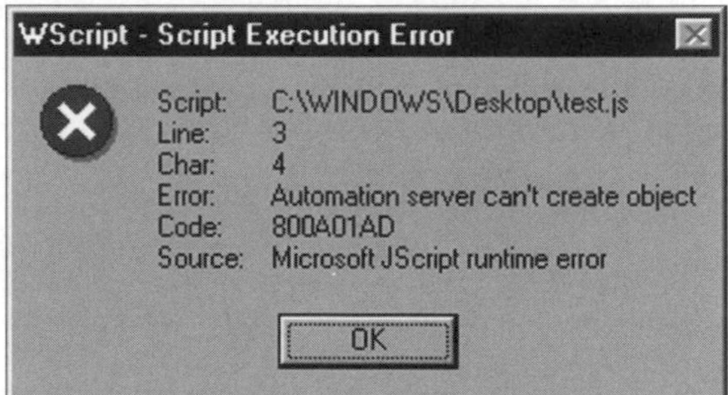

The instanceof Operator

Finally, the `instanceof` operator is worthy of a few words. It returns a Boolean value that indicates whether the object it acts upon is an instance of the specified class. This operator accompanies the existing `typeof` operator that returns the data type name of a particular expression. The syntax required is:

```
result = object instanceof class
```

As you saw earlier, *`object`* is the object you want to check, and *`class`* is any class defined within the scope in which the operator is being used.

Summary

In this chapter, we've looked at some of the latest developments that affect WSH and the way you use it. In particular, I examined the new Windows script (`.ws`) files that are available with WSH 2.0, and the changes in the 5.0 versions of the VBScript and JScript scripting engines. We also had a quick look at how the WSH object model is evolving.

This chapter marks the end of our survey of Windows Script Host native functionality, old and new. It has been my assertion from the very beginning that much of the power of WSH resides in its ability to link with other objects and object models, and it's that case I'll be championing in the rest of the book. In the next chapter, we'll discuss how the functionality you've seen so far can be combined with that of other standard Windows objects to provide a way of performing operations on the file system from your script code.

6

Accessing the Windows File System

It is surely the case that the most pervasive use of MS-DOS batch files was to automate the process of copying, moving, renaming and deleting files and directories. If WSH scripts are truly the modern replacement for batch files, as I've suggested on a number of occasions, it must be possible to use them for manipulating the file system.

Perhaps surprisingly, there is nothing in the WSH object model that enables access to the file system — surprising, that is, until you hear the explanation. The truth is that together with the VBScript and JScript runtime engines, Microsoft is delivering the **Scripting Run-time Library**, a hierarchy of COM objects that allows easy manipulation of files and folders. Strictly speaking, this library isn't a part of WSH, VBScript, or JScript, but as it *comes with* VBScript and JScript, it is definitely valid to describe it as being part of your WSH arsenal.

In this chapter I'm going to cover:

- The objects that form the Microsoft Scripting Run-time Library (SRL)
- How to combine these objects together to obtain more powerful functionality
- How to extend the same functionality to non-file system folders, through the Shell Automation objects

The Scripting Run-time Library, which is implemented in a single binary module (`scrrun.dll`), is also available for download as a stand-alone component. Take a look at http://msdn.microsoft.com/scripting *for details.*

The Scripting Run-time Library

The Scripting Run-time Library covers all the main requirements of providing programmatic access to the file system. It also provides a couple of objects to do accessory tasks, such as I/O on text files and creating dynamic collections of data. The main object in the library is called `FileSystemObject`, and it serves the purpose of allowing manipulation of files and folders. It is listed along with the other objects in the library in the following table:

Object	Description
`Dictionary`	An object that works like an associative array, storing items and retrieving them via keys. It is directly creatable from script; its ProgID is `Scripting.Dictionary`.
`Drive`	Lets you manage the properties of a drive, be it a floppy drive, a local hard drive, or a shared drive on a network. This object is not directly creatable, but an instance is returned by the method of `FileSystemObject` called `GetDrive()`. It is also the type that's used for items of the `Drives` collection.
`File`	Accesses the properties of a file, such as its path, parent folder, 'last modified' date, size, long name and short name. This object is not directly creatable, but an instance is returned by the method of `FileSystemObject` called `GetFile()`. It is also the type that's used for items of the `Files` collection.
`FileSystemObject`	Your entry point into the file system. This object lets you manage files and folders, and governs some file I/O operations. It is directly creatable from script; its ProgID is `Scripting.FileSystemObject`.
`Folder`	Very similar to `File`, but works on file system directories. This object is not directly creatable, but an instance is returned by the method of `FileSystemObject` called `GetFolder()`. It is also the type that's used for items of the `Folders` collection.
`TextStream`	Lets you control I/O operations on a text file, such as writing and reading individual lines. This object is not directly creatable, but an instance is returned by either `CreateTextFile()` or `OpenTextFile()`, both of which methods of the `FileSystemObject` object.

In addition, there are three collections, as hinted at by the previous table:

Collection	Description
`Drives`	Contains all the available drives, including network shares. A reference to this collection is returned by the `Drives` property exposed by the `FileSystemObject` object.
`Files`	Contains all the files in a given folder. A reference to this object can be obtained through the `Files` property of any `Folder` object.
`Folders`	Contains all the folders in a given folder. A reference to this object can be obtained through the `SubFolders` property of any `Folder` object.

The important thing about the SRL is that it offers the possibility to use the familiar, object-based notation when you're working with files and folders. All the information about any file system object (drive, file, folder) is available as a property, and any action can be performed through a method.

The following diagram depicts the hierarchy of the SRL object model:

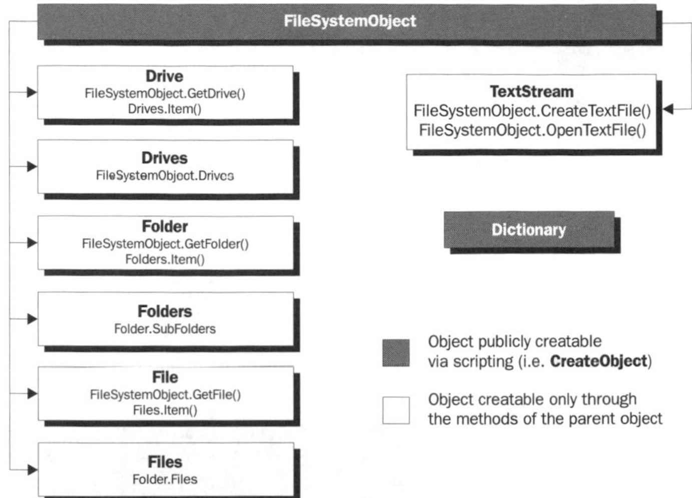

As you can see, a central role is played by `FileSystemObject`, which is responsible (directly or indirectly) for the creation of almost all the other objects. The sole exception to this is the `Dictionary` object, which is also creatable independently. In fact, the `Dictionary` object is not *strictly* tied to the file system at all — it's really a helper object that can be used in lieu of VBA collection objects in VBScript and JScript.

The picture also makes evident the types of the objects that form the hierarchy. There are three pairs of related objects that map to the constituent elements of the file system: `Drive` and `Drives`, `Folder` and `Folders`, `File` and `Files`. In each case, the plural means that the object is a collection of single objects of the same type. Out on a limb is `TextStream`, another helper object that lets you read and write from text files.

The File System Object

The main object of the SRL is undoubtedly `Scripting.FileSystemObject`, which gives you the ability to create, edit, move and delete files and folders. It also allows you to check whether a particular folder exists, and returns file- and folder-specific information such as names, creation dates, sizes, types and attributes.

`FileSystemObject` has several methods and a single property called `Drives` that returns the `Drives` collection mentioned above:

Property	Description
`Drives`	Returns a reference to a `Drives` collection. Each object in the collection is a `Drive` object that identifies a drive available to the system.

The various drives include removable units, local partitions, network shares, CD-ROM, and even RAM disks. This simple script shows how to enumerate the drives available on a given machine:

```
// Drives1.js
// Enumerates the drives available on a given machine
// ---------------------------------------------------------

var fso, drives;
fso = new ActiveXObject("Scripting.FileSystemObject");
drives = fso.Drives;

types = new Array("Unknown", "Removable", "Local Partition",
                  "Network Share", "CD-Rom Drive", "RAM Disk");
var e, strDrives;
e = new Enumerator(drives);

strDrives = "Drive\tType of the drive\tVolume\n\n";
for(; !e.atEnd(); e.moveNext())
{
   var d = e.item();
   var strLabel = (d.IsReady ? d.VolumeName : "<Not Ready>");
   strDrives += d.Path + "\t" + types[d.DriveType] + "\t" + strLabel + "\n";
}

WScript.Echo(strDrives);
```

On my machine, the resulting dialog box looked like this:

The code above makes use of some properties of the `Drive` object that I'll examine in more detail in a moment, but for now I want to concentrate on `FileSystemObject`. This has several methods that I've grouped into seven categories that describe their areas of application:

- ❑ Manipulating path names
- ❑ Copying files and folders
- ❑ Moving files and folders
- ❑ File and folder creation
- ❑ Deleting files and folders
- ❑ Checking the existence of drives, folders and files
- ❑ Getting objects representing file system entities

Manipulating Path Names

The methods that fall into this category are listed in the following table. Where it appears, `fso` should be assumed to be an object of type `FileSystemObject`:

Method	Description

`BuildPath()`	Takes two path names and concatenates them, adding a backslash only if necessary. The first path name can be a relative or an absolute path. The function doesn't check the existence of the involved folders and files; it just ensures that the returned string is a well-formatted path name. For example:
	`fso.BuildPath("c:","win")      ' Returns c:win`
	`fso.BuildPath("c:","\win")     ' Returns c:\win`
	`fso.BuildPath("c:\win","sys") ' Returns c:\win\sys`

`GetAbsolutePathName()`	Returns a fully qualified path name from a relative path. It resolves and expands paths like `c:` and those that contain the 'parent folder' (`..`) symbol. If the current directory is `c:\sys\temp`, for example, it returns `c:\sys\bin` when you pass it `..\bin`.

`GetBaseName()`	Returns the name component in the given path, regardless of whether it's a file or a folder. For example:
	`fso.GetBaseName("c:\")          ' Returns ""`
	`fso.GetBaseName("c:\windows")   ' Returns windows`
	`fso.GetBaseName("c:\file.txt") ' Returns file`
	The function doesn't attempt to resolve the path name, or to check for its existence.

`GetDriveName()`	Returns the drive name from a path string, if any. It never includes the backslash. For example:
	`fso.GetDriveName("c:\windows") ' Returns c:`
	`fso.GetDriveName("\windows")   ' Returns ""`

`GetExtensionName()`	Returns the extension (if any) of the last component in the path name provided. For example:
	`' Returns txt`
	`fso.GetExtensionName("c:\win\one.txt")`
	Note that the string so returned *doesn't* include the dot.

Table Continued on Following Page

<table>
<tr><th>Method</th><th>Description</th></tr>
<tr><td><code>GetFileName()</code></td><td>Works in much the same way as <code>GetBaseName()</code>, except that it returns filename and extension, if any:<pre>
fso.GetFileName("c:\")   ' Returns ""
fso.GetFileName("c:\windows")   ' Returns windows
fso.GetFileName("c:\file.txt") ' Returns file.txt
</pre></td></tr>
<tr><td><code>GetParentFolderName()</code></td><td>Returns the name of the parent folder of the last component in the path. In most cases, this means drive and path components.<pre>
' Returns ""
fso.GetParentFolderName("c:\")

' Returns c:\win
fso.GetParentFolderName("c:\win\sys\")

' Returns c:\win\sys
fso.GetParentFolderName("c:\win\sys\file.txt")

' Returns ..\win
fso.GetParentFolderName("..\win\file.txt")
</pre>The function doesn't attempt to resolve the path name, or to check for its existence.</td></tr>
<tr><td><code>GetSpecialFolder()</code></td><td>Returns the local path on the current machine of three special folders: the <code>Windows</code> folder, the <code>Windows\System</code> folder, and the folder for temporary files. It takes a constant that identifies the folder; the options available are shown below:<pre>
fso.GetSpecialFolder(0)   ' The Windows folder
fso.GetSpecialFolder(1)   ' Windows\System folder
fso.GetSpecialFolder(2)   ' The Temp folder
</pre>If you pass a value other than 0, 1 or 2, you'll get a run-time error.</td></tr>
<tr><td><code>GetTempName()</code></td><td>Returns a randomly generated name that is guaranteed to be unique. You might want to use this if you need to create a temporary file or folder. (This method doesn't create any files or folders; it just returns a name.)</td></tr>
</table>

To demonstrate some of these methods in use, the following example shows how to create a temporary file to save some information:

```
' Temp.vbs
' Creates a temporary file in the Temp folder
' --------------------------------------------------------

Const TemporaryFolder = 2          ' The index for the Windows Temp folder

Dim fso, folder, tempFile, tempName
Set fso = CreateObject("Scripting.FileSystemObject")

' Get the Windows Temp folder
Set folder = fso.GetSpecialFolder(TemporaryFolder)

' Get the name of a temporary file
tempName = fso.GetTempName
MsgBox tempName

' Creates a file by this name in the folder
Set tempFile = folder.CreateTextFile(tempName)
tempFile.Close
```

Copying Files and Folders

The previous group of functions endows you with a set of tools for manipulating path names and extracting various components such as the drive name, the folder name and the filename, with or without the extension. Manipulating path names is a basic task you need to be able to do before you can start fundamental file operations such as copying files and folders. `FileSystemObject` provides two methods with these jobs in mind: one for copying files and one for copying folders.

The CopyFile Method

`CopyFile()` is a method that mimics the MS-DOS `copy` command. It follows this prototype:

```
fso.CopyFile source, destination [, overwrite]
```

The `source` argument specifies one or more files to be copied to the given destination. (You can specify multiple files by using wildcards.) The `destination` *cannot* contain wildcards, and must be either a file or a folder. Note that unlike the MS-DOS `copy` command, the destination isn't optional — the method does not default to the current directory to copy files. The simplest way of using this method is something like:

```
fso.CopyFile "c:\foo.txt", "d:\file.txt"
```

This just copies the file `c:\foo.txt` to `d:\file.txt`, but there are some subtleties that you need to consider in order to exploit this method successfully. For one thing, while the `source` argument can contain wildcards, this is only allowed in the last component of the name. The following code, for example, is valid. Provided that at least one file matches the given specification, it will copy all the `.bmp` files from the `My Pictures` folder on disk C into a folder with the same name on disk D:

```
fso.CopyFile "c:\My Pictures\*.bmp", "d:\My Pictures"
```

This line, however, is unacceptable:

```
fso.CopyFile "c:\My*\*.bmp", "d:\My Pictures"
```

The intention here is presumably to copy all .bmp files from all folders whose names begin with My into the My Pictures folder on disk D, but it won't work. The MS-DOS copy command also has this limitation.

Specifying the Destination

Another aspect to consider is that if the source argument specifies just one file (that is, it doesn't contain wildcards) then the destination argument is taken to be a file *unless* you add a final backslash to the destination name. This, for example,

```
fso.CopyFile "c:\foo.txt", "d:"
```

causes an error, because d: is not considered to be a directory (it lacks the final backslash) and it isn't a valid filename either. The following two instructions, on the other hand, work just fine:

```
fso.CopyFile "c:\foo.txt", "d:\"
fso.CopyFile "c:\foo.txt", "d:\NewFolder\"
```

If you try these, you'll obtain a foo.txt file in the root of d: and in its NewFolder folder respectively. If you omit the final backslash, like this:

```
fso.CopyFile "c:\foo.txt", "d:\NewFolder"
```

the result is that the foo.txt file is copied to a file in the root of disk D that is simply called NewFolder.

Things are different if the source includes wildcards. In this case, the destination can *only* be a directory, irrespective of whether it has a final backslash. A line like this:

```
fso.CopyFile "c:\*.txt", "d:"
```

works exactly as you'd expect it to do — all the .txt files from c:\ are moved into the root directory of d:. The following code also works without surprises:

```
fso.CopyFile "c:\*.txt", "d:\NewFolder"
```

This time, the files are copied into a folder called NewFolder. A final, but important aspect to remember is that the destination folder *must* always exist. The method will not create any missing folders on your behalf.

The Overwrite Flag

The CopyFile() method has an optional Boolean argument that denotes whether the destination file should be overwritten. (Of course, this flag makes sense only when the destination *is* a file.) This flag is set to True by default, but if you set it to False and attempt to overwrite an existing file, you'll get a run-time error. If the target file is marked as read-only, the copy will fail regardless of the value of this flag.

To prevent an existing file being overwritten, then, you can do the following:

```
fso.CopyFile "c:\foo.txt", "d:\foo.txt", False
```

However, it's not a very elegant solution, because if you do run into a situation where the operation fails, you'll get a message box like this:

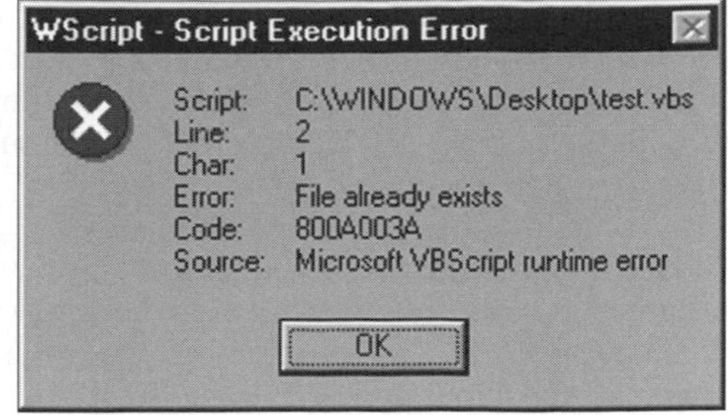

A better way to prevent overwriting is to make a preliminary check to see if the file already exists by exploiting the `FileExists()` method of the `FileSystemObject` object:

```
If Not fso.FileExists(sourceFile) Then
   fso.CopyFile sourceFile, destFile
End If
```

The CopyFolder Method

`CopyFolder()` takes care of copying folders. It has the following prototype:

```
fso.CopyFolder source, destination [, overwrite]
```

The `source` argument can include wildcards to select more than one folder, but if you provide a specification that may also include files, you'll get an error. The destination is the name of a folder that you can force to be created by not adding a final backslash.

```
fso.CopyFolder "c:\MyFolder", "d:\NewFolder"
```

In this case, a folder called `NewFolder` is created if one doesn't already exist. However, if there is a final backslash in the destination name, the method is forced to consider it as an existing directory to be overwritten. If the folder *doesn't* exist, there will be an error.

The copy is always recursive, but the creation of missing directories is not. Suppose you want to copy a folder to a path like this:

```
fso.CopyFolder "c:\MyFolder", "d:\MyApp\NewFolder"
```

If the `MyApp` directory doesn't exist (of course, `NewFolder` then won't exist either!), the script will produce a "path not found" error. To fix this, you need to divide the operation into two parts: make sure the directory tree exists, and then go ahead with the copy.

Making Sure a Directory Tree Exists

Creating a missing directory is easy if all you need to do is append a new directory to an existing path. But what if you have multiple directories to create in sequence? For example, consider a tree like this:

```
d:\MyApp\NewFolder
```

Neither the MS-DOS `mkdir` command nor the `CreateFolder()` method of the SRL provides the ability to create a nested structure like this one. (Until the advent of Windows 95, the Windows SDK was also lacking a function of this nature.) Despite this, there's nothing particularly tricky about providing this behavior yourself: you just have to walk the branches of the tree and create the missing folders at each step.

Having a piece of script code that does this turns out to be very helpful when used in conjunction with `CopyFolder()`. In general, `CopyFolder()` assumes the existence of whatever the `FileSystemObject.GetParentFolderName()` method would return for the folder you're trying to create. In this case, the parent folder of the destination path is just `d:\MyApp`, and if this doesn't exist, you'll get an error copying the folder. An elegant way to work around this is:

```
destFolder = "d:\MyApp\NewFolder"
MakeSureDirectoryTreeExists destFolder
fso.CopyFolder "c:\MyFolder", destFolder
```

`MakeSureDirectoryTreeExists()` is a function of my own devising that creates any folders and subfolders in the given path that are missing. In this way, it does exactly what its name suggests. The following script both defines this function and demonstrates its use.

```
' NewFolder.vbs
' Creates multiple nested directories from a FULLY-QUALIFIED path name.
' ---------------------------------------------------------------------

' Get the name of the (compound) folder to create
Dim dirName
If WScript.Arguments.Count = 0 Then
   dirName = InputBox("Enter the FULLY-QUALIFIED name of the folder:")
Else
   dirName = WScript.Arguments.Item(0)
End if

If dirName = "" Then
   WScript.Quit
End If

MakeSureDirectoryTreeExists dirName


Function MakeSureDirectoryTreeExists(dirName)
   ' Create the FSO object
   Set fso = CreateObject("Scripting.FileSystemObject")

   ' Check the folder's existence
   If Not fso.FolderExists(dirName) Then
      ' Split the various components of the folder's name
      aFolders = split(dirName, "\")

      ' Get the root of the drive
      newFolder = fso.BuildPath(aFolders(0), "\")

      ' Scan the various folder and create them
      For i = 1 To UBound(aFolders)
         newFolder = fso.BuildPath(newFolder, aFolders(i))

         If Not fso.FolderExists(newFolder) Then
            fso.CreateFolder newFolder
         End If
      Next
   End If
End Function
```

Doing the same thing in WSH 2.0 looks much tidier, because we can save the function into a separate file called (say) `direxists.vbs` and import it into any `.ws` script file, like this:

```
<?xml version="1.0"?>
<!-- NewFolder.ws -->

<job>
   <script language="VBScript" src="direxists.vbs" />

   <script language="VBScript">
      Dim dirName
      If WScript.Arguments.Count = 0 Then
         dirName = InputBox("Enter the FULLY-QUALIFIED name of the folder:")
      Else
         dirName = WScript.Arguments.Item(0)
      End if

      If dirName = "" Then
         WScript.Quit
      End If

      MakeSureDirectoryTreeExists dirName
   </script>
</job>
```

Moving Files and Folders

Moving files and folders works in the same way as copying them with one exception: you can't overwrite existing files. The prototypes of `MoveFile()` and `MoveFolder()` are therefore very similar to `CopyFile()` and `CopyFolder()` apart from the fact that they lack the optional flag to force overwriting:

```
fso.MoveFile source, destination
fso.MoveFolder source, destination
```

To avoid overwriting errors when you try to move a file (or a group of files) from one folder to another, you can use the error handling mechanism that your scripting language makes available. If you're moving a single file, this is fairly trivial: you just check whether the target file exists. If you're using wildcards, however, things are a little trickier.

In VBScript, for example, you can use the `On Error` instruction to resume execution after an error. This works fine, but it's up to you to figure out whether, after a critical instruction, an error was raised or not. A possible solution is to check the value of the `Number` property of VBScript's `Err` object:

```
On Error Resume Next
fso.MoveFile "c:\*.txt", "d:\foo.txt"
If Err.Number <> 0 Then
   ' An error occurred
End if
```

This same result can be obtained more elegantly in JScript 5.0 by using the `try-catch` construct we saw in Chapter 5. Here's the code:

```
// SafeMove.js
// Move files using a try/catch mechanism
// -------------------------------------------------------

var fso;
fso = new ActiveXObject("Scripting.FileSystemObject");
msg = "Done!";

try
{
   fso.MoveFile("c:\\foo.txt", "d:\\");
}
catch(e)
{
   msg = "An error occurred: " + e.description;
}

WScript.Echo(msg);
```

File and Folder Creation

To create a new folder, you can use the `CreateFolder()` method which has the following syntax:

```
fso.CreateFolder folderName
```

As I've already pointed out, though, this method is unable to create multiple, nested directory trees in one shot. If you need to obtain this result, you may wish to resort to the `MakeSureDirectoryTreeExists()` function that I presented earlier.

The SRL doesn't provide great support for file creation — the only thing available for this purpose is `CreateTextFile()` which, as its name suggests, isn't very helpful if you need to create binary files. However, if you *do* just need to create simple text files, this method does its job very well. It returns a reference to a `TextStream` object that exposes handy methods for reading and writing lines of text from and to the file. To create a text file, use:

```
fso.CreateTextFile fileName [,overwrite] [,unicode]
```

Of course, `fileName` denotes the name of the file to be created. If the file exists, the behavior of the function is driven by the `overwrite` parameter. This is a Boolean argument that is set to `False` by default, preventing overwriting. If you try to overwrite an existing file without specifying `True`, you'll get a run-time error. Finally, the last parameter lets you request an ASCII file or a Unicode file. Pass `True` to obtain a Unicode file; the default is ASCII.

Opening an Existing Text File

While we're talking about files, `FileSystemObject` also provides a method to open an existing text file, returning a `TextStream` object when it does so. This method is called `OpenTextFile()`:

```
fso.OpenTextFile fileName [,iomode] [,create] [,format]
```

The `iomode` argument lets you specify the operation you want to execute on the file. There are three options:

```
Const ForReading = 1
Const ForWriting = 2
Const ForAppending = 8
```

You can choose only one of these at a time; a file opened for reading can't accept write operations, and vice versa. In the same way, a file opened with the intention of appending data to it can't be read from the beginning.

If the `create` argument is set to `True` (which is *not* the default) then if a file doesn't exist with the given name, a new one is created. Finally, the `format` argument denotes how the file will be opened. This is the counterpart of the `unicode` argument defined by `CreateTextFile()`, and you have three options: 0, for ASCII, -1 for Unicode and -2 for the default system, which is ASCII under Windows 9x and Unicode under Windows NT.

The following example shows how to open a text file and read its content into an array. It utilizes the methods of the `TextStream` object for reading:

```
// Array.js
// Reads a text file to an array
// ------------------------------------------------------------

ForReading = 1;
FormatASCII = 0;

var fso, ts, str;
fileName = "c:\\servers.txt"
fso = new ActiveXObject("Scripting.FileSystemObject");

// Reads the whole file in one shot
ts = fso.OpenTextFile(fileName, ForReading, false, FormatASCII);
str = ts.ReadAll();

// Converts it to an array
aText = new Array();
aText = str.split("\n");

// Displays the elements of the array
for(i = 0; i < aText.length; i++)
   WScript.Echo(aText[i]);

ts.Close();
```

The content of the file is read in one go by the `ReadAll()` method of the `TextStream` object. Then it is split into an array, using the newline (`\n`) character as the separator of the various lines.

Deleting Files and Folders

A file can be deleted by calling the `DeleteFile()` method and specifying the name of the file (or files) to remove. To get rid of several files at the same time, use wildcards.

```
fso.DeleteFile filespec [,force]
```

This, for example,

```
fso.DeleteFile "c:\myApp\*.ini"
```

removes all the `.ini` files from the specified path. If no files match the specification, an error is raised. The `force` argument is an optional Boolean flag that forces the automatic deletion of any files marked as read-only. Hidden and system files are deleted in any case.

To remove an entire folder, use the `DeleteFolder()` method:

```
fso.DeleteFolder folderspec [, force]
```

The `folderspec` argument can accept wildcards, but you'll run into an error if no folder matches the specification you supply. The folder doesn't need to be empty for deletion to take place, and all files and subfolders are also removed. The `force` argument has the same role it had in the `DeleteFile()` prototype.

Also note that if you execute code like this:

```
fso.DeleteFolder "c:\myApp\System\TempFolder"
```

only the last folder in the path (in this case, `TempFolder`) will be deleted.

Note that these functions remove files and folders from disk *completely*. The items you delete *don't* go to the Recycle Bin.

Checking the Existence of Drives, Folders and Files

There are three basic constituent objects of the Windows file system: drives, folders and files. In the SRL, these elements are rendered through objects and collections. However, the `FileSystemObject` also provides three simple methods to test whether a given drive, folder or file exists. To test the existence of a given drive, for example, you use:

```
fso.DriveExists drivename
```

It returns a Boolean value denoting whether the drive exists or not. The argument `drivename` is the name of the drive, formed from the drive letter followed (optionally) by a colon and a final backslash:

```
fso.DriveExists("A")                    ' True
fso.DriveExists("A\")                   ' False
fso.DriveExists("C:\")                  ' True
fso.DriveExists("C:\WINDOWS")           ' False
```

What you should pass to `DriveExists()` is just the name of the drive as returned by the `GetDriveName()` method you saw earlier. If you need to test the existence of `c:\windows`, as in the last example here, you can use `FolderExists()` instead!

Note that `DriveExists()` *simply tells you whether a given drive exists on the machine. It doesn't say anything about the drive being ready or not. To find out about the working state of a drive, you need to resort to the* `Drive` *object's* `IsReady` *property.*

Indirect confirmation of a drive's existence can be obtained by `FolderExists()` and `FileExists()`, two other methods of `FileSystemObject` that return Boolean values according to the existence of the specified folder or file. Their prototypes are nearly identical:

```
fso.FolderExists foldername
fso.FileExists filename
```

Both methods accept relative and absolute path names.

Getting Objects Representing File System Entities

As I mentioned earlier in this chapter, the SRL provides objects for the three basic elements of the file system. As a faithful mirror of the Windows file system, `FileSystemObject` exposes methods that simply return instances of the `Drive`, `Folder` and `File` objects initialized on a specific drive, folder or file. These methods are:

```
fso.GetDrive drivespec
fso.GetFolder folderspec
fso.GetFile filespec
```

`GetDrive()` accepts a drive letter (with or without a trailing colon and backslash), instantiates a `Drive` object and set it to work on the specified drive. In this case, of course, the method performs checks to verify that the drive exists. `GetFolder()` takes a relative or absolute path and returns a `Folder` object for that path name. Finally, `GetFile()` returns an instance of the `File` object from an existing filename.

These objects are grouped in homogeneous collections (`Drives`, `Folders`, and `Files`) that are obtained in various ways. `Drives` is provided by a property of `FileSystemObject`, as I showed earlier in the chapter. A reference to a `Folders` object can be obtained from the `SubFolders` property of a `Folder` object. Finally, `Files` is a collection exposed by a `Folder` object. In the following sections, I'm going to cover these objects and collections in detail.

The Drive Object

This object represents a drive, be it hard or floppy; local or remote; fixed or removable. `Drive` has no methods, but many properties, as listed in this table:

Property	Description
`AvailableSpace`	Returns the number of bytes presently available for the current user on the specified drive. This value is not necessarily the free disk space (see later).
`DriveLetter`	Returns the drive letter — A, C, D, and so forth.
`DriveType`	Denotes the type of the drive: 1 = removable, 2 = fixed, 3 = network, 4 = CD-ROM, 5 = RAM disk. If there is an error or an unknown drive, 0 is returned.

Table Continued on Following Page

Property	Description
`FileSystem`	Returns a string that specifies the file system: FAT, FAT32, NTFS and CDFS are the possible options.
`FreeSpace`	Returns the number of free bytes on the specified drive (see later).
`IsReady`	`True` or `False` depending on whether the drive is ready for access.
`Path`	Returns the path of the drive, although the root backslash is not included. For example, `D:` is returned for the D drive.
`RootFolder`	Returns the root folder of the drive. For the D drive, `D:\` is returned.
`SerialNumber`	Returns the decimal serial number of the disk.
`ShareName`	Returns the share name of a specified drive, if it is a network drive. Otherwise, an empty string is returned.
`TotalSize`	Returns the size of the disk for the current user in bytes.
`VolumeName`	Gets/sets the volume name of the specified drive.

Using the `Drive` object is not particularly problematic, except for some difficulty in finding a reliable technique for discovering the free disk space.

Calculating Disk Space

Getting the exact amount of space available for a given user on a given disk might be something you need to do when you're copying files from one place to another. If there's not going to be enough room, it's likely that you'd be better off not starting the operation at all than getting stopped short halfway through the process.

However, finding this information can be tricky, despite a couple of promising properties like `FreeSpace` and `AvailableSpace`. There are two issues you need to be aware of:

- The presence of disk quotas
- A bug in the Windows 95 system routine that calculates free disk space

A **disk quota** is a slice of a disk drive that is assigned to a user on a shared disk. Imagine that you, as a system administrator, give a quota of 2Gb to a single user on a disk that is 10Gb in size. This means that any WSH script they run will always see 2Gb as the maximum available space. The `AvailableSpace` property returns the free disk space for the current user, taking the presence of disk quotas into account. `FreeSpace`, on the other hand, always returns the total amount of free disk space regardless of disk quotas.

Disk quotas are to be introduced to the Windows world with the release of Windows 2000, and only then on NTFS partitions. In all other cases, `AvailableSpace` *and* `FreeSpace` *are equivalent.*

Working with Very Large Disks

There can be problems in calculating disk space on very large disks. Try running this script on a disk that's larger than 2Gb in size:

```
Dim fso, disk
Set fso = CreateObject("Scripting.FileSystemObject")
Set disk = fso.GetDrive("d:")
MsgBox "Disk free space using FSO is: " & disk.AvailableSpace
```

Depending on which operating system you're running, the number returned by this code could be incorrect. The space-based properties like `AvailableSpace` rely on a kernel function called `GetDiskFreeSpace()` that contains a bug in the first release of Windows 95. Since release 2 of the operating system (OSR2), the function has been superseded by `GetDiskFreeSpaceEx()`, which the operating system will call automatically if present. As a result, you'll get incorrect values on machines running Windows 95 prior to OSR2, but accurate results on computers with more recent versions of the operating system.

There would be little to worry about were it not for another nasty problem. The sizes of very large disks can't be stored using `long` integers (`GetDiskFreeSpaceEx()` uses 64-bit integers rather than 32-bit `long`s), but scripting languages simply don't support anything bigger. If you think this might be a problem for you, I've written a new object called `WshKit.DiskSpace` that you'll find on the Wrox web site along with the rest of the code for the book. This object returns a preformatted string that uses large integers internally and converts them into Kb, Mb and Gb as appropriate.

The Folder Object

A `Folder` object renders a file system directory and provides a number of descriptive properties that make available not only status information (such as the creation date and the size of the folder), but also structural data (such as attributes). `Folder` objects are returned by the `FileSystemObject.GetFolder()` method.

Here's a full list of the properties supported by objects of this type:

Property	Description
`Attributes`	Sets and retrieves the attributes of a folder. (More on this later on.)
`DateCreated`	Read-only property that returns the date when the folder was created. This property is not available for root folders, or the `Windows` and `Windows\System` folders.
`DateLastAccessed`	Read-only property that returns the date when the folder was last accessed. This property isn't supported under Windows 9x, which always just returns the creation date. It is not available for root folders.
`DateLastModified`	Read-only property that returns the date when the folder was last modified. This property isn't supported under Windows 9x, which always just returns the creation date. It is not available for root folders.

Table Continued on Following Page

Property	Description
Drive	Read-only property that returns the letter of the drive that contains the folder. The string returned is comprised of the letter followed by a colon (e.g., `c:`).
Files	Returns a `Files` collection that contains all of the files (whatever their attributes) contained in the folder. No filter (say, `*.txt`) can be applied, although I'll provide a workaround for this later in the chapter.
IsRootFolder	Boolean property that indicates whether the folder is a root folder. It returns `True` for `c:\`, but not for `c:\windows`.
Name	Returns the name of the folder, without path information. If the folder is `c:\windows`, you're returned `windows`. By changing the value of this property, you rename the folder.
ParentFolder	Returns the `Folder` object for the parent of the current folder.
Path	Returns the full path name of the folder. If the folder has a long filename, this property will return the whole thing correctly.
ShortName	Returns the 8.3 version of the folder name. If the folder is called `c:\windows\application data`, you'll get a string like `applic~1`.
ShortPath	Returns the 8.3 version of the folder path. If the folder is called `c:\windows\application data`, you'll get a string like `c:\windows\applic~1`.
Size	Calculates and returns the amount in bytes occupied by the folder. Using this property may take a few moments to complete as the property scans the folder on the fly and tots up the space required by each file and subfolder.
SubFolders	Returns a `Folders` collection including all the subfolders (whatever their attributes) the given folder contains. The collection comprises only the folders that are *direct* children of the current folder. If the folder is `c:\windows`, you'll find `c:\windows\system` in the collection, but not `c:\windows\system\dcom`.

Type	Returns a string that describes the type of folder; in most cases this is `File Folder`. The string is actually what appears in the Type column of Explorer's Details view. This, for example:
	`set f = fso.GetFolder("c:\windows\favorites")`
	`msgbox f.Type`
	returns `Shell Favorite Folder`.

The script file below demonstrates how to get all kinds of information about a folder. Most of the information it shows is also available through the Properties window, but you can't read that programmatically! I have a shortcut to this script on my desktop, and sometimes I prefer typing in the name of the folder to starting Explorer and going through a series of right and left clicks.

```
' FolderProperties.vbs
' Provides all the information available on a given folder
' -----------------------------------------------------------

Const ReadOnly = 1
Const Hidden = 2
Const System = 4
Const Directory = 16

Dim dirName
If WScript.Arguments.Count = 0 Then
   dirName = InputBox("Enter the FULLY-QUALIFIED name of the folder:")
Else
   dirName = WScript.Arguments.Item(0)
End if

If dirName = "" Then
  WScript.Quit
End If

Set fso = CreateObject("Scripting.FileSystemObject")

' Attempt to get the folder
If Not fso.FolderExists(dirName) Then
   MsgBox "Sorry, but the folder doesn't exist!"
   WScript.Quit
End If
Set f = fso.GetFolder(dirName)

If f.IsRootFolder Then
   Set drive = fso.GetDrive(f.Drive)
   aText = Array( _
     "Folder Name:" & vbTab & fso.BuildPath(f.Path, f.Name), _
     "Short Name:" & vbTab & fso.BuildPath(f.ShortPath, f.ShortName), _
     "Type of folder:" & vbTab & f.Type, _
     "File System:" & vbTab & drive.FileSystem, _
     "Volume Name:" & vbTab & drive.VolumeName, _
     "Serial Number:" & vbTab & drive.SerialNumber, _
     "Available Space: " & vbTab & FormatNumber(drive.AvailableSpace/1024), _
     "Total Size: " & vbTab & drive.TotalSize)
Else
   aText = Array( _
     "Folder Name:" & vbTab & fso.BuildPath(f.Path, f.Name), _
     "Short Name:" & vbTab & fso.BuildPath(f.ShortPath, f.ShortName), _
     "Type of folder:" & vbTab & f.Type, _
     "Created on:" & vbTab & f.DateCreated, _
     "Accessed on:" & vbTab & f.DateLastAccessed, _
     "Modified on:" & vbTab & f.DateLastModified, _
     "Attributes: " & vbTab & FormatAttrib(f.Attributes), _
     "Total Size: " & vbTab & f.Size)
End if

MsgBox Join(aText, vbCrlf)


Function FormatAttrib(attr)
   str = ""
   If attr And ReadOnly Then str = str & "Readonly, "
   If attr And Hidden   Then str = str & "Hidden, "
   If attr And System   Then str = str & "System, "
   str = str & "Directory"
   FormatAttrib = str
End Function
```

Continued on Following Page

```
Function FormatDriveType(drivetype)
   types = Array("Unknown", "Removable", "Local Partition", _
                 "Network Share", "CD-Rom Drive", "RAM Disk")
   FormatDriveType = types(drivetype)
End Function
```

The following pictures demonstrate the output of this script in the case of both a root and an ordinary folder.

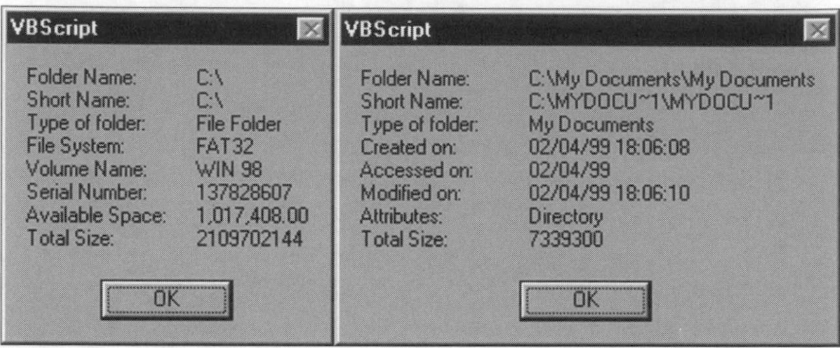

Notice how the information displayed is slightly different in each case. A root folder is slightly different from ordinary folders, because it has additional properties. To access these properties you need to resort to the `Drive` object, as the script demonstrates.

Operations on Folders

There are other ways of performing the basic operations on a folder than the methods of `FileSystemObject` that you saw earlier. If you need to copy a folder somewhere, you can use the `CopyFolder()` method of the root object and specify the source and the target, but you can also get a reference to the source folder and copy it to the destination. This, for example:

```
fso.GetFolder("c:\NewFolder")
fso.Copy "d:\"
```

is equivalent to this:

```
fso.CopyFolder "c:\NewFolder", "d:\"
```

Is there any difference at all? Actually, there is. The `FileSystemObject` methods allow you to specify wildcards in your folder operations, but if you're using the methods of a specific folder object, wildcards don't make sense at all.

The first of the above snippets exploits one of the four methods exposed by the `Folder` object, as listed in the table opposite.

Method	Description
`Copy()`	Copies the current folder to the specified folder. The syntax is nearly identical to that of FSO's `CopyFolder()`: `folder.Copy destination [,overwrite]`
`CreateTextFile()`	Creates a text file in the current folder, so you don't need to specify a fully qualified path. The syntax is identical to that of the corresponding FSO method: `folder.CreateTextFile fileName [,overwrite] [,unicode]`
`Delete()`	Deletes the current folder. The syntax is nearly identical to that of FSO's `DeleteFolder()`: `folder.Delete [force]`
`Move()`	Moves the current folder to the specified folder. The syntax is nearly identical to that of FSO's `MoveFolder()`: `folder.Move destination`

Changing the Folder's Attributes

The `Attributes` property contains a numerical value that denotes the file system attributes of the folder. For a folder, this number is a combination of the following constants:

```
Const ReadOnly = 1
Const Hidden = 2
Const System = 4
Const Directory = 16
```

A folder is first and foremost a directory, and only secondarily is it read-only, hidden, or a system folder, so the attributes of a folder always combine to a value not less than 16. In case you're wondering why it's necessary for a folder to have an attribute that says it's a directory ("Aren't folders and directories the same thing?"), *all* entities in the Windows file system are represented by attributes from this set, and the fact that folders have this attribute distinguishes them from other entities.

`Attributes` is a read/write property, which means that by assigning it a new value, you change the folder's attributes. When you try to do this, however, be aware that not all the styles can be changed — you can't remove the 'directory' attribute, for example. For this reason, when you're assigning a new value to the `Attributes` property, you should make sure that you're not overwriting a protected style. For folders, this means that you should use a bit mask to prevent modifications to the 'directory' style, and I'll demonstrate how to employ this technique in the next chapter.

The Folders Collection

The `Folder.Subfolders` property returns a read/write `Folders` collection to which you can add new elements — that is, new folders. This collection exposes two properties:

Property	Description
`Count`	Read-only property that returns the number of the folders in the collection.

`Item`	Takes a folder name and returns the corresponding `Folder` object, if any. This property doesn't accept an index value. For example, here's how to get the `Windows` folder:
	`Set f = fso.GetFolder("c:\")`
	`Set subf = f.SubFolders`
	`Set winfolder = subf.item("windows")`

Interestingly, it also has an `Add()` method:

```
folders.Add foldername
```

When you call this method and specify a folder name, you add a new item to the collection and cause a new folder to be created. The `Count` and `Item` properties are updated, and can detect the new folder immediately. The following code:

```
Set fso = CreateObject("Scripting.FileSystemObject")
set f = fso.GetFolder("c:\")
set subf = f.SubFolders
subf.Add "NewFolder"
```

is equivalent to using the `FileSystemObject.CreateFolder()` method:

```
Set fso = CreateObject("Scripting.FileSystemObject")
fso.CreateFolder "c:\NewFolder"
```

It represents the way in which you create a new sub-folder from the current folder.

The File Object

A `File` object renders a system file and describes it through a number of properties and methods. The properties are mostly for informational purposes — to find out easily about creation dates, types and attributes. An instance of this object is returned by calling the `GetFile()` method of the `FileSystemObject` object.

The properties supported by `File` are a subset of those supported by `Folder` — sensibly, it doesn't expose the `Files`, `IsRootFolder` and `Subfolders` properties. In addition, you should note that for this object, the various date fields (`DateCreated`, `DateLastAccessed`, `DateLastModified`) are fully supported on Windows 9x.

Here's the business end of a script that's rather like my earlier program that dealt with `Folder` objects. It demonstrates the properties of the `File` object in use, and provides all the information for a file at a glance:

```
Const ReadOnly = 1
Const Hidden = 2
Const System = 4
Const Archive = 32
```

...

```
Set fso = CreateObject("Scripting.FileSystemObject")
Set f = fso.GetFile(fileName)

aText = Array("File Name:" & vbTab & f.Path, _
              "Short Name:" & vbTab & f.ShortPath, _
              "Type of file:" & vbTab & f.Type, _
              "Created on:" & vbTab & f.DateCreated, _
              "Accessed on:" & vbTab & f.DateLastAccessed, _
              "Modified on:" & vbTab & f.DateLastModified, _
              "Attributes: " & vbTab & FormatAttrib(f.Attributes), _
              "Total Size: " & vbTab & f.Size)

MsgBox Join(aText, vbCrlf)


Function FormatAttrib(attr)
   str = ""
   If attr And Archive  Then str = str & "Archive, "
   If attr And ReadOnly Then str = str & "Readonly, "
   If attr And Hidden   Then str = str & "Hidden, "
   If attr And System   Then str = str & "System, "
   str = str & "Normal"
   FormatAttrib = str
End Function
```

If you arrange for `fileName` to contain the full path name of a file that exists somewhere in the file system, you can expect to get output something like this:

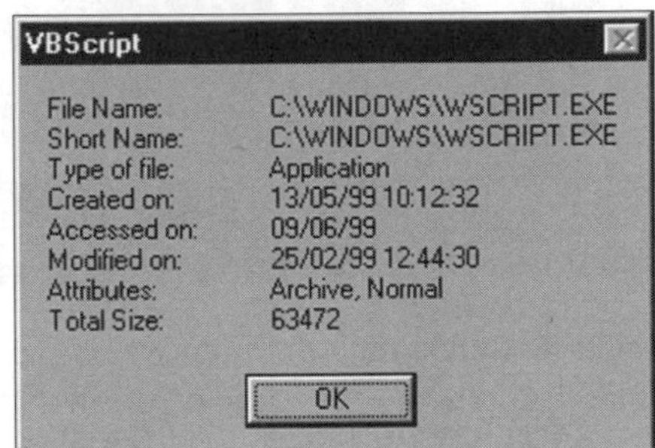

Operations on Files

The `File` object has four methods that let you execute basic operations on the file directly. You can copy or move a file to a different folder, delete it, and even open it as a text stream. Specifically, the methods are:

Method	Description
`Copy()`	Copies the current file to the specified folder. The syntax is nearly identical to that of FSO's `CopyFile()`: `file.Copy destination [,overwrite]`
`Delete()`	Deletes the current file. The syntax is nearly identical to that of FSO's `DeleteFile()`: `file.Delete [force]`

Table Continued on Following Page

Method	Description
`Move()`	Moves the current file to the specified folder. The syntax is nearly identical to that of FSO's `MoveFile()`: `file.Move destination`
`OpenAsTextStream()`	Opens the current file as a text stream. It returns a `TextStream` object for you to read or modify. The syntax is similar to that of FSO's `OpenTextFile()` method: `File.OpenAsTextStream [iomode] [,format]` The mode and the format follow the same specification as for `OpenTextFile()`.

Changing the File's Attributes

Changing the attributes of a file is less problematic than for a folder, because all the styles you might want to use are read/write. You can simply read the current value, do your modifications and set it back. Here's how to do it with JScript:

```
ReadOnly = 1;

fso = new ActiveXObject("Scripting.FileSystemObject");
file = fso.GetFile("c:\\foo.txt");
oldAttr = file.Attributes;

if(oldAttr & ReadOnly)
   file.Attributes = oldAttr & (~ReadOnly);
else
   file.Attributes = oldAttr | ReadOnly;
```

And with VBScript:

```
Const ReadOnly = 1

Set fso = CreateObject("Scripting.FileSystemObject")
Set file = fso.GetFile("c:\foo.txt")
oldAttr = file.Attributes

If oldAttr And ReadOnly Then
   file.Attributes = oldAttr And (Not ReadOnly)
Else
   file.Attributes = oldAttr Or ReadOnly
End If
```

The Files Collection

The `Files` collection is an object returned by the `Files` property of the `Folder` object. Unlike the apparently similar `Folders` object, it doesn't have an `Add()` method. The structure, therefore, is extremely straightforward.

Property	Description
`Count`	Read-only property that returns the number of the files in the collection.

`Item`	Takes a file name and returns the corresponding `File` object, if any. It doesn't accept an index value. Here's how to get the object for `autoexec.bat`:
	`Set f = fso.GetFolder("c:\")`
	`Set files = f.Files`
	`Set file = files.item("autoexec.bat")`
	`MsgBox file.Type`

This collection has no methods, and it can't be modified at runtime by adding or removing new items; you can only rename the existing ones.

The TextStream Object

This object was introduced to facilitate working with text files. It exposes methods for reading and writing any number of bytes from and to a file, but it can also manage whole lines at a time. Here, a "line" is a sequence of characters that ends with a carriage return/linefeed pair (the `vbCrLf` constant in VBScript, or `\r\n` in JScript).

It's this support for lines of text that makes the `TextStream` object particularly suitable for use with text files. It's not a very powerful object, but it turns out to be pretty handy if all you have to do are some simple read/write operations. Here are the methods it supports:

Method	Description
`Read()`	Reads the specified number of characters and returns the string thereby obtained. Reading starts at the current position and moves the **file pointer** forward. (I'll describe the file pointer in detail shortly.)
`ReadAll()`	Reads from the current position to the end of the file. After you've called this method, any other reading operation will fail. The function moves the file pointer to a position after the end of the file.
`ReadLine()`	Reads from the current position up to the first CR/LF pair, but the latter characters aren't returned. Reading moves the pointer forward to the start of the next line.
`Skip()`	Moves the file pointer forward by the specified number of characters. You *can't* pass a negative number to move the pointer backwards.
`SkipLine()`	Reads and discards all the characters from the current position up to the next CR/LF pair. It moves the pointer to the start of the next line.

Table Continued on Following Page

Method	Description
`Write()`	Writes the specified string at the current position in the file. Moves the file pointer forward.
`WriteLine()`	Writes the specified string at the current position and adds a CR/LF pair at the end. Moves the file pointer forward. If you omit the string, the call is equivalent to `WriteBlankLines(1)`.
`WriteBlankLines()`	Writes the specified number of CR/LF pairs at the current position, and moves the file pointer forward.
`Close()`	Closes a file that was opened using `CreateTextFile()` or `OpenTextFile()`.

`TextStream` also exposes a number of read-only properties:

Property	Description
`AtEndOfLine`	Indicates whether the file pointer is located just before the CR/LF characters that mark the end of the line.
`AtEndOfStream`	Indicates whether the file pointer is located just before the end of the file.
`Column`	Returns the position of the file pointer in the line.
`Line`	Returns the line in which the file pointer is located. Lines are recognized via CR/LF pairs.

The two great limitations of `TextStream` may have become apparent to you while you've been reading these tables: you can't move the file pointer backwards, and you can't skip bytes when you're writing. This means that you can't write a handful of bytes at specific positions.

You saw an example of the `TextStream` object in action earlier in this chapter, in a script that read the contents of a file into an array. In that example, I used the `ReadAll()` method to read all of the file in a single operation and then split the string into array elements using JScript strings' `split()` method. Let's examine a more flexible way of doing the same thing that loads the lines one after another. This approach gives you much more control over what happens, and lets you decide whether to read or skip a line according to content. In the following script, for example, I attempt to read a text file skipping all the blank lines:

```
// TexttoArray.js
// Reads a text file to an array line by line skipping blank lines
// ------------------------------------------------------------------

ForReading = 1;
FormatASCII = 0;

var fso, ts, str;
var i = 0;
fileName = "c:\\foo.txt"
fso = new ActiveXObject("Scripting.FileSystemObject");
```

```
// Reads the whole file
aText = new Array();
ts = fso.OpenTextFile(fileName, ForReading, false, FormatASCII);
while(!ts.atEndOfStream)
{
   var str = ts.ReadLine();
   if(str.length)
      aText[i++] = str;                  // Adds only non-empty lines
}
ts.Close();

// Displays the elements of the array
for(i = 0; i < aText.length; i++)
   WScript.Echo(aText[i]);
```

The File Pointer

When you're working with files (binary or text files), and whether you're aware of it or not, a **file pointer** is being used to keep track of the position where you're reading or writing. Opening a file for reading, for example, places the pointer at the first byte of the file. Reading *n* bytes of a file moves the pointer forward by those *n* bytes. If you want to start reading in the middle of the file, you have to skip over the bytes you don't want.

When you're using the `TextStream` object, you have to use the `Skip()` or `SkipLine()` methods for this purpose, despite their serious drawback: they don't allow backward movement. If you try calling (say) `Skip(-3)`, you'll get a syntax error. The only workaround for this is to close the file, reopen it, and start again from the beginning!

Writing to a File

Worse still, you're not even given the *possibility* of skipping bytes when the file is open for writing — `Skip()` and `SkipLine()` require the exclusive `ForReading` open mode. When you open a file for writing, the pointer is at the beginning of the file and you can only write from there onwards, overwriting all the existing material you find on your way. If you open for appending, the pointer is placed at the end of the file, but you can't move it backwards. Overall, it's not a very flexible object.

The `TextStream` object is at its best when you have to create little text files from scratch, such as `.ini` files for storing configuration settings, lists of user and server names, installation log files, and so on. I've shown how to load such information into an array, but often you need to write it back to the file if that information changes. Here's a quick JScript function that serializes an array to disk:

```
// ArrayToFile.js
// Writes the contents of an array to the specified text file
// ---------------------------------------------------------------

var fso, ts;
var i = 0;
fileName = "c:\\foo.txt";
fso = new ActiveXObject("Scripting.FileSystemObject");

aText = new Array("one", "two", "three");

// Dumps the array reads all the files
ts = fso.CreateTextFile(fileName, true);
for(i = 0; i < aText.length; i++)
   ts.WriteLine(aText[i]);

ts.Close();
```

The Dictionary

The dictionary is a very versatile data repository that can store any kind of data and provides smart ways of retrieving it. Admittedly, it doesn't have a lot to do with the Windows file system, but it's a very interesting object, and it's part of SRL; reason enough for me to provide a quick overview here.

The data structure that a dictionary looks like most is an **associative array** — that is, a collection of heterogeneous data that's indexed using ordinal positions or strings. You could, for example, ask the object to return the element at position 2 (the index is 0-based), or to retrieve the one called `Third`.

In general, a dictionary item is identified through a unique key, which can be any simple data type, although it's usually a number or a string. The `Dictionary` object exposes a programming interface that is akin to a VBA collection:

Method	Description

`Add()`	Inserts a new element in the dictionary. The method requires two arguments: the key and the data. The data can be anything at all, including an array:
	`Set dict = CreateObject("Scripting.Dictionary")`
	`a = Array(1, 3)`
	`dict.Add "First", a`

`Exists()`	Given a key, this method returns a Boolean value denoting whether an item exists with that key.
`Items()`	Creates and returns an array containing all the items in the dictionary in the order they were entered.
`Keys()`	Creates and returns an array containing all the keys in the dictionary.
`Remove()`	Given a key, this method removes the corresponding element from the dictionary.
`RemoveAll()`	Takes no arguments and simply empties the dictionary.

There are also some properties:

Property	Description

`Item`	Retrieves the item with the specified key. You can use it on both sides of an assignment instruction.
	`v = dict.Item("thisKey")`
	If an item with the specified key doesn't exist, the variable `v` is returned uninitialized. (Its type name is `Empty`.)
	`dict.Item("thisKey") = v`
	This time, if an item with the given key doesn't exist, one will be added to the dictionary. Otherwise, the value gets modified.

Property	Description
`Key`	Lets you modify the key of an existing item. If the specified key doesn't exist, an error occurs. `dict.key("thisKey") = newKey`
`Count`	Returns the number of items in the dictionary.

`CompareMode`	Global setting that applies to the dictionary object. It sets the way in which the object searches for the item that matches a given key. This property defaults to 0, which means that a binary, byte-to-byte comparison is done. It can also assume a value of 1, meaning that a textual comparison will take place. In the latter case, you have a case-insensitive, string-to-string comparison. For example, this code:
	`Set dic = CreateObject("Scripting.Dictionary")`
	`dic.CompareMode = 1     ' Textual comparison`
	`dic.Add "First", "First Element"`
	`dic.Add "FIRST", "An uppercase first element"`
	produces a "duplicate key" error, because we've set the textual comparison. By omitting (or setting to 0) the `CompareMode` property, the dictionary would have stored two different keys.
	You can set this property only when the dictionary is empty.

A Word about Performance

You may have noticed that I never mentioned anything about the *position* of the insertion when I wrote about the `Add()` method. This is due to the fact that the `Dictionary` object is implemented using a data structure (it's called a **hash table**) that provides consistent access times to any of its elements, regardless of their actual location in the structure. This is the reason why you can expect great performance when using the `Scripting.Dictionary` object, and also why you can never be exactly sure where in the object the new element will be inserted.

Filtering the Files Collection

The `Files` property of any `Folder` object returns a collection that includes all the files contained by that folder. However, the SRL object model doesn't provide a way of filtering this collection — that is, of asking for only those files that match a given pattern. You can't obtain a collection containing only those files that match `*.txt`, for example. To work around this, we need to:

- Scan the `Files` collection
- Add each file that matches the given pattern to a new collection
- Return the newly created collection

After all, we really have two problems to solve: how to verify whether a filename matches a given pattern, and how to create and fill a collection. Once we solve these issues, we'll have a very flexible and versatile tool that lets us apply some code only to the selected objects: a kind of modern `dir` command that outputs to memory. Neither the SRL nor the Shell Automation objects I'll describe later provide this feature, but I'm going to build a solution that uses nothing more than script code.

Does the File Match the Pattern?

The beauty of the `dir` command, and of wildcards in general, is that you can use the '`*`' and the '`?`' to define a match string. In this case, though, we need to figure out a way of verifying whether a certain filename is compatible with a specified pattern for ourselves. For example, given `f*.txt`, we need a (reliable) engine that tells us that `foo.txt` matches while `bar.txt` does not.

Visual Basic for Applications has an operator that would be helpful for accomplishing this kind of task: `Like`. It lets you compare two strings and returns `True` or `False` depending on whether the former string respects the pattern defined in the latter. For example:

```
MsgBox "Dino" Like "D*"                           ' Returns True
MsgBox "Dino" Like "E*"                           ' Returns False
```

Unfortunately, the `Like` operator isn't available in VBScript. However, writing a surrogate that resolves the most common file-related situations is not really a difficult task. The following listing shows a function called `IsLike()` that takes two strings, the first being the filename to process, and the second being the pattern:

```
Msgbox IsLike("config.sys", "c*.bat")             ' Returns False
Msgbox IsLike("autoexec.bat", "*.bat")            ' Returns True
Msgbox IsLike("command.com", "c*.*m")             ' Returns True
Msgbox IsLike("command.com", "c*.*")              ' Returns True
Msgbox IsLike("fpo.txt", "*y.*")                  ' Returns False
```

For the sake of simplicity, the function supports only the `*` wildcard, and it's case-insensitive.

```
Function IsLike(strText, match)
   Dim i, str, spec, temp, token, nPos

   ' Turn strings to lower case
   str = LCase(strText)
   spec = LCase(match)

   ' Split the various components of the match string
   aInput = split(spec, "*")       ' "c*.*m" becomes Array("c", ".", "m")

   ' Walk the array of specification sub-components
   i = 0
   For Each token In aInput

      ' The first token plays an important role: the file name must begin
      '  with a substring identical to the token.
      If i = 0 Then
         temp = Left(str, Len(token))

         ' Don't match...
         If temp <> token Then
            IsLike = False
            Exit Function
         End If
```

```
        ' Removes the leading substring before next step
        str = Right(str, Len(str) - Len(token))
     Else
        temp = str

        ' For each asterisk we come across, we check that what remains of
        ' the filename contains the next token of the match string.
        nPos = Instr(1, temp, token)

        ' Don't match...
        If nPos = 0 Then
           IsLike = False
           Exit Function
        End If

        ' Removes the leading substring before next step
        str = Right(str, Len(str) - nPos + 1)
     End If

     i = i + 1
  Next

  IsLike = True
End Function
```

The idea behind the algorithm is shown in the figure below, which demonstrates how the function matches `command.com` with `c*.*m`. The file specification is split into the various tokens (in the `aInput` array) that are processed sequentially. At each step, we can increase the portion of the string that's being recognized as correct.

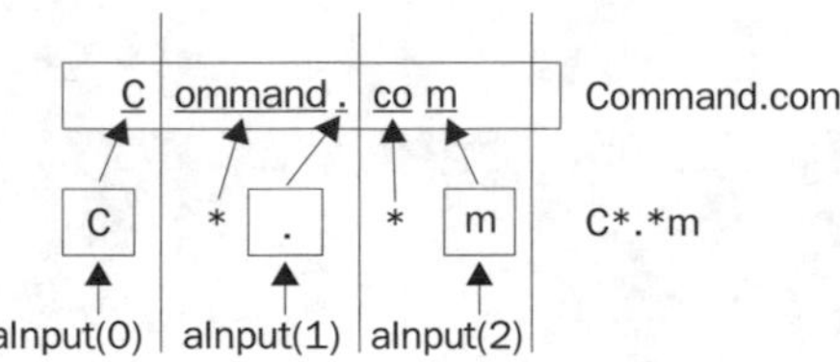

Now that we have a way to verify whether a filename matches a specification, we have almost finished. What remains is to find a way of getting matching filenames back to the user.

Creating a Dictionary

A dictionary is exactly the kind of object we need in order to store dynamic data in a way that is easily traversable and accessible. The body of the function we're building, then, will just enumerate the `Files` collection, check any filename against the pattern using regular expressions, and add the file to the dictionary if the test is successful. Let's see all this in practice:

```
Function FileQuery(dirName, filespec)

  ' Creates the required objects
  Set fso = CreateObject("Scripting.FileSystemObject")
  Set dic = CreateObject("Scripting.Dictionary")

  ' Gets the Files collection for the folder
  If Not fso.FolderExists(dirName) Then
     Exit Function
  End If
  Set f = fso.GetFolder(dirName)
  Set files = f.Files
```

Continued on Following Page

```
   ' Enumerates and processes the files
   For Each file In files
      fileName = file.Name
      If IsLike(fileName, filespec) Then
         dic.Add file.Name, file.Name
      End If
   Next

   Set FileQuery = dic
End Function
```

The following listing, on the other hand, demonstrates a short script that enumerates all the files that match such a pattern:

```
' filter.vbs
' Lets you query for files using wildcards
' ---------------------------------------------------------------------------

' Get the name of the folder to query
Dim dirName
If WScript.Arguments.Count = 0 Then
   dirName = InputBox("Enter the FULLY-QUALIFIED name of the folder:", _
                      , dirName)
   filespec = InputBox("Enter the file specification:", , filespec)
Else
   dirName = WScript.Arguments.Item(0)
   filespec = WScript.Arguments.Item(1)
End if

If dirName = "" Or filespec = "" Then
   WScript.Quit
End If

' Get the filtered collection and dump out the filenames
Set coll = FileQuery(dirName, filespec)

If coll.Count > 0 then
   msg = ""
   For Each file In coll
      msg = msg & vbCrLf & file
   Next
   MsgBox msg
End If
```

As usual, using WSH 2.0 makes all this code a bit more elegant:

```
<?xml version="1.0"?>
<!-- Filter.ws: Query for files using wildcards -->

<job>
   <script language="VBScript" src="filequery.vbs" />

   <script language="VBScript">
      <![CDATA[
         Dim dirName
         If WScript.Arguments.Count = 0 Then
            dirName = InputBox("Enter the folder name:", , dirName)
            filespec = InputBox("Enter the file specification:", , filespec)
         Else
            dirName = WScript.Arguments.Item(0)
            filespec = WScript.Arguments.Item(1)
         End If

         If dirName = "" Or filespec = "" Then
            WScript.Quit
         End If
```

```
            ' Get the filtered collection and dump out the file names
            Set coll = FileQuery(dirName, filespec)
            If coll.Count > 0 then
               msg = ""
               For Each file In coll
                  msg = msg & vbCrLf & file
               Next
               MsgBox msg
            End If
         ]]>
   </script>
</job>
```

Beyond the File System Objects

The file system objects that come with the SRL extend the power of scripting languages, and they form an excellent additional module for WSH developers. However, the SRL is not perfect. You can use it to manage operations that involve files and directories in quite a natural way, but:

- It doesn't provide support for I/O operations on binary files
- It isn't aware of Windows special folders, such Printers, Recycle Bin, and so on

With regard to the first point, the FileSystemObject documentation that's available with the latest VBScript and JScript user guides announces the availability of support for binary files in future releases of the SRL. The second point, on the other hand, is well handled by the **Shell Automation objects**.

I'm not going to cover these objects in detail, as much of their functionality has very little to do with the common tasks that are likely to be accomplished via WSH scripts. In addition, there's plenty of documentation available through the MSDN and my *Visual C++ Windows Shell Programming* book.

What I will address here is an issue that can't otherwise be resolved using the SRL. I'll show you how to enumerate the content of Windows special folders.

Getting a Folder Object

Confusingly, just like the SRL, the Shell Automation objects include an object by the name of Folder. *This* Folder object can be obtained in a couple of steps:

```
Dim shell, folder
Set shell = CreateObject("Shell.Application")
Set folder = shell.NameSpace(folderName)
```

First you create Shell.Application, the root object of the Shell Automation library, and then you call its NameSpace() method to get a reference to a particular folder.

Let's try to map these steps to the SRL components. The Shell object is similar to FileSystemObject. In addition, though, the shell object exposes a number of further methods to let you manipulate the Start menu and the taskbar, and allow you to invoke some standard system dialogs such as Find Files or Folders.

The NameSpace() method is similar to the FileSystemObject.GetFolder() method, the only difference being its support for special folders:

```
Set folder = NameSpace(folderName)
```

You can specify the folder to be returned in three different ways:

- The fully qualified path name. For example, `c:\myapp`. This is equivalent to what you can do with the SRL.
- A constant that identifies one of the special folders.
- A string in the form `::{CLSID}` to address all those special folders that don't have a constant. In practice, when the function detects that you passed one of the predefined constants, it just translates it automatically to a string in the form `::{CLSID}`.

The next script provides all the constants you may need to identify a folder.

```
' SpecFolders.vbs
' Special Folders Constants
' ---------------------------------------------------------------------

' Folder Constants
Const ssfDESKTOP = &H0                  ' Desktop
Const ssfPROGRAMS = &H2                 ' Programs folder on Start menu
Const ssfCONTROLS = &H3                 ' Control Panel
Const ssfPRINTERS = &H4                 ' Printers
Const ssfPERSONAL = &H5                 ' My Documents
Const ssfFAVORITES = &H6                ' Favorites
Const ssfSTARTUP = &H7                  ' Startup folder on Start menu
Const ssfRECENT = &H8                   ' Recent Files
Const ssfSENDTO = &H9                   ' Send To
Const ssfBITBUCKET = &HA                ' Recycle Bin
Const ssfSTARTMENU = &HB                ' Start menu
Const ssfDRIVES = &H11                  ' My Computer
Const ssfNETWORK = &H12                 ' Network Neighborhood
Const ssfFONTS = &H14                   ' Fonts
Const ssfTEMPLATES = &H15               ' Web templates

' Define the pseudo-path names for just a few of these folders
F_MYCOMPUTER      = "::{20D04FE0-3AEA-1069-A2D8-08002B30309D}"
F_DESKTOP         = "::{00021400-0000-0000-C000-000000000046}"
F_INTERNET        = "::{871C5380-42A0-1069-A2EA-08002B30309D}"
F_RECYCLEBIN      = "::{645FF040-5081-101B-9F08-00AA002F954E}"
F_PRINTERS        = F_MYCOMPUTER & "\::{2227A280-3AEA-1069-A2DE-08002B30309D}"
F_CONTROLPANEL    = F_MYCOMPUTER & "\::{21EC2020-3AEA-1069-A2DD-08002B30309D}"
F_DIALUP          = F_MYCOMPUTER & "\::{992CFFA0-F557-101A-88EC-00DD010CCC48}"
F_SCHEDULEDTASKS = F_MYCOMPUTER & "\::{D6277990-4C6A-11CF-8D87-00AA0060F5BF}"
```

And the following script shows how to use this file to connect to the `Scheduled Tasks` folder:

```
<?xml version="1.0"?>
<!-- WS script to connect to the Scheduled Tasks folder: Tasks.ws -->

<job>
   <script language="VBScript" src="SpecFolders.vbs" />

   <script language="VBScript">
      Set shell = CreateObject("Shell.Application")
      Set folder = shell.Namespace(F_SCHEDULEDTASKS)
      MsgBox folder.Title
   </script>
</job>
```

Other examples of valid calls to `NameSpace()` are this:

```
      Set folder = shell.Namespace(ssfDrives)
```

which returns a reference to `My Computer`, and this:

```
Set folder = shell.Namespace("c:\myapp")
```

which simply returns a `Folder` object for the `c:\myapp` directory.

> **Remember that this `Folder` object has nothing whatsoever to do with the `FileSystemObject`'s `Folder` object. They come from completely different object models.**

The Shell's Folder Object

The `Folder` object encapsulates two other objects (`FolderItem`, `FolderItemVerb`) and two collections (`FolderItems` and `FolderItemVerbs`). Their relationship is illustrated in the diagram below:

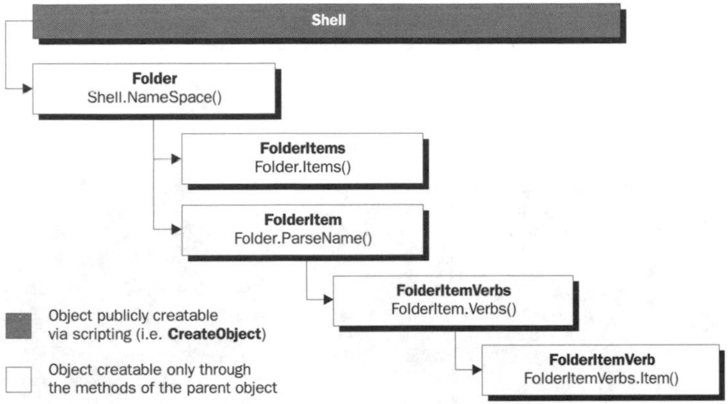

The descriptive name of the `Folder` object is exposed through its `Title` property, while the `Folder` object that precedes this one in the hierarchy (the parent folder) is identified through the `ParentFolder` property. The following table lists the methods of the object:

Method	Description
`CopyHere()`	Copies one or more file objects into the folder.
`GetDetailsOf()`	Returns column-based information about the specified folder item, in the same way as it is displayed in a shell view. The first column has an index of 0. The first argument to this method is the folder item to which you're referring. Pass the empty string to get the title of the column: `heading0 = folder.GetDetailsOf("", 0)`
`Items()`	Returns a collection of `FolderItem` elements. This collection is of type `FolderItems`.

Table Continued on Following Page

Method	Description
`MoveHere()`	The same as `CopyHere()`, but moves files.
`NewFolder()`	Creates a new folder within the given folder.
`ParseName()`	Creates a `FolderItem` object, starting from a name.

Enumerating the Content of a Special Folder

Once you have a reference to a `Folder` object, you can enumerate its contents, whether it's a special folder or an ordinary file system directory. All you need to do is scan the object returned by the `Items()` method, which is a `FolderItems` collection whose constituent elements are objects of type `FolderItem`.

```
<?xml version="1.0"?>
<!-- WS script to connect to the Scheduled Tasks folder: Tasks.ws -->

<job>
   <script language="VBScript" src="SpecFolders.vbs" />

   <script language="VBScript">
      <![CDATA[
         Set shell = CreateObject("Shell.Application")
         Set folder = shell.Namespace(F_SCHEDULEDTASKS)

         ' Displays information about the folder item
         heading0 = folder.GetDetailsOf("", 0) & vbTab & vbTab
         heading1 = folder.GetDetailsOf("", 1) & vbTab & vbTab
         heading2 = folder.GetDetailsOf("", 2) & vbTab

         For Each folderItem In folder.Items
            str = heading0 & folder.GetDetailsOf(folderItem, 0) & vbCrLf & _
                  heading1 & folder.GetDetailsOf(folderItem, 1) & vbCrLf & _
                  heading2 & folder.GetDetailsOf(folderItem, 2)
            MsgBox str
         Next
      ]]>
   </script>
</job>
```

As you'll surely have noticed, the overall design of this series of objects is similar to what we saw with the SRL. The difference is that the Shell Automation objects let you manage *any* item a folder can contain; not just files. The listing above, for example, enumerates the current scheduled tasks that you can see in Explorer if you browse to the special folder `C:\Windows\Tasks`. You should see a series of message boxes like this one:

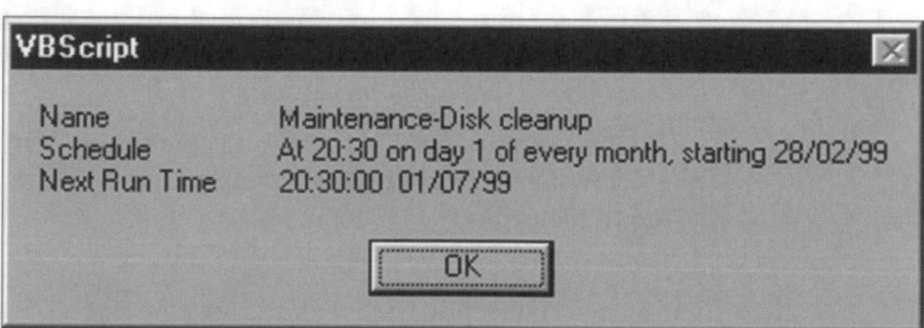

The underlying similarity between the FolderItem object and the SRL File object is that both are contained by a folder and both expose a number of properties. With a folder item object, these properties are somewhat dynamic, as they vary from folder to folder and aren't coded in the object model. The reason why you need to use GetDetailsOf() to read information that's specific to an item is that the details of a scheduled task are different from those that belong to (say) a printer, a deleted file or a normal system file.

Copying and Moving Files

This Folder object provides you with the ability to copy and move files with an additional set of parameters. Of course you can have automatic renaming on collision and directory creation, but you can also have the animations that Explorer displays when you copy or move files. The methods available are CopyHere() and MoveHere().

CopyHere

The method copies one or more files (or rather, file objects) from their original location to the current folder. The source files may be specified as strings, as individual FolderItem objects, or as a FolderItems collection of objects.

```
folder.CopyHere vFiles [, vOptions]
```

As it performs the copy operation, the function displays Explorer's usual animated dialog. The options available to you for customizing its behavior are:

```
Const FOF_SILENT =                &H4     ' No progress dialog is displayed
Const FOF_RENAMEONCOLLISION = &H8         ' Automatically adds "Copy Of"
Const FOF_NOCONFIRMATION =        &H10    ' No confirmation before overwriting
Const FOF_FILESONLY =             &H80    ' Files are copied, but not folders
Const FOF_SIMPLEPROGRESS =        &H100   ' Filenames not displayed during copy
Const FOF_NOCONFIRMMKDIR =        &H200   ' No confirmation before creating dirs
Const FOF_NOERRORUI =             &H400   ' Error codes instead of message boxes
```

If you wish, you can add these to the SpecFolders.vbs file, and you should feel free to combine them with the Or operator.

MoveHere

This method comes with all the same considerations as CopyHere(), with the eminently predictable difference that MoveHere() moves files instead of copying them. The prototype is:

```
folder.MoveHere vFiles [, vOptions]
```

Let's take a quick look at an example that uses CopyHere():

```
Set shell = CreateObject("Shell.Application")
Set folder = shell.Namespace("d:\My Pictures")
folder.CopyHere "c:\My Pictures\*.bmp"
```

These few lines copy all the .bmp files from c:\My Pictures into d:\My Pictures. Although the documentation isn't completely clear on the matter, the Shell Automation Folder object *does* support wildcards.

Any call to the `CopyHere()` method (or to the syntactically similar `MoveHere()`) causes Explorer's animation window to appear, while this slightly modified snippet:

```
Const FOF_SIMPLEPROGRESS = &H100
Set shell = CreateObject("Shell.Application")
Set folder = shell.Namespace("c:\My Pictures")
folder.CopyHere "d:\My Pictures\*.bmp", FOF_SIMPLEPROGRESS
```

Demonstrates how to show the Copying... progress dialog, but hide the actual names of the files being copied or moved:

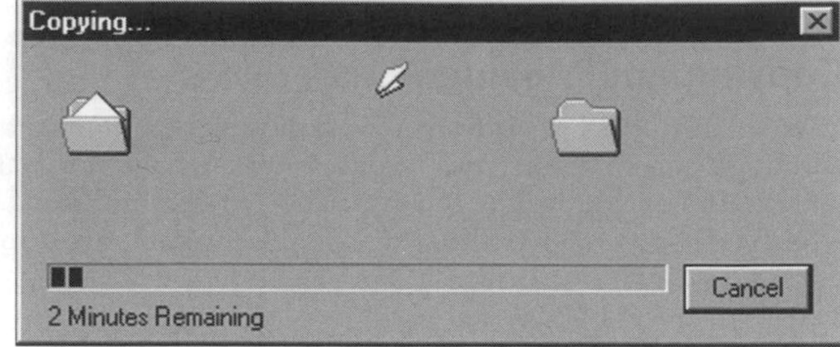

Aborting the Copy

If you abort the copy started by the above script by clicking the Cancel button, you'll sometimes get the (not particularly clear) error message opposite:

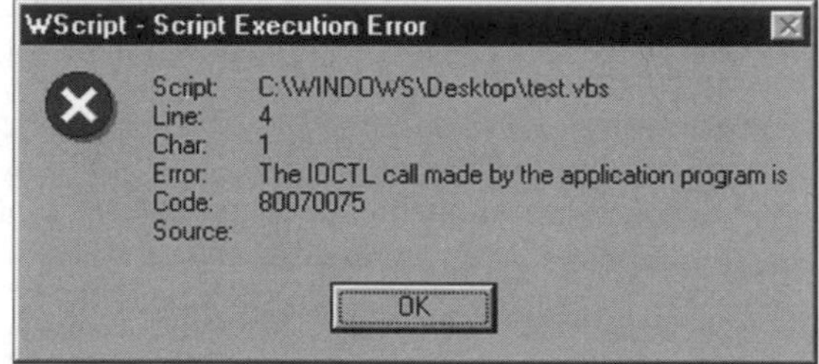

All this really means is that the API function working under the hood to accomplish the operation has raised an exception that the `wscript.exe` runtime has caught and reported using the above window. One way to avoid this in a VBScript program would be to add the following statement before the copy instruction:

```
On Error Resume Next
```

However, the VBScript exception handling technique is not very powerful, and sometimes it can hide bugs in your code. Better would be to move the code to JScript and exploit version 5.0's `try-catch` mechanism:

```
var FOF_SIMPLEPROGRESS = 0x100;
shell = new ActiveXObject("Shell.Application");
folder = shell.Namespace("c:\\My Pictures");

try
{
   folder.CopyHere("d:\\My Pictures\\*.bmp", FOF_SIMPLEPROGRESS);
}
catch(e)
{
   // If you want, you can display a message here to inform the user that the
   // copy aborted. This is also a good place to close any open objects, and
   // in general to perform any necessary cleanup after the copy operation.
}
```

Installation Scripts

One of the chief applications for operations that deal with the file system is in writing simple scripts for software installation. I *know* that there are lots of ready-to-use installers already available in the marketplace, but they're not free of charge, and sometimes they require you to invest some time learning how to get the most out of them. If you don't have a software product to package and sell, and if all you need is an automatic way to install files at certain locations on users' machines, WSH can be of considerable help.

In the right circumstances, WSH can be a great replacement for commercial installation programs: it's flexible enough to let you accomplish non-standard operations, it doesn't require you to learn new things, and it's easily modifiable. Unless you're dealing with complex and sophisticated deployment policies and supporting several storage media, all you lose by choosing WSH instead of a commercial installer is the colorful user interface.

Replacing Files in Use

A common problem that can arise in an installation script is the need to replace files that are in use at the time the process is being run. To reduce the chances of this being an issue, some installation programs ask their users to close all running applications before going any further, but even this doesn't guarantee success.

Replacing a file is a two-stage process: you have to delete the existing file and then copy the new one in its place. This means that you have to resolve the "permission denied" error that code like this will produce if the specified file is in use:

```
fso = new ActiveXObject("Scripting.FileSystemObject");
fso.DeleteFile("c:\\myFile.txt");
```

Using the JScript 5.0 language, trapping such an error is relatively easy:

```
fso = new ActiveXObject("Scripting.FileSystemObject");
try
{
   fso.DeleteFile("c:\\myFile.txt");
}
catch(e)
{
   // e is an instance of the new JScript Error object
   WScript.Echo("[" + e.number + "]  " + e.description);
}
```

The message box that results is shown opposite:

In general, it's most unlikely that you'll be replacing system files from Windows Script Host installation programs, so asking your users to close all applications and wrapping your code with error handling will suffice in the majority of cases. Evidently, though, there must be a way to work around this situation and have the file in use actually replaced — after all, any commercial installation program worth its salt is quite capable of dealing with the problem.

Moving Files Until Reboot

The Win32 SDK defines a function called `MoveFileEx()` that is capable of moving a file from one location to another only upon the next reboot. In other words, the function marks a file as being subject to deletion and replaces it with another one the next time the system starts up. Unfortunately, however, this function is only supported under Windows NT, and it can't be called from script code. Worse still, it's the only way of providing this behavior on that operating system, so if you're using WSH to deploy software on NT machines, you will always have the restrictions described above.

Happily, the situation under Windows 9x is completely different — all you need is a `.ini` file! On startup, Windows 9x looks for a file called `wininit.ini` in the `Windows` folder. If it succeeds, it scans its content and processes any lines of text it encounters. The file is supposed to adhere to the following schema:

```
[rename]
destination1=source1
destination2=source2
:
destinationn=sourcen
```

All the names you specify must be in the 8.3 short format, and the system just copies the source file over the destination. If the destination is the string "`NUL`" then the source file is deleted. As far as our code is concerned, if the `wininit.ini` file doesn't exist, then it should be created. If it does exist, it must be opened for appending.

```
// Replace.js
// Demonstrates how to replace files in use
// (Requires JScript 5.0)
//-------------------------------------------------------------

PERMISSION_DENIED = -2146828218        // From the dialog above

fso = new ActiveXObject("Scripting.FileSystemObject");
try
{
   // To cause this function to fail, open the document with Word.
   fso.DeleteFile("c:\\myFile.txt");
}
catch(e)
{
   WScript.Echo("[" + e.number + "]  " + e.description);
   if(e.number == PERMISSION_DENIED)
   {
      WindowsFolder = 0;
      ForAppending = 8;
```

```
        // Get the Windows folder and set up the full path name to wininit.ini
        sWinDir = fso.GetSpecialFolder(WindowsFolder);
        sWinInit = sWinDir + "\\WinInit.ini";
        if(fso.FileExists(sWinInit))
           f = fso.OpenTextFile(sWinInit, ForAppending);
        else
        {
           f = fso.CreateTextFile(sWinInit);
           f.WriteLine("[rename]");
        }

        // Deletes c:\myFile.txt
        f.WriteLine("nul=c:\\myFile.txt");

        // Replaces c:\yourFile.txt with the file saved in c:\temp
        f.WriteLine("c:\\yourFile.txt=c:\\temp\\yourFile.txt");
        f.Close();
    }
}
```

If it finds that `c:\myfile.txt` is in use, this code produces the following output:

```
[rename]
nul=c:\myFile.txt
c:\yourFile.txt=c:\temp\yourFile.txt
```

The next time the system reboots, `c:\myFile.txt` is deleted and `c:\yourFile.txt` is replaced by the file with the same name stored in the `c:\temp` directory.

The program that's responsible for processing `wininit.ini` is called `wininit.exe`. In most cases, a program that requires you to reboot the system in order to finalize installation will have written something to `wininit.ini`. Next time the machine boots, you'll see some text informing you that the system is updating its configuration. This means that `wininit.exe` is working and the files marked for deletion or renaming are being processed.

For a bigger example of what you can do with installation scripts written using WSH, take a look at the program that installed the source code for this book on your machine!

The SRL vs. Shell Automation Objects

The SRL and Shell Automation objects have some things in common, but also several significant differences. The former is quite powerful and has a clearer and more focused design: to make the functionality of the file system available to the script programmer. It handles the fundamentals of the file system very well, but doesn't take some of the more advanced features into account.

The Shell Automation objects, on the other hand, deal with most of the advanced features of Windows but lack some elementary methods — for deleting files, for example. I still think that there's room for an object model that manages files *and* folders, and copes with basic *and* advanced features of the Windows file system. Until that comes along, though, you should consider Shell Automation objects *and* the SRL when you're faced with problems of this kind.

Summary

This chapter has presented an annotated overview of the tools available for manipulating the Windows file system. We started with a look at the major features of the SRL library: a library of COM objects that are distributed with the scripting engines. I also highlighted some of the areas that it doesn't cover, and saw how the Shell Automation objects can come to the rescue. In particular, I demonstrated:

- How to use the `FileSystemObject` to access files and folders on your hard disk
- The good and bad aspects of the `TextStream` object for manipulating text files
- How to obtain a collection of files that match a specification containing wildcards
- The highlights of the `Dictionary` object for holding and navigating collections of data with WSH
- How to manage special folders with Shell Automation objects

Fundamentally, what I've demonstrated in this chapter is that there are some standard Windows objects that are enormously useful to WSH programmers, even though they're not strictly a part of the Windows Script Host itself. In the next chapter, we'll go one step further and start to write some custom objects using the same philosophy.

7

Writing Reusable WSH Code

In previous chapters, I've talked about **code reusability** being one of the weakest points of the Windows Script Host. The ability to import proven, pre-written code into your projects is an important one, and when it's missing you notice its absence, in scripting as in any other programming context.

WSH 1.0 itself doesn't provide any facilities for reusing script code. However, as we discussed briefly in Chapter 5, JScript has always provided the `eval()` function that can be used to import external files, and VBScript 5.0 is now capable of the same trick. While it works acceptably, though, using the languages in this way *is* just a workaround, and the good news is that WSH 2.0 provides a native instruction to get the same result.

When you start exploiting the real power of WSH and VBScript/JScript, you begin to build more and more complex applications. When programming becomes harder, reusability becomes a serious issue. In WSH programming, you will eventually need the following:

- A mechanism for injecting external code into the current script file
- A mechanism for creating your own objects
- A mechanism for aggregating heterogeneous data in more sophisticated, user-defined data components such as classes

If you utilize version 2 of WSH and version 5 of the scripting engines, you can choose the best solution for each of these requirements from a range of choices available to you. Whatever the version of WSH you're addressing, however, you can always rely on **Windows Script Components**, which are COM objects written in VBScript and/or JScript.

In this chapter, I'll analyze all the possible approaches you could take to satisfy the three points listed above.

The WSH Handbook for Reusable Code

When I talk about code reuse, I mean techniques that allow you to write code that spans across multiple projects. This goal can be achieved in two ways:

- By importing general-purpose, structured code (subroutines, functions, constants, etc.) into your script files
- By building complex objects that either the language or the surrounding environment can put to work (classes or WSC components)

As you can see, the second point expands in two directions, bringing us back to the three options listed in the introduction to the chapter.

The solutions available to you are not compatible across all versions of WSH and the scripting engines. The following table summarizes the system requirements for using each of them; you should make sure that these requirements are met on your development machine *and* your clients' machines. I've explained ways of testing the version numbers of WSH and the scripting engines in earlier chapters.

Technique	Requirement	Description
'Including' code	VBScript 5.0	A function I presented in Chapter 5 that evaluates code at runtime and adds symbols to the global scope. (Similar versions of this technique have been circulating for some time on the WSH newsgroups.) It exploits a new feature of VBScript 5.0 that can also be easily simulated in any version of JScript.
Importing source code	WSH 2.0	A feature of the new `.ws` format supported by WSH 2.0 that lets you import code in a script through a `src` attribute, just as you would in an HTML page.
Classes	VBScript 5.0	With VBScript 5.0, you can define your own classes in much the same way you would define JScript objects. Unlike JScript, however, VBScript 5.0 lets you bring these objects into the global scope, making them visible outside the file in which they're defined. (This is the same feature that I exploit in the 'include' function.)
Windows Script Components	WSH 1.0	This is the most language-independent solution. You can write an XML-based file that is treated and used as a fully-fledged COM Automation object.

I covered the new features of WSH 2.0 and VBScript 5.0 in Chapter 5, but in this chapter I'm going to provide a practical demonstration of all these techniques. As my first example, I've chosen a piece of software that lets you customize the appearance of a file system folder. I'll begin by briefly discussing the characteristics of this problem and the strategy to be applied during the development of a solution, and then I'll start my analysis of the first potential approach.

An Example: Changing Folder View Properties

Since Windows 95, it has been possible to modify the appearance of a system folder (that is, a folder tied to a specific directory, rather than a special folder such as `Printers`). Usually, you'd do this through the View | Folder Options... menu command of Explorer, which brings up a tabbed dialog. When you select the View tab, you're presented with something like this:

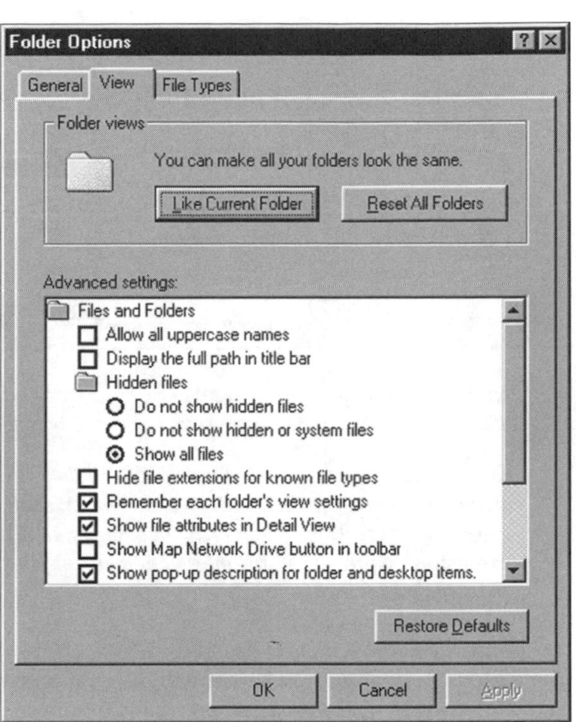

The advent of the Active Desktop for Windows 95 and Windows NT 4.0, and then the introduction of Windows 98, considerably increased the number of settings available. The above screenshot comes from a Windows 98 machine, and it's much richer than the corresponding dialog on a Windows 95 machine.

The Active Desktop is a layer of code you can choose to install during the setup procedure of Internet Explorer 4.x. It comes as an integrated component of both Windows 98 and Windows 2000.

Though it's largely undocumented, there's a way to set all these preferences programmatically. Each setting maps to a specific value under a key in the system registry, so to read or change an option, you just need to read or change the right value of the right key. If you had a script file that performed these operations, you could use it to ensure that all the employees in your organization have identical settings, making your support task much simpler.

The Active Desktop also introduced the ability to provide any system folder with a custom icon and some descriptive text. The icon is drawn next to the folder's name in the left pane of Explorer, while the text is used to display a description of the folder's content in the right pane when View | as Web Page is turned on. (It is also used as the content of a tooltip that pops up when the mouse hovers over the folder name in either Explorer or the Open/Save File dialogs.)

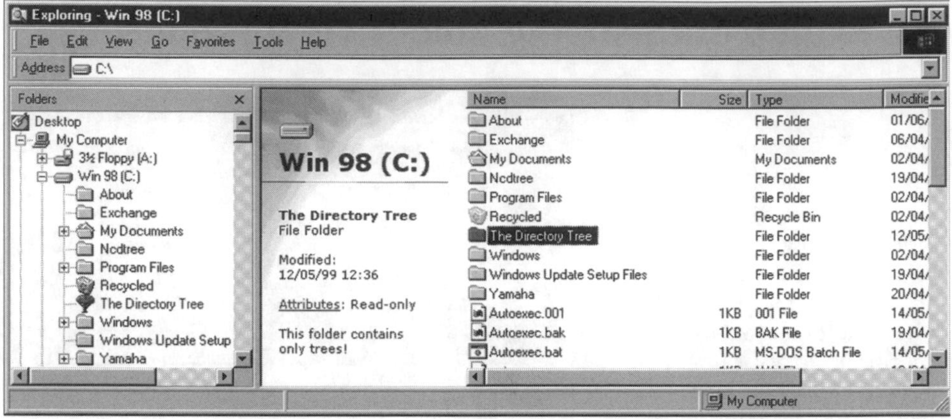

Note that the folder called `The Directory Tree` *has a custom icon, and when it's selected in the right pane, some text tells us something about it.*

Custom icons were a common feature of Windows before this feature came along, but only for folders with special content, such as `Printers` *or the* `Recycle Bin`*. These folders rely on binary modules called* **namespace extensions** *to provide all the information and support that Explorer needs in order to display them.*

To assign a custom icon and descriptive text, we just need to create a small text file in the folder. My goal in this chapter will be to demonstrate how to accomplish this via scripting code and, above all, in a reusable manner.

The Programming Interface

Throughout these examples, I'll be using various techniques to create myself a programming interface that I can call from script code. It will include the following methods and properties:

Method	Description
`CustomizeFolder()`	Takes a folder name, the name of the file that contains the icon, the index of the icon and some text. It arranges things in such a way that the specified folder is assigned with a custom icon and a description.

As far as the Boolean folder view options are concerned, I have chosen just three, but there are several others available. Feel free to enhance and extend the final source code to cover more settings. As everything will be written in VBScript or JScript, it shouldn't be hard to do.

Property	Description
HideFileExtension	If this is set, Explorer won't show the extension for known file types. (A 'known file type' is a file type for which an associated program exists.)
MapNetworkButton	If this is set, Explorer adds two new buttons to its toolbar. One is for adding a new network connection, while the other is for removing it.
ShowAttributes	If this is set, Explorer adds a final column to its 'details' view that shows the attributes (read-only, hidden, archive) of the various files.

The Tools we Need

In order to set the folder options, we just need to create an instance of the `WshShell` object and figure out exactly which registry key to work with. Adding a custom icon is a bit trickier, and for this we need to follow a two-step procedure:

- Create a text file called `desktop.ini` in the folder to be customized, and add a few lines to it.
- Turn on the 'read-only' attribute of the folder to be customized, in order to tell Explorer to treat it in a particular way. The custom icon feature works if (and only if) the folder contains a properly filled `desktop.ini` file, and has the 'read-only' attribute set.

To create a text file, we can use the `FileSystemObject` object that we met in Chapter 6. To read and write file attributes, there are two roads we can take:

- Resort to the `attrib` MS-DOS command
- Use the features of the `Folder` object that's part of the Scripting Runtime Library

In the former case, you should consider running code like this:

```
shell = new ActiveXObject("WScript.Shell");
shell.Run("command.com /c attrib +r folderName");
```

The above snippet shows how to set the 'read-only' attribute for the folder called *folderName*. The only drawback with this solution is that you'll see the DOS window appear for a moment while the command is executing. Apart from this minor irritation, the code works just fine.

If you choose to use the methods of a `Folder` object for the same task, however, things get a little trickier. When I read the documentation and then tried it, the first code I wrote looked like this:

```
Const ReadOnly = 1

' Attempt to toggle on/off the readonly attribute
Set fso = CreateObject("Scripting.FileSystemObject")
Set f = fso.GetFolder(folderName)

oldAttr = f.Attributes
If oldAttr And ReadOnly Then
   f.Attributes = f.Attributes - ReadOnly
Else
   f.Attributes = f.Attributes + ReadOnly
```

However, this didn't work, because the `Folder.Attributes` property has some protected bits (see the documentation). In particular, the 5th bit (16 decimal) that makes it a folder can't be modified programmatically. When you read the value of the `Attributes` property, you're returned a value with that bit set. Subsequently, when you try to set a new value, you end up attempting to modify a protected bit and provoke a run-time error. To make a folder read-only, you need code like this:

```
Const ReadOnly = 1
Const Hidden = 2
Const System = 4
Const Archive = 32

' Attempt to toggle on/off the readonly attribute
Set fso = CreateObject("Scripting.FileSystemObject")
Set f = fso.GetFolder(foldername)

' Prepare the bit mask to access ONLY the read/write bits of the property
bitMask = ReadOnly + Hidden + System + Archive
oldValue = f.Attributes And bitMask

If oldValue And ReadOnly Then
   f.Attributes = oldValue And (Not ReadOnly)    ' toggles off
Else
   f.Attributes = oldValue Or ReadOnly           ' toggles on
End If
```

The bit mask ensures that you will only be modifying read/write bits when setting a new value for the `Folder.Attributes` property. The bits listed in the `bitMask` variable are the only bits you can access without restrictions.

At this point, we're ready to start building some reusable WSH code to obtain the results we require. In particular, I'm going to develop:

- A `.vbs` module that exposes this functionality through procedures. This module can be used from VBScript scripts and WSH 2.0's `.ws` script files.
- A VBScript 5.0 class, and its JScript counterpart.
- A script-based COM object that can also be used outside the WSH environment.

Writing General-Purpose VBScript Functions

Writing a VBScript function to create a text file on the fly and set some folder attributes is actually not the most difficult task you could ever be assigned. The following code shows how to accomplish it in a **script-level procedure**. (A script-level procedure is a global procedure, rather than a method of a class.)

```
' CustomizeFolder()
' Assign a custom icon and a description to the specified folder
Public Function CustomizeFolder(folderName, folderIcon, folderDesc)
   Dim fso, f, shell, aIconInfo

   ' Creates the objects that we need
   Set fso = CreateObject("Scripting.FileSystemObject")
   Set shell = CreateObject("WScript.Shell")

   ' Splits the icon name into components: "file,index"
   aIconInfo = split(folderIcon, ",")

   ' Creates the desktop.ini file
   Set f = fso.CreateTextFile(folderName & "\desktop.ini", 1)
   f.WriteLine "[.ShellClassInfo]"
   f.WriteLine "IconFile=" & aIconInfo(0)
   f.WriteLine "IconIndex=" & aIconInfo(1)
   f.WriteLine "InfoTip=" & folderDesc
   f.Close

   ' Makes the folder readonly
   shell.Run "command.com /c attrib +r " & Chr(34) & folderName & Chr(34)
End Function
```

This function does exactly what it has to do, and no more.

Identifying the Icon for the Folder

To identify the icon for the folder, we need two separate pieces of information: the name of the file (`.ico`, `.exe`, `.dll`, etc.) that contains it, and the 0-based index of the icon within the file. (If you specify an `.ico` file, then 0 will almost always be the only available index.) A compact and common way to represent file and index is to use a comma-separated (`filename,index`) pair, like this: `shell32.dll,41`.

If a string like this is passed as an argument, it means we have to split it into its constituent parts in the body of the function. VBScript and JScript both support a very handy routine called `split()` that tokenizes a string, using a character that you supply as the separator. Each sub-string it finds is then stored in an array, so processing our sample string with this code:

```
aIconInfo = split(folderIcon, ",")
```

would return an array with the following two elements:

```
aIconInfo(0)      shell32.dll
aIconInfo(1)      41
```

Creating a desktop.ini File

The `CreateTextFile()` method of `FileSystemObject` lets you create an ASCII file with the name you specify as an argument. You can also dictate whether to overwrite an existing file with the same name silently, and whether to employ the Unicode character set. The following call:

```
Set f = fso.CreateTextFile(folderName & "\desktop.ini", 1)
```

creates an ASCII file called `desktop.ini`, overwriting any existing file with the same name. (Of course, you get a 'permission denied' error if the file is read-only.) The method returns a `TextFile` object that can be used to accomplish read and write operations. These lines:

```
f.WriteLine "[.ShellClassInfo]"
f.WriteLine "IconFile=" & aIconInfo(0)
f.WriteLine "IconIndex=" & aIconInfo(1)
f.WriteLine "InfoTip=" & folderDesc
```

produce the following result:

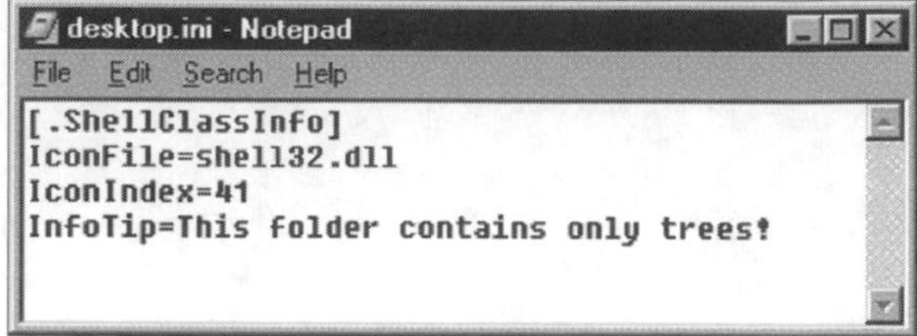

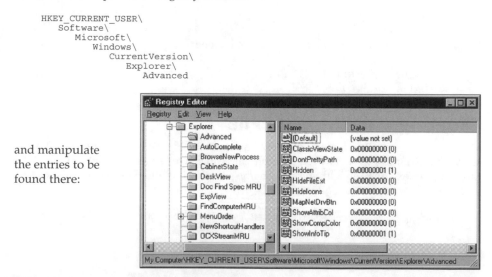

assuming of course that you call the `CustomizeFolder()` function with the following arguments:

```
CustomizeFolder "c:\the directory tree", _
                "shell32.dll,41", _
                "This folder contains only trees!"
```

Finally, to complete the customization, we need to assign the 'read-only' attribute to the folder:

```
Set shell = CreateObject("WScript.Shell")
shell.Run "command.com /c attrib +r " & Chr(34) & folderName & Chr(34)
```

Get/Set Functions for Folder Options

As I stated earlier, we also want to be able to set a few of the folder options that are available from the View | Folder Options... dialog programmatically. The states of these properties are kept in the registry on a per-user basis, so to read or modify them we need to access a particular registry location:

```
HKEY_CURRENT_USER\
   Software\
      Microsoft\
         Windows\
            CurrentVersion\
               Explorer\
                  Advanced
```

and manipulate the entries to be found there:

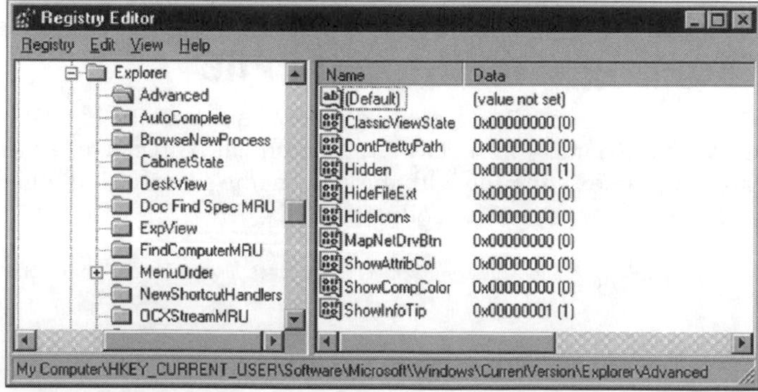

A complete description of the subject is beyond the scope of this book, but all you really need to know here is that all the entries listed above map to the options in the Folder Options dialog box. I defined two generic functions to get and set any of these properties:

```
' Helper functions to read/write the folder options

' Registry locations
Private Const L_REG_HKCU_WINDOWS = _
              "HKCU\Software\Microsoft\Windows\CurrentVersion\"
Private Const L_REG_FOLDER_OPTIONS = _
              "Explorer\Advanced\"

Private Function GetFolderSetting(propName)
   Dim shell
   Set shell = CreateObject("WScript.Shell")
   v = shell.RegRead(L_REG_HKCU_WINDOWS & L_REG_FOLDER_OPTIONS & propName)
   GetFolderSetting = v
End Function

Private Function SetFolderSetting(propName, v)
   Dim shell
   Set shell = CreateObject("WScript.Shell")
   shell.RegWrite L_REG_HKCU_WINDOWS & L_REG_FOLDER_OPTIONS & propName, _
                  v, "REG_DWORD"
End Function
```

The functions just manipulate the entry you specify as an argument, and they can be employed to build more specific functions that let you set and get the `HideFileExt`, `MapNetDrvBtn` and `ShowAttribCol` entries explicitly — reusable code! Let's see how that might work.

Hiding Extensions for Known File Types

In the Windows shell, you can ask Explorer to hide the extensions of those files that have programs registered to handle them. For example, `.txt` files have Notepad as their default handler, and are therefore considered to be a 'known' file type. By default, the option to hide these extensions is turned on, which can cause problems when you try to rename a file directly from the Explorer because you can't modify the extension. If you have a file called `foo.txt`, and you want to rename it to `foo.vbs`, you can't do it from within the shell when the `HideFileExt` option is toggled on. What you get is a file named `foo.vbs.txt`!

To toggle this feature on and off programmatically, we need to write a `DWORD` value (0 or 1) in the `HideFileExt` entry:

```
' Get/Set the HideFileExt flag
Public Function GetHideFileExtension()
   GetHideFileExtension = GetFolderSetting("HideFileExt")
End Function

Public Function SetHideFileExtension(bFlag)
   SetFolderSetting "HideFileExt", bFlag
End Function
```

To call these functions, you could then employ code like this:

```
SetHideFileExtension 1
MsgBox GetHideFileExtension()
```

Toggling the 'Map Drive' Button

The File Manager program that shipped with Windows for Workgroups had a couple of buttons in its toolbar for mapping and 'un-mapping' network drives quickly. The same feature is not automatically available in Windows 9x; to enable it, you should check the Show Map Network Drive button in toolbar option in the Folder Options window.

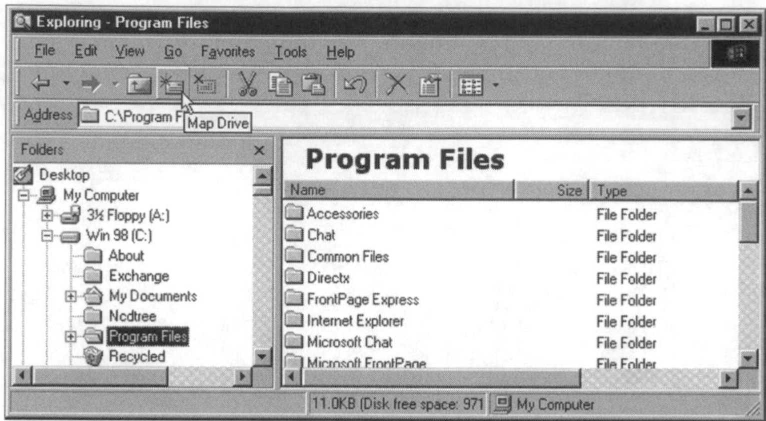

The same effect can be obtained programmatically this way:

```
' Get/Set the MapNetDrvBtn flag
Public Function GetShowNetworkButton()
   GetShowNetworkButton = GetFolderSetting("MapNetDrvBtn")
End Function

Public Function SetShowNetworkButton(bFlag)
   SetFolderSetting "MapNetDrvBtn", bFlag
End Function
```

Using these functions is no harder than using the previous ones:

```
SetShowNetworkButton 1
MsgBox GetShowNetworkButton()
```

Adding an Attributes Column

Explorer's 'details' view of folders usually includes four columns: name, size, type, and date modified. However, it's possible to add a fifth column containing the file's attributes, and this requires you to change another option in the settings:

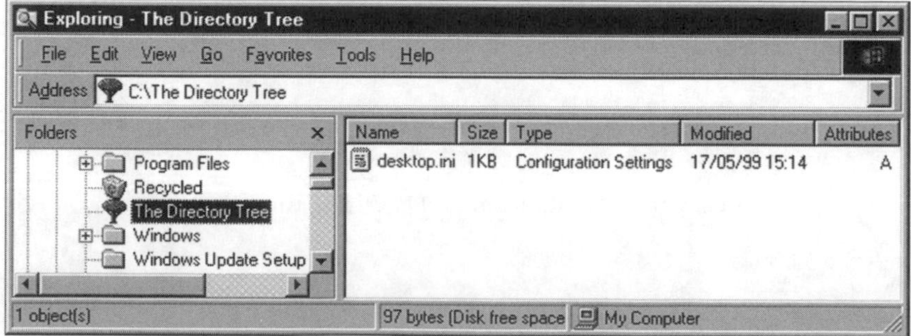

The option involved this time is `ShowAttribCol`:

```
' Get/Set the ShowAttribCol flag
Public Function GetShowAttributes()
   GetShowAttributes = GetFolderSetting("ShowAttribCol")
End Function

Public Function SetShowAttributes(bFlag)
   SetFolderSetting "ShowAttribCol", bFlag
End Function
```

Some Points to Consider

There are a few points that we need to consider about the solutions I've presented so far. In particular:

- The use of `Public` and `Private` qualifiers
- Custom folder icons under Windows 9x and Windows 2000
- The role of the `ShowInfoTip` option

Public and Private

The primary goal of this demonstration is not to show you how to assign custom icons or set folder options, but to explain how to write reusable code. In this first approach, I've written some global VBScript functions that will be imported into a VBScript module through the `Include()` function I demonstrated in Chapter 5.

I used the `Private` and `Public` keywords while declaring the functions to be imported, in the hope that a function declared as `Private` wouldn't be visible in the host module. Unfortunately, this is not the case with `.vbs` files running through WSH 1.0, as in this context using a `Private` or `Public` (or neither) qualifier has no effect. As I'll show you in a moment, though, things will change when we come to look at WSH 2.0.

Custom Icons in Windows 9x and Windows 2000

The technique presented for assigning a custom icon to a folder works fine under Windows 98 and under Windows 95/NT 4.0 if the Active Desktop is installed. With Windows 2000, it works even better, at least judging from the Beta 3 release! The thing is, Windows 9x doesn't display custom icons for normal (as opposed to special) folders in Open File dialogs or Explorer's right pane, but this feature has been added to Windows 2000. The Open File dialog that comes with the Office 97 products also supports custom icons, but then that's not one of the common dialogs!

The ShowInfoTip Option

The pop-up descriptions of folders that you can set via the `desktop.ini` file are enabled only if you have the following flag turned on:

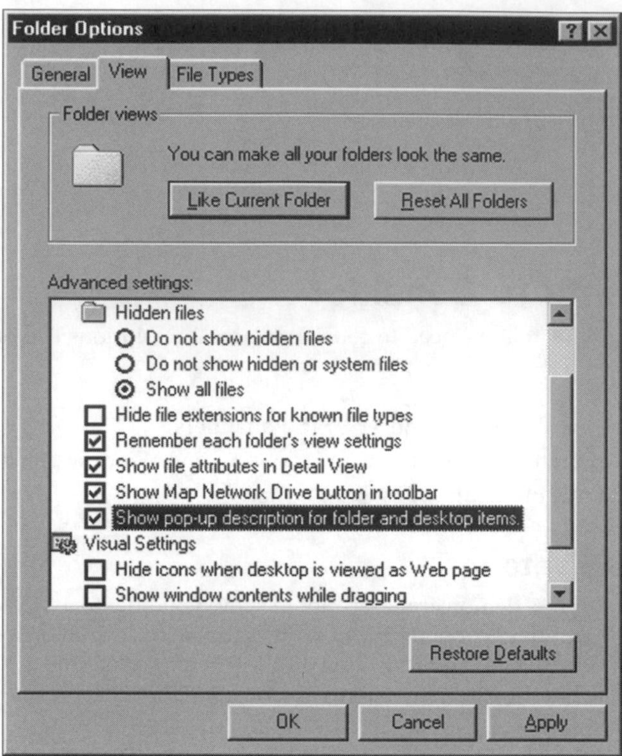

Of course, this flag can be read or written programmatically, in the same way as `HideFileExt` and the others. The registry entry involved is `ShowInfoTip`.

A Full Demonstration using VBScript 5.0

Suppose now that you have a file called `FolderOption.vbs` that defines all the functions we've discussed so far. You'll see that I've also added a little extra code to the `SetFolderSetting()` function to validate the values that get passed to it:

```
' FolderOption.vbs
' Collection of VBS functions to manipulate folders' styles

' Insert the listing for the CustomizeFolder() function here

' Insert the Get/SetHideFileExtension() function listings here

' Insert the Get/SetShowNetworkButton() function listings here

' Insert the Get/SetShowAttributes() function listings here

' Helper functions to read/write the settings
Private Const L_REG_HKCU_WINDOWS = _
            "HKCU\Software\Microsoft\Windows\CurrentVersion\"
Private Const L_REG_FOLDER_OPTIONS = _
            "Explorer\Advanced\"

Private Function GetFolderSetting(propName)
   Dim shell
   Set shell = CreateObject("WScript.Shell")
   v = shell.RegRead(L_REG_HKCU_WINDOWS + L_REG_FOLDER_OPTIONS + propName)
   GetFolderSetting = v
End Function
```

```
Private Function SetFolderSetting(propName, v)
   Dim shell

   ' Validate the input data
   If (v <> 0) And (v <> 1) Then
      Exit Function
   End If

   Set shell = CreateObject("WScript.Shell")
   shell.RegWrite L_REG_HKCU_WINDOWS + L_REG_FOLDER_OPTIONS + propName, _
                  v, "REG_DWORD"
End Function
```

How are we going to arrange for this code to be reused in multiple scripts? Sticking with the facilities of VBScript 5.0, and eschewing the rather uninspiring cut-and-paste option, we can use the `Include()` function that I provided in Chapter 5.

This function reads a VBScript file and inserts the source code at the engine's global scope. This code is therefore visible to (and accessible from) any VBScript function:

```
' SetOptions.vbs
' Demonstrates importing FolderOption.vbs

' This line imports all the code included in the specified file
Include "FolderOption.vbs"

' The code in Folderoption.vbs can now be accessed freely...

' (Re)Using the code to manipulate folder settings
CustomizeFolder "c:\The Directory Tree", _
                "shell32.dll,41", _
                "This folder contains only trees!"

SetHideFileExtension 0
SetShowAttributes 1
SetShowNetworkButton 1
MsgBox GetShowNetworkButton

' Unfortunately, you need to copy this short subroutine into
'  any VBScript WSH script that uses Include()
Sub Include(file)
   Dim fso, f
   Set fso = CreateObject("Scripting.FileSystemObject")
   Set f = fso.OpenTextFile(file, 1)
   str = f.ReadAll
   f.Close
   ExecuteGlobal str
End Sub
```

This is quite an easy way to import external code into your own scripts. The solution requires the VBScript 5.0 engine to work, but you can use it with any version of WSH. Before analyzing a better approach that uses the features of WSH 2.0, I want to spend a moment or two explaining why an `Include()` function like this one can't be written in JScript, and what we can do to fix that.

A Rather Similar JScript Demonstration

The `Include()` function in the code above does two things: it reads the contents of the specified file and adds it to the global scope of the engine. There's nothing preventing you from writing a function that reads the contents of a file in JScript, but there's no way to get the same *global* effect from within a function that `ExecuteGlobal()` provides in the above sample. Before you give up, though, there's one more card to play.

Since its inception, JScript has had an `eval()` function for evaluating code at runtime. However, the string you pass to the function is evaluated in the same context as the call to the method, so if we make a call to `eval()` within the `Include()` function, the code just gets inserted into the context of `Include()`! No other function can see the new functions you've tried to introduce.

Is there a workaround? Of course there is. Just make your `Include()` function return a string, and call `eval()` on that! This is demonstrated in the following code:

```
// SetOptions.js
// Demonstrates importing JS code

// This line imports all the code included in the specified file.
eval(Include("folderoption.js"));

// The code in Folderoption.js can now be accessed freely...

// (Re)Using the code to manipulate folder settings
CustomizeFolder("c:\\the directory tree",
                "shell32.dll,41",
                "This folder contains only trees!");

SetHideFileExtension(0);
SetShowAttributes(1);
SetShowNetworkButton(1);
WScript.Echo(GetShowNetworkButton());

// Unfortunately, you need to import this short subroutine into
//  any JScript WSH script that uses Include()
function Include(file)
{
   var fso, f;
   fso = new ActiveXObject("Scripting.FileSystemObject");
   f = fso.OpenTextFile(file, 1);
   str = f.ReadAll();
   f.Close();
   return str;
}
```

This approach is actually even more portable than the one we used in the VBScript example. `eval()` has been supported since JScript 1.0, and it's part of the ECMAScript specification.

The `FolderOption.js` *file is nearly identical to its VBScript counterpart, and you can download it from the Wrox web site (*http://www.wrox.com*).*

A Full Demonstration using WSH 2.0

If using WSH 2.0 doesn't present you with any potential compatibility problems, then you can get rid of all these tricks and workarounds, and exploit the ability to import files that WSH 2.0 offers automatically:

```
<!-- Windows script file to set folder options: SetOptions.ws -->

<job>
   <script language="VBScript" src="FolderOption.vbs" />

   <script language="JScript">
      CustomizeFolder("c:\\the directory tree",
                      "shell32.dll,41",
                      "This folder contains only trees!");

      // This call generates an error, since GetFolderSetting() is declared
      //  as a private function
      // GetFolderSetting("HideFileExt");

      SetHideFileExtension(0);          // Toggle HideFileExt off
      SetShowAttributes(1);             // Toggle ShowAttribCol on
      SetShowNetworkButton(1);          // Toggle MapNetDrvBtn on
   </script>
</job>
```

The first `<script>` element includes the content of the file specified by the `src` attribute in the current job, and while the `src` and `language` attributes must refer to the same language, the source code of other `<script>` elements in the same job can access the imported functions even if their language is different. The listing above, in fact, demonstrates JScript code calling into the public members of the `folderoption.vbs` file.

Reusability Through Classes

Classes provide a way to model complex data types, making them easily accessible and their use more understandable. Classes are also a key element in achieving reusability. I don't want to embark on a discussion about the difference between a class and an object here; in this context, my definition is:

In VBScript, a class is a user-defined type with properties and methods.

In these terms, VBScript 5.0 classes and JScript objects are both examples of classes. When I use the term 'object', I'll be talking about *COM* objects written in any language, including scripting languages.

Writing VBScript Classes

Classes were introduced in VBScript version 5.0, and I gave you an overview of the syntax required to use them in Chapter 5. Once you've defined the structure of a class, you instantiate it using the `New` operator and then start programming it using the familiar object-based notation.

```
Dim cls
Set cls = New MyClass
```

Classes wouldn't be very helpful if you couldn't reuse them across multiple projects. By combining the power of VBScript 5.0 and WSH 2.0, you can isolate a class in a `.vbs` file and import it through a `<script>` block, as I demonstrated above for global functions. You can even get the same result using WSH 1.0, provided that you return again to the services of `ExecuteGlobal()`.

The FolderOption VBScript Class

This class is a 'wrapper' around the functions we've discussed so far, with a few minor alterations. In order to turn our earlier code into a class, you just have to make these changes:

```
' ClsFolderOption.vbs
' A VBS class to manipulate folders' styles

Private Const L_REG_HKCU_WINDOWS = _
              "HKCU\Software\Microsoft\Windows\CurrentVersion\"
Private Const L_REG_FOLDER_OPTIONS = _
              "Explorer\Advanced\"

Class FolderOption

   ' Assign a custom icon to the given folder
   Public Function Customize(folderName, folderIcon, folderDesc)

      ' The body of the function as before

   End Function

   ' Toggles visibility of the extensions for known file types
   Public Property Get HideFileExtension()
      HideFileExt = GetFolderSetting("HideFileExt")
   End Property

   Public Property Let HideFileExtension(bFlag)
      SetFolderSetting "HideFileExt", bFlag
   End Property

   ' Add/Remove the Map Network button to the Explorer's toolbar
   Public Property Get ShowNetworkButton()
      HideFileExt = GetFolderSetting("MapNetDrvBtn")
   End Property

   Public Property Let ShowNetworkButton(bFlag)
      SetFolderSetting "MapNetDrvBtn", bFlag
   End Property

   ' Add the Attributes column to Details view
   Public Property Get ShowAttributes()
      HideFileExt = GetFolderSetting("ShowAttribCol")
   End Property

   Public Property Let ShowAttributes(bFlag)
      SetFolderSetting "ShowAttribCol", bFlag
   End Property

   ' GetFolderSetting() and SetFolderSetting() exactly as before

End Class
```

The class has one method named `Customize()` and three properties called `HideFileExtension`, `ShowNetworkButton` and `ShowAttributes`. The two helper functions that actually read and write the settings are declared as `Private`, while all the rest are `Public`.

A WSH 1.0 Demonstration

To import classes into VBScript files, you need to include them in the same way that we incorporated global functions in a previous section:

```
' SetOptCls.vbs
' Demonstrates using ClsFolderOption.vbs

Include "ClsFolderOption.vbs"

Dim folder
Set folder = New FolderOption

With folder
   .Customize "c:\the directory tree", _
              "shell32.dll,41", _
              "This folder contains only trees!"
   .HideFileExtension = 0
   .ShowAttributes = 1
   .ShowNetworkButton = 0
End With

Sub Include(file)
   Dim str, fso, f
   Set fso = CreateObject("Scripting.FileSystemObject")
   Set f = fso.OpenTextFile(file, 1)
   str = f.ReadAll
   f.Close
   ExecuteGlobal str
End Sub
```

Once again, the `Include()` routine turns out to be a very useful piece of code!

A WSH 2.0 Demonstration

Importing and using this class from a WSH 2.0 script is straightforward. Here's an example:

```
<!-- WS script to set folder options: SetOptCls.ws -->

<job>
   <script language="VBScript" src="ClsFolderOption.vbs" />

   <script language="VBScript">
      Dim Folder
      Set Folder = New FolderOption
      With folder
         .Customize "c:\the directory tree", _
                    "shell32.dll,41", _
                    "This folder contains only trees!"
         .HideFileExtension = 0
         .ShowAttributes = 1
         .ShowNetworkButton = 0
      End With
   </script>
</job>
```

Note that you *can't* use VBScript classes from within JScript `<script>` elements. More precisely, you can't create an instance of a VBScript class from within JScript. However, you *can* use an already-created instance of a VBScript class from JScript — it's just treated like an ActiveX control. The following code demonstrates just this:

```
<!-- WS script to set folder options: SetOptCls1.ws -->

<job>
   <script language="VBScript" src="ClsFolderOption.vbs" />
```

Continued on Following Page

```
   <script language="VBScript">
      Function CreateAndReturnClass()
         Dim f
         Set f = New FolderOption
         Set CreateAndReturnClass = f
      End Function
   </script>

   <script language="JScript">
      f = CreateAndReturnClass();
      f.Customize("c:\\the directory tree",
                  "shell32.dll,41",
                  "This folder contains only trees!");
      f.HideFileExtension = 0;
   </script>
</job>
```

Writing JScript Classes

You can write almost identical code with JScript, even without employing the latest engine. JScript's objects can be adapted to work in a rather similar way, and to expose properties and methods. The only drawback is that you *can't* expose properties that need special routines in order to be read or written. In other words, in JScript you haven't got the `Property Get`, `Property Let`, and `Property Set` statements.

The above VBScript class has three properties, but each has its own 'get' and 'set' routines that allow you to read and write the property as if it were a member variable. This leaves the task of identifying the right piece of code for carrying out the I/O operation to the VBScript runtime. JScript's properties, on the other hand, are just variables that you expose directly. If you need special code for 'get' and 'set' operations (as is the case for the `FolderOption` class), you have to resort to explicit `GetXxx()` and `SetXxx()` methods.

> *A JScript class that exposes identical functionality to the VBScript class demonstrated above is available for download along with the rest of the source code for this book from the Wrox Press web site at* http://www.wrox.com.

Pros and Cons

We've now looked at a number of techniques for writing reusable code to be used with WSH, and it's about time we considered their relative merits. Used correctly, classes and objects let you model problems better than functions — that, after all, is the tenet on which object-oriented programming in based. Moreover, starting off with a powerful environment that has effective native functionality is better than resorting to tricks — it saves time, and it lets you write more maintainable and readable code. Remember, however, that classes present a number of potential compatibility issues:

- VBScript classes require the VBScript 5.0 engine (or higher) on all the machines that will be running the script. This might mean that you have to update lots of machines, which is not always an easy task.
- While you can construct similar data types in VBScript and JScript, the classes of the former and the objects of the latter are different kinds of entity. You can use instances of VBScript classes from within JScript and vice versa, but you can't *create* such components from the other language.

- JScript's objects aren't as rich with features as VBScript's classes but they are supported by any version of JScript.

If you can utilize WSH 2.0 and the 5.0 versions of the scripting engines, then by all means always try to choose classes over global functions, but you don't need to be religious about it. Classes allow a higher level of expressiveness and let you create complex data types, but if you just want to reuse a few lines of code that execute a one-shot, stand-alone task, using classes could be overkill. If you needed a piece of code to change just one folder setting, then a function could be the right choice. If you wanted to control all the attributes of a folder, a class would be the better option.

As I said earlier in the book, performance is always an issue you should have at the back of your mind, but it's not as important when you're scripting as it is at other times. You should accord a higher development priority to the readability and maintainability of your code. A script is likely to be subject to change during its lifetime, and frequently many different people will be responsible for this work. My advice is that you should try to write your code in a self-describing way. Classes are an excellent way of doing this, but they can add unnecessary complexity when the task to be accomplished is fairly simple.

COM Objects with Scripting Languages

To conclude this chapter, I want to discuss yet another way of producing reusable code: writing Automation-compatible COM objects with a scripting language. This may sound a bit strange at first, but I can assure you it's completely true, and it works.

If we had a COM object called `WshKit.FolderOption`, we could simply use it like this:

```
f = new ActiveXObject("WshKit.FolderOption");
f.Customize("c:\\the directory tree",
            "shell32.dll,41",
            "This folder contains only trees!");
```

It wouldn't matter what language was used to write the component. All that's important is the ProgID and the methods and properties (and events) it makes available. Furthermore, COM objects have a number of advantages over classes and functions, as listed below:

- A COM object is language neutral and portable to any COM-aware environment. You can use it with Visual Basic, Visual J++, Visual C++ and Delphi, and also with other scripting languages such as Perl.
- A COM object doesn't require you to import anything into your script. You just create an instance of the object.
- A COM object is unaffected by the version of WSH you or your clients are using. (Note, though, that script-based COM objects are tied to the version-dependent features of the language you use to write them.)
- A COM object can be used remotely through DCOM or HTTP.
- A COM object can fire events, a feature that neither VBScript classes nor JScript objects support.

As I'll show you in a moment, the technology known as **Windows Script Components** has a freely available Wizard and an overall architecture that completely shield you from knowing the details of COM programming. Designing a script-based COM object is identical to designing a VBScript class, so my suggestion is that you should strongly consider using COM objects when you need to implement a short piece of reusable code for use with the Windows Script Host.

Script-based COM Objects

When I first heard about COM objects written with VBScript or JScript, I wondered, "Where's the magic?" The first questions I had were:

- A COM object is a binary file. What has that to do with VBScript or JScript?
- A COM object needs registration and a CLSID. Who deals with that?
- A COM object exposes interfaces. How is that possible with a scripting language?
- A COM object has a well-known binary layout. Who provides that for a script file?

As I was formulating the last question, however, I started to figure out a possible way of getting such an incredible result.

A Similar Case

At this time, I was working with OLE DB providers (specifically, with OLE DB simple providers in Visual Basic), and the pattern by which they work is exactly the same as the one used by Windows Script Components. OLE DB simple providers are two-tiered components made up of your simple Visual Basic (or Java) code and a DLL. The DLL processes the code you've written and exposes a regular OLE DB programming interface to its consumers.

The Scripting Runtime Engine

Windows Script Components (WSCs, previously known as Scriptlets) work in much the same way. Once they've been registered, all script-based COM objects point to the same COM-compliant executable: `scrobj.dll`. Furthermore, all script-based COM objects have an additional key in the registry pointing to a script file. This file contains metadata defining both the executable code and the interfaces to be made externally available.

Creating a Windows Script Component

A WSC is an XML file that contains all the information about the object (methods, properties, events) and the script code that is called when the object is used. In addition, it includes a special section containing registration information. This block is used by `regsvr32.exe` to add the proper entries to the registry when the WSC is registered.

The WSC kit is available from the http://msdn.microsoft.com/scripting site. Once you've installed it, any file with a `.wsc` extension will have menu commands available to register it, un-register it, and generate a type library from it:

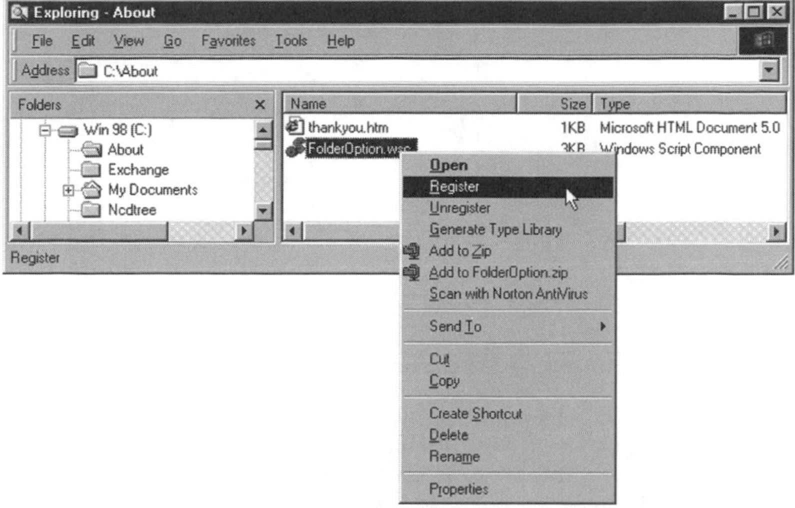

Another invaluable download from the Microsoft scripting site is the Windows Script Component Wizard, which makes it incredibly easy to write WSCs:

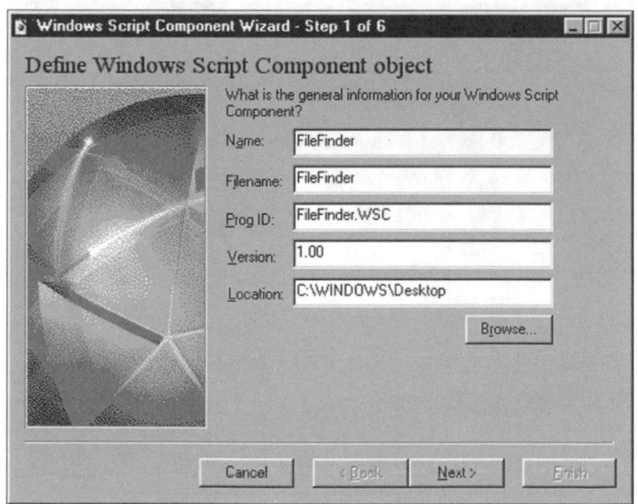

The above screenshot shows the first screen of the Wizard, in which you decide the name of the component, its ProgID, and where it should be stored. The next step then lets you specify characteristics such as the language to be used and "special interface support". If you select the latter, the Wizard will provide help with implementing the interfaces required to work with Active Server Pages or DHTML behaviors, but neither is an issue if you're creating a WSC to be used with WSH. Leave step 2 as it is, and move on:

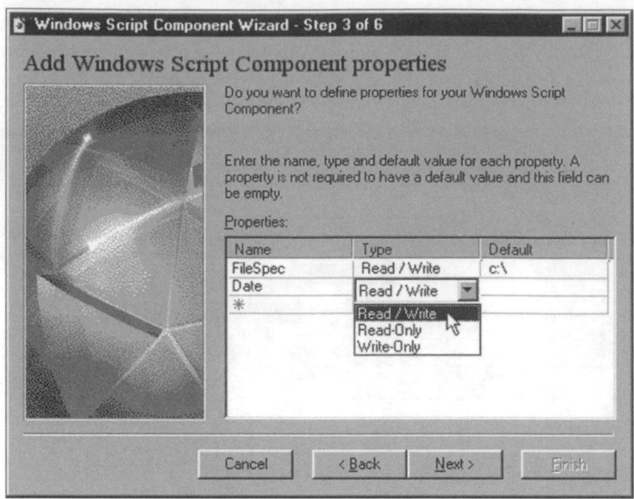

Steps 3 to 5 let you define the properties, methods and events for your component. As an example, I'm going to put together a component that enumerates all the files matching a given date and specification. Start off by defining two read/write properties called `FileSpec` and `Date`, as in the previous figure, and then move to the next step and add a method called `Search()`. This will start the search and return a collection of files that match the parameters set by the properties:

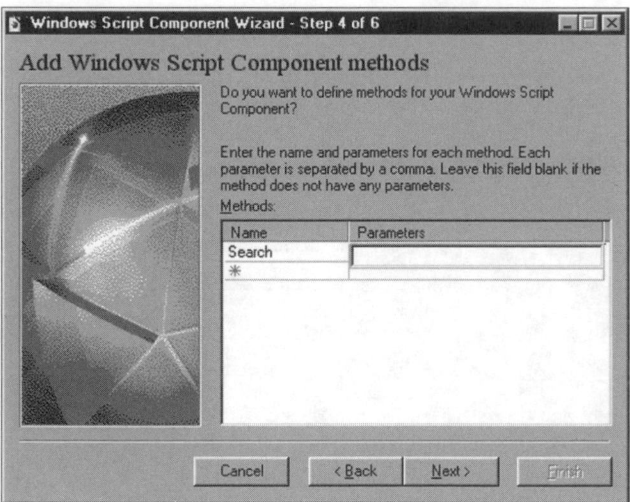

This component is not going have any events, so you can skip the fifth step and go directly to the final screen to confirm the creation of your WSC:

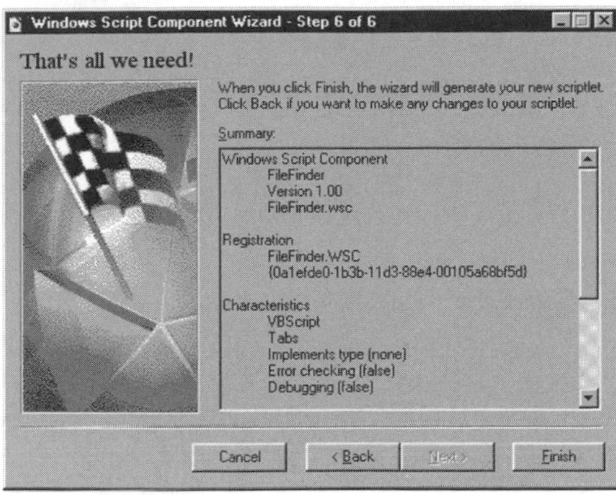

Notice that the Wizard has generated a CLSID for us. The source code that's generated and placed in the file called `FileFinder.wsc` is shown below:

```
<?xml version="1.0"?>

<component>
   <registration description="FileFinder"
                 progid="FileFinder.WSC"
                 version="1.00"
                 classid="{e8c35060-1879-11d3-b17c-00c0dfe39736}">
   </registration>

   <public>
      <property name="FileSpec">
         <get/>
         <put/>
      </property>

      <property name="Date">
         <get/>
         <put/>
      </property>

      <method name="Search">
      </method>
   </public>

   <script language="VBScript">
      <![CDATA[
         dim FileSpec
         FileSpec = "c:\"

         dim Date

         function get_FileSpec()
            get_FileSpec = FileSpec
         end function

         function put_FileSpec(newValue)
            FileSpec = newValue
         end function

         function get_Date()
            get_Date = Date
         end function
```

Continued on Following Page

```
        function put_Date(newValue)
           Date = newValue
        end function

        function Search()
           Search = "Temporary Value"
        end function
     ]]>
   </script>
</component>
```

A Look at the Syntax

On examination, you can see that the syntax is not unlike that of the .ws files we examined in Chapter 5. A .wsc file follows an XML schema in which the main element is named <component>, and this has three subsidiary elements: <registration>, <public> and <script>. If you find yourself doing a lot of work with WSCs, these aren't the only elements you'll ever encounter, but they're all you need for writing WSC components for WSH scripts.

The <component> Element

This is the main element that encloses the entire source code of a single component. It can have an id attribute, but this is only required if you have more than one component in the same file, in which case it lets you identify a specific component. To embed several components in the same .wsc file, you can use a <package> element, just as we did for the <job> elements of .ws files. For example:

```
<package>
   <component id="one">
      <!-- code here -->
   </component>

   <component id="two">
      <!-- code here -->
   </component>
</package>
```

If the .wsc file contains only a single component, using the <package> element is optional.

The <registration> Element

The code in a <registration> element stores information about how the COM object should be registered. Attributes of the <registration> tag can specify the CLSID, the ProgID, a version number and a description, as in the Wizard-generated code of the above listing:

```
<registration description="FileFinder"
              progid="FileFinder.WSC"
              version="1.00"
              classid="{e8c35060-1879-11d3-b17c-00c0dfe39736}">
</registration>
```

The Wizard helps by providing all this code automatically, but in fact some of these attributes aren't essential. If you omit the classid, for example, one will be generated for you during the registration process, but you must always specify *either* a classid *or* a progid. The description and version attributes are also optional.

If you omit to specify a ProgID, you won't be able to create an instance of the object using the native object creators of VBScript or JScript. Your only option then is to use the `<object>` *tag of a WSH 2.0* `.ws` *file.*

The complete syntax of the `<registration>` tag also includes a `remotable` attribute that can be set to `true` or `false` to denote whether an instance of the component can be created over the network, through DCOM. The following is therefore a valid `<registration>` element for a Windows Script Component:

```
<registration progid="MyComponent.WSC" remotable=true />
```

You can then instantiate an object registered in this way over the network, like so:

```
Set obj = CreateObject("MyComponent.WSC", "\\server\components")
```

Finally for this element, you can specify that some script code should be executed when the component is registered, as shown:

```
<registration description="FileFinder"
              progid="FileFinder.WSC"
              version="1.00"
              classid="{e8c35060-1879-11d3-b17c-00c0dfe39736}">
   <script language="VBScript">
      Function register()
         MsgBox "FileFinder.WSC registered."
      End Function

      Function unregister()
         MsgBox " FileFinder.WSC unregistered."
      End Function
   </script>
</registration>
```

All you have to do is supply a `register()` and/or an `unregister()` function in the body of the `<registration>` element.

The <public> Element

The next major element you can see in the Wizard-generated code is `<public>`, which is used to indicate the properties, methods and events exposed by the component. Here's what the Wizard gave us:

```
<public>
   <property name="FileSpec">
      <get/>
      <put/>
   </property>

   <property name="Date">
      <get/>
      <put/>
   </property>

   <method name="Search">
   </method>
</public>
```

Although it's probably fairly clear to you what's going on here just by looking at the code, this doesn't fully describe the range of facilities offered by these elements. It's possible, for example, to specify the arguments that methods and events will take, and we should look at each one in more detail.

The <property> Element

It will come as no surprise that each <property> element defines a property, but they can be expressed in two different ways. First, you can implement a property directly by using a public variable and let the user write and read it without restriction. In that case the declaration would be:

```
<property name="FileSpec" internalname="m_FileSpec" />
```

This code just defines a public variable called m_FileName that will be read and written from script code that uses the name FileName:

```
obj.FileName = "c:\"
```

The above ends up writing "c:\" to the internal variable called m_FileName. If you omit the optional internalname attribute, the internal variable will be given the same name as the name attribute, which is compulsory.

The limitation of this approach is that you can't validate the values that the user assigns to the variable, or execute any other operations related to the property (updating other internal variables, for example). Another drawback is that you can't make this kind of property read-only or write-only — all of them are read/write.

By placing <get> and <put> tags within the <property> element, you permit the specification of a function to read and write the contents of that property. These tags correspond to the Property Get and Property Let methods of VBScript classes. As you've seen, this is the approach that the Wizard takes, and in general I recommend that you do it this way too:

```
<property name="FileSpec">
   <get/>
   <put/>
</property>
```

If you specify the <get> tag, the property is considered readable. If you specify the <put> tag, it is also considered writeable. Specifying both means that the property is read/write. Omitting <put> makes the property read-only, while omitting <get> makes it write-only. Omitting both makes the variable read/write through a public variable, as seen a moment ago.

The presence of <get> and <put> implies that reading and writing are operations to be accomplished by two specialized functions. The names of these functions can optionally be set through the internalname attribute, but they default to get_Xxx() and put_Xxx(), where Xxx is the name of the property. Again, this is what the Wizard does:

```
dim FileSpec
FileSpec = "c:\"

function get_FileSpec()
   get_FileSpec = FileSpec
end function
```

Behind these functions, there's always a private variable that holds the value, to which you're free to give whatever name you want — the Wizard just chooses the same name as the property for convenience. When you specify `<get>` or `<put>`, you *must* have the relative function defined in the `<script>` section.

The <method> Element

You make a method available by using the `<method>` element, within which each `<parameter>` tag specifies a formal parameter. The `<method>` tag can have two attributes, `name` and `internalname`, the first of which is compulsory and denotes the name by which you can invoke it from script code. The `internalname`, on the other hand, is optional and identifies the internal procedure that implements the method. By default, the internal name coincides with the public name. Here's an example where both are specified:

```
<method name="Read" internalname="DoRead">
   <parameter name="fileName" />
   <parameter name="maxLen" />
</method>

...

<script language="VBScript">
function DoRead
   ' Code here...
end function
</script>
```

The <event> Element

We haven't added one to our component, but the `<event>` element declares an event that the component can fire. The syntax lets you specify the name of the event through the `name` attribute:

```
<event name="Completed" />
```

This name will be used by sinks to define the procedure that handles the event in script code. It's not explained in the documentation, but you can also use `<parameter>` tags to specify the parameters that the event will pass back to the sink, like this:

```
      <event name="FileFound">
         <parameter name="fileName" />
      </event>
```

An event can be raised by the component using the `FireEvent()` function defined by the WSC runtime in `scrobj.dll`. This function takes a compulsory argument that is the name of the event, plus as many additional arguments as are needed to match the specified parameters.

The <script> Element

The third major element is `<script>`, which has the same role here as it does in Windows Script files: it encloses all the script code for the various elements we've looked at so far.

```
<script language="VBScript">
   <![CDATA[
      dim FileSpec
      FileSpec = "c:\"

      dim m_Date

      function get_FileSpec()
         get_FileSpec = FileSpec
      end function

      function put_FileSpec(newValue)
         FileSpec = newValue
      end function

      function get_Date()
         get_Date = Date
      end function

      function put_Date(newValue)
         Date = newValue
      end function

      function Search()
         Search = "Temporary Value"
      end function
   ]]>
</script>
```

Notice how the Wizard-generated code includes `CDATA` delimiters in order that you can use characters such as < and `&` in the usual way, and the code remains compliant with the XML 1.0 standard.

Implementing the Component

You now know how the various elements in the `.wsc` file work, and it's about time we got round to making our component do something. Just before that, though, let's ensure that what we have right now really does work. So that we can see something happening, add a line to the implementation of the `Search()` function:

```
      function Search()
         MsgBox "Searching for " & FileSpec & " files..."
         Search = "Temporary Value"
      end function
```

Testing the component requires that we register it, and this can be done simply by right clicking on the `.wsc` file in Explorer and choosing Register. The following code will then create an instance of the `FileFinder.WSC` object and execute the `Search()` method:

```
Dim o
Set o = CreateObject("FileFinder.WSC")
o.Search
```

At this point, we just need to fill in the various script blocks to give the component the behavior we require. We want the files contained in the folder specified by `FileSpec` to be enumerated and the date of their last modification to be compared to the one set in `Date`. If the difference expressed in days is zero, then the file will be added to the collection to be returned.

The first thing we need to do is give `Date` a default value. We were able to give one of these to `FileSpec` in step 3 of the Wizard, but I want to set `Date` using VBScript's `Now()` function, and if we'd tried to do that, we'd have got the *string* "Now" instead:

```
dim FileSpec
FileSpec = "c:\"

dim Date
Date = Now
```

`Search()` returns the list of the files through a newly instantiated `Dictionary` object. (This is one of the helper objects in the Scripting Runtime Library that we looked at in the last chapter.) To enumerate the files in a folder, I use the `Folder` object that's returned by the `FileSystemObject.GetFolder()` method. The list of files is stored in the `Files` object, and the `Search()` method just compares the dates and adds to the dictionary accordingly:

```
function Search()
   set fso = CreateObject("Scripting.FileSystemObject")
   set fld = fso.GetFolder(FileSpec)
   set files = fld.Files

   set dic = CreateObject("Scripting.Dictionary")
   for each f in files
      d = DateDiff("d", f.DateLastModified, Date)
      if d = 0 then
         dic.add f.Name, f.Name
      end if
   next

   set Search = dic
end function
```

We also need to add some validation code to the `put_Xxx()` functions to make sure that an existing folder and a valid date are specified:

```
function put_FileSpec(newValue)
   set fso = CreateObject("Scripting.FileSystemObject")
   if fso.FolderExists(newValue) then
      FileSpec = newValue
   end if
end function

function put_Date(newValue)
   if IsDate(newValue) then
      Date = newValue
   end if
end function
```

A typical use of this object is demonstrated in the following VBScript example, which concatenates and then prints out all the names of the files in the root of drive C that have been modified during the day:

```
' FF.vbs
' Demonstrates the use of the FileFinder WSC component
' -------------------------------------------------------

Dim oFF, fileName, files, str
Set oFF = CreateObject("FileFinder.WSC")

oFF.FileSpec = "c:\"
oFF.Date = Now

set files = oFF.Search()
for each fileName in files
   str = str & fileName & vbCrLf
next

WScript.Echo str
```

To make the script a bit more versatile, let's make it accept arguments that set the folder and the date through the command line, and prompt you if they're missing:

```
' FF.vbs
' Demonstrates the use of the FileFinder WSC component
' Usage: FF [path] [date]
' -------------------------------------------------------

Dim oFF, fileName, files, str
Set oFF = CreateObject("FileFinder.WSC")

if WScript.Arguments.Count > 0 then
   if WScript.Arguments.Item(0) = "/?" then
       WScript.Echo "Usage: FF [path] [date]"
       WScript.Quit
   end if
end if

if WScript.Arguments.Count = 2 then
   oFF.FileSpec = WScript.Arguments.Item(0)
   oFF.Date = WScript.Arguments.Item(1)
else
   if WScript.Arguments.Count = 1 then
      oFF.FileSpec = WScript.Arguments.Item(0)
      oFF.Date = Now
   else
      oFF.FileSpec = InputBox("Enter the folder name:",, "c:\")
      if oFF.FileSpec <> "" then
         oFF.Date = InputBox("Enter the date as a string:",, Date)
      else
         WScript.Echo("You must provide the name of an existing folder.")
         WScript.Quit
      end if
   end if
end if

set files = oFF.Search()
for each fileName in files
   str = str & fileName & vbCrLf
next

if str = "" then
   str = "No file found."
end if

WScript.Echo str
```

Basically, the `ff.vbs` script now looks at the `Arguments` collection and does the following:

- If `/?` is specified as the single argument, it just displays a line with usage information
- If only the path is specified, then the date defaults to the current date
- If both the arguments are specified, then they are assigned to the appropriate properties
- If no argument is specified, the script prompts you for them

Adding Events

To complete this demonstration of Windows Script Components, let's add the ability to fire events to the `FileFinder` component. This requires two steps:

- Declare the event name in the `<public>` section, using the `<event>` tag
- Fire the event from within the script code by using the `FireEvent()` global function

I'm going to add an event called `FileFound` that will be raised each time a new file is added to the dictionary. This event will take one parameter containing the name of the file being added. The following snippet shows how `FileFinder.wsc` evolves:

```
<public>
   <property name="FileSpec">
      <get/>
      <put/>
   </property>

   <property name="Date">
      <get/>
      <put/>
   </property>

   <method name="Search">
   </method>

   <event name="FileFound">
      <parameter name="fileName" />
   </event>
</public>
```

The `Search()` function then becomes:

```
function Search()
   set fso = CreateObject("Scripting.FileSystemObject")
   set fld = fso.GetFolder(FileSpec)
   set files = fld.Files

   set dic = CreateObject("Scripting.Dictionary")
   for each f in files
      d = DateDiff("d", f.DateLastModified, Date)
      if d = 0 then
         FireEvent "FileFound", f.Name
         dic.add f.Name, f.Name
      end if
   next

   set Search = dic
end function
```

Finally, we need to make changes to `ff.vbs` to take advantage of the new support for events. For example, we can build the final string with all the names of the selected files as soon as we're notified that a given file has been added, saving us from visiting the collection when `Search()` terminates. I called this new file `ffx.vbs`.

```
' FFX.vbs
' Demonstrates the use of the FileFinder WSC component (with events)
' Usage: FF [path] [date]
' ---------------------------------------------------------------------

Dim oFF, str
Set oFF = WScript.CreateObject("FileFinder.WSC", "FileFinder_")

if WScript.Arguments.Count > 0 then
   if WScript.Arguments.Item(0) = "/?" then
      WScript.Echo "Usage: FF [path] [date]"
      WScript.Quit
   end if
end if

if WScript.Arguments.Count = 2 then
   oFF.FileSpec = WScript.Arguments.Item(0)
   oFF.Date = WScript.Arguments.Item(1)
else
   if WScript.Arguments.Count = 1 then
      oFF.FileSpec = WScript.Arguments.Item(0)
      oFF.Date = Now
   else
      oFF.FileSpec = InputBox("Enter the folder name:",, "c:\")
      if oFF.FileSpec <> "" then
         oFF.Date = InputBox("Enter the date as a string:",, Date)
      else
         WScript.Echo("You must provide the name of an existing folder.")
         WScript.Quit
      end if
   end if
end if

oFF.Search()

if str = "" then
   str = "No file found."
end if

WScript.Echo str

' -------------------------------------------------------
' Event handler
' -------------------------------------------------------
sub FileFinder_FileFound(fileName)
   str = str & fileName & vbCrLf
end sub
```

In order to sink event, we have to resort to the `WScript.CreateObject()` method that allows for an additional prefix name used to identify the script functions that actually sink events.

```
Set oFF = WScript.CreateObject("FileFinder.WSC", "FileFinder_")
```

To sink the `FileFound` event, we just write a `FileFinder_FileFound()` function that will receive any argument specified in the event declaration.

Generating a Type Library

A WSC is a COM object, so it may need a type library to inform clients of its potential. A type library is not always necessary, but if you plan to use the object in, say, Visual Basic, having it available makes working with the component much more comfortable and more efficient. The environment can use the type library information to provide the IntelliSense auto-completion feature, and to bind the component early.

Whatever the reason, if you need a type library for the WSC, just right-click on the filename in Explorer and choose Generate Type Library, or run a script like this to get more control over the properties:

```
' TypeLib.vbs
' Generating a type library for the specified WSC file
' ----------------------------------------------------

Set oTL = CreateObject("Scriptlet.TypeLib")
oTL.AddURL "FileFinder.wsc"                 ' Source name
oTL.Path = "FileFinder.tlb"                 ' Target name
oTL.Doc = "FileFinder Type Library"         ' Appears in the References
oTL.Name = "FileFinderTLB"                  ' Appears in the Object Browser
oTL.Write
oTL.Reset
```

By writing a script file, you can control all the available settings, rather than passively accepting the defaults of the context menu command. Moreover, you can insert some script code into the `register()` function mentioned above to generate a type library each time you register the component.

In the above listing, `Path` lets you decide the output name of the type library, while `Doc` and `Name` specify handy names to be used with Visual Basic and similarly friendly clients. Here's how the References window of Visual Basic looks once you've selected `FileFinder.tlb`:

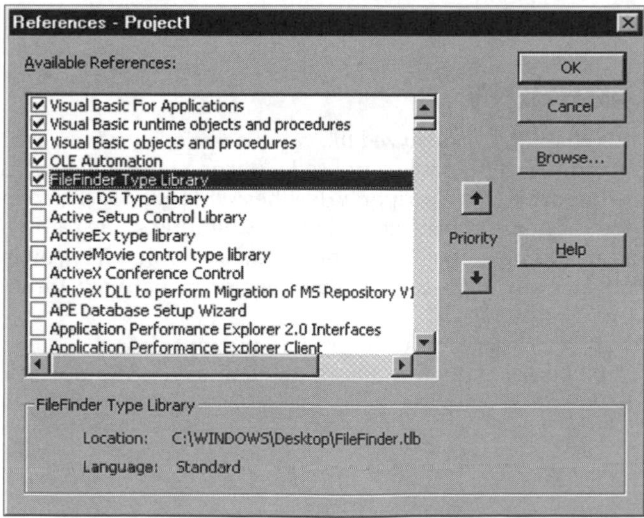

And here's how the component looks inside the Visual Basic 6 Object Browser:

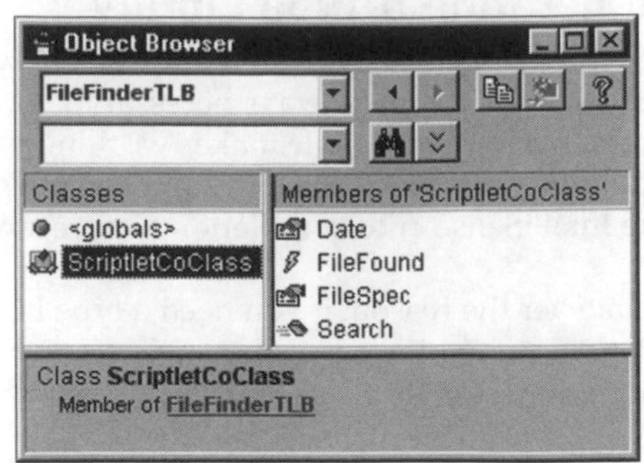

Note that some documentation still refers to the ProgID of the type library generator as `Scriptlet.GenerateTypeLib`*, but the latest WS development kit uses* `Scriptlet.TypeLib`.

Further Reading

WSC is a technology that's evolved incredibly quickly over recent months, and I strongly recommend that you keep an eye on the http://msdn.microsoft.com/scripting site for the latest news. However, the principles of the technology haven't changed very much. This is the reason that leads me to recommend a couple of my articles that appeared in the April 98 issue of MIND (*Server Scriptlets*) and the November 99 edition of MSDN News (*Writing COM Objects with Scripting Languages*) as further reading. Neither is up-to-date with the latest features, but both should give you a grasp of the underlying technology.

Summary

In this chapter, I've analyzed the various options you can choose when you want to plan and realize reusable script code, starting with a look at global functions that need to be imported into a script file. Neither WSH 1.0 nor the scripting engines provide native support for this feature, but by exploiting some features of VBScript and JScript you can end up with a kind of macro expander that lets you inject source code into a script. Happily, WSH 2.0 supports this feature natively, through a direct instruction.

I also had a closer look at VBScript and JScript classes and concluded with a discussion of COM objects written with scripting languages: Windows Script Components.

8

Dialog Boxes and the User Interface

The WSH object model encapsulates some of the features of the Windows operating system into scriptable objects, and lets you work with them quite easily. It is not a *complete* encapsulation of the OS, but then it was never supposed to be! The support for COM that WSH offers is the lever that allows you to write external components tailored to your own needs, making the model as complete as you need it to be.

You'll often use WSH scripts to do batch processing, involving operations such as moving files across the network or tweaking the registry, and in those situations you won't need an interactive user interface. However, this is not the only way to use WSH scripts, and in many other cases you *will* end up needing to ask the user for some information. For example, you may need to know the folder where the files to be moved should be taken from, or the configuration information to be stored in the registry. The facilities offered by VBScript and JScript for data acquisition are not impressive; what you need is an approach that is flexible and powerful enough to let you design fully-fledged interfaces for requesting and receiving information, not just simple modal input boxes.

In this chapter, I'll design and develop a COM module that works as a dialog provider — it will take a user's specification for how the dialog should look, and produce a modal window that contains it. I'll also supply you with a new component that provides a superior set of options for requesting simple data from your scripts' clients.

A Better Input Box

VBScript's `InputBox()` function lets you ask the user for a line of text. You can specify some default text, the prompt that explains the reason for the input, the title of the dialog, its position, and even a help page. The easiest way of using `InputBox()` is shown below:

```
Dim strInput
strInput = InputBox("Enter your user ID", "Testing InputBox", "despos")
If strInput <> "" Then
   MsgBox("Your user ID is: " & strInput)
End If
```

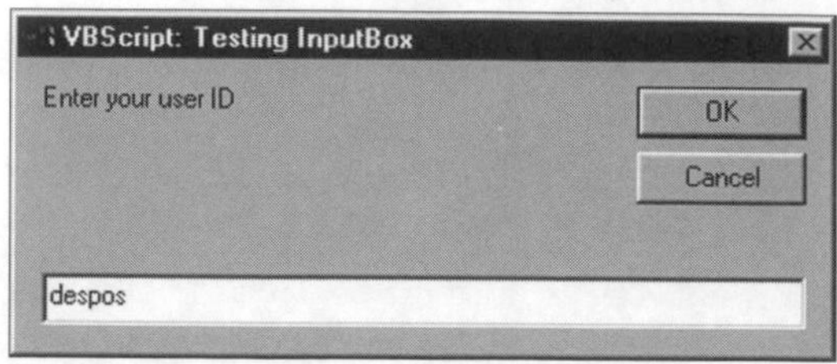

If you click OK, the function returns the contents of the edit box. Otherwise, the empty string is returned. The prompt string (Enter your user ID in the example) can occupy more than one line, provided that you use the `vbCrLf` constant to separate the various lines of text.

As you've seen in earlier chapters, this function can be quite useful, but there are some drawbacks with it:

- The title bar always prefixes the title with VBScript:
- The edit box only accepts one line of text, so you can only ask for one thing at a time
- There's no way of showing an icon to help the user understand the dialog
- There's no way to align or limit the length of the text
- There's no way to validate the text entered in place

Another potential problem is that there's no JScript counterpart of this function. If you can guarantee availability of WSH 2.0, which permits JScript and VBScript to be used in the same job, you can write a VBScript function that wraps `InputBox()` and then call that from within a JScript block. If just one of your clients is tied to using WSH 1.0, however, that's not an acceptable solution.

A WSC Component for InputBox

In the last chapter, I made much of the assertion that Windows Script Components are an excellent way to achieve code reuse across scripts and across languages. Let's turn this into practice by writing a WSC that lets you use `InputBox()` from JScript in a way that's compatible with WSH 1.0:

```
<!-- InputBox.wsc -->
<component>
   <registration progid="InputBox.WSC" />

   <public>
      <method name="Show">
         <parameter name="prompt" />
         <parameter name="title" />
         <parameter name="default" />
      </method>
   </public>

   <script language="VBScript">
      function Show(prompt, title, default)
         Show = InputBox(prompt, title, default)
      end function
   </script>
</component>
```

This short script just exposes a slightly simplified version of the `InputBox()` function in a language-independent manner. You can take advantage of this `InputBox.WSC` component from VBScript, JScript, or indeed any other scripting language:

```
// UseInputBox.js
// Uses VBScript's InputBox() from within JS code
// -----------------------------------------------------------

var obj, str;

obj = new ActiveXObject("InputBox.WSC");
str = obj.Show("Enter some text", "Title of the dialog", "<Default Value>");
WScript.Echo(str);
```

This short example is a good demonstration of the advantages of using WSCs over other language-specific techniques (such as classes and functions) to reuse code.

Improving InputBox

Even though we've solved the problem of using it from different languages, the main problem with `InputBox()` is that it's not very versatile or powerful. For my first stab at improving the situation regarding WSH dialog boxes, I'm going to provide a COM component that you can use in place of `InputBox()`, whatever your chosen scripting language. Compared with `InputBox.WSC`, this new component provides an enhanced programming interface and lets you control many more aspects of the window.

I took my inspiration for several of the facilities provided by this component from questions I've seen posted on the WSH newsgroups, and I implemented it using C++ and ATL. Annotated source code for the project is available from the Wrox Press web site, but the component can also be downloaded in binary form for immediate use. In this chapter I will document the programming interface and demonstrate the use of `WshKit.InputBox`, and so we start with a description of its single method:

Method	Description
`Show()`	Displays a dialog box, taking into account the state of the object's properties. Returns the contents of the edit box it contains as a string.

And its eleven properties:

Property	Description
`Label`	Text that describes the purpose of the dialog, in the same way as `InputBox()`'s prompt text.
`Title`	The title of the window. (No prefix is added automatically.)

Table Continued on Following Page

Property	Description
Icon	A comma-separated string specifying the name of the file containing the icon to be used, and the 0-based index of the icon within that file. The 2nd icon in the file `shell32.dll`, for example, would be indicated like this: `shell32.dll,1` The string must not contain spaces, unless the filename itself contains spaces. If you don't specify a path for the filename, make sure the file is in a searchable folder.
Text	The default text for the edit box. After the `Show()` method has returned successfully, this property is updated with the text entered. It retains its value if the dialog is canceled.
Multiline	A Boolean property that you can set in order to specify a multi-line or a single-line edit box. Set to `False` by default.
Password	A Boolean property that you can set in order to hide any characters typed in. I've made it work only for single-line text boxes; it is ignored if `Multiline` is set to `True`.
NumberOnly	A Boolean property that you can set in order to make the text box accept only numbers. I've made it work only for single-line text boxes; it is ignored if `Multiline` is set to `True`.
Uppercase	A Boolean property that automatically converts any character to upper case. It works while you're typing, and applies to both single- and multi-line windows.
MaxLen	An integer value that contains the maximum number of characters you can type. It applies to both single- and multi-line windows.
Align	A case-insensitive string that indicates the text alignment you prefer (it can be `left`, `center` or `right`). It applies to both single- and multi-line windows. For single-line text boxes, this feature only works under Windows 98 and Windows 2000.
Format	A string that can be set to a pattern compatible with those used by the `RegExp` object we saw in Chapter 5. When set, this property is used to validate the text in the box. If you don't set it, no validation is performed.

Using the InputBox Object

I created the `WshKit.InputBox` object to be as similar as possible (in simple use) to VBScript's `InputBox()` function, but so that you can see the differences, let's start with a VBScript example:

If you haven't done so yet, you'll need to register the component on your machine before this code will work. Navigate to the directory that contains `WshKit.dll`*, and type* `'regsvr32.exe WshKit.dll'` *at the command line.*

```
' InputBox.vbs
' Demonstrates a more powerful InputBox object
'-----------------------------------------------
Option Explicit

Dim dlg
Dim strText

Set dlg = CreateObject("WshKit.InputBox")

dlg.Title = "Good Morning, Dino!"
dlg.Label = "Please enter your user ID"
dlg.Icon = "shell32.dll,44"
dlg.Text = "despos"

strText = dlg.Show
If strText <> "" Then
   MsgBox strText
End If
```

This script prompts you with a dialog box and then displays a message box containing the text you entered. Beyond the changes to the syntax, the logic and structure of this routine is the same as that of the simple `InputBox()` demonstrated above. Look at the output of this script:

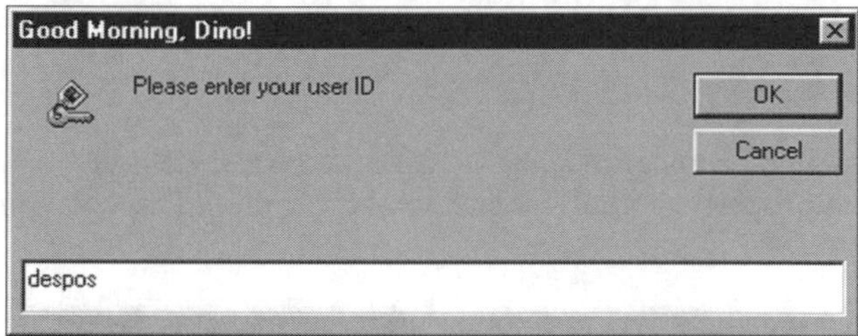

As you can see, it's not so very different from what we had earlier. If you neglect to set any of the properties and just invoke the `Show()` method from scratch, you'll get the following dialog box:

When you dismiss the dialog, `Show()` returns the contents of the edit box. This value is also stored back in the `Text` property, which means that when the dialog is dismissed with the OK button, the following code is equivalent to the previous sample:

```
...
dlg.Show
If dlg.Text <> "" Then
   MsgBox dlg.Text
End If
```

If you cancel the dialog, however, `Show()` returns the empty string while `Text` retains any pre-assigned value.

Entering Multi-line Text

The `Multiline` property lets you switch between a single line of input text (like in all the previous pictures) and a multi-line control (like an HTML `<textarea>` tag). This is useful if you need to collect a larger amount of text that's structured across more than one line, like an address or a feature list. Using the property is simple indeed:

```
// MultiLine.js
// A JScript multi-line textbox
//-----------------------------------------------------------------

var dlg;
var strText;

dlg = new ActiveXObject("WshKit.InputBox");

dlg.Title = "Good Morning, Dino!";
dlg.Label = "Please write your comments below";
dlg.Icon = "shell32.dll,41";
dlg.Multiline = true;
dlg.Text = "Type your\r\ntext here...";

strText = dlg.Show();
if(strText != "")
   WScript.Echo(strText);
```

After you've created an instance of the `WshKit.InputBox` object, you just need to set the `Multiline` property to `true` (or any non-zero value). This code produces the following output:

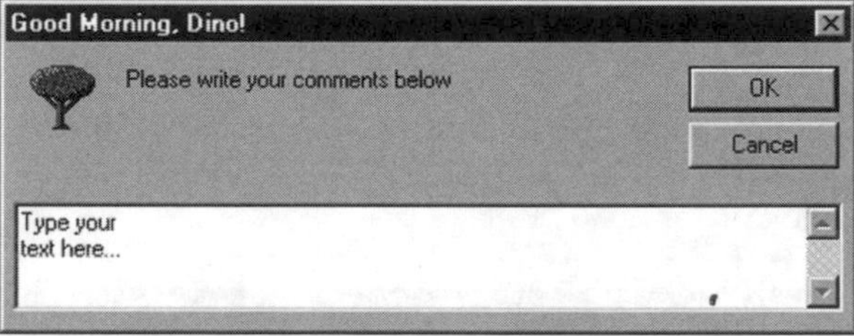

Note that you can split the default text across multiple lines by using the `\r\n` special characters in JScript, and the equivalent `vbCrLf` constant in VBScript. When you click the OK button, the text displayed is exactly what you typed:

Advanced Features of InputBox

The `WshKit.InputBox` object provides a whole series of properties addressing many different features, and all you need to do in order to use them is assign appropriate values. In this section I'm going to go through each one in turn, demonstrating how it works and suggesting when it might be useful.

Upper Case Text

The `Uppercase` property is implemented by means of a Boolean flag, and uses an inbuilt feature of the Windows edit controls to convert any character to upper case. Interestingly, this also works for accented vowels in the languages that require them, like Italian and French. The `Uppercase` property works with either single- or multi-line text boxes.

I've found this feature useful when asking the user for short answers (usually a single character) that are to be compared against a range of choices. For example:

```
// UCase.js
// Demonstrates Uppercase in a textbox
//-----------------------------------------------------------

var dlg, strText, strLabel;
var strA, strC, strM;

strA = "A - Analyst";
strC = "C - Consultant";
strM = "M - Manager";
strLabel = "\n" + strA + "\n" + strC + "\n" + strM;

dlg = new ActiveXObject("WshKit.InputBox");

dlg.Title = "Good Morning, Dino!";
dlg.Label = "Enter your administrative level:" + strLabel;
dlg.Icon = "shell32.dll,41";
dlg.Uppercase = true;
dlg.MaxLen = 1;

strText = dlg.Show();
if(strText != "")
{
   switch(strText)
   {
      case "A":
         strText = "You're an analyst";
         break;
      case "C":
         strText = "You're a consultant";
         break;
      case "M":
         strText = "You're a manager";
         break;
      default:
         strText = "What are you doing here?";
   }

   WScript.Echo(strText);
}
```

Instead of the property, an alternative way of implementing this feature would have been to convert the returned string in the client code, using a language-dependent technique such as JScript's `toUpperCase()` method:

```
strText = dlg.Show();
strText = strText.toUpperCase();
```

However, applying the conversion at this stage in the proceedings would mean that the string being manipulated by the program would differ (by case) from the one entered by the user — not an ideal state of affairs. Because the conversion being used here is automatic, you can assign any text to the object programmatically and still be sure that it will be displayed correctly, in upper case characters.

Limiting the Length of the Text

Another feature that many dialogs require (and not only in the realm of WSH) is the ability to limit the number of characters a user can type into a text box. In my component, you can do this by setting the `MaxLen` property to the size you need. Beware, though, that if you set the maximum allowed size below the length of some text being assigned programmatically:

```
dlg.MaxLen = 10
dlg.Text = "Type your text here..."
```

The text will be truncated. Also, if you set the property to a value less than 1, the text box will assume a default size that is different under Windows 9x and Windows NT. Windows 9x imposes a limit of 32Kb for single-line controls and 64Kb otherwise, while the maximum sizes under Windows NT are 2Gb for a single-line control and 4Gb for multi-line.

The above listing has already demonstrated a scenario in which limiting the length of the text to be entered was a reasonable thing to want to do. Like `Uppercase`, the `MaxLen` property works seamlessly with either single- or multi-line text boxes.

Hiding the Input String

When set to `True`, the `Password` property forces the `WshKit.InputBox` object to display an asterisk (`*`) for each character typed into the text box. As you can imagine, this is very helpful if you're requesting the entry of a password, and the following code demonstrates this behavior:

```
// Password.js
// Using the InputBox object to get a password
//---------------------------------------------------------

var dlg;

dlg = new ActiveXObject("WshKit.InputBox");

dlg.Title = "Enter Password";
dlg.Label = "Please enter your password (max 8 chars)";
dlg.Icon = "shell32.dll,44";
dlg.MaxLen = 8;
dlg.Password = true;

dlg.Show();
if(dlg.Text != "")
   WScript.Echo("Your password is: " + dlg.Text);
else
   WScript.Echo("No password specified.");
```

This results in the following dialog:

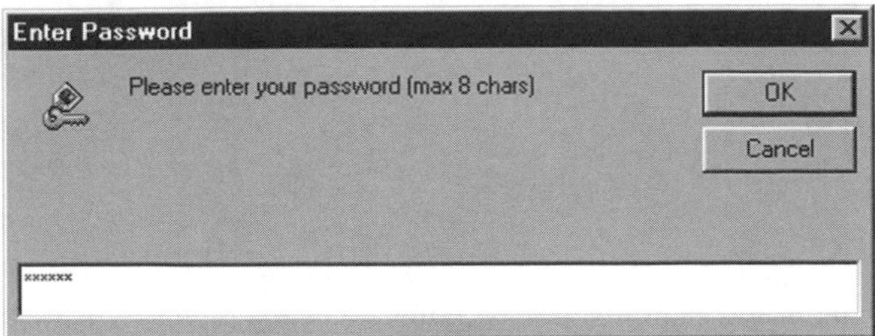

Text Alignment

There are many circumstances in which right-aligned text is more natural and intuitive than left-aligned text — perhaps the most obvious case is when you need to request numbers that represent monetary values. By setting the `Align` property to one of `left`, `center` or `right`, the `WshKit.InputBox` dialog will display the text justified accordingly.

You can actually assign *any* string to `Align`; if the object doesn't recognize it, it will simply default to standard left alignment. In addition, you don't have to worry about the case of the keyword, as `InputBox` will normalize it internally before making its checks. Once again, this property works fine with either single- or multi-line text boxes.

Regardless of the alignment, the string returned by the `Show()` method is just the sequence of characters you typed in. No padding or special formatting is performed.

> *Until the release of Windows 98, the Win32 SDK only allowed text alignment for multi-line text boxes. Since* `WshKit.InputBox` *is built using the Win32 edit controls, it inherits this behavior too. For this reason, the* `Align` *property won't work for single-line text boxes under Windows 95 or NT 4.0.*

Formatting Numbers

As I mentioned above, numbers often need to be right aligned in order to reflect their role in a specific context. From the standpoint of an input dialog box, this means a couple of things. Firstly, you should make sure that only numbers are typed in. Secondly, you should ask the dialog to display them from the right.

The `Align` property we discussed earlier satisfies the second of these points, while the `NumbersOnly` property filters the input characters and discards anything that's not a number.

```
' Number.vbs
' Demonstrates numeric styles in InputBox
'------------------------------------------------------------------
Option Explicit

Dim dlg
Dim str

Set dlg = CreateObject("WshKit.InputBox")
```

Continued on Following Page

```
dlg.Title = "Enter Price"
dlg.Label = "Please enter the suggested price for the specified item in US$"
dlg.Icon = "moricons.dll,48"
dlg.NumberOnly = true
dlg.MaxLen = 4
dlg.Align = "right"

str = dlg.Show
If str <> "" Then
   MsgBox "The price is: $" & dlg.Text
End If
```

This example demonstrates an `InputBox` object that only accepts numbers composed of 4 (or fewer) digits and right-justifies its content. The dialog it produces looks like this:

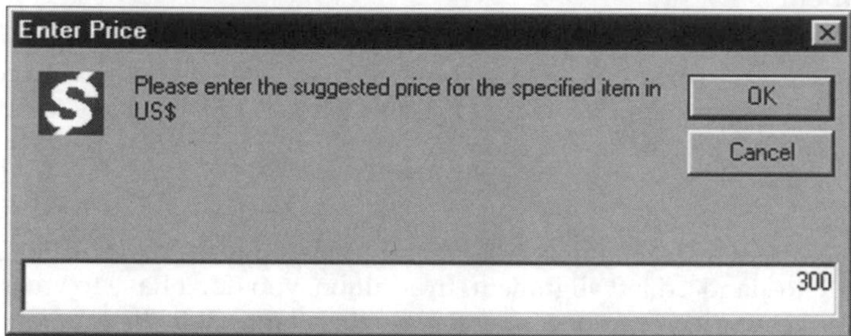

Regular Expressions

I talked about the introduction of regular expressions into the VBScript language in Chapter 5, and while it would be entirely possible to perform that kind of validation in client code after the dialog is dismissed, I chose to add it right into my component. When you set the `InputBox.Format` property to the pattern you want to be matched, the `InputBox.Show()` method won't return until the dialog is cancelled or a correct string is entered. Let's revisit that e-mail example you saw in Chapter 5:

```
' Validate.vbs
' Demonstrates the use of regular expressions with InputBox
'---------------------------------------------------------------

Dim dlg
Set dlg = CreateObject("WshKit.InputBox")
dlg.Title = "E-mail Address"
dlg.Label = "Please type your e-mail address in the edit box " & _
            "below, in the format (account@server.ext):"
dlg.Icon = "shell32.dll,46"
dlg.Format = "\w+\@\w+\.\w+"       ' Matches anything like word@word.word
dlg.Show

If dlg.Text <> "" Then
   MsgBox "Your e-mail address is: " & dlg.Text
End If
```

The rather less than intuitive string "`\w+\@\w+\.\w+`" means that the dialog requires a string made up of a word, followed by a `@` plus another word, followed by a period, followed by a word. The pattern that is created (which is matched by `account@server.ext`) is a bit more precise than the one we had in Chapter 5. The dialog displayed is:

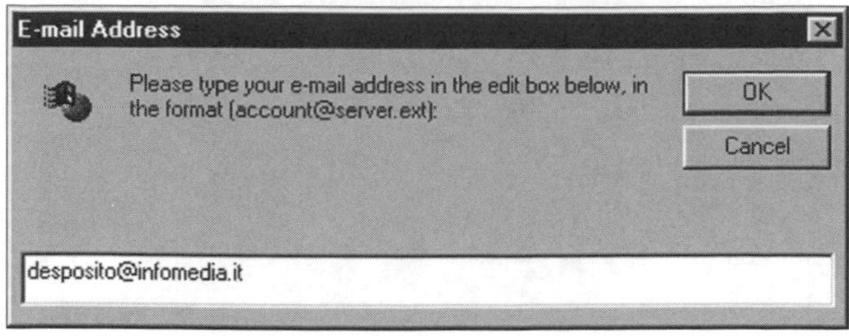

Since the text here matches the pattern, the dialog box can be dismissed with the OK button, and the final message box is displayed as usual.

> *Note that the pattern string shown above (*`\w+\@\w+\.\w+`*) also matches e-mail addresses like* `john.smith@my.server.com` *since the expression* `\w+` *permits strings that contain periods.*

If the text entered does not match the regular expression, the dialog will remain stubbornly in place, and a beep will sound to warn you that something is wrong.

Regular expressions and enhanced input dialogs that provide automatic support for them are a quick way to validate user input. Every time you need the user to enter text in a given format, you can associate a regular expression with the edit box rather than having to use `RegExp` code in your client script, like this:

```
While Not bOK
   str = dlg.Show()
   If str <> "" Then
      Ret re = CreateObject("VBScript.RegExp")
      re.Pattern = "\w+\@\w+\.\w+"
      If re.test Then
         bOK = True
      End If
   End If
Wend
```

Do remember, though, that regular expressions aren't a replacement for manual validation in all cases — you can't use them to perform comparisons against database fields, for example. Also, because you're placing a restriction on what the user can enter, it's a good idea to provide a visual cue for the format of the data, as I did in the `InputBox.Label` property above. Failing to do this will likely result in frustration for your users.

Putting it All Together

Let's take a look at a sizable example that demonstrates the potential of an input box component like the one I've written. In it, I'll simulate the steps required to make an expense claim. The user must enter their ID, and then answer some questions about the amount payable and the date. The amount payable will be validated according to the seniority of the user and their time in post.

```
<?xml version="1.0"?>
<!-- UserData.ws:  Collects data about a user -->
```

```
<job>
   <script language="JScript" src="adminlevel.js" />
   <script language="VBScript" src="employeeid.vbs" />
   <script language="JScript" src="expenseclaim.js" />
   <script language="VBScript" src="dateofclaim.vbs" />

   <script language="VBScript">
      Function CleanUp()
         MsgBox "Procedure aborted."
         WScript.Quit(1)
      End Function
   </script>

   <script language="VBScript">
      <![CDATA[
         Dim AdminLevel
         Dim EmpID
         Dim AmountPayable

         ' Get your administrative level
         AdminLevel = GetAdminLevel()
         If AdminLevel = "" Then
            CleanUp
         End If

         ' Get the employee ID
         EmpID = GetEmployeeID(AdminLevel)
         If EmpID = "" Then
            CleanUp
         End If

         ' Get the amount
         AmountPayable = GetExpenseClaim(EmpID)
         If AmountPayable = "" Then
            CleanUp
         End If

         ' Get the date of the claim
         DateOfBill = GetDateOfClaim(EmpID)
         If DateOfBill = "" Then
            CleanUp
         End If

         MsgBox "Your bill has been approved.",, "Congratulations!"
      ]]>
   </script>
</job>
```

This is the main part of the application. Each of the individual steps is accomplished by a specific function written either in VBScript or JScript that basically requests some input and then validates it.

Entering the Administrative Level

We ran into a procedure like this one when we were testing the `Uppercase` property of the `WshKit.InputBox` object. The user just has to enter a letter denoting their position in the company:

```
// AdminLevel.js
// Lets you enter a letter identifying your position in the company
//-------------------------------------------------------------------

function GetAdminLevel()
{
   var dlg;
   var strA, strC, strM, strLabel;

   strA = "A - Analyst";
   strC = "C - Consultant";
   strM = "M - Manager";
   strLabel = "\n" + strA + "\n" + strC + "\n" + strM;

   dlg = new ActiveXObject("WshKit.InputBox");
```

```
   dlg.Title = "Good Morning!";
   dlg.Label = "Enter your position:" + strLabel;
   dlg.Uppercase = true;
   dlg.MaxLen = 1;
   dlg.Format = "[ACM]";                  // Enter only A, C, M

   return dlg.Show();
}
```

The only notable aspect here is the pattern of the regular expression: `[ACM]` means any one of those three letters. The string is case-sensitive, but that's OK because the `Uppercase` property has been set to `true`.

Entering the Employee ID

In this demonstration, the employee ID will have a format of `A-nnnnn-n`. The first character, a letter, will represent their job title; the (up to five) numbers in the middle are a standard code issued by the company; and the final number represents the employee's time in post. I've chosen this format to illustrate the power of the `InputBox` component.

```
' EmployeeID.vbs
' Lets you enter a formatted employee ID number
'-----------------------------------------------------------

Function GetEmployeeID(AdminLevel)
   Dim dlg
   Dim strDesc, strPatt, strForm

   Select Case AdminLevel
      Case "A"
         strDesc = "Analyst"
         strPatt = "[A]\-\d{1,5}\-[1-3]$"
         strForm = "A-99999-9"         ' Clue for the user

      Case "C"
         strDesc = "Consultant"
         strPatt = "[C]\-\d{1,4}\-[1-4]$"
         strForm = "A-9999-9"

      Case "M"
         strDesc = "Manager"
         strPatt = "[M]\-\d{1,3}\-[1-5]$"
         strForm = "A-999-9"
      End Select

   Set dlg = CreateObject("WshKit.InputBox")

   dlg.Title = "Good Morning, " & strDesc & "!"
   dlg.Label = "Enter your employee ID (" & strForm & "):"
   dlg.UpperCase = true
   dlg.MaxLen = Len(strForm)
   dlg.Format = strPatt

   GetEmployeeID = dlg.Show()
End Function
```

Notice how the pattern string is adapted to the job title, as this ID is intended to change over time. Managers have IDs beginning with M, while consultants' IDs begin with C.

Entering the Expense Claim

This procedure accepts a value denoting an amount payable. It is validated against a maximum that depends upon the user's position, and the length of time they've been in that position:

```
// ExpenseClaim.js
// Lets you enter a monetary value
//-----------------------------------------------------------

function GetExpenseClaim(EmpID)
{
   var dlg, maxAmount, maxLen, strDesc1, strDesc2, shell;
   var empName, empNo, empAdminLevel, empCatLevel;
   var bOK = false;

   empName = LookupName(EmpID);   // Retrieve the user's name from a database

   a = empID.split("-");
   empAdminLevel = a[0];
   empNo = a[1];
   empCatLevel = eval(a[2]);      // Time in position

   switch(empAdminLevel)
   {
      case "A":
         maxAmount = 500;
         maxLen = 3;
         break;

      case "C":
         maxAmount = 1000 + (empCatLevel - 1) * 200;
         maxLen = 4;
         break;

      case "M":
         maxAmount = 2500 + (empCatLevel-1)*1000;
         maxLen = 4;
         break;
   }

   strDesc1 = "Enter the amount of your expense claim. ";
   strDesc2 = "(Up to $" + maxAmount + ")";

   dlg = new ActiveXObject("WshKit.InputBox");
   dlg.Title = "Good Morning, " + empName + "!";
   dlg.Label = strDesc1 + strDesc2;
   dlg.Align = "right";
   dlg.MaxLen = maxLen;

   shell = new ActiveXObject("WScript.Shell");

   // Validate the amount
   while(!bOK)
   {
      var money;
      money = dlg.Show();
      if(money > maxAmount)
      {
         var str1, str2;
         str1 = "I'm afraid you spent too much. Your maximum is ";
         str2 = "Sorry, " + empName;
         shell.Popup(str1 + maxAmount, 0, str2);
      }
      else
      {
         bOK = true;
         return dlg.Text;
      }
   }
   return "";
}

function LookupName(empID)
{
   // The world's simplest one!
   return empID;
}
```

Regular expressions can't validate input against a maximum value, so we have to use script code to make the comparison.

Entering the Date of the Claim

Finally, your users have to enter a valid date for the claim. Again, the correctness of the date is not something that can be easily checked with regular expressions, so I've chosen a different approach: I validate the date using script, and in particular VBScript's `IsDate()` function. We can, however, force the edit box only to accept strings of the form `mm/dd/yy`:

```
' DateOfClaim.vbs
' Lets you enter a date
'-----------------------------------------------------------

Function GetDateOfClaim(empName)
   Dim dlg
   Dim bOK
   Dim theDate

   Set dlg = CreateObject("WshKit.InputBox")
   dlg.Title = "Good Morning, " & empName & "!"
   dlg.Label = "Enter the date (mm/dd/yy):"
   dlg.MaxLen = 8
   dlg.Format = "\d{1,2}\/\d{1,2}\/\d{2}"

   bOK = False
   While Not bOK
      theDate = dlg.Show()
      If IsDate(theDate) Then
         bOK = True
         GetDateOfClaim = theDate
      Else
         MsgBox "Please enter a valid date."
         GetDateOfClaim = ""
      End If
   Wend
End Function
```

It would be fair to say the example has been a little contrived, but we've successfully used `WshKit.InputBox` to receive and perform validation on four different kinds of data, something that would have required a great deal more work in client code had we tried to do it with the `InputBox()` function alone.

Towards More Structured Dialogs

What was intended to be a simple, text-based dialog box has evolved to include many features. For all its assets, though, `InputBox` has a structural limitation: there's only one textual input element. It would be useful to have a more complex dialog in which several controls integrate and cooperate to provide a real 'console' for entering data — you wouldn't use `InputBox()` to collect all the data for an invoice, for example!

What you need is a component that's general enough not to force you to reinvent the wheel each time you use it, and smart enough to let you concentrate on presentation issues rather than implementation details.

Complex HTML-based Dialogs

When I think about dialog boxes, my mind naturally turns to Visual Basic and Delphi forms — container windows full of child controls. Some of these controls are static, but most of them are interactive and exist to get input from users. Dialog boxes of this type allow users to provide different kinds of data at the same time. In some senses, a dialog box is to complex data structures what `InputBox` is to a simple string of text.

Of course, a 'complex data structure' could be anything at all, and can't necessarily be identified with a single control (or even several controls) in the way that a text string can. An invoice, for example, is completely different from a date or a sales report. Furthermore, not all invoices include the same fields in the same order. Visual Basic, Delphi and Visual C++ provide tools for creating dialog boxes and integrating them with the rest of an application, but this facility is lacking in WSH.

The goal of the following sections is to fill this gap by developing a generic WSH container for any combination of controls. The final component will be a WSH dialog provider that you initialize by passing a template and then display modally. In creating this component, we'll have to face and resolve three issues:

- To decide what the dialog template is, and how to write one
- To decide how to let the dialog writer glue together the various dialog controls programmatically and have them interact
- To provide a programming interface to set and read back the contents of the constituent controls

If we start by getting satisfactory answers to these questions, it will help considerably in the design and coding of a brand new `WshKit.DialogBox` component.

A Flashback to Win32

Let's start by looking at how things work at the level of the Win32 platform. A dialog box is rendered via script code that describes its constituent controls. This script code is called the **dialog template**, and it's processed by the Win32 API functions that create dialog boxes, such as `CreateDialog()` and `DialogBox()`. Normally, the dialog template is stored in the application's resource (`.rc`) file; it is then compiled and attached to the final executable. When the application tries to create a dialog box, the dialog template is loaded into memory and processed. Broadly speaking, each line in the dialog template describes the style and position of a child control in the host window.

Looking at Visual Basic Forms

The above description covers the 'pure' Win32 approach that's typical of Visual C++-based programs, and despite the fact that different actors are playing, exactly the same things happen in Visual Basic and Delphi. Here, the container window is called a **form**, and the script is generated behind the scenes by the development environment. If you open a Visual Basic `.frm` file with an ASCII editor (say, Notepad), you'll find that it is composed of a descriptive section where all the controls are listed, each with their own properties. You manage the content of this data through visual tools in the IDE — the Property window, for example.

> *A* `.frm` *file also has a section containing all the code you've attached to the events of the various controls.*

What emerges clearly from these descriptions is the presence of two types of element:

- The constituent controls themselves (edit boxes, buttons, combo boxes, tree views, labels, etc.)
- A layer of code that glues all these controls together, providing the overall behavior of the dialog

We need to reproduce this in our WSH component too, but the problem is that Visual Basic, Delphi and Visual C++ all use an IDE to help with creating the dialog template and entering the code. While a WSH development environment would be most welcome, it's not something we have right now.

A Flashback to Internet Explorer

The Dynamic HTML object model provides a `window` object that has a method called `showModalDialog()`. You use it like this:

```
<html>
   <script>
      function init()
      {
         window.showModalDialog("template.htm");
      }
   </script>

   <body onload="init()">
   </body>
</html>
```

Now, provided that the content of `template.htm` is the following:

```
<html>
   <body>
      <H1>This is the dialog template</H1>
      <HR>
      <input type="text" size=10 value="Enter text">
   </body>
</html>
```

You'll get the result shown in this screenshot:

This is a pretty easy way to display a modal dialog whose template is defined by an HTML page. Of course, this solution is targeted to showing modal dialogs within the browser, and `showModalDialog()` is a method you can only use from within Internet Explorer. However, the idea of using HTML as the template language is rather intriguing, as there are a number of advantages to this approach:

- There is no need for a special IDE to create your own dialog templates — any HTML authoring tool will suffice.
- Following the 'two types of elements' design identified above, an HTML file has a code section (the `<SCRIPT>` tag) and a presentation section (the `<BODY>` tag). You can gather the controls and the code that makes them interact together, in the same HTML template.
- The chances are that because this is HTML, you don't need to learn anything new to use it.
- HTML lets you embed almost anything in your template, from complex graphics to animation, and from ActiveX controls to applets.

The fact that `showModalDialog()` is a feature of the Internet Explorer Dynamic HTML object model (and therefore not directly exploitable from WSH) isn't a big problem. You could create an instance of Internet Explorer object, load the document and access the method via script. Furthermore, there's an API function called `ShowHTMLDialog()` that's exported by `mshtml.dll` and does the same job. You could write an Automation wrapper for it in a matter of minutes, and solve the problem this way.

> *See the latest Platform SDK for documentation about* `ShowHTMLDialog();` *a working example is available in the* `SAMPLES\INTERNET\IE\HTMLDLG` *folder.*

The weakest point of this idea lies elsewhere, and has to do with the underpinnings of the technique. When you write a dialog, you need a way to accomplish the following three basic tasks:

- Initialize the controls
- Display the dialog
- Read the contents of the controls once the dialog has been dismissed

The first and last of these requirements aren't directly addressed by `showModalDialog()`. You still have to initialize the controls before the dialog is displayed and retrieve their values afterwards. Unfortunately you can only do this via script code embedded in the dialog template page. That's not very elegant, and worse still it's not particularly readable or maintainable.

> *Internet Explorer 5.0 has introduced **HTML applications** (HTAs), which are basically HTML files viewed through a very lightweight browser that produces the same effect as calling* `showModalDialog()`. *While this approach is great for the easy deployment of DHTML applications, it has th same drawbacks as* `showModalDialog()` *from the WSH point of view.*

The Definitive Solution

The Internet Explorer approach to dialogs advocates the use of HTML as the language for specifying the dialog template. This is a good approach, as HTML lets you host any number of any kind of object and use script code to glue them together. However, the definitive solution must provide a way to manage the components of the page from *WSH* script code, and not just from the HTML code. I want to be able to set the content of a text box from WSH, but still have the textbox update (say) the status bar when its content is modified. The page must have a life of its own, and contain code that lets the various components interact.

Providing the structure of the dialog by using an HTML page is a great solution, but the content of that HTML page must be externally visible in order to enable a WSH script to initialize the page elements before the dialog is displayed, and to read their values when the dialog is no longer visible. Happily, the DHTML object model lets us access the internals of an HTML page in this way.

Our HTML-based dialog will be made up of a template given by an HTML page, and a COM component that displays that page and returns a reference to the `Document` object of the page to us. To make things even simpler my implementation will include a group of `Get/Set` functions that recognize elements in the page by ID, so that you can assign or read the value of an element (say, an `<INPUT>` textbox) just by specifying its name. This saves you from knowing the details of the DHTML object model.

> *The name of the file containing this control is calle* `UIWshKit.dll`*, and if you don't want to go through the process of creating it from scratch that's described later on, you should register it on your machine now by issuing* `'regsvr32.exe UIWskKit.dll'` *at the command line.*

The Programming Interface of the DialogBox Object

The `WshKit.DialogBox` object provides a programming interface for creating a dialog, starting from an HTML page. It lets you control the content of any item in the page, whatever the HTML tag that identifies it:

Method	Description

`Create()`	Creates the dialog without displaying it. The method takes one argument — the HTML template:
	`dlg.Create("invoice.htm")`
	In order to let you initialize its controls properly the dialog isn't displayed immediately. You can use a special notation to specify that the template is to be found in the folder of the script:
	`dlg.Create("path://invoice.htm")`
	The `path://` pseudo-protocol just tells the component to add the current path to the filename. The function returns a Boolean value to denote success or failure.

Table Continued on Following Page

<table>
<tr><th>Method</th><th>Description</th></tr>
<tr><td><code>Show()</code></td><td>Displays a dialog that was previously created with the <code>Create()</code> method. You can also (optionally) specify the logical position of the window:

<code>dlg.Show([strPosition])</code>

Legal values for <code>strPosition</code> are: <code>center</code>, <code>topleft</code>, <code>topright</code>, <code>bottomleft</code> and <code>bottomright</code>. Note that this method always considers the size of the whole screen without compensating for the taskbar.

The dialog that is displayed is modal with respect to the calling application and window, and fully resizable.</td></tr>
<tr><td><code>Move()</code></td><td>Sets the absolute position and size of the dialog. It takes four parameters (left, top, right and bottom), all of which are required. The logical position you can specify through <code>Show()</code> overwrites these settings.

If you don't call <code>Move()</code> or pass a position to <code>Show()</code>, the dialog is displayed at the center of the screen with a fixed size.</td></tr>
<tr><td><code>GetItemText()</code>,
<code>SetItemText()</code></td><td>These methods read and write the <code>innerHTML</code> property of the page element with the ID you specify. The method won't work if there are several page elements with the same ID.

<code>obj.SetItemText "total", 0</code>

The above example sets the contents of an HTML tag with an ID of <code>total</code> to 0.</td></tr>
<tr><td><code>GetItemValue()</code>,
<code>SetItemValue()</code></td><td>These methods read and write the <code>value</code> property of the page element with the ID you specify. The method won't work if there are several page elements with the same ID.

<code>obj.SetItemValue "invoicedate", Now</code>

The above example sets the HTML tag with an ID of <code>invoicedate</code> to the current time.</td></tr>
<tr><td><code>GetItemSrc()</code>,
<code>SetItemSrc</code></td><td>These methods read and write the <code>src</code> property of the page element with the ID you specify. The method won't work if there are several page elements with the same ID.

<code>obj.SetItemSrc "companylogo", "company.gif"</code>

The above example assigns the specified image to the HTML tag with an ID of <code>companylogo</code>.</td></tr>
<tr><td><code>GetItemHref()</code>,
<code>SetItemHref</code></td><td>These methods read and write the <code>href</code> property of the page element with the ID you specify. The method won't work if there are several page elements with the same ID.

<code>obj.SetItemHref "recipient", "www.wrox.com"</code>

The above example sets the target URL for the HTML tag with an ID of <code>recipient</code>.</td></tr>
</table>

Together, these methods provide a great deal of control over the content of the HTML page you're displaying. Of course, the HTML tag you want to initialize or retrieve must have an ID, and you can assign an ID to any HTML tag with the `id` attribute:

```
<input type="text" id="invoiceID" size="10">
```

The `innerHTML` property denotes the HTML text associated with a given element. It's a read-write property, which means that by setting it you can change the content of the page being viewed. For example, if you have this:

```
<a id="wroxSite" href="www.wrox.com"><b>Go to the Wrox web site</b></a>
```

the `innerHTML` property contains `<b>Go to the Wrox web site</b>`. The DHTML object model also defines an `innerText` property, which differs in that it removes all the HTML tags from the string. In the case above, `innerText` would evaluate to just `Go to the Wrox web site`.

The methods listed in the table don't let you program any *objects* that you may have on the page, and for this reason I've added a property called `Document` that just returns a reference to the page's `HTMLDocument` object. Once you have that, you can make your WSH script do anything that you could do within an HTML page! I'll demonstrate this later on in this chapter.

Property	Description
`Document`	Returns a reference to the DHTML document object model

A further difference between the `DialogBox` object and the `showModalDialog()` function is that you don't need to worry about the OK and Cancel command buttons that are used to confirm or close the dialog; they are provided and handled by the object. If your dialog needs more specific buttons, however, then you *will* have to supply and deal with those yourself.

Using the DialogBox Component

To see this component in action, let's consider a plausible scenario such as collecting the information needed to prepare an invoice. In a realistic example of this exercise, there are many fields to fill in: the recipient, the invoicing company, the details of items, the price, the amount payable, the date, the invoice number, and so on. Using `InputBox` for all this would be completely impractical, but `DialogBox` can provide an HTML page with all the input controls and tables you need.

> *My goal in this chapter is to develop the* `DialogBox` *component and prove that it works. You'll find a more involved example of how to use this component in Chapter 10.*

```
' Invoice.vbs
' Demonstrates HTML-based dialog boxes in VBScript
' ----------------------------------------------

Dim dlg
Set dlg = CreateObject("WshKit.DialogBox")
If dlg.Create("path://invoice.htm") = True Then
   dlg.Move 0, 0, 700, 450
   dlg.Show
End If
```

The listing above causes `DialogBox` to search for an `invoice.htm` file in the folder containing the script. If it's found, this file is loaded and displayed in a window with the given size.

A Demonstration Dialog

To explore the potential of `DialogBox`, let's consider a fairly complex HTML page, like the one in this figure:

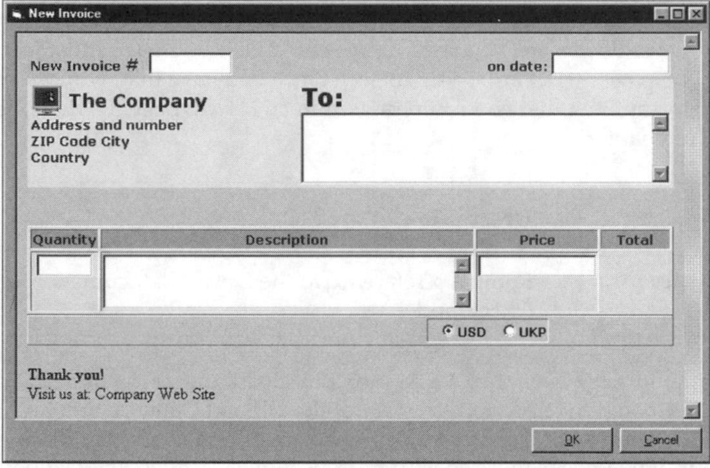

There are a number of placeholders in the dialog: there's the section about the invoicing company (logo, company name, address), the section about the recipient, and the invoice details. In addition, the invoice template also supports different currencies: you can choose between US dollars and UK pounds, and always have the equivalent value displayed in Italian lire.

I'm not going to present the entire source code for `invoice.htm` here, but you can find it on our web site together with the source for `DialogBox` itself. The page elements that have IDs are:

ID	Tag Description
`CompanyLogo`	An `<IMG>` tag representing the logo of the company
`CompanyName`	A `<SPAN>` tag for the name of the company
`CompanyAddress`	A `<SPAN>` tag for the address

ID	Tag Description
CompanyCity	A <SPAN> tag for the ZIP code and city
CompanyCountry	A <SPAN> tag for the province and the country
CompanyPhone	A <SPAN> tag for the company phone number
InvoiceID	An <INPUT> tag for the invoice number
InvoiceDate	An <INPUT> tag for the invoice date
Recipient	A <TEXTAREA> tag for all the details of the recipient
Quantity	An <INPUT> tag for the quantity of the invoice items
Description	A <TEXTAREA> tag for the item description
Price	An <INPUT> tag for the item price
Total	A <SPAN> tag for the total price
Payable	A <SPAN> tag for the total amount payable
Lire	A <SPAN> tag for the total amount payable in Italian lire
CompanySite	An <A> tag for a link to the company web site

All of these elements are addressable using the `Get/Set` methods I listed earlier, and you can enhance the `invoice.vbs` script to customize the look of the page like this:

```
' Invoice.vbs
' Demonstrates HTML-based dialog boxes in VBScript
' ------------------------------------------------

Dim dlg
Set dlg = CreateObject("WshKit.DialogBox")
If dlg.Create("path://invoice.htm") = True Then
   dlg.SetItemSrc "companylogo", "expoware.gif"
   dlg.SetItemText "companyname", "Expoware Soft"
   dlg.SetItemText "companyaddress", "One Expoware Way, 1"
   dlg.SetItemText "companycity", "00000 Roundmond"
   dlg.SetItemText "companycountry", "Rome, Italy"
   dlg.SetItemText "companyphone", "+39 06 12345678"
   dlg.SetItemValue "invoiceID", "7"
   dlg.SetItemValue "invoicedate", Now
   dlg.SetItemValue "quantity", 1
   dlg.SetItemValue "description", "Royalties for WSH Book"
   dlg.SetItemValue "price", "<lots of money>"
   dlg.SetItemText "total", "0"
   dlg.SetItemText "lire", "<i>No lire</i>"
   dlg.SetItemText "companysite", "our web site."
   dlg.SetItemHref "companysite", "http://www.expoware.com"
   dlg.SetItemValue "recipient", "Wrox Press" & vbCrLf & _
                                 "Arden House" & vbCrLf & _
                                 "1102 Warwick Road, Acock's Green" & _
                                 vbCrLf & "Birmingham, UK. B27 6BH"
   dlg.Move 0, 0, 700, 450
   If dlg.Show("center") = True Then
      MsgBox "You sent an invoice to:" & vbCrLf & vbCrLf & _
               dlg.GetItemValue("recipient") & vbCrLf & vbCrLf & _
             "for an amount payable of " & _
               dlg.GetItemText("lire"),, "New Invoice"
   End If
Else
   MsgBox "Template not found.", 64, "New Invoice"
End If
```

The dialog box now appears at the center of the screen, and contains all the information we've set using script code:

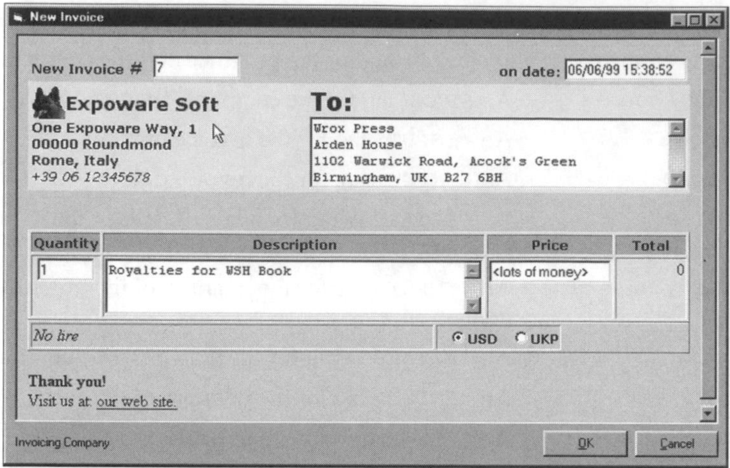

You have full control over the dialog template from your WSH code, and you can also add script code to the HTML template in order to arrange specific behaviors. In my page, as soon as you enter a number in the Price field and press *Enter*, the `Total`, `Payable` and `Lire` elements are automatically updated. The `SetItemXxx()` methods allow you to set the various tags, while the `GetItemXxx()` methods retrieve their values when the dialog is dismissed. Click OK, and you'll get the following message box from the code shown above:

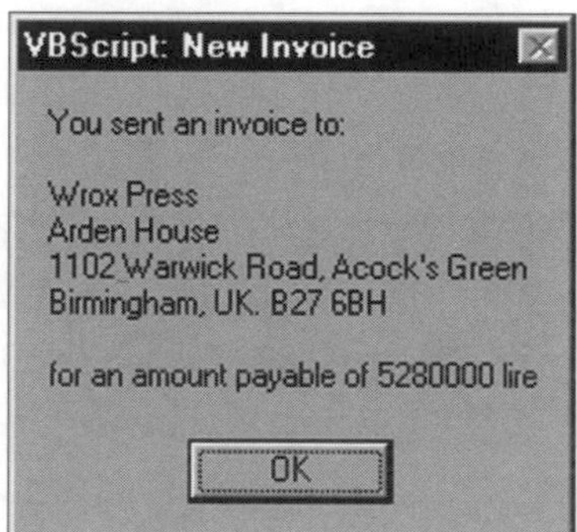

Of course, you should use the `Get/Set` methods as you would from within HTML code, so (for example) you can't use `GetItemText()` to retrieve the content of an `<INPUT>` tag.

Scripting Inside the Page

With the `DialogBox` object, you don't need to add script code to the page to retrieve initialization parameters (As mentioned above, this is what you need to do if you use `showModalDialog()`). However, if you want *interactive* controls, you will still have to employ scripting within the page. Here's the script code in `invoice.htm` that updates fields when you change the price of an item:

```
USDLIRE = 1780;
UKPLIRE = 2870;

function Price_OnKeyPress()
{
   if(window.event.keyCode == 13)
   {
      total.innerHTML = quantity.value * price.value;
      payable.innerHTML = total.innerHTML;

      if(usd.checked)
         lire.innerHTML = total.innerHTML * USDLIRE + " lire"
      else
         lire.innerHTML = total.innerHTML * UKPLIRE + " lire"
   }
}
```

Displaying Help Text

One of the dialogs shown above has an interesting feature: the mouse pointer is hovering over the name of the company, and a little explanatory note has appeared below the page, in the status bar. This is a built-in ability of the `DialogBox` object. Whenever the mouse hovers over an item with custom attribute called `tip`, the dialog displays the string associated with that attribute, for example:

```
<td tip="Invoicing Company" width="50%">
```

I could have used the `title` attribute for the same purpose, but that would have resulted in lots of tooltips that I didn't want— Internet Explorer supports the `title` attribute automatically.

Full Access to the Page

So far, I've demonstrated how to access tags throughout the HTML page, but only through specialized methods. The various `Get/Set` functions don't allow you to access *any* component in the page; each of them just addresses a particular property of a particular type of tag. What if you need to check some properties before setting or getting a value, or to access the properties of an embedded ActiveX control?

In these situations, the `Document` property comes to the rescue. Once you have that, there's no difference between executing a WSH script and manipulating an HTML page from within Internet Explorer. Through the reference returned by `Document`, you can access every part of the dialog template page. You can access and modify any element *at runtime*, getting the most out of DHTML. For example, here's how to add a tooltip to the company's logo from your WSH script:

```
Set wbDoc = dlg.Document
wbDoc.all("companylogo").alt = "Expoware Soft"
If dlg.Show("center") = True Then
   ...
```

Among other things, `Document` lets you work around the fact that the (admittedly fairly simple) `Get/Set` functions don't allow you to manage collections of items with the same ID:

```
Set wbDoc = dlg.Document
Set coll = wbDoc.all("price")
msgbox coll.item(0)
```

The above snippet, for example, would access the first item in the collection of all items whose ID is `price`.

Implementation Details

The WshKit.DialogBox component was written in Visual Basic 6.0. Basically, it's an ActiveX DLL made up of a class (dialogbox.cls) and a form (dialog.frm):

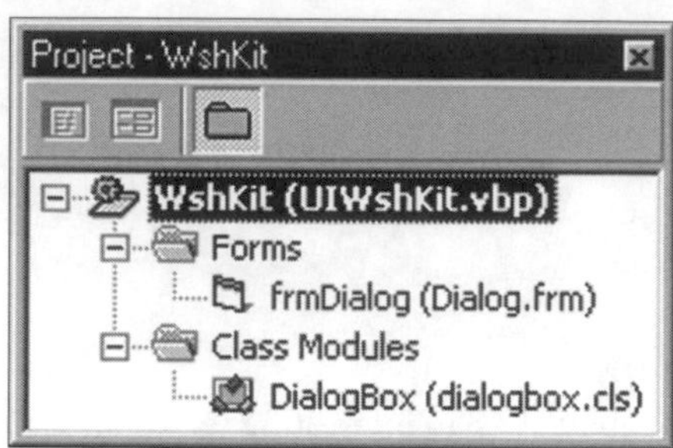

The class provides the public programming interface, while the form encompasses all the working logic. The project references the mshtml.tlb type library, which contains information about the Dynamic HTML object model implemented in mshtml.dll. Here's the complete listing of dialogbox.cls.

```
Option Explicit

Private Declare Function GetCurrentDirectoryA Lib "kernel32" _
        (ByVal nBufferLength As Long, ByVal lpBuffer As String) As Long

Private g_htmlPage As HTMLDocument      ' Document object reference
Private g_dlgTempl As Form              ' Dialog template


' Creates the form without displaying it. The HTML file contains the template
Public Function Create(ByVal szHtml As String) As Boolean
   Create = True

   ' Loading from the current path...
   Dim s As String
   s = Left(szHtml, 7)

   Dim s1 As String * 260
   Dim s2 As String
   Dim pathLen As Integer
   pathLen = GetCurrentDirectoryA(260, s1)
   s2 = Left(s1, pathLen)

   If s = "path://" Then
      szHtml = s2 & "\" + Right(szHtml, Len(szHtml) - 7)
   End If

   ' Store a reference to the form being displayed
   Set g_dlgTempl = frmDialog

   ' Force the form (that contains a WebBrowser) to navigate to the
   '  specified HTML page. The page will work as the dialog template.
   Set g_htmlPage = frmDialog.SetTemplate(szHtml)

   If g_htmlPage Is Nothing Then
      Create = False
      Exit Function
   End If

   ' The page title goes on the caption
   frmDialog.Caption = g_htmlPage.Title
End Function
```

```
' Returns a reference to the Document object of the page
Public Property Get Document() As Object
   Set Document = g_htmlPage
End Property

' Displays the dialog
Public Function Show(Optional ByVal pos As String) As Boolean
   Select Case pos
      Case "center"
         frmDialog.Move (Screen.Width - frmDialog.Width) / 2, _
                        (Screen.Height - frmDialog.Height) / 2, _
                        frmDialog.Width, frmDialog.Height
      Case "topleft"
         frmDialog.Move 0, 0, frmDialog.Width, frmDialog.Height
      Case "topright"
         frmDialog.Move Screen.Width - frmDialog.Width, _
                        0, frmDialog.Width, frmDialog.Height
      Case "bottomleft"
         frmDialog.Move 0, Screen.Height - frmDialog.Height, _
                        frmDialog.Width, frmDialog.Height
      Case "bottomright"
         frmDialog.Move Screen.Width - frmDialog.Width, _
                        Screen.Height - frmDialog.Height, _
                        frmDialog.Width, frmDialog.Height
   End Select

   frmDialog.Show vbModal
   Show = frmDialog.RetVal
End Function

Public Sub Move(ByVal l As Integer, ByVal t As Integer, _
                ByVal cx As Integer, ByVal cy As Integer)
   Dim tppx As Integer
   Dim tppy As Integer
   tppx = Screen.TwipsPerPixelX
   tppy = Screen.TwipsPerPixelY

   frmDialog.Left = l * tppx
   frmDialog.Top = t * tppy
   frmDialog.Width = cx * tppx
   frmDialog.Height = cy * Screen.TwipsPerPixelY
End Sub

' Get/Set the innerHTML property of a given tag, identified by its ID
Public Sub SetItemText(ByVal strID As String, ByVal strText As String)
On Error Resume Next
   g_htmlPage.All(strID).innerHTML = strText
End Sub

Public Function GetItemText(ByVal strID As String) As String
On Error Resume Next
   GetItemText = g_htmlPage.All(strID).innerHTML
End Function

' Get/set the value property of a given tag
Public Sub SetItemValue(ByVal strID As String, ByVal strText As String)
On Error Resume Next
   g_htmlPage.All(strID).Value = strText
End Sub

Public Function GetItemValue(ByVal strID As String) As String
On Error Resume Next
   GetItemValue = g_htmlPage.All(strID).Value
End Function

' Get/set the src property of a given tag
Public Sub SetItemSrc(ByVal strID As String, ByVal strSrc As String)
On Error Resume Next
   g_htmlPage.All(strID).src = strSrc
End Sub

Public Function GetItemSrc(ByVal strID As String) As String
On Error Resume Next
   GetItemSrc = g_htmlPage.All(strID).src
End Function
```

Continued on Following Page

```
' Get/set the href property of a given tag
Public Sub SetItemHref(ByVal strID As String, ByVal strHref As String)
On Error Resume Next
   g_htmlPage.All(strID).href = strHref
End Sub

Public Function GetItemHref(ByVal strID As String) As String
On Error Resume Next
   GetItemHref = g_htmlPage.All(strID).href
End Function
```

All the internal coordinates are expressed in twips rather than pixels, which is the default in Visual Basic. At the user level, though, twips aren't particularly friendly, and so the code makes it possible to specify the size and the position of the dialog in pixels. The `DialogBox` still needs to translate the pixels into twips, however, and this is done in `Move()`.

A twip is a unit of length. There are approximately 1440 twips to a logical inch, or 567 twips to a logical centimeter. A logical inch or centimeter is the length of an item on the screen that measures one inch or one centimeter when printed. Unlike pixels, therefore, twips are resolution independent.

Displaying the Form

The `DialogBox` controls a form that contains a WebBrowser control. The key function that connects the high-level interface with the form is `SetTemplate()`. This takes the name of the HTML template file, navigates to it and (if all goes well) returns a reference to the document object model. The reference is then made available through the `Document` property. `SetTemplate()` is a public method of the form object.

```
Set g_htmlPage = frmDialog.SetTemplate(szHtml)
```

`SetTemplate()` causes the WebBrowser (called `wb` in the sample code) to navigate to the specified page. Despite the fact that all this occurs before the window is actually displayed, the various navigation events are raised as usual. After instigating the navigation process, `SetTemplate()` waits for the `DocumentComplete` event that indicates that the page was loaded and its object model was initialized properly:

```
Private Sub wb_DocumentComplete(ByVal pDisp As Object, URL As Variant)
   g_bIsReady = True

   If LCase(URL) = LCase(g_htmlPage) Then
      g_bNavigateError = False
   Else
      g_bNavigateError = True
   End If

   Set g_htmlDoc = wb.Document
End Sub
```

To detect a possible error condition (typically this will be a "page not found" error), I compare the event's `URL` argument with a global variable that holds the name of the page. The two must coincide, or the `Create()` method will fail.

The next picture shows the layout of the form that's used to host the template page. All the controls are adjusted at runtime during the `Resize` event, which ensures that you can resize the dialog without restriction.

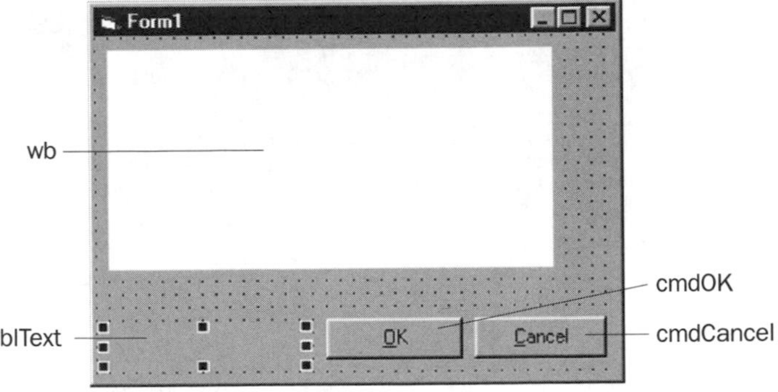

Here's the full source code for the `dialog.frm` file:

```
Option Explicit

Private Declare Function IsIconic Lib "user32" (ByVal hwnd As Long) As Long

Private WithEvents g_htmlDoc As HTMLDocument

Private g_bIsReady As Boolean
Private g_bNavigateError As Boolean
Private g_htmlPage As String

Public RetVal As Boolean

Private Const DLG_PADDING = 100
Private Const DLG_CAPTION = 500
Private Const DLG_2BORDER = 100

Private Sub cmdCancel_Click()
   RetVal = False
   Unload Me
End Sub

Private Sub cmdOK_Click()
   RetVal = True
   Unload Me
End Sub

Private Sub Form_Load()
   RetVal = False

   ' Default size and position
   frmDialog.Width = 2 * Screen.Width / 3
   frmDialog.Height = Screen.Height / 2
   frmDialog.Move (Screen.Width - frmDialog.Width) / 2, _
                  (Screen.Height - frmDialog.Height) / 2, _
                  frmDialog.Width, frmDialog.Height
End Sub

' Resizes the form, moving the constituent controls
Private Sub Form_Resize()
   Dim frmRealWidth As Integer
   Dim frmRealHeight As Integer

   ' Skip if minimizing...
   If IsIconic(frmDialog.hwnd) Then
      Exit Sub
   End If

   ' Get real width and height by removing twips for borders and caption
   frmRealWidth = frmDialog.Width - DLG_2BORDER
   frmRealHeight = frmDialog.Height - DLG_CAPTION
```

Continued on Following Page

```
   ' Position WebBrowser
   wb.Move DLG_PADDING, DLG_PADDING, _
           frmRealWidth - 2 * DLG_PADDING, _
           frmRealHeight - 2 * DLG_PADDING - cmdOK.Height

   ' Position OK and Cancel
   cmdCancel.Move frmRealWidth - cmdCancel.Width - DLG_PADDING, _
                  wb.Top + wb.Height + DLG_PADDING
   cmdOK.Move cmdCancel.Left - cmdOK.Width - DLG_PADDING, _
              wb.Top + wb.Height + DLG_PADDING

   ' Position the status text
   lblText.Move DLG_PADDING, wb.Top + wb.Height + 2 * DLG_PADDING, _
             frmRealWidth - (cmdOK.Width + cmdCancel.Width + 5 * DLG_PADDING)
End Sub

' Navigate to the page
Public Function SetTemplate(ByVal htmlPage As String) As HTMLDocument
   ' Navigate to the page
   g_htmlPage = htmlPage
   wb.navigate htmlPage

   ' Wait for the document to be completely loaded
   g_bIsReady = False
   g_bNavigateError = False
   While Not g_bIsReady
      DoEvents
   Wend

   ' Return the reference to the document object model
   If g_bNavigateError = False Then
      Set SetTemplate = wb.Document
   Else
      Set SetTemplate = Nothing
   End If

   ' Set the status bar
   lblText.Caption = htmlPage
End Function

' Fired when document loading completed
Private Sub wb_DocumentComplete(ByVal pDisp As Object, URL As Variant)
   g_bIsReady = True

   If LCase(URL) = LCase(g_htmlPage) Then
      g_bNavigateError = False
   Else
      g_bNavigateError = True
   End If

   Set g_htmlDoc = wb.Document
End Sub

' Fired when the status text should change
Private Sub wb_StatusTextChange(ByVal Text As String)
   lblText.Caption = Text
End Sub


' DHTML Events
' Fired when you right-click the document
Private Function g_htmlDoc_oncontextmenu() As Boolean
   g_htmlDoc_oncontextmenu = False
End Function

' Fired when the mouse is over an element
Private Sub g_htmlDoc_onmouseover()
On Error Resume Next
   Dim obj As IHTMLElement
   Dim strHelpText As String
```

```
    ' Retrieve the element that originated the event
    Set obj = g_htmlDoc.parentWindow.event.srcElement

    ' Get the help text if any and display it
    strHelpText = obj.getAttribute("tip")
    lblText.Caption = strHelpText
End Sub
```

Returning the Value

The form is displayed using its `Show()` method with the `vbModal` argument. There's nothing at the system level that informs us about how the dialog was closed, but this information is absolutely necessary, because it determines the return value to the calling script.

For this reason, the form maintains a global variable called `RetVal`, which it uses to store how the dialog was closed — through either OK or Cancel. This is the value that's returned to the WSH script via the `DialogBox.Show()` method.

DHTML Events

When you host a WebBrowser control with the intention of viewing some HTML pages, it's pretty likely that you'll want to 'hook' for events that take place at the document level. In other words, you might want to know about clicks and right-clicks on the document. Two typical scenarios for this are when you want to prevent the standard context menu from appearing, and when you want to know whether the mouse is moving over a certain tag.

These would be easy tasks to accomplish if we were within an HTML page being viewed with Internet Explorer, rather than a Visual Basic form. However, Visual Basic provides help in this area with the `WithEvents` keyword. If you declare an object variable like this:

```
Private WithEvents g_htmlDoc As HTMLDocument
```

you'll be able to write handlers for any of the events exposed by the `HTMLDocument` object, which is the COM object that represents the DHTML document object model (DOM). The following code shows how to suppress the context menu when the user right-clicks on the page being viewed through WebBrowser:

```
Private Function g_htmlDoc_oncontextmenu() As Boolean
   g_htmlDoc_oncontextmenu = False
End Function
```

Note that the `oncontextmenu` *event is only exposed by the IE 5.0 DOM.*

Likewise, to display help text when the mouse hovers over a certain tag, you can do this:

```
Private Sub g_htmlDoc_onmouseover()
On Error Resume Next
   Dim obj As IHTMLElement
   Dim strHelpText As String

   ' Retrieve the element that originated the event
   Set obj = g_htmlDoc.parentWindow.event.srcElement

   ' Get the help text if any and display it
   strHelpText = obj.getAttribute("tip")
   lblText.Caption = strHelpText
End Sub
```

The trickiest part of this code is retrieving the reference to the element that originated the event.

Summary

Do these objects cover all possible data acquisition and presentation requirements? Certainly not — a report-style component capable of displaying recordsets or arrays would be helpful, as would a hierarchical, tree view-based component for showing structured (possibly XML-driven) data. The list could go on and on. In this chapter, I've described and demonstrated two interesting and insightful components to enrich your programming arsenal. Interesting because they cover an area that is common to many applications, but neglected by the WSH object model. Insightful because the examples provided open up a window on some Windows features that you might exploit to build even better new components.

In the samples provided, I've been able to use VBScript and JScript interchangeably because of the language-independence of COM. You should feel free to use them anywhere in Windows. Elsewhere, this chapter discussed:

- An enhanced, COM-based version of VBScript's `InputBox()` function
- The use of HTML as a language for constructing dialog templates
- A COM component for controlling HTML-based dialog boxes

The next chapter will develop upon some of the things we've discussed in this one. I'm going to provide some more custom controls that can be used to augment the existing WSH object model, and show you how they can be useful in everyday situations.

9

A WSH Component Gallery

The fact that its object model is so open to augmentation poses some problems for the author of a book about WSH. He must both demonstrate the power of the script host as supplied by Microsoft, and provide some ideas and inspiration for extensions that go beyond this native functionality. The trouble with this is that it's very hard to come up with examples that are simultaneously non-trivial and useful to a wide range of readers.

In this chapter my goal is to provide a kind of WSH 'component gallery', with the intention of giving you the starting point for a repository of short solutions for *your* common tasks. I have chosen and will demonstrate three objects to address problems that have been raised at various times on the WSH newsgroups. The selection I have made tries to encompass the following issues:

- Problems for which a consolidated and commonly accepted solution is missing from WSH
- Programming topics that could reasonably be of interest to all WSH and script developers

The components in this chapter were variously developed using Visual Basic and Visual C++, but this book is not the place for a discussion of their internal construction. Instead, I shall restrict myself to describing the reasons that drove me to create them, documenting their programming interfaces, and demonstrating their use.

> *The binary files you need in order to use the components I'll be discussing in this chapter are available from the Wrox web site at* http://www.wrox.com. *If you're interested, the complete, annotated source code can also be downloaded from the same location.*

Before you begin to experiment with the samples in this chapter, ensure that you have run the installation script that's included with the source code for this book. Doing so will make certain that all the examples behave correctly.

Our List of WSH Components

The three COM objects that I am going to cover in the rest of this chapter are each intended to help with the solution of a specific problem that WSH developers may face in their everyday work. The complete list is as follows:

Component	Description	Useful when
`Browse`	Browses for files or folders	You need to select a file or files of a certain type
`Modeless`	Lets you display a modeless dialog box	You want to display messages to monitor a lengthy operation
`Process`	Returns a collection of all the process that are running at a certain time	You need to know whether a certain process is running, or which is the version number of any executable

Browsing for Files

A common requirement for developers is to browse the file system or the Windows desktop in order to pick up a certain file. The Shell Automation objects we met in detail in Chapter 6 provide an easy way of browsing for *folders*, via an interface based on a tree view, but the object I'm going to introduce here has slightly different features. The combination of the two objects will give you a range of choices when it comes to selecting files and folders.

The `Browse` object lets you browse for files using *either* the typical interface of the File | Open... dialog boxes *or* the tree view-based look of Explorer, and there are two methods to accomplish this: `Browse()` and `Explore()`. Using them, you can:

- Apply a filter to the files being displayed
- Select an initial folder
- Select any number of files
- Customize the title of the window

Let's examine the programming interface of the object:

Method	Description
`Browse()`	Displays the typical File | Open... dialog box with a given title, and lets you select multiple files subject to a filter that you can specify. If you select just one file, the method will return its fully qualified name. If you select more than one, you're returned a string like this: `folder, file1, file2, ..., filen`, where `folder` includes the full path and the various `files` are just name and extension. A zero-length string means that no file was selected. The method also takes an optional argument: `strFiles = object.Browse([pathName])` Where `pathName` is the folder to open initially. The method doesn't support non-file system folders such as `Printers` or `Scheduled Tasks`. By default, it opens the current folder.
`Explore()`	Displays a tree view-based dialog box that lets you explore the Windows shell searching for a folder or a file. This method doesn't support a filter string or multiple selections, but it *does* support non-file system folders and items. If you select one of these, its display name is returned. (A display name is the name Explorer uses to render the element, such as Printers for the printer folder.)

The properties that the object exposes are:

Property	Description
`FileCount`	A read-only property that returns the number of the files selected. It is supported by both `Browse()` and `Explore()`, although the latter always sets it to 1. If you cancel either of the dialogs, this property is set to 0.

`Filter`	Defines a tokenized string to specify which files should be shown in the `Browse()` dialog box. It must have the following syntax:
	
	`Display|filespec|` ... `Display|filespec|`
	
	Here, `Display` is a descriptive string and `filespec` is the wildcard string to be matched. Note that the final | is always required. For example:
	
	`JScript|*.js|All files|*.*|`
	
	The value of this property is ignored by `Explore()`.

`Title`	Sets the title of the dialog box in slightly different ways for `Browse()` and `Explore()`. In the former case, it is just the caption of the window; in the latter, it is the text of an embedded label.

Using the Browse Object

Let's examine how to take advantage of the `Browse` object. Its ProgID is `WshKit.Browse`, and the simplest way of using it from JScript code is like this:

```
var obj = new ActiveXObject("WshKit.Browse");
WScript.Echo(obj.Browse());
```

This results in the window opposite, from which you can choose the files you want. As I didn't specify an initial path, the dialog opened in the current folder, which in this case was the folder from which I started the script:

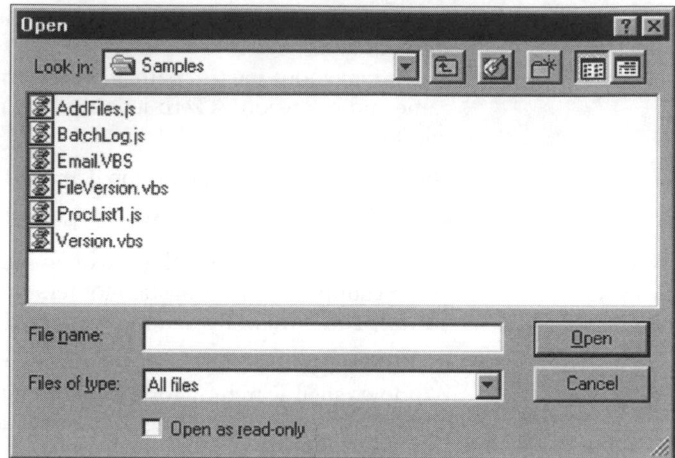

The first enhancement offered by the object's properties is the ability to change the caption of the dialog box, for which you just need to assign a string to the `Title` property. Furthermore, if you want to restrict the files that the dialog window can show, you can use the `Filter` property. The following snippet demonstrates how to select just `.js` or `.vbs` files:

```
var obj = new ActiveXObject("WshKit.Browse");
obj.Title = "Choose one or more files";
obj.Filter = "JScript|*.js|VBScript|*.vbs|";
WScript.Echo(obj.Browse());
```

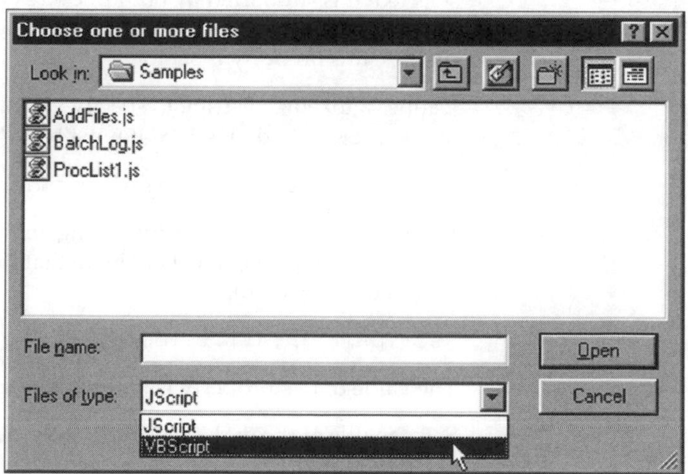

If you want the dialog to open on a specific folder, you simply have to specify it as an argument to `Browse()`:

```
var obj = new ActiveXObject("WshKit.Browse");
obj.Title = "Choose one or more files";
obj.Filter = "JScript|*.js|VBScript|*.vbs|"
WScript.Echo(obj.Browse("c:\\"));
```

Now the dialog will open in the root of the C drive. Note once again that this method doesn't support folders that aren't part of the file system, such as `Printers` or `Dial-up Networking`.

Multiple File Selection

As I mentioned earlier, the `Browse()` method allows you to select multiple files at the same time. In this case, you're returned a semicolon-separated string in which the first item is the fully qualified folder name, and the remaining items are just the filenames. Using a semicolon as the separator makes it easy to split the string later on and lets you manage long filenames that contain spaces with ease.

The following example shows a way to manage single and multiple selections seamlessly:

```
' Browse.vbs
' Demonstrates how to select script files using the OpenFile dialog.
'--------------------------------------------------------------------
Option Explicit

Dim browse
Dim files, strFiles
Dim arrayFiles

Set browse = CreateObject("WshKit.Browse")
browse.Title = "Pick up a script file"
browse.Filter = "JScript|*.js|VBScript|*.vbs|"

files = browse.Browse("c:\windows\samples\wsh")

' Splits the string to an array
If browse.FileCount > 1 Then
   arrayFiles = split(files, ";")

   ' 0th item is the folder path
   Dim i
   For i = 1 To browse.FileCount
      strFiles = strFiles & arrayFiles(0) & "\" & arrayFiles(i) & vbCrLf
   Next
Else
   strFiles = files
End If

' Show the result using MsgBox()
MsgBox strFiles,, browse.FileCount & " file(s) selected"
```

If you were to select files as shown in this figure:

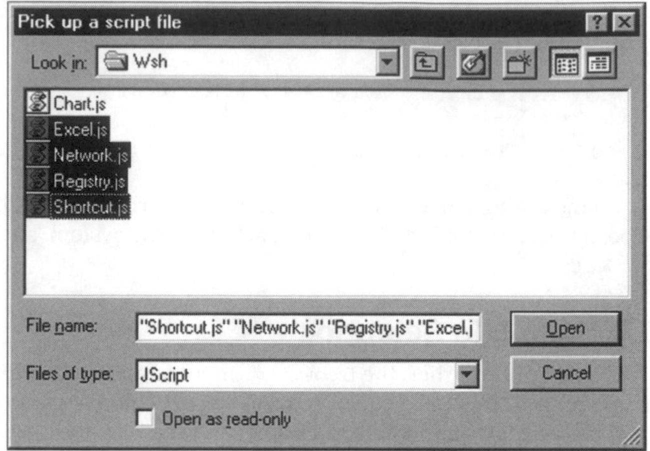

You would get a final message box that looked like this:

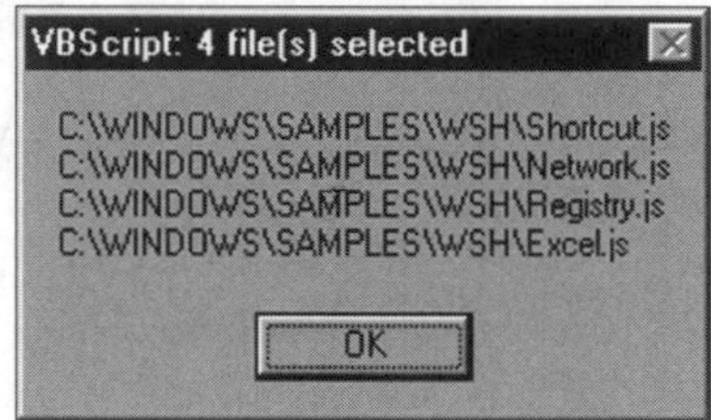

The code works because the string returned by `Browse.Browse()` is structured in the following fashion:

```
C:\Windows\Samples\Wsh;
Shortcut.js;
Network.js;
Registry.js;
Excel.js
```

I've broken it onto separate lines for readability purposes, but you should imagine it as a continuous string. When this string is processed by VBScript's `split()` function:

```
arrayFiles = split(files, ";")
```

it results in a new array in which the 0th element is the folder, and the remaining items are the selected filenames. A simple loop like the one below then produces a multi-line string like the one shown above:

```
For i = 1 to browse.FileCount
   strFiles = strFiles & arrayFiles(0) & "\" & arrayFiles(i) & vbCrLf
Next
```

Things are no different when you're using JScript, because it has a `split()` method that does the same job as the VBScript function. The full JScript code for the example is reproduced below. As you can see, there are only minor syntax-dependent differences:

```
// Browse.js
// Demonstrates how to select script files using the OpenFile dialog.
//--------------------------------------------------------------------

var browse
var files, strFiles
var arrayFiles

browse = new ActiveXObject("WshKit.Browse");
browse.Title = "Pick up a script file";
browse.Filter = "JScript|*.js|VBScript|*.vbs|";

files = browse.Browse("c:\\windows\\samples\\wsh");

if(browse.FileCount > 1)
{
   arrayFiles = files.split(";");
   strFiles = "";

   // 0th item is the folder path
   for(i = 1; i <= browse.FileCount; i++)
      strFiles += arrayFiles[0] + "\\" + arrayFiles[i] + "\r\n";
}
else
   strFiles = files;

WScript.Echo(strFiles);
```

The next figure shows the output of this code when you select just two files:

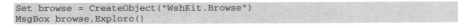

Exploring for Files and Folders

If you don't want an interface based on the File | Open... dialog, you can use the `Explore()` method to display an Explorer-like view instead:

```
Set browse = CreateObject("WshKit.Browse")
MsgBox browse.Explore()
```

As you can see, this window lets you browse for files too, but it doesn't support multiple selections. With `Explore()`, you can select a file *or* a folder, while `Browse()` only allows you to pick up files. The `Title` property affects the label that appears at the top of the dialog — Choose a file or folder: in the picture here.

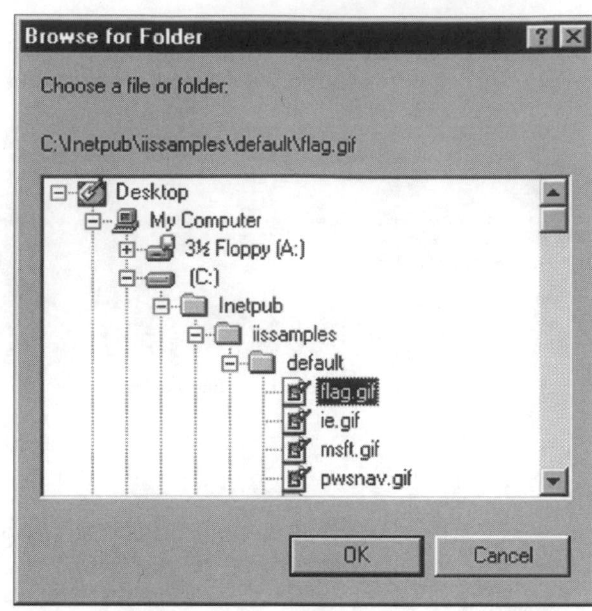

You can force `Explore()` to go straight to a specified folder at startup by passing the folder name on the command line. The following code, for example, automatically displays the contents of the `Favorites` folder. Notice the use of the `SpecialFolders` collection that I introduced in Chapter 4:

```
Set browse = CreateObject("WshKit.Browse")
browse.Title = "Pick up a file from the Favorites folder:"

Set shell = CreateObject("WScript.Shell")
Set folders = shell.SpecialFolders

MsgBox browse.Explore(folders.item("Favorites"))
```

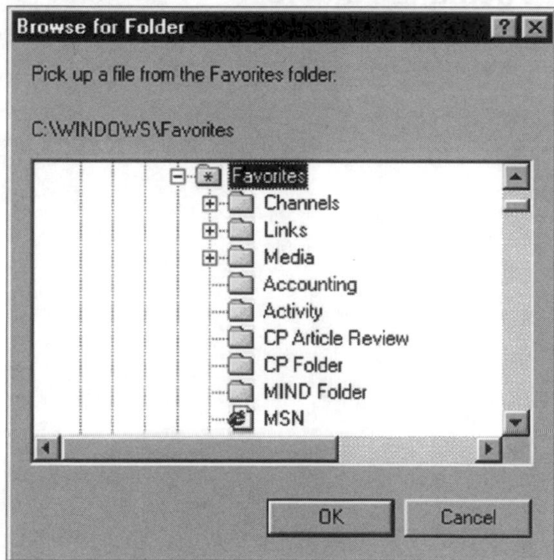

`Explore()` is based on the API function `SHBrowseForFolder()`, a peculiarity of which is that it provides support for special folders regardless of whether they are based on a file system directory. `Favorites` is a special folder, for example, but it's a kind of shortcut for an ordinary directory like `c:\windows\favorites`. The `Explore()` method is also capable of returning *non* file system items, like printers.

A Whiteboard Component

If you need to display some messages then WSH provides you with a range of choices, from VBScript's `MsgBox()` to `WScript`'s `Echo()` and `Popup()`. The last of these, in particular, has an interesting feature that we examined in Chapter 4: it can be made to close automatically after a certain number of seconds.

All these functions, however, share a common trait: they halt execution of the script until the user has dismissed the message box. In Windows terms, these message boxes are called **modal dialogs**, and from the Windows Script Host's perspective they are effectively breakpoints in your script code. The instruction that follows a call to `MsgBox()`, for example, will not execute until you dismiss the dialog by clicking one of its buttons.

Of course, there are circumstances in which this is exactly what you need. If you have a message for the user to reply to, or the dialog requires the user's attention, you don't want the script to continue until that has been dealt with. The choices offered by WSH are then quite adequate.

But what if you're starting a lengthy operation and want to give some feedback to the user without stopping the operation itself — if you want to update a progress bar according to the completion of an operation, for example? Or how about when you want to log the activity of a script? Sure, you could write the various messages to disk in a text file, but to look at them you need to stop the script and then load the file in a text editor.

These two scenarios are different sides of the same coin: you need a component that is visible to the user (through a window), but whose content can be updated over time until the user closes the window. It must be possible to hide or show the window as many times as required, and in such a way that it doesn't interfere with script execution. This means, for example, that you could start a lengthy task like uploading a file over a network and update a report of the number of bytes transferred every so often. In this way, the user has some feedback about what's going on.

In essence, we're talking about a **modeless dialog**, which differs from a modal dialog in that once the dialog has been created, the method that caused it simply returns. The script is responsible for the window and must take care of displaying and destroying it upon exit or before. Modal dialogs, on the other hand, do all this by themselves.

A method that creates a modal dialog (say, `WScript.Echo()`) causes the following steps to take place:

- Creation of the window
- Looping until the user clicks one of the available buttons
- Dismissal of the window

- Destruction of the window
- Returning a value to the script

The last four steps make the difference between modal and modeless dialogs. Once the window prompted by `WScript.Echo()` has been closed, there's no way to call it back to the screen to display another message. Exactly this feature, however, is provided by modeless dialogs.

A Modeless Dialog Component

As a script programmer, it so happened that I needed a component like this one for my own business. When I came to design it, there were two main issues: displaying *non-blocking* messages during script execution, and providing a log window.

In the end, I found myself making double use of the window: as a kind of 'watch window' for debugging during development (I confess to having no great affection for the Microsoft Script Debugger), and as a log window for the script to leave messages for the user. Its third potential use would be as a very simple framework to display a collection of data.

Let's start, then, by looking at how I designed this component. It was written in Visual Basic 6.0, and it has a ProgID of `WshKit.Modeless`.

The Programming Interface

The `Modeless` component is based on a form with a fixed layout. It has a window to hold and display the text, and a button. The component can work in two modes: as a normal status window, or as a more specialized log window. The difference is that in the former case, the window to hold the text is a simple label and any new assignment overwrites the previous one. In log mode, the window is a list box to which you just add messages in the order they arrive. The button has customizable text (Cancel by default) and fires an event when it's clicked.

The modeless dialog is created as soon as an instance of the `Modeless` component is generated with `CreateObject()` or `ActiveXObject`. It is not shown by default, and you must destroy it before exiting the script.

Method	Description
`Show()`	Makes the window appear. The window retains position, size and content. When the window is displayed, you can resize it.
`Hide()`	Hides the window but doesn't destroy it.
`Destroy()`	Destroys the window.
`WriteLine()`	Adds a line of text to the log window.
`Save()`	Saves the content of the log window (if any) to a text file. This method takes the name of the output file as an argument.

The component has the following properties:

Property	Description
`Title`	Specifies the text to be displayed in the window's caption bar. By design, the window has a tiny caption.
`Label`	Specifies the text to be displayed when the component is not working in log mode. When you set this text, any existing label is overwritten.
`ButtonText`	Specifies the caption of the button.
`LogMode`	Boolean value that determines whether the component is working in log or normal mode. Set to `False` by default (which means normal mode). When in log mode the window can be resized and is larger by default.
`Log`	When the control is working in log mode, it displays text through a list box, and this property returns a reference to that list box object. By calling the standard methods and properties of a list box, you can add and delete lines and even change its colors.

Switching to log mode while an instance of the component is running hides the label but doesn't delete it, and the same thing happens to the list box when you go in the opposite direction. In other words, switching back and forth between normal and log mode hides the text associated with the other mode, but doesn't erase it.

Event	Description
`Click`	This event is fired when the button is clicked. Typical use of the button is to cancel a lengthy operation.

Let's have our first example of how to use this component. The script below simulates a lengthy operation during which you display a progressive value to represent the amount of work already done:

```
' Progress1.vbs
' Sample VBS script to demonstrate non-blocking messages
' ----------------------------------------------------------
Option Explicit

Dim obj
Set obj = CreateObject("WshKit.Modeless")

obj.Title = "WSH Whiteboard"
obj.Show

' Simulates a lengthy operation
Dim i
For i = 1 To 4000

    ' Do something here
```

Continued on Following Page

```
   ' Update the progress bar
   Dim nPerc, str
   nPerc = (i \ 40)
   str = "Completed " & nPerc & "%"
   obj.Label = str
Next

' Final message
MsgBox "Finished!"

' Destroy the dialog
obj.Destroy
```

The result is shown in the figure:

A more interesting exercise is to find a way of stopping an operation in progress. For this to occur, of course, the operation itself must be interruptible — displaying feedback (and subsequently interrupting) while a certain task is accomplished is possible only if that task takes place under the control of the script. If all you're doing is invoking a method on an object, it's quite impossible to obtain this level of control.

For example, let's suppose that you want to retrieve and process all the e-mail messages you've received from a given user:

```
' Email.vbs
' Processes e-mail messages from a given sender
' ---------------------------------------------------------
Option Explicit

' Sender to search for
Dim senderName
If WScript.Arguments.Count = 0 Then
   senderName = InputBox("Enter the name of the sender:")
Else
   senderName = WScript.Arguments.Item(0)
End if

If senderName = "" Then
   WScript.Quit
End If

Const olFolderInbox = 6           ' Identifies the Outlook Inbox folder

Dim obj
Set obj = CreateObject("WshKit.Modeless")
obj.Title = "Messages from: " & senderName
obj.Label = "No messages found."
obj.Show

' Initializes Outlook
Dim oMsgs, oInbox, oNS, outlook
Set outlook = CreateObject("Outlook.Application")
Set oNS = outlook.GetNamespace("MAPI")
Set oInbox = oNS.Session.GetDefaultFolder(olFolderInbox)
Set oMsgs = oInbox.Items
```

```
Dim msg, nMsgs, i
nMsgs = 0
i = 0
For Each msg In oMsgs
   i = i + 1

   ' Process each message
   If InStr(1, msg.SenderName, senderName) Then
      nMsgs = nMsgs + 1
   End If

   Dim nPerc, str
   nPerc = (i * 100 \ oMsgs.Count)
   str = CStr(nMsgs) & " message(s) found. " & nPerc & "% loaded."

   obj.Label = str
Next

' Final message
MsgBox nMsgs & " message(s) found."
obj.Destroy
```

If you do something like this — that is, handle the whole operation from your script code — you should be able to add some code that will stop the processing. Here's what you could get from this script:

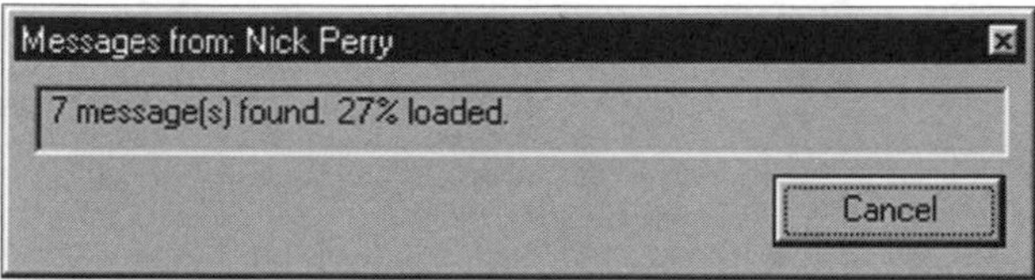

However, if you're using (perhaps for performance reasons) a custom component that does the work internally and just returns the number of messages, there's no way for our dialog (or indeed any other component) to 'break in' and get progress information.

Interrupting the Operation

The `Modeless` component exposes an event that you can employ to break the operation when the button is clicked. (Remember that you can change the text of the button by using the `ButtonText` property.) There are a few changes to the code:

```
' Email2.vbs
' Processes e-mail messages from a given sender and handles events
' ---------------------------------------------------------------------
Option Explicit

' Sender to search for
Dim senderName
If WScript.Arguments.Count = 0 Then
   senderName = InputBox("Enter the name of the sender:")
Else
   senderName = WScript.Arguments.Item(0)
End if

If senderName = "" Then
   WScript.Quit
End If

Const olFolderInbox = 6          ' Identifies the Outlook Inbox folder
```

Continued on Following Page

```
Dim obj
Dim bExit
Set obj = WScript.CreateObject("WshKit.Modeless", "Message_")
obj.Title = "Messages from: " & senderName
obj.Label = "No messages found."
obj.Show

' Initializes Outlook
Dim oMsgs, oInbox, oNS, outlook
Set outlook = CreateObject("Outlook.Application")
Set oNS = outlook.GetNamespace("MAPI")
Set oInbox = oNS.Session.GetDefaultFolder(olFolderInbox)
Set oMsgs = oInbox.Items

bExit = False
Dim msg, nMsgs, i
nMsgs = 0
i = 0
For Each msg In oMsgs
   i = i + 1

   ' Process each message
   If InStr(1, msg.SenderName, senderName) Then
      nMsgs = nMsgs + 1
   End If

   Dim nPerc, str
   nPerc = (i * 100 \ oMsgs.Count)
   str = CStr(nMsgs) & " message(s) found. " & nPerc & "% loaded."

   obj.Label = str

   If bExit Then
      Exit For
   End If
Next

' Final message
If bExit = True Then
   MsgBox "Stopped when: " & obj.Label
Else
   MsgBox nMsgs & " message(s) found from " & senderName
End If

obj.Destroy

Function Message_Click()
   bExit = True
End Function
```

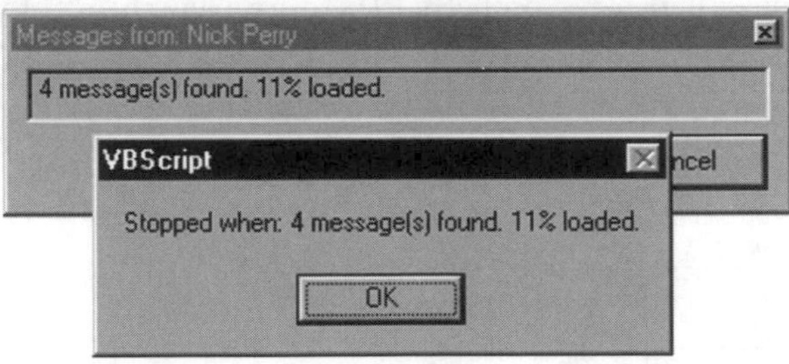

Basically, you need to create an instance of `WshKit.Modeless` using `WScript.CreateObject()` in order to exploit the final argument to sink events:

```
Set obj = WScript.CreateObject("WshKit.Modeless", "Message_")
```

The event exposed is named `Click`, so the event handler must be a procedure named `Message_Click()`:

```
Function Message_Click()
   bExit = True
End Function
```

You can do whatever you need here, but in order to stop the iteration it's enough to set a Boolean variable to `True` and then check it in the body of the loop:

```
If bExit Then
   Exit For
End If
```

When it is detected that the flag has been set to `True`, the loop is abandoned, resulting in the pair of dialogs you can see in the above screenshot.

Switching to Log mode

In normal mode, the only thing the component makes available for displaying text is a simple label. If you need more — say, a list of strings that track the evolution of the application — you should switch the `Modeless` object to work in log mode.

Log mode makes it unlikely that you'll want a button named Cancel; more probable is that you'll need to keep the window visible for the lifetime of the script, or at least until the user closes it. For this reason, the caption on my button for this part of the demonstration will be Close.

The following script shows how to use `Modeless` to log the various steps a script takes during execution. On this occasion, the example doesn't do anything particularly interesting — it just scans all the available drives — but the program does make use of all the features of the `Modeless` object's log mode.

```
' LogMode.vbs
' Demonstrates Log mode
' ----------------------------------------------------------
Option Explicit

Const Fixed = 2
Dim aDriveType
aDriveType = Array("Unknown", "Removable", "Fixed", _
                   "Network", "CdRom", "RAM Disk")

Dim obj
Set obj = WScript.CreateObject("WshKit.Modeless", "Log_")

obj.Title = "WSH Log Window"
obj.LogMode = True
obj.ButtonText = "Close"
obj.Show

MsgBox "Starting the script... I recommend that you resize the window."

AddToLog("Creating the FileSystemObject object")
Dim fso
Set fso = CreateObject("Scripting.FileSystemObject")

AddToLog("Ready to scan for drives...")
```

Continued on Following Page

```
Dim d
For Each d In fso.Drives
   AddToLog("Scanning disk " & d.DriveLetter & ":")
   ScanDisk(d)
Next

' Save to disk?
Dim answer
answer = MsgBox("Work completed successfully. Would you save to disk?", _
                vbYesNo)

If answer = vbYes Then
   obj.Save "c:\myfile.log"
End If

' Destroy the dialog
obj.Destroy


Function ScanDisk(d)
   AddToLog("Drive " & d.DriveLetter & ":" & _
            " is " & aDriveType(d.DriveType))

   If d.DriveType = Fixed Then
      AddToLog("Getting the Folder object for " & d.RootFolder)
      Dim f
      Set f = fso.GetFolder(d.RootFolder)

      AddToLog("Getting the Files object for " & d.RootFolder)
      Dim files
      Set files = f.Files

      Dim file
      For Each file In Files
         AddToLog("Processing: " & file)
      Next
   End If
End Function

Function AddToLog(s)
   obj.WriteLine s
End Function

Function Log_Click()
   obj.Hide
End Function
```

As the lines of code that call `AddToLog()` execute, information is added to the log window. At the end of the process, it really does look like the output window of a debugger:

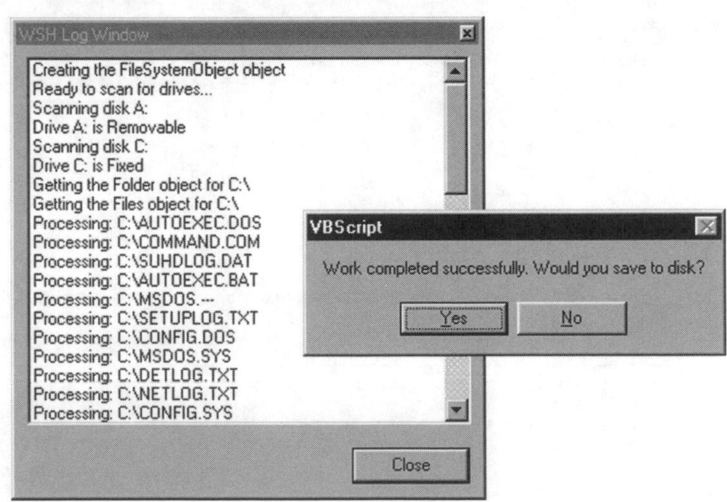

By clicking on the Close button, you cause the window to be hidden, but this doesn't stop the script from doing its processing.

Configuring the Log Window

As I mentioned earlier, the window that hosts all the messages is a list box, and this has methods and properties of its own that we can exploit. The `WriteLine()` method that writes to the log window is actually just adding an item to the list box, while the `Modeless.Log` property simply returns a reference to it.

This means that you can use the list box's programming interface to remove one, several or all of the entries it contains, or to change the colors in which things are displayed. These two lines, for example, result in white text on a blue background:

```
obj.Log.BackColor = &HFF
obj.Log.ForeColor = &HFFFFFF
```

A third and final way of using this component is to display nothing at all while processing takes place, and then show the window to the user when the task has completed, like this:

```
// BatchLog.js
// Demonstrates Log mode
// -----------------------------------------------------------
var obj
obj = new ActiveXObject("WshKit.Modeless");

// Settings
obj.Title = "WSH Log Window";
obj.LogMode = true;
obj.ButtonText = "Close";

// Adds some lines to the window
for(i = 1; i < 100; i++)
   obj.WriteLine("This is line #" + i);

// Processing has finished. Ask to see the log.
shell = new ActiveXObject("WScript.Shell")
answer = shell.Popup("Would you like to see the log?", 0, "Log Window", 4);

if(answer == 6)
{
   obj.Show();
   shell.Popup("Click here to close.");
}

obj.Destroy();
```

Running Processes

A question that arises time and again on the newsgroups is, "Is there a way to know whether a certain program is running?" With Windows 95, Microsoft provided a group of functions that return the list of running processes in a memory structure, which has the advantage of being quite easy to manage. The problem with these functions, however, is that they aren't supported under Windows NT 4.0, although it seems they will be incorporated in Windows 2000 (they were there in the Beta 3 version I tested).

Even assuming that we *do* have the tools to find out which programs are running at any moment in time, though, how is it possible to get at this information from script code? We encountered one situation where it would have been useful to know about the running processes in Chapter 3, when we discussed the `GetObject()` function, but there are others. The following are all reasons I've found (other than pure curiosity) for wanting a component with this functionality:

- The need to know whether a particular (usually large) program is already running so that you can exploit its services instead of launching a brand new instance
- The need to make sure that a certain program is running because a script requires its services and otherwise cannot work properly
- The need to ascertain whether a certain group of programs *isn't* running (this is common if you have to write setup scripts)

In a similar vein, it's often extremely useful to know the version number of an installed file. In the time between Windows 95 and Windows 98, so many direct and indirect updates have been made that versioning is an ever-increasing problem. It's annoyingly common to find that an application will run on one machine but not on another due to the wrong version of a file being installed.

The library for Common Controls (toolbar, tree view, list view) is certainly one file that tends to suffer from this problem, but so too is `shell32.dll`, which is a basic Windows library. Lots of features that are available by default under Windows 98 and the betas of Windows 2000 are only available under Windows 95 and Windows NT 4.0 if you're running at least version 4.71 of the shell library. How can you know (simply and programmatically) which version is installed on the machine your script finds itself being executed on?

The `WshKit.Process` object lets you take a snapshot of the processes that are running at a certain moment and places them in a collection. It wraps each one in another custom object called `WshKit.ProcessObject`, which has properties that return the full name, ID, version number and priority of the process. In addition, you're given the ability to kill the process, and to display a table with all the processes listed. Let's start with a look at the programming interface:

Method	Description
`Load()`	Scans the list of running processes and stores their names in an internal collection that you can access using `Item()` and `Count`. Each time you run this method, any existing collection is freed. (The list of running processes may change at any time, but the list held by this object does not.)
`ShowUI()`	Displays a modal dialog box containing a report of the running processes.

Method	Description
`Find()`	Given the name of an `.exe` file, this method returns a nonzero number representing the index of the `ProcessObject` object that identifies it in the collection. If the program isn't running, it returns 0. If you pass the name of a non-executable file (say, a `.txt` file), it works as if you had passed the name of the executable file registered to handle that type of document.
`Item()`	Lets you navigate the collection prepared by the most recent call to `Load()`. Given a non-zero index, it returns a `ProcessObject` object.
`GetVersion()`	Given the name of an executable or library file, this method returns a string containing its version number (if any). It works on *any* file, whether or not it's running when the method is called. The method returns the string unknown if it is unable to read the information.
`FindProgram()`	Takes the name of a file as input, and returns the name of the executable file registered to handle it. The function also accepts non-existing files, and it isn't necessary to specify a path.

The single property of this component is:

Property	Description
`Count`	Returns a count of the currently running processes

The subsidiary `WshKit.ProcessObject` object, on the other hand, has one method:

Method	Description
`Kill()`	Terminates the process abruptly

And four properties:

Property	Description
`ExeName`	The full name of the executable
`Version`	A `n.n.n.n` string denoting the version number of the specified module
`ProcessID`	Returns the ID of the process
`Priority`	Returns the priority of the running process

As I said earlier, obtaining the list of running processes requires a different approach under Windows 9x, Windows 2000 and Windows NT 4.0, and the `WshKit.Process` *component only addresses Windows 9x and Windows 2000. If you need one, a similar component that only supports NT can be found at* http://factory.glazier.co.nz.

The List of Processes

The `ShowUI()` method of the `Process` component returns a modal window with a report of the running processes. If you just need a quick display of the running applications, use this method. Its output is illustrated in the picture:

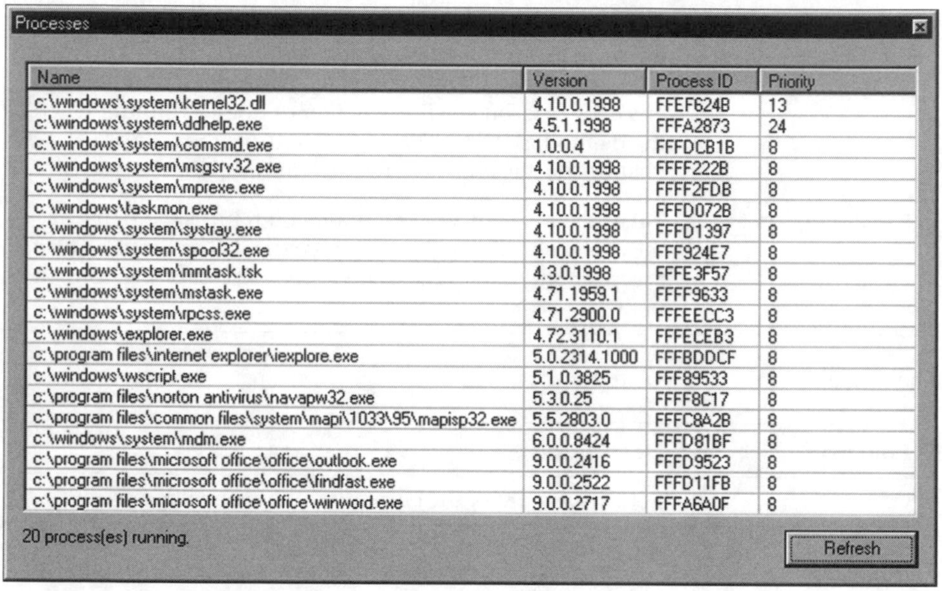

Processes

Name	Version	Process ID	Priority
c:\windows\system\kernel32.dll	4.10.0.1998	FFEF624B	13
c:\windows\system\ddhelp.exe	4.5.1.1998	FFFA2873	24
c:\windows\system\comsmd.exe	1.0.0.4	FFFDCB1B	8
c:\windows\system\msgsrv32.exe	4.10.0.1998	FFFF222B	8
c:\windows\system\mprexe.exe	4.10.0.1998	FFFF2FDB	8
c:\windows\taskmon.exe	4.10.0.1998	FFFD072B	8
c:\windows\system\systray.exe	4.10.0.1998	FFFD1397	8
c:\windows\system\spool32.exe	4.10.0.1998	FFF924E7	8
c:\windows\system\mmtask.tsk	4.3.0.1998	FFFE3F57	8
c:\windows\system\mstask.exe	4.71.1959.1	FFFF9633	8
c:\windows\system\rpcss.exe	4.71.2900.0	FFFEECC3	8
c:\windows\explorer.exe	4.72.3110.1	FFFECEB3	8
c:\program files\internet explorer\iexplore.exe	5.0.2314.1000	FFFBDDCF	8
c:\windows\wscript.exe	5.1.0.3825	FFF89533	8
c:\program files\norton antivirus\navapw32.exe	5.3.0.25	FFFF8C17	8
c:\program files\common files\system\mapi\1033\95\mapisp32.exe	5.5.2803.0	FFFC8A2B	8
c:\windows\system\mdm.exe	6.0.0.8424	FFFD81BF	8
c:\program files\microsoft office\office\outlook.exe	9.0.0.2416	FFFD9523	8
c:\program files\microsoft office\office\findfast.exe	9.0.0.2522	FFFD11FB	8
c:\program files\microsoft office\office\winword.exe	9.0.0.2717	FFFA6A0F	8

20 process(es) running.

Refresh

This is similar to what tools like the Process Viewer do under Windows 9x, but it includes the version number that other tools often forget.

```
// ProcList1.js
// Displays the list of the running processes
// -----------------------------------------------------------

var obj
obj = new ActiveXObject("WshKit.Process");
obj.Load();
obj.ShowUI();
```

As you can see, this is an extremely simple script. The `Load()` method performs the important task of loading the process information into memory, and is therefore the key that allows all the other methods to work properly. One of the benefits of `Load()` is that it creates a collection that may be explored with either a `For...Next` or a `For...Each` statement.

Walking the List of Processes

The next example demonstrates how you can handle any process separately. The list created by the `Load()` method can be stepped through using any of VBScript's typical methods. Here's a script that enlists the help of the `Modeless` object to generate a report view of the processes that are running:

```
' ProcList2.vbs
' Walking the list of running processes
' ---------------------------------------------------------

Dim proclist, log
Set proclist = CreateObject("WshKit.Process")
Set log = CreateObject("WshKit.Modeless")

log.Title = "Process List"
log.LogMode = true
log.Show

proclist.Load

' Walking the processes
For i = 1 To proclist.Count
   log.WriteLine proclist.item(i).ExeName & _
                 " (" & proclist.item(i).version & ")"
Next

' Final message
MsgBox "Click here to finish."

' Destroy the log
log.Destroy
```

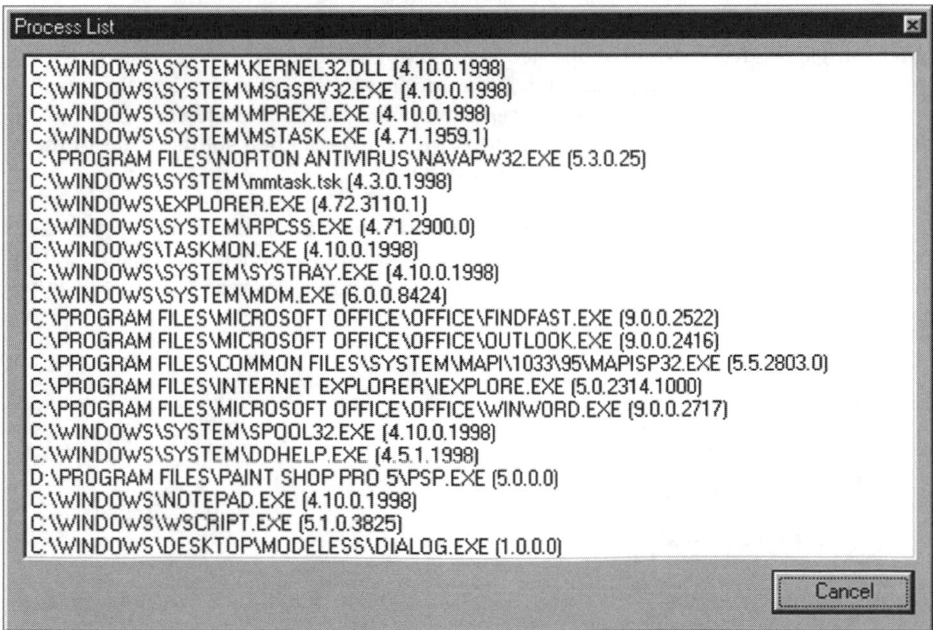

Is This Process Running?

I guess that while having a report of all the processes active at a certain moment in time is useful, the most typical way in which you would take advantage of this component is to find out if there is a process running that originated from a particular file — in other words, an application.

The `Process.Find()` method can do just that. It takes a full path name denoting an application, and returns an index number that is either 0, or the position where the process is stored in the internal collection of processes. The following code snippet, for example, shows how to find out whether the Registry Editor (`regedit.exe`) is running:

```
Dim proclist, procobj
Set proclist = CreateObject("WshKit.Process")

proclist.Load

' Finds the process and displays its version number
n = proclist.Find("c:\windows\regedit.exe")
If n > 0 Then
   Set procobj = proclist.item(n)
   MsgBox procobj.version
End If
```

This approach requires you to know the full path name of a given executable, but sometimes you may be in a different position: you don't know the full path name of a program, but you *do* know the name of a document that the program might be working on.

For example, I once had to write a script to be run on about fifty machines that, among other things, needed to copy an updated version of a document. Since it was a frequently-used document, I needed to make sure it was closed at the time the script was run. Unsurprisingly, sending the users a message asking them to close the document so that I could run my script didn't prove to be a great solution: lots of them ignored it, and I just got 'permission denied' errors.

Instead, I decided to make the check myself. The problem then was to figure out the exact path on each machine where the program to kill was installed, but I realized that the path of the *document* was common to all the machines. I was therefore able to solve the problem using a script like this:

```
' FindAndKill.vbs
' Find a given process from EXE/document name and kill it
' ---------------------------------------------------------

' Program/document name to search for
If WScript.Arguments.Count = 0 Then
   prgName = InputBox("Enter the full path name of the program/document:")
Else
   prgName = WScript.Arguments.Item(0)
End if

If prgName = "" then
  WScript.Quit
End If

Dim proclist, procobj
Set proclist = CreateObject("WshKit.Process")
```

```
proclist.Load

n = proclist.Find(prgName)
If n > 0 Then
   Set procobj = proclist.item(n)
   answer = MsgBox(prgName & _
                " is running at the moment with a process ID of " & _
                Hex(procobj.processID) & ". Its version number is " & _
                procobj.version & "." & vbCrLf & _
                "Do you want to kill it?", vbYesNo)
   If answer = vbYes Then
      procobj.Kill
   End If
Else
   MsgBox prgName & " isn't running."
End If
```

Of course, my specific solution didn't contain all these informative message boxes! To kill the process, I use the `Kill()` method exposed by the `ProcessObject`. It makes use of the process ID to identify the running process uniquely, and then asks the system to stop it.

Multiple Instances

A process is an instance of an application that is running, but at any given moment there could be several processes in the system that were all originated by the same program. The `WshKit.Process` component, however, identifies and kills just one process at a time. If you want to make sure to kill *all* the running instances of, say, `notepad.exe`, use a script like this:

```
' KillAll.vbs
' Find and kill all the running instances of a given EXE
' -----------------------------------------------------------

' Program name to search for
If WScript.Arguments.Count = 0 Then
   prgName = InputBox("Enter the full path name of the program:")
Else
   prgName = WScript.Arguments.Item(0)
End if

If prgName = "" Then
  WScript.Quit
End If

Dim proclist, procobj, moreInstances
Set proclist = CreateObject("WshKit.Process")

moreInstances = True
While moreInstances
   proclist.Load
   n = proclist.Find(prgName)
   If n > 0 Then
      Set procobj = proclist.item(n)
      procobj.Kill
   Else
      moreInstances = False
      MsgBox prgName & " is no longer running."
   End If
Wend
```

The script loops, looking for the specified program name in the list of running processes. It kills any matching processes it finds one by one, until none remains.

Who Handles This Document?

While we're talking about programs and documents, another little problem I have encountered has to do with an automatic and script-based way to know which program is registered to open a certain type of document. There are (as we have discussed) several ways of *running* a program given the name of a document, but the problem I had was a little different: I wanted to know about the path of the program that manages a certain file.

On one occasion, I needed to verify automatically whether a certain program was installed on a number of machines. I suspect that the context in which this problem originated is fairly common: there are lots of computers in an organization, and different people use them for different tasks. Each machine is subject to the occasional 'clean-up', however, and you can never be absolutely sure that all the important programs have been retained or reinstalled. If your script needs to use a program, it's sensible to check that it's present before you try.

Is This Program Installed?

If you need to know whether (say) Microsoft Word is installed on a given machine, you can do a very simple thing: ask the `Process` component to return the name of the program registered to handle `.doc` documents. Of course, this technique may not work in all cases, because in theory you could have another program registered to manage certain types of document — if you don't have Word, for example, it's likely that WordPad will be set to open `.doc` files by default. In my particular case, however, the document type was a proprietary one, and it's seldom that another program will be set up to manage those.

For my solution, I developed and used the `Process.FindProgram()` method, which accepts the name of a document and checks the registry for a match. The following script is a quick tool for checking whether a given program exists:

```
' WhoRunsWhom.vbs
' Find the program that manages a document
' --------------------------------------------------------------

' Document name to search for
Dim docName
If WScript.Arguments.Count = 0 Then
   docName = InputBox("Enter the document template name (file.ext):")
Else
   docName = WScript.Arguments.Item(0)
End if

If docName = "" Then
   WScript.Quit
End If

' Find the program to handle that document
Dim proclist, prgName
Set proclist = CreateObject("WshKit.Process")
prgName = proclist.FindProgram(docName)

If prgName = "" Then
   MsgBox "No program is registered to handle documents like " & docName
Else
   str1 = "The program you're searching for is " & UCase(prgName)
   str2 = vbCrLf & "Would you like to check that it exists?"
```

```
    answer = MsgBox(str1 & str2, vbYesNo, docName)
    If answer = vbYes Then
       Set fso = CreateObject("Scripting.FileSystemObject")
       If fso.FileExists(prgName) Then
          MsgBox prgName & " exists."
       Else
          MsgBox prgName & " doesn't exist."
       End If
    End If
End If
```

If you pass `image.bmp` to this script, here's what you get:

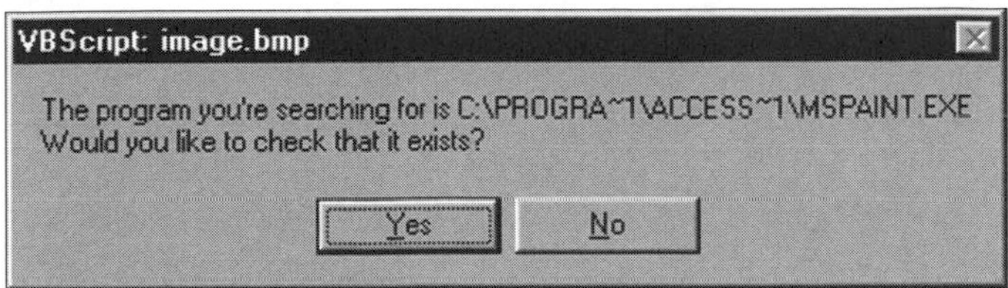

Note that you don't need to specify a path name, or even the name of an existing file! The name you pass is taken as a template for which to search the registry. Incidentally, the question that the message box above proposes is not as silly as it may at first appear. Just because a program is registered to handle a certain type of document doesn't necessarily mean that it exists on the disk! To be (more) certain, you can check for the file's existence using the `FileExists()` method of `FileSystemObject`.

Bear in mind that even in this case you might not have the right answer. A program usually needs other modules that could still be missing or incorrectly registered despite our tests. WSH is not a land of certainty!

The Problem of Version Numbers

The `Process` component can also return the version number of any running program. The version number is actually an array of four numbers that are usually formatted by putting periods between them. For example:

```
4.1.123.0
```

In this string, the first two numbers are commonly taken to be the major and the minor version number, the third is usually called the build number, and the fourth seems to be at the disposal of the team that wrote the program. Sometimes it's the year, sometimes it's 0, and sometimes it's apparently just arbitrary.

A couple of the sample scripts you've already seen have demonstrated how to get the version number of a running process, but while this can be interesting in itself, it is not always what you really need. Knowing the version of a running program is fine, but it would be much better if you could do the same for *any* executable, regardless of its extension or its status. (Reading the version number from the collection of running processes limits you to `.exe` files only.)

To work around this, the `Process` component comes with a `GetVersion()` method that takes a full path name and returns a string containing the version number of the file at that location. Because not all of the files you pass will have a version information block inside, the method returns the string <unknown> if it is unable to read it.

Earlier in this discussion, I mentioned the potential for problems to occur as a result of an old version of the Windows shell library being present, so let's see how to test that:

```
' FileVersion.vbs
' Retrieve the version of the specified executable file
' ----------------------------------------------------------

' Name of the executable
Dim exeName
If WScript.Arguments.Count = 0 Then
   exeName = InputBox("Enter the full path name of the executable to test:")
Else
   exeName = WScript.Arguments.Item(0)
End if

If exeName = "" Then
   WScript.Quit
End If

Dim proclist, ver
Set proclist = CreateObject("WshKit.Process")

ver = proclist.GetVersion(exeName)
MsgBox "Your " & UCase(exeName) & " has a version number of " & ver
```

When you run this script on a Windows 98 machine, passing `shell32.dll` as the filename, this is what you get:

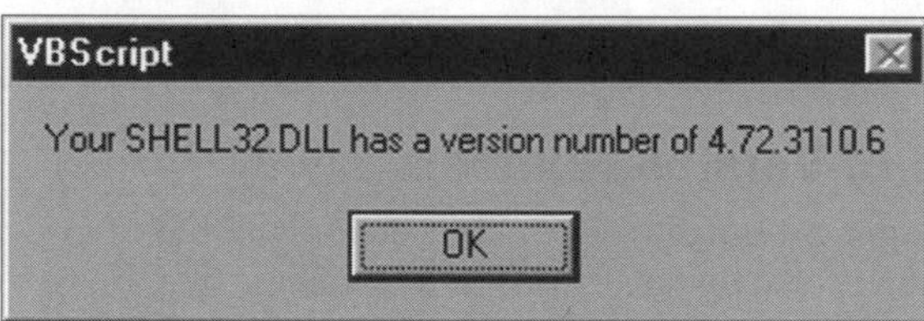

The drawback of this, however, is that `GetVersion()` returns a string rather than a numerical value, and therefore doesn't allow for serious comparisons. The question we *really* want to answer with this component is, "How can I make sure that at least shell version 4.71 is running on this machine?" It's as easy as running a script like this:

```
' ShellVer.vbs
' Verify whether the PC running this file has the Active Desktop Shell Update
'  installed. (The version of shell32.dll must be 4.71 or higher.)
' ------------------------------------------------------------------

Dim prgName
prgName = "shell32.dll"

Dim proclist
Set proclist = CreateObject("WshKit.Process")

' Split the string into its numeric components
ver = proclist.GetVersion(prgName)
aVersion = split(ver, ".")
```

```
' Compares against 4.71
major = aVersion(0)
minor = aVersion(1)

Dim net
Set net = CreateObject("WScript.Network")
pcName = net.ComputerName

If (major >= 4) And (minor >= 71) Then
   MsgBox pcName & " is running the Active Desktop shell update.",,ver
Else
   MsgBox "Sorry, but the Active Desktop isn't installed.",, ver
End If
```

The key technique to understand here is how to convert the string into its numeric components. As the string is dot-separated, extracting its components into an array just requires a call to the very useful VBScript `split()` function:

```
ver = proclist.GetVersion(prgName)
aVersion = split(ver, ".")
```

Following this call, `aVersion` is an array that contains four elements: the various numeric components of the string. Given this, comparing the major and the minor version numbers against 4 and 71 respectively is completely straightforward.

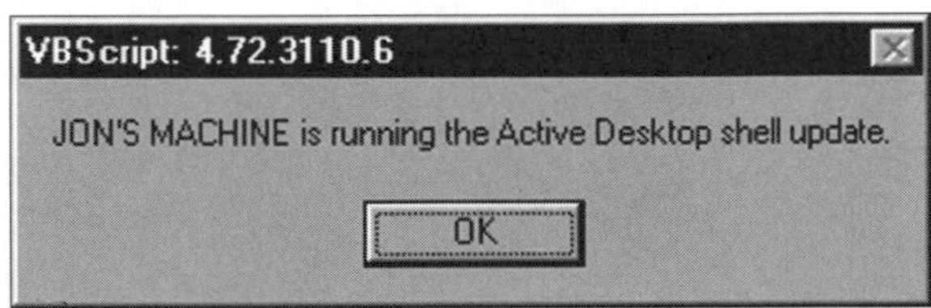

Note that this script can be easily adapted to work on any file, and to make any kind of version comparison. Furthermore, by providing a network path you should also be able to test a remote computer.

With this example, our WSH component gallery is complete — at least, for this book. However, there are other ready-to-use objects with full documentation that can be found on the Wrox Press web site along with the rest of the code for my *Visual C++ Windows Shell Programming* book, Chapter 13 of which includes information on the creation of WSH-compatible objects for reading and writing text from and to the clipboard, formatting disks, choosing icons, and enumerating the contents of the registry.

At this point, I would also like to mention another web site where you can find a very rich and interesting download section: http://cwashington.netreach.net. To share your knowledge and learn new tricks, I suggest regular perusal of http://wsh.glazier.co.nz as well.

Summary

This chapter has documented the programming interfaces and potential applications of a (small) gallery of custom COM components designed for use with WSH. I have tried to make them address problems that I or others have had while developing WSH scripts, and also to make them as generic as possible. These three components are available in source and binary form from the Wrox web site, and you should feel free to use or modify them as you see fit.

In the final chapter that follows, I will be reusing custom and standard components that you have seen here and elsewhere in the book to build WSH scripts that address some more complex tasks, including the so-called "WSH is glue" scenario. I will also try to improve the limited support that the shell offers to WSH programs by default.

10

Windows Script Host Tidbits

In this chapter, I'm going to illustrate some quite complex, real-world scenarios in which you might find yourself using WSH scripts. The idea behind this is that the WSH and COM-based technologies available within Windows give you enormous power when it comes to automating tasks, and I'm going to give you a sizable example of doing so.

In particular, I'll show you how to write a real application that spans across three different components (MS Word, MS Access and MS Outlook) and uses various technologies including Active Data Objects (ADO) and Dynamic HTML (DHTML). Although the specific example may not necessarily meet your needs, it will demonstrate how you can set any existing application that exposes an Automation interface to work for you.

The more you work with WSH, the more you find yourself looking for advanced tools and system-wide facilities, and I'll provide a few of those here too. Specifically, I'll show you how to add `.vbs` and `.js` files to the system's New menu, and how to have these files support drag-and-drop. Finally, I'll examine the problem of code security by discussing the new script encoder for VBScript and JScript files. In summary, this chapter will discuss:

- How to create Word documents on the fly
- How to query databases using ADO
- How to add `.vbs` and `.js` files to the system's New menu
- A shell drag-and-drop handler for `.vbs` and `.js` files
- How to encode script files

Creating Documents Dynamically

It's not as often as I'd like it to be, but sometimes I need to prepare, print and send out invoices. This is a task that usually requires a Word document template to be filled out, printed, and attached to an e-mail message. I may also need to keep a record of it in a database. Unless you have an administration department to take care of this stuff on your behalf, you have to deal with it yourself, so let's break the process down into a series of steps to be accomplished:

- Get the number of any previous invoice
- Collect information about the client that will receive the invoice
- Create a new Word document using a ready-made template
- Update the database
- Print the document
- Send the document out to its final recipient

In a typical scenario, this will involve using MS Word, MS Access, and your favorite mail program. By exploiting the Automation capabilities of the Microsoft Office suite, the ADO object model, and a few custom objects that we've discussed earlier in the book (see Chapters 7 thru 9), we can write a WSH program that executes all of these steps in a semi-automatic way.

What You Need to Get Started

To define the operational parameters of the example, I'm going to make a few assumptions. Let's suppose that you have a database whose ODBC system data source name (DSN) is `Invoices`:

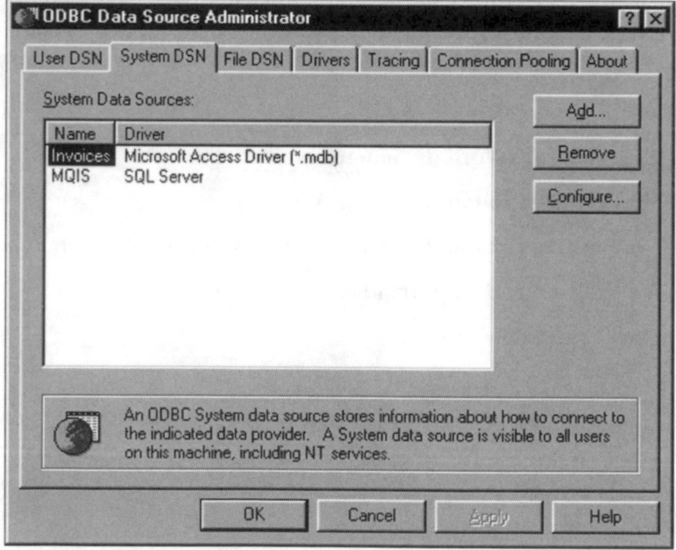

For this example, I'll assume that it's an MS Access database with the following layout. It contains a single table (also called `Invoices`) that's indexed on the `InvoiceNo` field:

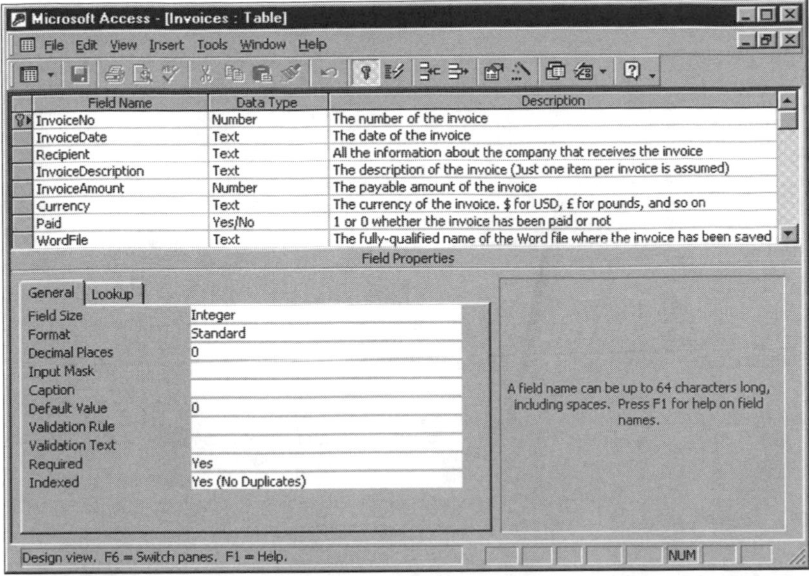

An invoice will be saved to a Word file that's built from a predefined template document called `InvoiceTemplate.dot`, which is located in the `Templates` subfolder of your Microsoft Office installation. It could look something like this:

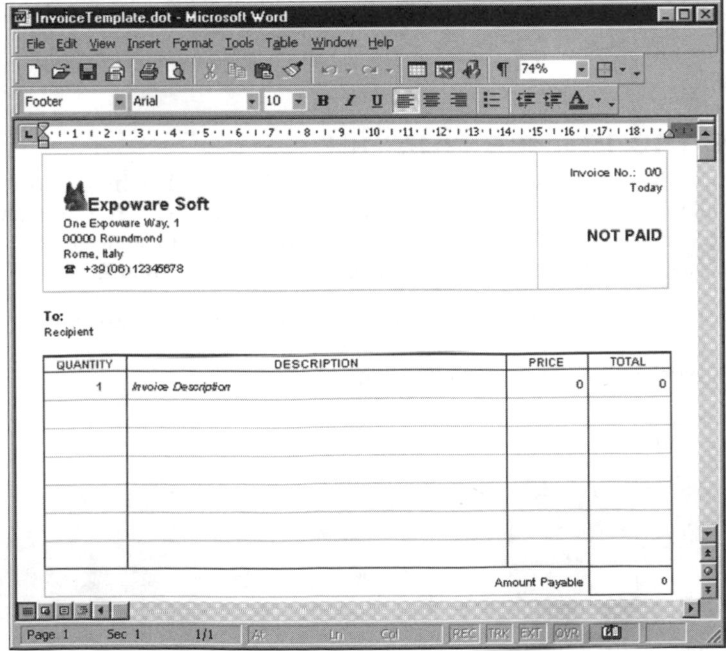

The programmatic steps to match the ones I described in the bulleted list above will be placed into the following skeleton VBScript file:

```
' NewInvoice.vbs
' Creates, prints and sends invoices through e-mail
' ---------------------------------------------------------------------

' ---------------------------------------------------------------------
' Gets the number for the new invoice
' ---------------------------------------------------------------------
' Accesses [Invoices] via ADO, gets a sorted recordset and
'  increases the previous invoice number by one.

' ---------------------------------------------------------------------
' Collects all the information needed to prepare the invoice
' ---------------------------------------------------------------------
' Displays a DHTML-based dialog box and retrieves all the data entered.
' Makes use of the WshKit.DialogBox object presented in Chapter 8.

' ---------------------------------------------------------------------
' Creates a new Word document
' ---------------------------------------------------------------------
' Exploiting the Word Automation model, creates a new document based
'  on the specified template, fills it and saves it to disk.

' ---------------------------------------------------------------------
' Records the invoice in the database
' ---------------------------------------------------------------------
' Adds a new record to the [Invoices] database via ADO.

' ---------------------------------------------------------------------
' Prints the invoice
' ---------------------------------------------------------------------
' Prints out the Word document using either Word's Automation interface
'  or the shell Automation facilities.

' ---------------------------------------------------------------------
' Sends the document through e-mail
' ---------------------------------------------------------------------
' Gets the e-mail address of the recipient and sends an e-mail
'  message with the Word document attached. This step could be
'  accomplished in a variety of ways - using CDO, CDONTS, the
'  simple Mailto: protocol or the Outlook object model.
```

Let's examine in detail how to accomplish each of these steps using a Windows Script Host program.

Getting the Invoice Number

An invoice must have a unique number. One way to obtain such a thing is to get the numbers of all the records in the `Invoices` database, and choose a number that's one bigger than the highest you find. This is not necessarily the best way to do the job, but it does let me show you how to work with ADO 2.x from within a WSH script!

> *I'm assuming some basic knowledge of the ADO 2.x object model here. For more information, you might want to refer to* ADO 2.1 Programmer's Reference *(Wrox Press, 1-861002-68-8).*

```
' NewInvoice.vbs
' Creates, prints and sends invoices through e-mail
' ---------------------------------------------------------------------
Option Explicit

' Constants
Const adUseClient = 3
Const adLockOptimistic = 3
Const ssfDrives = &H11                    ' Reference to My Computer
Const myInvoiceFolder = "C:\Invoices\"
Const myInvoiceDlgTemplate = "invoice.htm"
Const myInvoiceDocTemplate = "InvoiceTemplate.dot"
```

```
' -----------------------------------------------------------
' Gets the number for the new invoice
' -----------------------------------------------------------
Dim rs, numNewInvoice
Set rs = CreateObject("ADODB.Recordset")
rs.CursorLocation = adUseClient
```

After defining a few constants that will be used in various places in the application that follows, the code above shows how to create an instance of the ADO recordset object and set it to work with a client-side cursor. The first two constants (`adXxx`) are specific to ADO, while `ssfDrives` serves to identify the `My Computer` folder.

With ADO 2.x, you don't need to set up an explicit connection to a database. Instead, you can try to open the recordset directly, specifying the connection string as an argument:

```
numNewInvoice = 1
rs.Open "select InvoiceNo from Invoices order by InvoiceNo desc", "Invoices"

If rs.RecordCount > 0 Then
   numNewInvoice = rs("InvoiceNo") + 1
End If

rs.Close
```

The query string selects a single-column recordset based on the `InvoiceNo` field. The recordset is also sorted in descending order, so that the highest number belongs to the first record.

If the database contains no records, the `numNewInvoice` variable remains set to 1; otherwise it contains the highest number plus 1. This variable will be used later on to initialize the DHTML dialog that gathers the information to prepare the invoice.

A Dialog Box for Data Entry

I presented a new COM object called `WshKit.DialogBox` in Chapter 8 (it was created to facilitate the creation of complex dialogs with WSH), and as an example I discussed the creation of an invoice. Basically, `WshKit.DialogBox` takes an HTML page and uses it as a dialog template, and I'm going to use exactly the same `invoice.htm` template page here that I introduced then. The next code snippet is therefore very similar to the examples you've seen previously:

```
' -----------------------------------------------------------
' Collects all the information needed to prepare the invoice
' -----------------------------------------------------------
Dim dlg
Set dlg = CreateObject("WshKit.DialogBox")
If Not dlg.Create("path://" & myInvoiceDlgTemplate) Then
   MsgBox "Unable to locate the [" & myInvoiceDlgTemplate & "] template"
   WScript.Quit
End If
```

At this point, the dialog has been created in memory but it's still hidden from view. This is a good time to initialize some fields, including the date and the invoice number:

```
Dim sMonth, sDay, sYear, sDate
sMonth = MonthName(Month(Date))
sDay = Day(Date)
sYear = Year(Date)
sDate = sMonth & " " & sDay & ", " & sYear
```

Continued on Following Page

```
' Initialize the fields of the dialog
dlg.SetItemSrc "companylogo", "expoware.gif"
dlg.SetItemText "companyname", "Expoware Soft"
dlg.SetItemText "companyaddress", "One Expoware Way, 1"
dlg.SetItemText "companycity", "00000 Roundmond"
dlg.SetItemText "companycountry", "Rome, Italy"
dlg.SetItemText "companyphone", "+39 06 12345678"
dlg.SetItemValue "invoiceID", numNewInvoice
dlg.SetItemValue "invoicedate", sDate
dlg.SetItemValue "quantity", 1
dlg.SetItemValue "description", "Description of the invoice"
dlg.SetItemText "companysite", "our Web site."
dlg.SetItemHref "companysite", "http://www.expoware.com"
```

Instead of formatting the date myself, I could have called VBScript's `FormatDateTime()` function, passing the `vbLongDate` constant as the second argument. I would have obtained a string representing the given date in the long format specified in the computer's regional settings:

```
FormatDateTime Date, vbLongDate
```

What I want here, however, is a very *particular* long date format: `MMMM d, YYYY`. The predefined long date format is *usually* like this, but not always, and that's why I chose to format it myself. The dialog box is then sized and displayed with the following code:

```
' Display the dialog box
dlg.Move 0, 0, 700, 450
If Not dlg.Show("center") Then
   WScript.Quit
End If
```

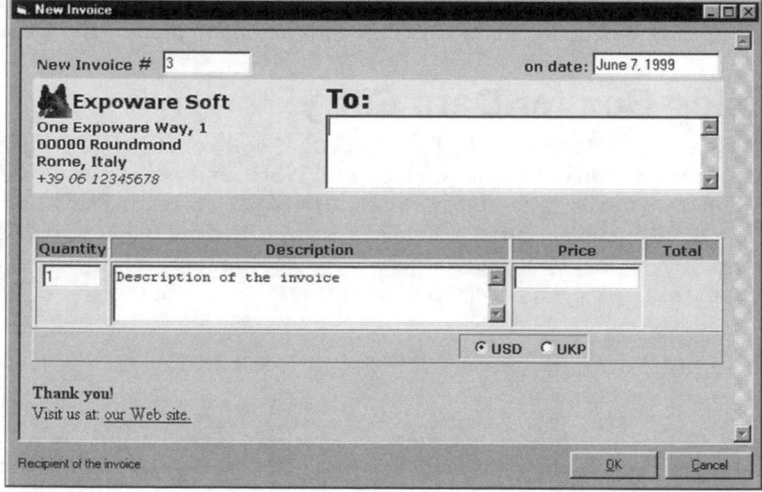

As I demonstrated in Chapter 8, the `DialogBox` object lets you set and read any element in the HTML page that has an `ID` attribute, so this code just assigns the contents of `newNumInvoice` to the HTML element with an ID of `invoiceID`:

```
dlg.SetItemValue "invoiceID", numNewInvoice
```

After the dialog is closed, the same technique is used to read back the values that the user entered:

```
' Store the data into variables
Dim dlgInvoiceNo, dlgInvoiceDate, dlgQuantity
Dim dlgPrice, dlgDesc, dlgTotal
Dim dlgTo, dlgCurrency

dlgTo = dlg.GetItemValue("recipient")
dlgInvoiceNo = dlg.GetItemValue("invoiceID")
dlgInvoiceDate = dlg.GetItemValue("invoiceDate")
dlgQuantity = dlg.GetItemValue("quantity")
dlgDesc = dlg.GetItemValue("description")
dlgPrice = FormatNumber(dlg.GetItemValue("price"),,,, -2)
dlgTotal = dlgQuantity * dlgPrice
dlgTotal = FormatNumber(dlgTotal,,,, -2)
```

All the data that's required for preparing the invoice is stored in variables. Notice the role of VBScript's `FormatNumber()` function, which returns a string in lieu of a number:

```
dlgTotal = FormatNumber(dlgTotal,,,, -2)
```

The final `-2` requires that the string groups the digits as specified in the regional settings for currency:

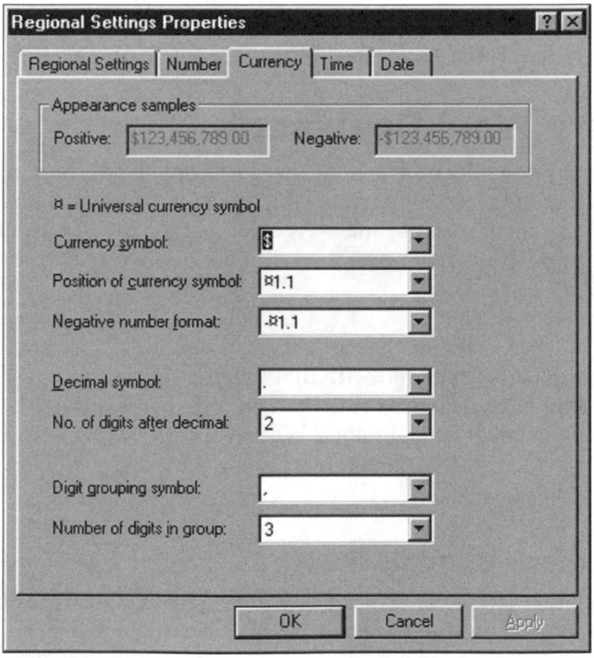

Given these settings, the final formatted string will assume the following form, which is fine for prices and any amount payable.

```
1,200.00
```

As you can see, there's no indication of the currency — to get that, I would have to have used `FormatCurrency()`. However, the invoice in the example can be expressed in more than one currency (say, USD and UKP), which means that I have to add the currency symbol myself:

```
' Get the currency
Dim wbdoc, ukp
Set wbdoc = dlg.Document
Set ukp = wbdoc.all("ukp")
dlgCurrency = "$"
If ukp.checked Then dlgCurrency = "£"
```

The `invoice.htm` template shown above employs a radio button to choose between the currencies; which one has been selected can only be detected with a bit of DHTML code. With this line:

```
Set wbdoc = dlg.Document
```

we get a reference to the HTML page's document object model. By accessing the `all` collection, we can create an instance of the element whose ID is `ukp` — the radio button:

```
Set ukp = wbdoc.all("ukp")
```

If it is checked, we use `£` as the currency symbol; if not, we use `$`.

When the dialog box gets closed, we have all the information we need to fill out a new Word document based on the `InvoiceTemplate.dot` template.

Preparing a Word Document

In most cases, invoices are documents that share a template but contain different information. Sharing the same template means that you can always identify points in the document where some specific data (say, a date, or the invoice number, or the item's description and price) is to be injected. But how do we keep track of these points?

A common way of creating similar documents is to define a `.dot` template, and to have a brand new document created with that schema whenever you select File | New.... Into this template you enter the information that is really significant, and which differentiates one document from another. When you're working with Word interactively, it's obvious where the data should go: you can see it. How can a WSH script do the same thing?

Using Document Bookmarks

A **bookmark** is an association between an identifying name and a specific position in a Word document. Bookmarks are a feature of Word documents that can be used to mark text, graphics, tables or indeed anything else you can put in a Word document. To add a bookmark, you select the item of which to keep track and click Insert | Bookmark.... The following dialog box will appear:

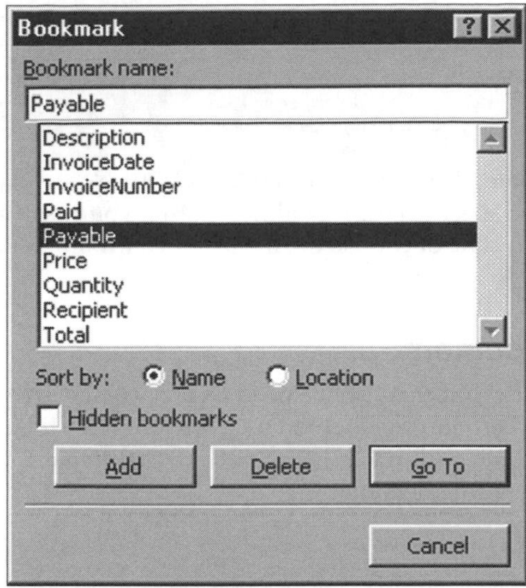

The names you can see in the window are the bookmarks I've defined for the `InvoiceTemplate.dot` document. To add a new bookmark, just type in the name and click Add. The bookmark will apply to the currently selected item; the next picture shows all of the bookmarks in the `InvoiceTemplate.dot` document:

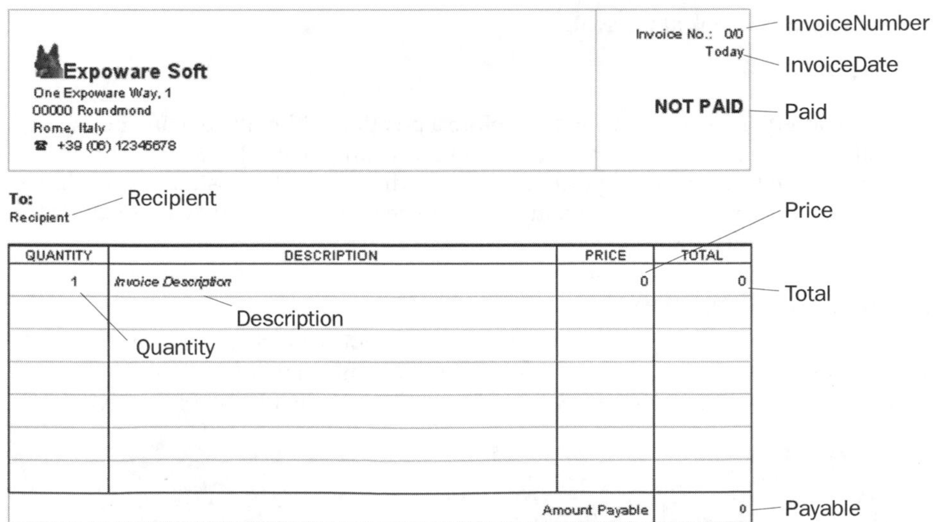

Initializing the Word Object Model

To create a new Word document programmatically, the first step is to create a new instance of the Word application. The following initializes the Word object model and adds a new document based on the specified template:

```
' ------------------------------------------------------------------
' Creates a new Word document
' ------------------------------------------------------------------
Dim word, doc, docName
Set word = CreateObject("Word.Application")
Set doc = word.Documents.Add(myInvoiceDocTemplate)
```

In this example, the template file must be located in MS Office's standard `Templates` subfolder, but you can also specify a fully-qualified path if you want. The `doc` variable being initialized in the third line of code is the means of controlling our new invoice from WSH.

Filling Out the Document

At this point, we have all the information we need to prepare the invoice in the variables that were set earlier. Through bookmarks, we also have links to the places where the data must be stored within the document. All that remains is to write the data to the file, and then save the document:

```
' Fill the bookmarks in the document
doc.Bookmarks("InvoiceNumber").Range.Text = dlgInvoiceNo
doc.Bookmarks("InvoiceDate").Range.Text = dlgInvoiceDate
doc.Bookmarks("Paid").Range.Text = "PAID"
doc.Bookmarks("Quantity").Range.Text = dlgQuantity
doc.Bookmarks("Recipient").Range.Text = dlgTo
doc.Bookmarks("Description").Range.Text = dlgDesc
doc.Bookmarks("Price").Range.Text = dlgCurrency & dlgPrice
doc.Bookmarks("Total").Range.Text = dlgCurrency & dlgTotal
doc.Bookmarks("Payable").Range.Text = dlgCurrency & dlgTotal
```

Let's have a closer look at the syntax.

```
doc.Bookmarks("...")
```

This code identifies an element, and therefore a position within the document. In general, a `Range` object represents a contiguous area in a Word document — it's defined by a starting character position and an ending character position. It also has a property called `Text` that will contain the text to be displayed there, with the formatting styles defined.

Saving the Document

So far, we've been working on a volatile new document. To save it, however, you just need to call the `SaveAs()` method, passing a path name. In this case, I assign the document a name like "`Invoice XX.doc`", where `XX` is the number of the invoice:

```
' Save the document as 'Invoice #.doc'
Dim myDocs, fso
Set fso = CreateObject("Scripting.FileSystemObject")
If Not fso.FolderExists(myInvoiceFolder) Then
   fso.CreateFolder(myInvoiceFolder)
End If

docName = myInvoiceFolder & "Invoice " & dlgInvoiceNo & ".doc"
doc.SaveAs docName
doc.Close
word.Quit
```

It's reasonable that you would want to store all your invoices in a common directory. The code above checks that this folder exists, and creates it if necessary. Then, it just builds the full path name for the document, saves it, and quits Word.

Recording the Invoice

The next step is to add a record to the `Invoices` database in order to keep track of the new document. Once again, we do this by using ADO and SQL:

```
' -----------------------------------------------------------
' Records the invoice in the database
' -----------------------------------------------------------
Set rs = CreateObject("ADODB.Recordset")
rs.CursorLocation = adUseClient
rs.Open "select * from Invoices", "Invoices",, adLockOptimistic
rs.AddNew
```

This code creates an instance of the ADO recordset object and opens it on the `Invoices` data source, requiring a client-side cursor and following an optimistic locking policy. By calling `AddNew()`, we add a new record to the current recordset.

Filling Out the Record

Naturally, the new record must be filled out before we update the table. Given the table structure I presented earlier in the chapter, the following code will do the job:

```
rs.Fields("InvoiceNo") = dlgInvoiceNo
rs.Fields("InvoiceDate") = dlgInvoiceDate
rs.Fields("Recipient") = dlgTo
rs.Fields("InvoiceDescription") = dlgDesc
rs.Fields("InvoiceAmount") = dlgTotal
rs.Fields("Currency") = dlgCurrency
rs.Fields("Paid") = 1
rs.Fields("WordFile") = docName
rs.Update
rs.Close
```

The dialog box doesn't perform any validation on the arguments the user enters, so if you changed the default invoice ID and chose an existing number, executing this code will cause an error.

Printing the Document

At this point, most things are done: the invoice has been created and registered in the database for my records. As far as printing it is concerned, there are two possible ways for you to proceed, and both rely on the same low-level technique. Firstly, you could ask Word to print the document directly:

```
doc.Print
```

Secondly, you could identify the document in its folder and ask the Windows shell to print it through the document's context menu. The ultimate action, though, is the same because a new temporary instance of Word is run just to print out the document. I'll discuss this latter approach in more detail.

Documents as Folder Items

In Chapter 6, I introduced the Shell Automation objects, by means of which you can (among other things) access the functions defined in any file's context menu. In order to do this, however, we have to transform a filename into a `FolderItem` object:

```
' --------------------------------------------------------------
' Prints the invoice
' --------------------------------------------------------------
Dim shell, f, fi
Set shell = CreateObject("Shell.Application")
```

The above code creates the main shell object, from which we can obtain the `My Computer` folder:

```
Set f = shell.Namespace(ssfDrives)
```

The variable `f` is an object of type `Folder`. (Remember that this `Folder` object has nothing to do with the `FileSystemObject`'s `Folder` object.) To get the `FolderItem` object that corresponds to a certain filename contained in the folder, you need to execute the following code:

```
Set fi = f.ParseName(docName)
```

Now, `fi` is a `FolderItem` object that exposes its context menu through the `InvokeVerb()` method:

```
fi.InvokeVerb("&Print")
```

Notice that `InvokeVerb()` takes as an argument a string that must exactly match the command string that appears on the context menu:

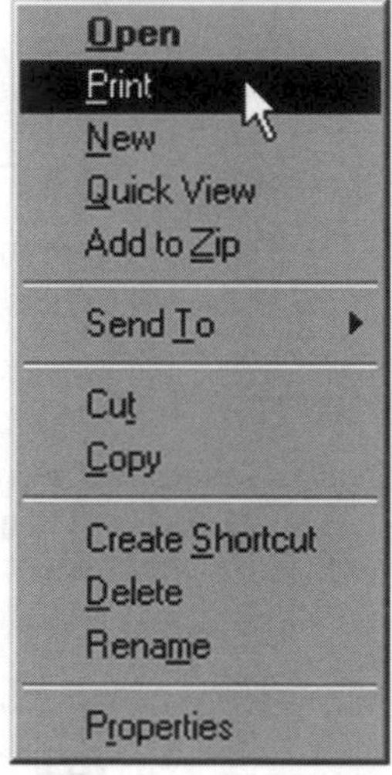

If you're running English versions of Windows and Microsoft Office then the command to print documents is Print. In the Windows environment, though, the underscore in menu commands equates to a preceding ampersand in the command string. That's why printing a document requires a rather unusual string like "`&Print`".

Be aware that with localized versions of either Windows or Microsoft Office, this string might be different. The rule is: look at the context menu's print command string, and insert an ampersand before the underlined letter. In Italian, for example, the menu string is Stampa, which evaluates to a command string `&Stampa`.

It's Always Word to Print

Invoking the context menu always causes Word to start up and print, so this approach is functionally equivalent to creating an instance of Word, opening the document, and asking it to print itself. It's up to you to decide which technique better suits your scenario.

Keep in mind that the Shell Automation approach requires you either to have installed Internet Explorer 4+ on a Windows 95 or Windows NT 4.0 machine, or to be running Windows 98 or later.

Sending the Invoice Through E-mail

Any real invoice is created not to be stored in a folder, but to be sent out to someone, and e-mail is an excellent means of transportation. There are several ways and technologies to send e-mails from within script programs. You can use:

- The Outlook object model
- The Collaboration Data Objects (CDO)
- The `mailto` protocol

In my opinion, using Outlook is fine, and recommended if it's your default mail program. CDO, on the other hand, is a pretty complex and powerful object model that requires you to do a lot of work to send even the world's simplest e-mail message. The `mailto` protocol would be my preferred solution, however, if only it were more configurable and less rigidly interactive:

```
Set shell = CreateObject("WScript.Shell")
shell.Run "mailto:despos@tin.it"
```

The above code is enough to display a window in which to compose messages, and the screenshot shows what happens if you use MS Outlook as your default mail program:

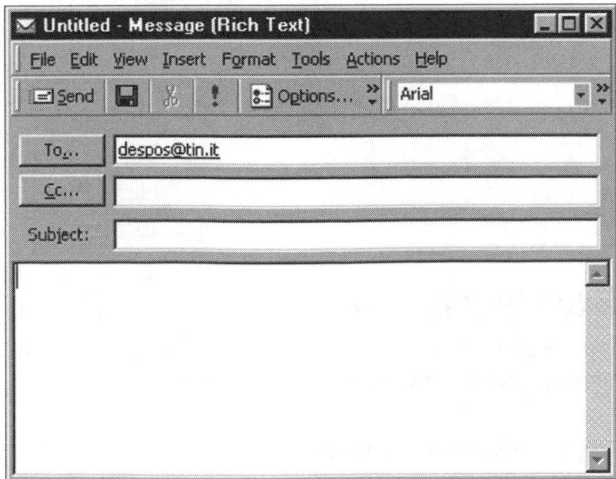

As you can see, there's no way to initialize the Cc: or the Subject: field, and there's no way to attach a file to send automatically. (For me, this is the most bothersome action when you send e-mails.)

The CDO for NT Server

CDO 1.21 is a vast library whose primary purpose is to work with Exchange 5.5 and Outlook 8.x, and I think it's overkill for sending a simple message with a file attached. A more compact COM object to be used with script files, however, is CDO for NT Server (CDONTS), a shrink-wrapped version of CDO that ships with IIS 4.0 and works on Windows NT Server.

With CDONTS, sending a message is as easy as this:

```
Set mail = CreateObject("CDONTS.NewMail")
mail.Send from, to, subject, body
```

You can also do more complicated things, such as attaching files and specifying additional recipients. However, CDONTS is a server-side component, and it isn't available on Windows 98 or NT Workstation machines.

A Very Simple COM Object for E-mail

In a moment, I'm going to demonstrate how to send the invoice using MS Outlook, and if it's your default e-mail program this is definitely the best way of doing it. However, if you use another program to read and send e-mail (Outlook Express, Eudora, Netscape Mail), then the messages you send using Outlook will never appear in your 'Sent' or 'Outbox' folder.

If you think you need a component that's as easy to use as Outlook but works in conjunction with *your* e-mail reader, there's one on the Wrox Press web site called `WshKit.SendMail`. This uses the simple MAPI (Messaging API) functions and sends full messages without authenticated logon. (In other words, you log on without specifying a profile name.) It isn't very flexible (from this standpoint, it's inferior to CDONTS), but on the other hand, it works everywhere! The following code illustrates its use:

```
Dim email
Set email = CreateObject("WshKit.SendMail")
email.Init
email.Subject = "Invoice"
email.Body = "Here's the invoice you were waiting for."
email.Attachment = docName
email.Send address
email.Close
```

Using Outlook to Send E-mail

Let's see now what you need to do in order to send an e-mail message using Microsoft Outlook 98. The main steps can be summarized in this way:

- Creating an instance of the Outlook application
- Creating an object that renders an e-mail message

- Filling the object with its recipient, subject line, body and attachment
- Sending the e-mail

If you're connected to the Internet, the message will be sent immediately. If not, it will be placed in the 'Outbox' folder ready to be sent next time you connect. The following code shows how to display an input box (based on the `InputBox` component you saw in Chapter 8) to accept the e-mail address of the recipient. You might want also to add a pattern based on a regular expression to make sure that what's entered is a valid address in the form `account@server.com`.

```
' -----------------------------------------------------------------
' Sends the document through e-mail
' -----------------------------------------------------------------
' Displays a dialog to accept the e-mail address of the recipient. It also
'  validates what you type in using a regular expression.
Dim address
Set dlg = CreateObject("WshKit.InputBox")
dlg.Title = "Send E-mail"
dlg.Label = "Type the e-mail address in the edit box below:"
dlg.Format = "\w+\@\w+\.\w+"       ' The reg. exp. for e-mail addresses
dlg.Show

If dlg.Text = "" Then
   WScript.Quit
End If

' Stores the address
address = dlg.Text
```

Once you have a valid e-mail address, you can start preparing the message. This means creating an instance of Outlook and a new mail item, which is not quite as simple as it sounds. The Outlook object model manages several types of item, including mail messages, appointments, Post-It notes, contacts, and tasks, and when you create a new one you must specify its type. The constant `olMailItem` (which equates to 0) serves this purpose in the code below.

```
Dim oApp
Dim mail
Const olMailItem = 0                ' A mail item in Outlook

' Starts the Outlook application
Set oApp = CreateObject("Outlook.Application")

' Creates a new mail item
Set mail = oApp.CreateItem(olMailItem)

' Fill in the message
mail.To = address
mail.Subject = "Invoice"
mail.Body = "Here's the invoice you were waiting for."
mail.Attachments.Add docName
mail.Send

' Closes Outlook
oApp.Quit
```

As you can see from the listing above, filling up the various fields of the message and then sending it is really quite straightforward.

With this code in place and operational, we have completed the lifecycle of the invoice and sent it out to the recipient. All that remains now is to wait for the check to arrive!

Shell Facilities for WSH Scripts

When you're doing a lot of work with WSH, you'll find (or at least, *I've* found) that having only a simple text editor and the Windows Explorer's double-click functionality to assist with the development process quickly becomes tedious. For this reason, I've come up with a couple of utilities that should help with writing and testing your scripts.

The first one demonstrates how to add the possibility of creating new Windows Script Host files directly from the Explorer's New menu, while the second is a module that handles drag-and-drop operations on `.ws`, `.vbs` and `.js` files. Once you've installed it, you'll be able to drag-and-drop files from Explorer onto your script's icon, and have it receive their names as if they had been specified on the command line — they'll be available through the `WScript.Arguments` collection.

WS, VBS and JS in the New Menu

When you right-click on the desktop, or in the background of a folder view in Windows Explorer, you can access a New menu that presents a list of document types you can create on the fly. By selecting one of these, you cause the system to perform some actions that result in the creation of a new document of that type in the current folder.

Usually, this menu (which is also available through Explorer's File menu) lets you create new folders and shortcuts, as well as text files, bitmaps and wave sounds. However, any application can add its own document types to the list. Indeed, any Windows-compliant application is *encouraged* to do just that. The figure below shows how this menu appears on my machine:

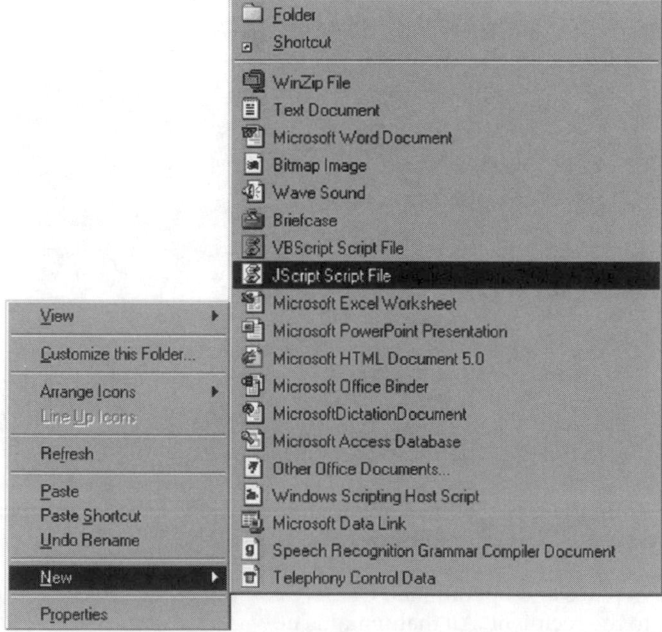

You can see entries for all the different types of Office documents, HTML pages, and (highlighted) the VBScript and JScript files that constitute WSH scripts.

The New Menu

Adding a new item to the menu is actually not particularly difficult — it just requires you to write a few entries in the registry and then decide the initial content of the new document. Windows supports several ways of defining this, but I'm just going to demonstrate the most reasonable way of doing it for Windows script, VBScript and JScript files.

Providing a Template File

When you click to create a new file, the shell creates a copy of a template file (that you have provided) in the current folder. On the road to adding documents to the New menu, then, the first step is to provide some appropriate template files. This is the code I chose for a VBScript file:

```
' New.vbs
' Sample VBS script
' ----------------------------------------------------------

Dim obj
' Set obj = CreateObject("ProgID")
```

While this is the template code for a JScript file:

```
// New.js
// Sample JS script
// ---------------------------------------------------------

var obj;
// obj = new ActiveXObject("ProgID");
```

And a new Windows script file will look like this:

```
<?xml version="1.0"?>
<!-- New.ws: A aample WS script -->

<job>
   <script language="VBScript">
   </script>
</job>
```

Of course, you should change or enhance these files as you see fit; just remember that what you write here is what you'll get in the current folder after creating a new document of one of these types. I've called them `new.vbs`, `new.js` and `new.ws`, but again you can change their names if you wish. For the following procedure to work, though, all three files must be stored in the `ShellNew` subfolder of the `Windows` directory.

Registering a New File Type

Having created our template files, we need to establish the link that tells the system to make copies of them whenever new files of their type are requested. Now, any kind of file that has an entry in the New menu must be a **registered file type**. In other words, it must have a known extension and a program that's registered to manage it. After WSH has been installed, this certainly applies to `.vbs`, `.js` and `.ws` files — they have icons of their own, and double-clicking them results in the invocation of `wscript.exe`.

Among other things, this means that there are nodes named `.vbs`, `.js` and `.ws` under the `HKEY_CLASSES_ROOT` key of the registry. Beneath these nodes, you need to create sub-keys like this:

```
.vbs\
   ShellNew
```

And this:

```
.js\
   ShellNew
```

And this:

```
.ws\
   ShellNew
```

Then, add a value called `FileName` that contains the name of the template file to be used — you don't need the whole path name, because it's always in the `ShellNew` directory. The following script registers `new.ws`, `new.vbs` and `new.js` as the templates to be used:

```
' AddToMenuNew.vbs
' Sample VBS script that registers WS, VBS and JS as members of the shell's
'  New menu. It needs files called new.ws, new.vbs and new.js in its folder.
' ---------------------------------------------------------------------------

Const REG_WSNEW = "HKCR\.ws\ShellNew\"
Const REG_VBSNEW = "HKCR\.vbs\ShellNew\"
Const REG_JSNEW = "HKCR\.js\ShellNew\"
Const REG_TEMPLATE = "FileName"

Const WS_FILE = "new.ws"
Const VBS_FILE = "new.vbs"
Const JS_FILE = "new.js"

Set shell = CreateObject("WScript.Shell")
Set fso = CreateObject("Scripting.FileSystemObject")

' Register WS, VBS and JS files
shell.RegWrite REG_WSNEW & REG_TEMPLATE, WS_FILE, "REG_SZ"
shell.RegWrite REG_VBSNEW & REG_TEMPLATE, VBS_FILE, "REG_SZ"
shell.RegWrite REG_JSNEW & REG_TEMPLATE, JS_FILE, "REG_SZ"

' Copies template files to the ShellNew folder
shellNewDir = fso.GetSpecialFolder(0) & "\ShellNew\"
wsFile = shellNewDir & WS_FILE
vbsFile = shellNewDir & VBS_FILE
jsFile = shellNewDir & JS_FILE

If Not fso.FileExists(wsFile) Then
   fso.CopyFile WS_FILE, wsFile
End If

If Not fso.FileExists(vbsFile) Then
   fso.CopyFile VBS_FILE, vbsFile
End If

If Not fso.FileExists(jsFile) Then
   fso.CopyFile JS_FILE, jsFile
End If
```

In this way, you've added the means to create new scripts anywhere in the Windows shell with a click of the right mouse button. The default name that is assigned to the new file is decided by the system: it's "`New` *`Xxx`*`.` *`ext`*", where *`ext`* stands for the file type extension and *`Xxx`* is the description of the type. Any new VBScript file, for example, has the default name "`New VBScript Script File.VBS`":

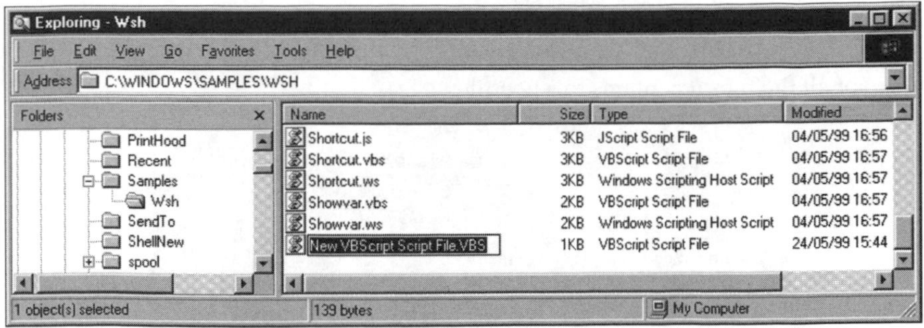

Note that you can use the `AddToMenuNew.vbs` *script shown above to install any other type of file in the* New *menu. All you need to do is change the name of the template file and the registry keys involved.*

Passing Arguments to Script Files

Many WSH applications need to accept arguments through their command lines, and as we saw back in Chapter 2, the WSH object model defines a specialized object called `WshArguments` to manage this very need. If you have a script file that uses command line arguments, you will find yourself writing code like this:

```
Var0 = WScript.Arguments.Item(0)
Var1 = WScript.Arguments.Item(1)
```

While the WSH object model provides you with almost everything you need to *manage* arguments, actually *passing* arguments to script files is less well supported.

When you're using the `WshArguments` *object, you never know what the whole command line passed to the script was — you always get the individual arguments, pre-parsed and split up into the elements of the collection. There's no way to know about the whole command line string, although you could try to rebuild it by concatenating all the individual arguments. This is not usually a problem,* unless *you need to pass arguments that contain quotes, or you want to use a custom algorithm to parse the command line string. Windows Script Host simply separates arguments by spaces or quotes.*

Running a Script File

If you launch a script from the Run dialog box, you can specify the arguments one after the other. This works fine, but I don't think it's the best way of doing things. The *easiest* way to run a script file is by double-clicking on it from within a folder, but in this case there's no way to pass it any arguments on the command line.

Getting external data to work on is one of the typical traits of script files, and so we have to consider whether there is a way to pass parameters to WSH script files through the Windows shell. It turns out that this *is* possible, provided that you have a specialized module to handle shell drag-and-drop.

A Drag-and-drop Handler for WSH Files

A **drag-and-drop handler** for WSH files is a COM module that, once installed, lets you drag-and-drop files (and, in principle, any other kind of data) onto `.vbs`, `.js` and `.ws` files throughout the Explorer. If your script needs to be passed some filenames, you just have to select them and drop them onto the script. It will then automatically receive these names through the `WshArguments` object.

Using the Command Line

Let's consider the following example that takes a folder name and dumps out the names of all the files it contains to a text file:

```
' EnumFiles.vbs
' Writes all the files found in a given folder to a TXT file.
'-------------------------------------------------------------------
Dim dir, coll, strFiles
Dim fileSpec, fso, f

' Get the folder to scan for files
fileSpec = InputBox("Enter the folder name with the final \:", _
                    "File Query", "c:\")
If fileSpec = "" Then WScript.Quit

' Check the folder name
Set fso = CreateObject("Scripting.FileSystemObject")
If Not fso.FolderExists(fileSpec) Then
   MsgBox "Sorry, the folder seems not to exist!",,fileSpec
   WScript.Quit
End If

' Executes a 'DIR' command into a collection
Set dir = fso.GetFolder(fileSpec)
Set coll = dir.Files
strFiles = ""

' Walk the collection and prints out names
For Each elem In coll
   strFiles = strFiles & elem & vbCrLf
Next

' Writes the result to a files.txt file, created in the script directory
filePath = fso.GetParentFolderName(WScript.ScriptFullName)
Set f = fso.CreateTextFile(filePath & "\files.txt", 1)
f.Write strFiles
f.Close
```

The script takes the name of the folder to work with through an `InputBox()` dialog, and this works perfectly well, but sometimes you may need to scan a directory with a very long name, at which point typing all the characters becomes tedious. Furthermore, you might want to run it programmatically and without interaction. Adding the possibility of receiving the folder name through the command line is a great enhancement that requires just a few more lines of code.

```
' EnumFilesEx.vbs
' Writes all the files found in a given folder to a TXT file.
'-------------------------------------------------------------

Dim dir, coll, strFiles
Dim fileSpec, fso, f

' Get the folder to scan for files
If WScript.Arguments.Length > 0 Then
   fileSpec = WScript.Arguments.Item(0)
   fileSpec = fileSpec & "\"
Else
   fileSpec = InputBox("Enter the folder name with the final \:", _
                       "File Query","c:\")
   If fileSpec = "" Then WScript.Quit
End If


' The remainder of the code as before
```

Wouldn't it be even nicer, though, if you could pass the name of the folder via drag-and-drop? Look at this screenshot:

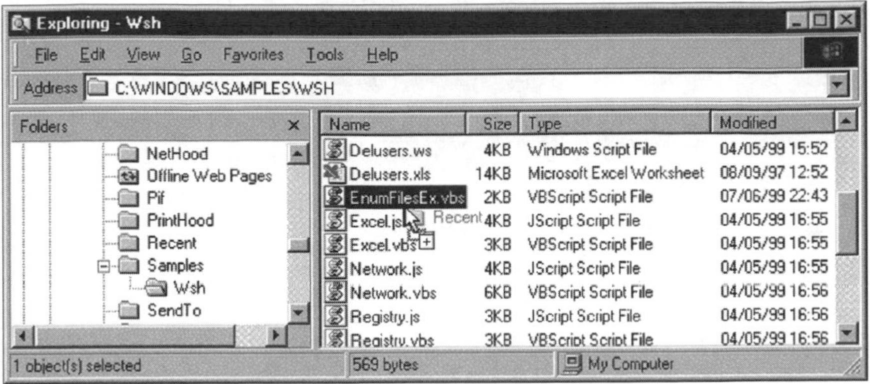

Here, the `EnumFilesEx.vbs` script is receiving the name of the folder to process via shell drag-and-drop. As a result, the following line of code:

```
fileSpec = WScript.Arguments.Item(0)
```

will set `fileSpec` to the full name of the `Recent` subfolder that's being dragged.

Shell Drag-and-drop

The Windows shell allows you to write and register special COM modules that handle what happens when things are 'dropped' over files of a certain type. These modules are called **DropHandler shell extensions**, and they're usually written in C++. (You could use Delphi as well, but it's very hard to write them with Visual Basic.)

Shell extensions are a huge topic well beyond the scope of this book, and once again I'm not going to cover the implementation details of this component here. As usual, though, it's available from our web site (it's called `wshdrop.dll`), and once you've registered it you can start dropping filenames and raw text over `.ws`, `.vbs` and `.js` files throughout the Windows shell.

Registering the Drop Handler

You can't just copy `wshdrop.dll` onto a computer and expect it to start working. Once it's there, you need to register it, which you can do by issuing the following command from the Run box or the command prompt. Make absolutely sure that you specify the full path name:

```
regsvr32.exe path\wshdrop.dll
```

For `wshdrop.dll` to start working, you also need to restart the Windows shell, which can be accomplished with a simple logoff or a more drastic reboot. At that point, you're ready to start trying it out.

Exploiting WSH Drag-and-drop

The next listing shows a simple script for testing the abilities of `wshdrop.dll`. It just dumps out all the parameters it receives through the command line.

```
// DropText.js
// Test for wshdrop.dll. Simply displays what it receives on command line.
// -----------------------------------------------------------------------
var shell = WScript.CreateObject("WScript.Shell");
var sDrop = "Arguments received:\n\n";

if(WScript.Arguments.Length > 0)
{
   for(i = 1; i <= WScript.Arguments.Length; i++)
      sDrop += i + ") " + WScript.Arguments.Item(i - 1) + "\n";
   shell.Popup(sDrop);
}
else
   shell.Popup("No arguments specified.");

WScript.Quit();
```

The next figure shows how it works. The text selected in the Word document can be dropped directly onto the `droptext.js` file:

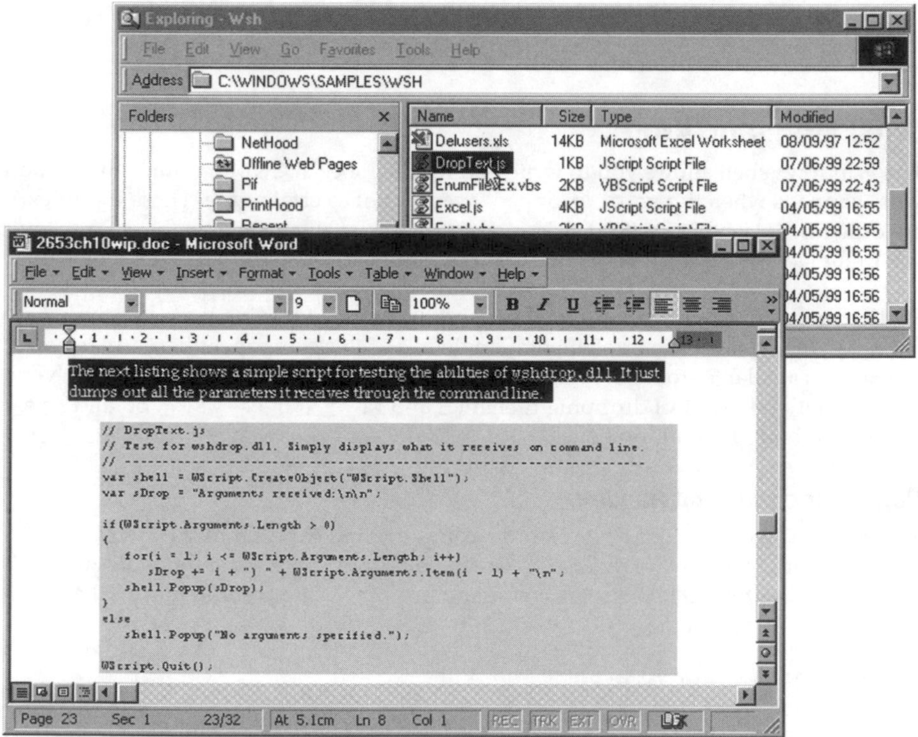

This causes the following message box to appear:

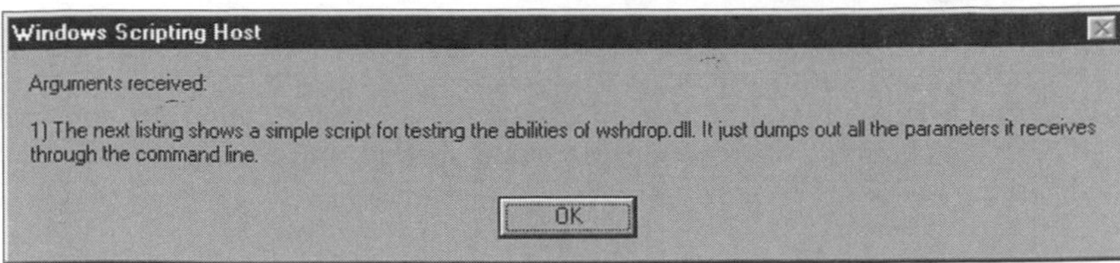

As you can see, this demonstration works perfectly, but it really just serves the purpose of demonstrating that the drop handler is up and running. What sort of operation could you use this functionality for in real life? Let's consider a practical scenario in which this component proves itself to be genuinely helpful.

File Deployment

If you're an administrator, it's likely that from time to time you'll need to copy files onto all the machines under your control — you may need to update the logon scripts, for example. Assuming that you have write access to the target machines, you might want to use the following script:

```
strFile = WScript.Arguments.Item(0)
Set fso = CreateObject("Scripting.FileSystemObject")
fso.CopyFile strFile, "\\PDC\netlogon\logon.vbs"
fso.CopyFile strFile, "\\BDC1\netlogon\logon.vbs"
fso.CopyFile strFile, "\\BDC2\netlogon\logon.vbs"
```

Save this in a `.vbs` file on the desktop or any other place to which you have easy access — the Quick Launch toolbar, perhaps. All you need to do then is drop your files over it, and they will automatically be deployed on all the specified computers. In other words, the shortcut to this script becomes a kind of network-wide dispatcher.

Towards a WSH IDE

The more you work with the Windows Script Host, the more often you come up with ideas for advanced tools that would assist with the development effort. I've provided a couple of shell facilities in this chapter, but I think it's about time that a real IDE (Integrated Development Environment) for WSH appeared.

For a start, we need a specialized text editor. While Notepad is fine to an extent, a better tool would help you with line numbers, syntax highlighting, debugging, on-line help, macro editing, and so forth. If you already own Microsoft Visual Studio, it is a good choice even though it's not particularly targeted to WSH.

Still, while we're waiting for such a tool to appear from Microsoft or one of the many third-party vendors, I'd like to turn your attention to the concept of **script encoding**.

Encoding WSH Scripts

Scripts are quick and easy to write and they don't require a compiler, but traditionally they have come at a cost: they can be easily altered — intentionally or not — and they don't allow you to protect your investments in time and effort. The scripts you write and deliver to the client are source code, plain and simple, and there's not much you can do about it.

The problem, then, is that scripts haven't provided protection of the intellectual property contained within them, or any assurance that users really will get what you intended. Anyone can pull your scripts apart, modify them (perhaps even maliciously) and pass them off as their own. Script blocks embedded into HTML or ASP pages suffer from the same problem.

The Microsoft Script Encoder

Microsoft has attempted to address the problem of script security by introducing the Script Encoder (MSE), a small command-line tool that's capable of encoding any VBScript or JScript file. It's available from http://msdn.microsoft.com/scripting.

The tool wouldn't be particularly exciting, however, were it not for the fact that encrypted files are supported and silently decrypted upon execution by the Windows Script layer. This means that you can now write your files, encode them, deploy them, and still have your users run them without problems. In this way, a WSH script file looks very much like a binary executable. The following picture shows how the `EnumFilesEx.vbs` file looks once it's been encoded:

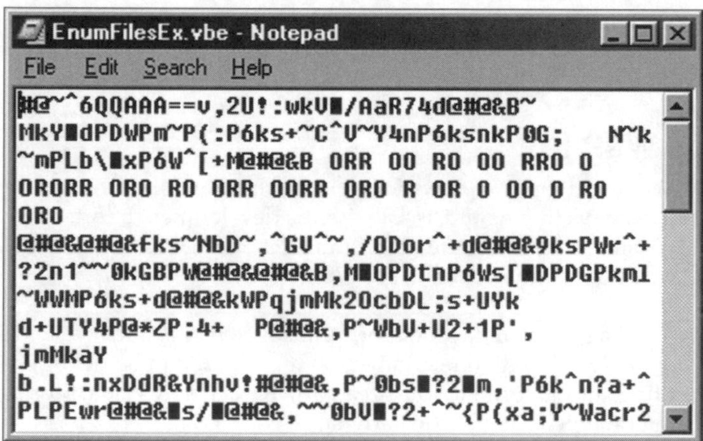

By default, the file now has a `.vbe` extension that makes the Windows Script-compliant scripting engine recognize it as an encoded file. (For JScript files the extension is `.jse`.)

To enable this feature and encrypt the script file, *you* need the Microsoft Script Encoder to be installed. *Your users* just need version 5.0 of the VBScript and JScript engines, plus some settings in the registry that permit WSH to manage encoded files. These settings are entered automatically by the MSE when it is installed.

This is an important point: as long as your users have the version 5.0 VBScript and JScript engines, they don't need the MSE installed in order to run your encrypted files. However, they do still need to make some tweaks to the registry that I'll cover in a moment.

How Encoding Works

To encode a script file, you simply call a program called `screnc.exe`, passing the source and destination filenames. Both parameters are mandatory:

```
screnc.exe myfile.vbs myfile.vbe
```

`screnc.exe` *supports many switches on the command line that are well described in the documentation that comes with the package. The usage shown above is sufficient for our purposes here.*

An encoded file is completely unintelligible to a human reader, and represents a guarantee for you. The source code will never be visible, and if someone alters even a single byte, the entire script will stop working.

Running Encoded Scripts

While the MSE is obviously necessary for creating encoded scripts, you don't strictly need it on the client machine in order to run those scripts. VBScript and JScript version 5.0 both incorporate the capability to decode such scripts, but since an encoded script file is no longer a `.vbs` or `.js` file, you should make sure that encoded scripts are registered on the client machine as types of document handled by `wscript.exe` or `cscript.exe`.

When you encode a VBScript file, it originates a new file with a `.vbe` extension that replaces the original `.vbs` version. This change automatically removes the file from the list of those that the WSH executable knows how to handle — in other words, a `.vbe` or `.jse` file won't be an executable file unless you enter some settings in the registry to register them with WSH.

Today, this kind of work is done automatically only by the MSE setup program. However, it wouldn't be surprising if future versions of the scripting engines were to add it to their setup procedures.

Tweaking the Registry for Encoded Scripts

Basically, the changes you need to make to the client machine's registry are the same as those you would have to make if you were adding a *new* scripting engine capable of processing encrypted files. The fact that the ability to execute encoded scripts lies in engines that are already used elsewhere is not an issue. To add a new engine, you need to:

- Define a new type of document (in this case, `.vbe` and `.jse`).
- Associate them with `wscript.exe` and `cscript.exe`.
- Add a value named `ScriptEngine` under the registry's document node. Make it point to the appropriate Windows Script-compliant engine.

Encoded script files don't use the standard VBScript or JScript engines, but new ones called `VBScript.Encode` and `JScript.Encode` respectively. When a module such as WSH or Internet Explorer 5.0 encounters one of these language engines, it loads a parser that first decrypts and then executes the code. For VBScript and JScript, these new modules are contained in the same `vbscript.dll` and `jscript.dll` files as the traditional parsers.

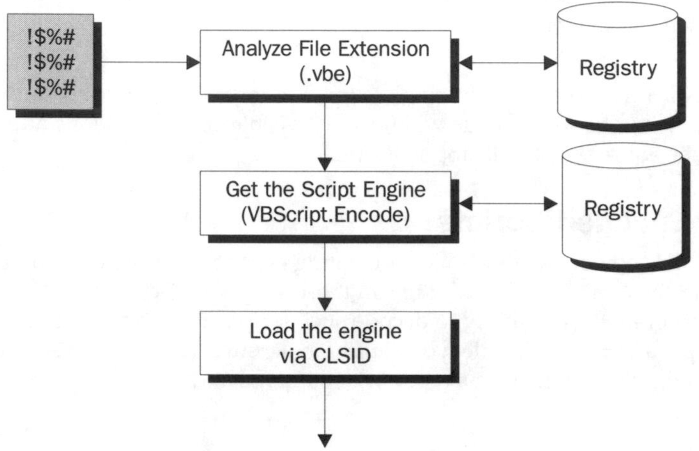

The diagram shows the sequence of steps that causes WSH to execute an encoded script — it's really no different from executing a regular `.vbs` file. In summary, to run encoded scripts you need:

- Version 5.0 of the `vbscript.dll` and `jscript.dll` libraries.
- The registry settings that cause WSH to load the `VBScript.Encode` and `JScript.Encode` engines when you run `.vbe` and `.jse` files. (These settings must be entered manually or by downloading and installing the MSE.)

Configuring Encoded Scripts to Run

In case you do need to arrange the settings for encoded scripts to be run manually, here's some help. I'm going to consider the case of `.vbe` files, but everything I say here also holds true for `.jse`. There are four groups of settings to enter:

- Registering the `.vbe` file extension
- Storing information for `.vbe` files
- Storing information for the `VBScript.Encode` scripting engine
- Registering the COM object that acts as the decoder

To illustrate the various steps, I'll be using the notation employed by `.reg` files. I'll also provide a couple of `.reg` files to edit and run on your machine.

> *`.reg` files might not illustrate the discussion as clearly as a script would do, but when you need to duplicate portions of the registry from PC to PC, they are a much safer bet — they can be created directly from the Registry Editor. If you select a node and choose* Registry | Export Registry File..., *you get a `.reg` file created on the fly, with all the keys and the values of that sub-tree. All you have to do then is copy that file and run it on the client PC.*

Dealing with the first of the settings just means creating a `.vbe` entry under `HKEY_CLASSES_ROOT` and assigning a name (`VBEfile`) to its `Default` value:

```
 [HKEY_CLASSES_ROOT\.VBE]
@="VBEFile"
```

Under `VBEFile`, you should duplicate all the information found under the standard `VBSFile` node, *except* for this one, which changes:

```
 [HKEY_CLASSES_ROOT\VBEFile\ScriptEngine]
@="VBScript.Encode"
```

To this point, we have stored a link to `VBScript.Encode`, but we're still missing the information for it. Add a new node with a `CLSID` sub-node:

```
 [HKEY_CLASSES_ROOT\VBScript.Encode]
@="VBScript Language Encoding"

[HKEY_CLASSES_ROOT\VBScript.Encode\CLSID]
@="{B54F3743-5B07-11cf-A4B0-00AA004A55E8}"
```

Of course, the `Default` value of `CLSID` will point to the CLSID of the COM object that works as the decoder and parser. Finally, you should register the COM object specifying, among other things, its local path.

The full source code for `vbefile.reg` is shown below, although I should point out that it makes use of paths that are specific to my computer; so don't forget to verify them on yours before you run it!

```
REGEDIT4

; ////////////////////////////////////////////////////////////////
; // .VBE
 [HKEY_CLASSES_ROOT\.VBE]
@="VBEFile"

; ////////////////////////////////////////////////////////////////
; // VBEFile
[HKEY_CLASSES_ROOT\VBEFile]
@="VBScript Encoded Script File"
```

Continued on Following Page

```
[HKEY_CLASSES_ROOT\VBEFile\DefaultIcon]
@="C:\\WINDOWS\\WScript.exe,2"

[HKEY_CLASSES_ROOT\VBEFile\ScriptEngine]
@="VBScript.Encode"

[HKEY_CLASSES_ROOT\VBEFile\Shell]

[HKEY_CLASSES_ROOT\VBEFile\Shell\Open]
@="&Open"

[HKEY_CLASSES_ROOT\VBEFile\Shell\Open\Command]
@="C:\\WINDOWS\\WScript.exe \"%1\" %*"

[HKEY_CLASSES_ROOT\VBEFile\Shell\Open2]
@="Open &with MS-DOS Prompt"

[HKEY_CLASSES_ROOT\VBEFile\Shell\Open2\Command]
@="C:\\WINDOWS\\COMMAND\\CScript.exe \"%1\" %*"

[HKEY_CLASSES_ROOT\VBEFile\Shell\Edit]
@="&Edit"

[HKEY_CLASSES_ROOT\VBEFile\Shell\Edit\Command]
@="C:\\WINDOWS\\Notepad.exe %1"

[HKEY_CLASSES_ROOT\VBEFile\Shell\Print]
@="&Print"

[HKEY_CLASSES_ROOT\VBEFile\Shell\Print\Command]
@="C:\\WINDOWS\\Notepad.exe /p %1"

[HKEY_CLASSES_ROOT\VBEFile\ShellEx]

[HKEY_CLASSES_ROOT\VBEFile\ShellEx\PropertySheetHandlers]

[HKEY_CLASSES_ROOT\VBEFile\ShellEx\PropertySheetHandlers\WSHProps]
@="{60254CA5-953B-11CF-8C96-00AA00B8708C}"

; ////////////////////////////////////////////////////////////
; // VBScript.Encode
[HKEY_CLASSES_ROOT\VBScript.Encode]
@="VBScript Language Encoding"

[HKEY_CLASSES_ROOT\VBScript.Encode\OLEScript]

[HKEY_CLASSES_ROOT\VBScript.Encode\CLSID]
@="{B54F3743-5B07-11cf-A4B0-00AA004A55E8}"

; ////////////////////////////////////////////////////////////
; // VBScript.Encode CLSID
[HKEY_CLASSES_ROOT\CLSID\{B54F3743-5B07-11cf-A4B0-00AA004A55E8}]
@="VBScript Language Encoding"

[HKEY_CLASSES_ROOT\CLSID\{B54F3743-5B07-11cf-A4B0-00AA004A55E8}\OLEScript]

[HKEY_CLASSES_ROOT\CLSID\{B54F3743-5B07-11cf-A4B0-00AA004A55E8}\ProgID]
@="VBScript.Encode"

[HKEY_CLASSES_ROOT\CLSID\{B54F3743-5B07-11cf-A4B0-
00AA004A55E8}\InprocServer32]
@="C:\\WINDOWS\\SYSTEM\\VBSCRIPT.DLL"
"ThreadingModel"="Both"

[HKEY_CLASSES_ROOT\CLSID\{B54F3743-5B07-11cf-A4B0-00AA004A55E8}\Implemented
Categories]

[HKEY_CLASSES_ROOT\CLSID\{B54F3743-5B07-11cf-A4B0-00AA004A55E8}\Implemented
Categories\{F0B7A1A1-9847-11CF-8F20-00805F2CD064}]

[HKEY_CLASSES_ROOT\CLSID\{B54F3743-5B07-11cf-A4B0-00AA004A55E8}\Implemented
Categories\{F0B7A1A2-9847-11CF-8F20-00805F2CD064}]

[HKEY_CLASSES_ROOT\CLSID\{B54F3743-5B07-11cf-A4B0-00AA004A55E8}\Implemented
Categories\{F0B7A1A3-9847-11CF-8F20-00805F2CD064}]
```

> **Note that the VBScript and JScript functions for performing run-time evaluation of source code, `ExecuteGlobal()` and `eval()`, don't support encoding. The `Include()` functions I built earlier in the book can therefore import neither `.jse` nor `.vbe` files.**

The good news about encoded files is that you can still pass arguments to them through the command line, just as you would have done with the corresponding `.vbs` and `.js` files:

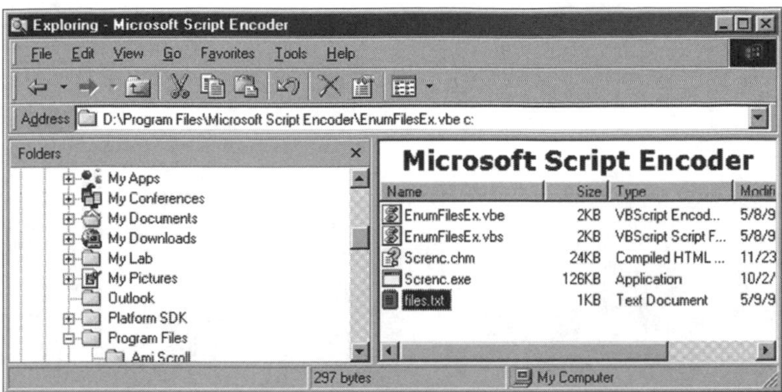

This feature lets us extend the `wshdrop.dll` module you saw earlier to support drag-and-drop for `.vbe` and `.jse` files as well, so that dropping text and filenames over `.vbs` and `.vbe` files has the same final effect.

As I stated earlier, having an encoded script is not very different from having a binary executable. Provided that you and your users have compatible (if not identical) configurations for script libraries and registry settings, all you will ever have to do is distribute the `.vbe` or `.jse` files, and your users will only ever have to double-click them.

Summary

This last chapter presented a couple more concrete examples of the things it's possible to do with WSH scripts. With the help of some of the objects we've discussed in earlier chapters, I demonstrated how to use script to tie together MS Office, Dynamic HTML and Messaging. I also showed you a couple of applications for a DropHandler shell extension.

Later in the chapter, I presented some ways of improving Windows' native support for script files, and introduced the Microsoft Script Encoder as a way of protecting your intellectual investments.

Using the COM components that are sprinkled around your hard disk, you can arrange little cross-product applications just like the invoicing tool shown above, and utility programs that will assist in your everyday work. The final, golden rule of WSH programming is that there are no limits apart from your imagination and your requirements.

VBScript Reference

Array Handling

Dim – declares a variable. An array variable can be static, with a defined number of elements, or dynamic, and can have up to 60 dimensions.
ReDim – used to change the size of an array variable that has been declared as dynamic.
Preserve – keyword used to preserve the contents of an array being resized (otherwise data is lost when ReDim is used). If you need to use this then you can only re-dimension the rightmost index of the array.
Erase – reinitializes the elements of a fixed-size array or empties the contents of a dynamic array:

```
Dim arEmployees ()
ReDim arEmployees (9,1)

arEmployees(9,1) = "Phil"

ReDim arEmployees(9,2)              ' loses the contents of element (9,1)
arEmployees(9,2) = "Paul"

ReDim Preserve arEmployees(9,3)     ' preserves the contents of (9,2)
arEmployees(9,3) = "Smith"

Erase arEmployees                   ' back to where we started - empty array
```

LBound – returns the smallest subscript for the dimension of an array. Note that arrays always start from the subscript zero so this function will always return the value zero.
UBound – used to determine the size of an array:

```
Dim strCustomers(10, 5)
intSizeFirst = UBound(strCustomers, 1)      ' returns SizeFirst = 10
intSizeSecond = UBound(strCustomers, 2)     ' returns SizeSecond = 5
```

The actual number of elements is always one greater than the value returned by UBound because the array starts from zero.

Assignments

Let – used to assign values to variables (optional).
Set – used to assign an object reference to a variable.

```
Let intNumberOfDays = 365

Set txtMyTextBox = txtcontrol
txtMyTextBox.Value = "Hello World"
```

Constants

Empty – an empty variable is one that has been created, but has not yet been assigned a value.
Nothing – used to remove an object reference:

```
Set txtMyTextBox = txtATextBox          ' assigns object reference
Set txtMyTextBox = Nothing              ' removes object reference
```

Null – indicates that a variable is not valid. Note that this isn't the same as Empty.
True – indicates that an expression is true. Has numerical value –1.
False – indicates that an expression is false. Has numerical value 0.

Error Constant

Constant	Value
vbObjectError	&h80040000

System Color Constants

Constant	Value	Description
vbBlack	&h000000	Black
vbRed	&hFF0000	Red
vbGreen	&h00FF00	Green
vbYellow	&hFFFF00	Yellow
vbBlue	&h0000FF	Blue
vbMagenta	&hFF00FF	Magenta
vbCyan	&h00FFFF	Cyan
vbWhite	&hFFFFFF	White

Comparison Constants

Constant	Value	Description
vbBinaryCompare	0	Perform a binary comparison.
vbTextCompare	1	Perform a textual comparison.

Date and Time Constants

Constant	Value	Description
vbSunday	1	Sunday
vbMonday	2	Monday
vbTuesday	3	Tuesday
vbWednesday	4	Wednesday
vbThursday	5	Thursday
vbFriday	6	Friday
vbSaturday	7	Saturday
vbFirstJan1	1	Use the week in which January 1 occurs (default)
vbFirstFourDays	2	Use the first week that has at least four days in the new year
vbFirstFullWeek	3	Use the first full week of the year
vbUseSystem	0	Use the format in the regional settings for the computer
vbUseSystemDayOfWeek	0	Use the day in the system settings for the first weekday

Date Format Constants

Constant	Value	Description
vbGeneralDate	0	Display a date and/or time in the format set in the system settings. For real numbers display a date and time. For integer numbers display only a date. For numbers less than 1, display time only.
vbLongDate	1	Display a date using the long date format specified in the computer's regional settings.
vbShortDate	2	Display a date using the short date format specified in the computer's regional settings.
vbLongTime	3	Display a time using the long time format specified in the computer's regional settings.
vbShortTime	4	Display a time using the short time format specified in the computer's regional settings.

Message Box Constants

Constant	Value	Description
`vbOKOnly`	0	Display OK button only
`vbOKCancel`	1	Display OK and Cancel buttons
`vbAbortRetryIgnore`	2	Display Abort, Retry, and Ignore buttons
`vbYesNoCancel`	3	Display Yes, No, and Cancel buttons
`vbYesNo`	4	Display Yes and No buttons
`vbRetryCancel`	5	Display Retry and Cancel buttons
`vbCritical`	16	Display Critical Message icon
`vbQuestion`	32	Display Warning Query icon
`vbExclamation`	48	Display Warning Message icon
`vbInformation`	64	Display Information Message icon
`vbDefaultButton1`	0	First button is the default
`vbDefaultButton2`	256	Second button is the default
`vbDefaultButton3`	512	Third button is the default
`vbDefaultButton4`	768	Fourth button is the default
`vbApplicationModal`	0	Application modal
`vbSystemModal`	4096	System modal

String Constants

Constant	Value	Description
`vbCr`	`Chr(13)`	Carriage return only
`vbCrLf`	`Chr(13) & Chr(10)`	Carriage return and linefeed (Newline)
`vbFormFeed`	`Chr(12)`	Form feed only
`vbLf`	`Chr(10)`	Line feed only
`vbNewLine`	-	Newline character as appropriate to a specific platform
`vbNullChar`	`Chr(0)`	Character having the value 0
`vbNullString`	-	String having the value zero (not just an empty string)
`vbTab`	`Chr(9)`	Horizontal tab
`vbVerticalTab`	`Chr(11)`	Vertical tab

`With` – executes a series of statements for a single object:

```
With myDiv.style
    .posLeft = 200
    .posTop = 300
    .color = Red
End With
```

Functions

VBScript contains several inbuilt functions that can be used to manipulate and examine variables. These have been subdivided into these general categories:

- Conversion functions
- Date/time functions
- Math functions
- Object management functions
- Script engine identification functions
- String functions
- Variable testing functions

For a full description of each function and the parameters it requires, see the Microsoft web site at http://msdn.microsoft.com/scripting.

Conversion Functions

These functions are used to convert values in variables between different types:

Function	Description
`Abs()`	Returns the absolute value of a number.
`Asc()`	Returns the numeric ANSI (or ASCII) code number of the first character in a string.
`AscB()`	As above, but provided for use with byte data contained in a string. Returns result from the first byte only.
`AscW()`	As above, but provided for Unicode characters. Returns the `Wide` character code, avoiding the conversion from Unicode to ANSI.
`Chr()`	Returns a string made up of the ANSI character matching the number supplied.
`ChrB()`	As above, but provided for use with byte data contained in a string. Always returns a single byte.

Table Continued on Following Page

Function	Description
`ChrW()`	As above, but provided for Unicode characters. Its argument is a `Wide` character code, thereby avoiding the conversion from ANSI to Unicode.
`CBool()`	Returns the argument value converted to a `Variant` of subtype `Boolean`.
`CByte()`	Returns the argument value converted to a `Variant` of subtype `Byte`.
`CCur()`	Returns the argument value converted to a `Variant` of subtype `Currency`.
`CDate()`	Returns the argument value converted to a `Variant` of subtype `Date`.
`CDbl()`	Returns the argument value converted to a `Variant` of subtype `Double`.
`CInt()`	Returns the argument value converted to a `Variant` of subtype `Integer`.
`CLng()`	Returns the argument value converted to a `Variant` of subtype `Long`.
`CSng()`	Returns the argument value converted to a `Variant` of subtype `Single`.
`CStr()`	Returns the argument value converted to a `Variant` of subtype `String`.
`Fix()`	Returns the integer (whole) part of a number. If the number is negative, `Fix` returns the first negative integer greater than or equal to the number.
`Hex()`	Returns a string representing the hexadecimal value of a number.
`Int()`	Returns the integer (whole) portion of a number. If the number is negative, `Int` returns the first negative integer less than or equal to the number.
`Oct()`	Returns a string representing the octal value of a number.
`Round()`	Returns a number rounded to a specified number of decimal places.
`Sgn()`	Returns an integer indicating the sign of a number.

Date/Time Functions

These functions return date or time values from the computer's system clock, or manipulate existing values:

Function	Description
`Date()`	Returns the current system date
`DateAdd()`	Returns a date to which a specified time interval has been added
`DateDiff()`	Returns the number of days, weeks, or years between two dates
`DatePart()`	Returns just the day, month or year of a given date
`DateSerial()`	Returns a `Variant` of subtype `Date` for a specified year, month and day
`DateValue()`	Returns a `Variant` of subtype `Date`
`Day()`	Returns a number between `1` and `31` representing the day of the month
`Hour()`	Returns a number between `0` and `23` representing the hour of the day
`Minute()`	Returns a number between `0` and `59` representing the minute of the hour
`Month()`	Returns a number between `1` and `12` representing the month of the year
`MonthName()`	Returns the name of the specified month as a string
`Now()`	Returns the current date and time
`Second()`	Returns a number between `0` and `59` representing the second of the minute
`Time()`	Returns a `Variant` of subtype `Date` indicating the current system time
`TimeSerial()`	Returns a `Variant` of subtype `Date` for a specific hour, minute and second
`TimeValue()`	Returns a `Variant` of subtype `Date` containing the time
`Weekday()`	Returns a number representing the day of the week
`WeekdayName()`	Returns the name of the specified day of the week as a string
`Year()`	Returns a number representing the year

Math Functions

These functions perform mathematical operations on variables containing numerical values:

Function	Description
`Atn()`	Returns the arctangent of a number
`Cos()`	Returns the cosine of an angle
`Exp()`	Returns `e` (the base of natural logarithms) raised to a power
`Log()`	Returns the natural logarithm of a number
`Randomize()`	Initializes the random-number generator
`Rnd()`	Returns a random number
`Sin()`	Returns the sine of an angle
`Sqr()`	Returns the square root of a number
`Tan()`	Returns the tangent of an angle

Miscellaneous Functions

Function	Description
`Eval()`	Evaluates an expression and returns a Boolean result (e.g. treats `x = y` as an *expression* which is either true or false)
`Execute()`	Executes one or more statements (e.g. treats `x = y` as a *statement* which assigns the value of `y` to `x`)
`RGB()`	Returns a number representing an RGB color value

Object Management Functions

These functions are used to manipulate objects, where applicable:

Function	Description
`CreateObject()`	Creates and returns a reference to an Automation-compatible object
`GetObject()`	Returns a reference to an Automation-compatible object
`LoadPicture()`	Returns a picture object

Script Engine Identification

These functions return the version of the scripting engine:

Function	Description
`ScriptEngine()`	A string containing the major, minor, and build version numbers of the scripting engine
`ScriptEngineMajorVersion()`	The major version of the scripting engine, as a number
`ScriptEngineMinorVersion()`	The minor version of the scripting engine, as a number
`ScriptEngineBuildVersion()`	The build version of the scripting engine, as a number

String Functions

These functions are used to manipulate string values in variables:

Function	Description
`Filter()`	Returns an array from a string array, based on specified filter criteria.
`FormatCurrency()`	Returns a string formatted as currency value.
`FormatDateTime()`	Returns a string formatted as a date or time.
`FormatNumber()`	Returns a string formatted as a number.
`FormatPercent()`	Returns a string formatted as a percentage.
`InStr()`	Returns the position of the first occurrence of one string within another.
`InStrB()`	As above, but provided for use with byte data contained in a string. Returns the byte position instead of the character position.
`InstrRev()`	As `InStr()`, but starts from the end of the string.
`Join()`	Returns a string created by joining the strings contained in an array.
`LCase()`	Returns a string that has been converted to lowercase.

Table Continued on Following Page

Function	Description
`Left()`	Returns a specified number of characters from the left end of a string.
`LeftB()`	As above, but provided for use with byte data contained in a string. Uses that number of bytes instead of that number of characters.
`Len()`	Returns the length of a string or the number of bytes needed for a variable.
`LenB()`	As above, but is provided for use with byte data contained in a string. Returns the number of bytes in the string instead of characters.
`LTrim()`	Returns a copy of a string without leading spaces.
`Mid()`	Returns a specified number of characters from a string.
`MidB()`	As above, but provided for use with byte data contained in a string. Uses that numbers of bytes instead of that number of characters.
`Replace()`	Returns a string in which a specified sub-string has been replaced with another sub-string, a specified number of times.
`Right()`	Returns a specified number of characters from the right end of a string.
`RightB()`	As above, but provided for use with byte data contained in a string. Uses that number of bytes instead of that number of characters.
`RTrim()`	Returns a copy of a string without trailing spaces.
`Space()`	Returns a string consisting of the specified number of spaces.
`Split()`	Returns a one-dimensional array of a specified number of sub-strings.
`StrComp()`	Returns a value indicating the result of a string comparison.
`String()`	Returns a string of the length specified made up of a repeating character.
`StrReverse()`	Returns a string in which the character order of a string is reversed.
`Trim()`	Returns a copy of a string without leading or trailing spaces.
`UCase()`	Returns a string that has been converted to uppercase.

Variable Testing Functions

These functions are used to determine the type of information stored in a variable:

Function	Description
`IsArray()`	Returns a `Boolean` value indicating whether a variable is an array
`IsDate()`	Returns a `Boolean` value indicating whether an expression can be converted to a date
`IsEmpty()`	Returns a `Boolean` value indicating whether a variable has been initialized
`IsNull()`	Returns a `Boolean` value indicating whether an expression contains no valid data
`IsNumeric()`	Returns a `Boolean` value indicating whether an expression can be evaluated as a number
`IsObject()`	Returns a `Boolean` value indicating whether an expression references a valid Automation-compatible object
`TypeName()`	Returns a string that provides `Variant` subtype information about a variable
`VarType()`	Returns a number indicating the subtype of a variable

Variable Declarations

`Class` – declares the name of a class, as well as the variables, properties, and methods that comprise the class.
`Const` – declares a constant to be used in place of literal values.
`Dim` – declares a variable.

Error Handling

`On Error Resume Next` – indicates that if an error occurs, control should continue at the next statement.
`Err` – this is the error object that provides information about run-time errors.

Error handling is very limited in VBScript and the `Err` object must be tested explicitly to determine if an error has occurred.

Input/Output

This consists of `Msgbox()` for output and `InputBox()` for input:

MsgBox

This displays a message, and can return a value indicating which button was clicked.

```
MsgBox "Hello There", 20, "Hello Message", "c:\windows\MyHelp.hlp", 123
```

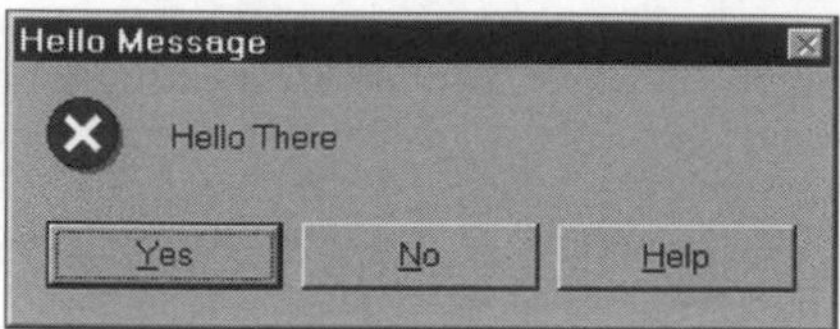

The parameters are:
`"Hello There"` – this contains the text of the message (the only obligatory parameter).
`20` – this determines which icon and buttons appear on the message box.
`"Hello Message"` – this contains the text that will appear as the title of the message box.
`"c:\windows\MyHelp.hlp"` – this adds a Help button to the message box and determines the help file that is opened if the button is clicked.
`123` – this is a reference to the particular help topic that will be displayed if the Help button is clicked.

The value of the icon and buttons parameter is determined using the following tables:

Constant	Value	Buttons
`vbOKOnly`	0	OK
`vbOKCancel`	1	OK, Cancel
`vbAbortRetryIngnore`	2	Abort, Retry, Ignore
`vbYesNoCancel`	3	Yes, No, Cancel
`vbYesNo`	4	Yes, No
`vbRetryCancel`	5	Retry, Cancel

Constant	Value	Buttons
`vbDefaultButton1`	0	The first button from the left is the default.
`vbDefaultButton2`	256	The second button from the left is the default.
`vbDefaultButton3`	512	The third button from the left is the default.
`vbDefaultButton4`	768	The fourth button from the left is the default.

Constant	Value	Description	Icon
vbCritical	16	Critical Message	
vbQuestion	32	Questioning Message	
vbExclamation	48	Warning Message	
vbInformation	64	Informational Message	

Constant	Value	Description
vbApplicationModal	0	The application stops until user clicks a button.
vbSystemModal	4096	On Win16 systems the whole system stops until user clicks a button. On Win32 systems the message box remains on top of any other programs.

To specify which buttons and icon are displayed you simply add the relevant values. So, in our example we add together `4 + 0+ 16` to display the Yes and No buttons, with Yes as the default, and the `Critical` icon. If we used `4 + 256 + 16` we could display the same buttons and icon, but have No as the default.

You can determine which button the user clicked by assigning the return code of the `MsgBox()` function to a variable:

```
intButtonClicked = MsgBox("Hello There", 35, "Hello Message")
```

Notice that brackets enclose the `MsgBox()` parameters when used in this format. The following table determines the value assigned to the variable `intButtonClicked`:

Constant	Value	Button Clicked
vbOK	1	OK
vbCancel	2	Cancel
vbAbort	3	Abort
vbRetry	4	Retry

Constant	Value	Button Clicked
vbIgnore	5	Ignore
vbYes	6	Yes
vbNo	7	No

InputBox

This accepts text entry from the user and returns it as a string.

```
strName = InputBox("Please enter your name", "Login", "John Smith", 500, 500)
```

The parameters are:
`"Please enter your name"` – this is the prompt displayed in the input box.
`"Login"` – this is the text displayed as the title of the input box.
`"John Smith"` – this is the default value displayed in the input box.
`500` – specifies the x position of the input box in relation to the screen.
`500` – specifies the y position of the input box in relation to the screen.

As with the `MsgBox()` function, you can also specify a help file and topic to add a **Help** button to the input box.

Procedures

`Call` – optional method of calling a subroutine.
`Function` – used to declare a function.
`Sub` – used to declare a subroutine.

Other Keywords

`Rem` – old style method of adding comments to code (it's now more usual to use an apostrophe (`'`).)
`Option Explicit` – forces you to declare a variable before it can be used (if used, it must appear before any other statements in a script).

Visual Basic Run-time Error Codes

The following error codes also apply to VBA code and many will not be appropriate to an application built completely around VBScript. However, if you have built your own components then these error codes may well be brought up when such components are used.

Code	Description
3	Return without `GoSub`
5	Invalid procedure call
6	Overflow
7	Out of memory
9	Subscript out of range
10	This array is fixed or temporarily locked
11	Division by zero
13	Type mismatch
14	Out of string space
16	Expression too complex
17	Can't perform requested operation
18	User interrupt occurred
20	Resume without error
28	Out of stack space
35	Sub or Function not defined
47	Too many DLL application clients
48	Error in loading DLL
49	Bad DLL calling convention
51	Internal error
52	Bad file name or number
53	File not found

Code	Description
54	Bad file mode
55	File already open
57	Device I/O error
58	File already exists
59	Bad record length
61	Disk full
62	Input past end of file
63	Bad record number
67	Too many files
68	Device unavailable
70	Permission denied
71	Disk not ready
74	Can't rename with different drive
75	Path/File access error
76	Path not found
91	Object variable not set
92	`For` loop not initialized
93	Invalid pattern string
94	Invalid use of Null
322	Can't create necessary temporary file
325	Invalid format in resource file

Table Continued on Following Page

Code	Description
380	Invalid property value
423	Property or method not found
424	Object required
429	OLE Automation server can't create object
430	Class doesn't support OLE Automation
432	File name or class name not found during OLE Automation operation
438	Object doesn't support this property or method
440	OLE Automation error
442	Connection to type library or object library for remote process has been lost. Press OK for dialog to remove reference.
443	OLE Automation object does not have a default value
445	Object doesn't support this action
446	Object doesn't support named arguments
447	Object doesn't support current locale setting
448	Named argument not found
449	Argument not optional
450	Wrong number of arguments or invalid property assignment
451	Object not a collection

Code	Description
452	Invalid ordinal
453	Specified DLL function not found
454	Code resource not found
455	Code resource lock error
457	This key is already associated with an element of this collection
458	Variable uses an OLE Automation type not supported in Visual Basic
462	The remote server machine does not exist or is unavailable
481	Invalid picture
500	Variable is undefined
501	Cannot assign to variable
502	Object not safe for scripting
503	Object not safe for initializing
504	Object not safe for creating
505	Invalid or unqualified reference
506	Class not defined
1001	Out of memory
1002	Syntax error

Code	Description
1003	Expected ':'
1004	Expected ';'
1005	Expected '('
1006	Expected ')'
1007	Expected ']'
1008	Expected '{'
1009	Expected '}'
1010	Expected identifier
1011	Expected '='
1012	Expected 'If'
1013	Expected 'To'
1014	Expected 'End'
1015	Expected 'Function'
1016	Expected 'Sub'
1017	Expected 'Then'
1018	Expected 'Wend'
1019	Expected 'Loop'
1020	Expected 'Next'
1021	Expected 'Case'
1022	Expected 'Select'
1023	Expected expression
1024	Expected statement
1025	Expected end of statement
1026	Expected integer constant
1027	Expected 'While' or 'Until'
1028	Expected 'While', 'Until' or end of statement
1029	Too many locals or arguments
1030	Identifier too long
1031	Invalid number
1032	Invalid character
1033	Un-terminated string constant
1034	Un-terminated comment
1035	Nested comment
1036	'Me' cannot be used outside of a procedure
1037	Invalid use of 'Me' keyword
1038	'loop' without 'do'
1039	Invalid 'exit' statement
1040	Invalid 'for' loop control variable
1041	Variable redefinition
1042	Must be first statement on the line
1043	Cannot assign to non-ByVal argument
1044	Cannot use parentheses when calling a Sub
1045	Expected literal constant
1046	Expected 'In'
1047	Expected 'Class'
1048	Must be defined inside a Class

Table Continued on Following Page

Code	Description
1049	Expected Let or Set or Get in property declaration
1050	Expected 'Property'
1051	Number of arguments must be consistent across properties specification
1052	Cannot have multiple default property/method in a Class
1053	Class initialize or terminate do not have arguments
1054	Property set or let must have at least one argument
1055	Unexpected 'Next'
1056	'Default' can be specified only on 'Property' or 'Function' or 'Sub'
1057	'Default' specification must also specify 'Public'

Code	Description
1058	'Default' specification can only be on Property Get
5016	Regular Expression object expected
5017	Syntax error in regular expression
5018	Unexpected quantifier
5019	Expected ']' in regular expression
5020	Expected ')' in regular expression
5021	Invalid range in character set
32811	Element not found

For more information about VBScript, visit Microsoft's VBScript site at http://msdn.microsoft.com/scripting.

JScript Reference

Values

JScript recognizes the following data types:

- **strings –** e.g. "Hello World"
- **numbers** – both integers (86) and decimal values (86.235)
- **Boolean** – `true` or `false` (case sensitive)

A null (*no value*) value is assigned with the keyword `null`.

JScript also makes use of 'special characters' in a similar way to the C++ programming language:

Character	Function
`\n`	new line
`\t`	tab
`\f`	form feed
`\b`	backspace
`\r`	carriage return

You may 'escape' other characters by preceding them with a backslash (\), to prevent the engine from trying to interpret them. This is most commonly used for quotes and backslashes, or to include a character by using its octal (base 8) value:

```
document.write("This shows a \"quote\" in a string.");
document.write("This is a backslash: \\");
document.write("This is a space character: \040.");
```

Variables

JScript is a **loosely typed** language. This means that variables do not have an explicitly defined variable type. Instead, every variable can hold values of various types. Conversions between types are done automatically when needed, as this example demonstrates:

```
x = 55;                         // x is assigned to be the integer 55
y = "55";                       // y is assigned to be the string "55"
y = '55';                       // an alternative using single quotes

z = 1 + y;

/* because y is a string, x will be automatically
   converted to a string value, so the result is z = 155. */

document.write(x);
/* the number 55 will be written to the screen. Even
   though x is an integer and not a string, JScript will
   make the necessary conversion for you. */

n = 3.14159;                    // assigning a real (fractional) number
n = 0546;                       // numbers starting 0 assumed to be octal
n = 0xFFEC;                     // numbers starting 0x assumed to be hex
n = 2.145E-5;                   // using exponential notation
```

The `parseInt()` and `parseFloat()` functions (discussed later in this appendix) can be used to convert strings for numeric addition.

Variable names must start with either a letter or an underscore. Beyond the first letter, variables may contain any combination of letters, underscores, and digits. JScript is case sensitive, so `this_variable` is not the same as `This_Variable`.

Variables do not need to be declared before they are used. However, you may use the `var` keyword to explicitly define a variable. This is especially useful when there is the possibility of conflicting variable names. When in doubt, use `var`.

```
var x = "55";
```

Assignment Operators

The following operators are used to make assignments in JScript:

Operator	Example	Result
`=`	`x = y`	x equals y
`+=`	`x += y`	x equals x plus y
`-=`	`x -= y`	x equals x minus y
`*=`	`x *= y`	x equals x multiplied by y
`/=`	`x /= y`	x equals x divided by y
`%=`	`x %= y`	x equals x modulus y

Each operator assigns the value on the right to the variable on the left.

```
x = 100;
y = 10;
x += y;                          // x now is equal to 110
```

Equality Operators

Operator	Meaning
==	is equal to
!=	is not equal to
>	is greater than
>=	is greater than or equal to
<	is less than
<=	is less than or equal to

Other Operators

<table>
<tr><th>Operator</th><th>Meaning</th></tr>
<tr><td>+</td><td>Addition</td></tr>
<tr><td>-</td><td>Subtraction</td></tr>
<tr><td>*</td><td>Multiplication</td></tr>
<tr><td>/</td><td>Division</td></tr>
<tr><td>%</td><td>Modulus</td></tr>
<tr><td>++</td><td>Increment</td></tr>
<tr><td>--</td><td>Decrement</td></tr>
<tr><td>-</td><td>Unary Negation</td></tr>
<tr><td>&</td><td>Bitwise AND</td></tr>
<tr><td>|</td><td>Bitwise OR</td></tr>
<tr><td>^</td><td>Bitwise XOR</td></tr>
<tr><td><<</td><td>Bitwise left shift</td></tr>
<tr><td>>></td><td>Bitwise right shift</td></tr>
<tr><td>>>></td><td>Zero-fill right shift</td></tr>
<tr><td>&&</td><td>Logical AND</td></tr>
<tr><td>||</td><td>Logical OR</td></tr>
<tr><td>!</td><td>Not</td></tr>
</table>

String Operators

Operator	Meaning
`+`	Concatenates strings, so `"abc" + "def"` is `"abcdef"`

`==`
`!=`
`>`
`>=`
`<`
`<=`
	Compare strings in a case-sensitive way. A string is 'greater' than another based on the Latin ASCII code values of the characters, starting from the left of the string. So `"DEF"` is greater than `"ABC"` and `"DEE"`, but less than `"abc"` (upper case letters come before lower case ones in the ASCII character set).

Comments

Operator	Meaning
`// a comment`	A single line comment
`/* this text is a` `multi-line comment */`	A multi-line comment

Input/Output

In JScript, there are three different methods of providing information to the user and getting a response back. (Note that these are methods of the window object and not JScript function calls.)

alert

This displays a message with an OK button:

```
alert("Hello World!");
```

confirm

Displays a message with both an OK and a Cancel button. `true` is returned if the OK button is pressed, and `false` is returned if the Cancel button is pressed:

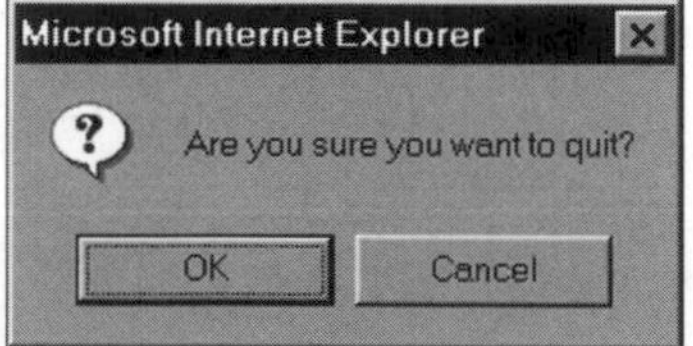


```
confirm("Are you sure you want to quit?");
```

prompt

Displays a message and a text box for user input. The first string argument forms the text that is to be displayed above the text box. The second argument is a string, integer, or property of an existing object, which represents the default value to display inside the box. If the second argument is not specified, "<undefined>" is displayed inside the text box.

The string typed into the box is returned if the OK button is pressed. `false` is returned if the Cancel button is pressed:

```
prompt("What is your name?", "");
```

Control Flow

There are two ways of controlling the flow of a program in JScript. The first involves **conditional** statements, which follow either one branch of the program or another. The second way is to use **repeated iteration** of a set of statements.

Conditional Statements

JScript has two conditional statements:

`if..then..else` – used to run various blocks of code, depending on conditions. These statements have the following general form in JScript:

```
if(condition)
{
   // code to be executed if condition is true
}
else
{
   // code to be executed if condition is false
};
```

In addition:

- The `else` portion is optional.
- `if` statements may be nested.
- Multiple statements must be enclosed by braces.

Here is an example:

```
person_type = prompt("What are you ?", "");
if(person_type == "cat")
   alert("Here, have some cat food.");
else
{
   if(person_type == "dog")
      alert("Here, have some dog food.");
   else
   {
      if(person_type == "human")
         alert("Here have some, er, human food!");
   }
};
```

Notice that the braces are only actually required where there is more than one statement within the block. Like many other constructs, they can be omitted where single statements are used. (Although not necessary, it can sometimes be a good idea to include all of the semi-colons and brackets that could be used, as this makes the code easier to modify.)

All statements in JScript are supposed to have a semicolon line terminator, because a statement can span more than one line without special continuation markers. However, JScript lets you leave it out in quite a few areas, as long as it can tell where a statement is supposed to end. The final semicolon is therefore not mandatory.

`switch` – used to run various blocks of code, depending on conditions. These statements have the following general form in JScript:

```
switch(expression)
{
   case label1 :
      // code to be executed if expression is equal to label1
      break;
   case label2 :
      // code to be executed if expression is equal to label2
   ...
   default :
      // code to be executed if expression is not equal to any of the labels
}
```

`break;` can be inserted following the code for a case, to prevent execution of the code running into the next case automatically.

Loop Statements

`for` – executes a block of code a specified number of times:

```
for(initialization; condition; increment)
{
   statements to execute
}
```

In the following example, `i` is initially set to zero, and is incremented by 1 at the end of each iteration. The loop terminates when the condition `i < 10` is false:

```
for(i = 0; i < 10; i++)
{
   document.write(i);
}
```

`while` – executes a block of code while a condition is true:

```
while(condition)
{
   // statements to execute...
}
```

`do...while` – executes a statement block once, and then repeats execution of the loop while a condition is true:

```
do
{
   // statements to execute...
} while(condition);
```

`break` – will cause an exit from a loop regardless of the condition statement:

```
x = 0;
while(x != 10)
{
   n = prompt("Enter a number or 'q' to quit", "");
   if(n == "q")
   {
      alert("See ya");
      break;
   }
}
```

`break` can also be used in `switch`, `for` and `do...while` loops.

`continue` – will cause the loop to jump immediately back to the condition statement.

```
x = 0;
while(x != 1)
{
   if(!(confirm("Should I add 1 to n ?")))
   {
      continue;
      // the following x++ is never executed
      x++;
   }
   x++;
}
alert("Bye");
```

`with` – Establishes a default object for a set of statements. The code:

```
x = Math.cos(3 * Math.PI) + Math.sin(Math.LN10)
y = Math.tan(14 * Math.E)
```

can be rewritten as:

```
with(Math)
{
   x = cos(3 * PI) + sin(LN10)
   y = tan(14 * E)
}
```

When you use the `with` statement, the object passed as the parameter is the default object. Notice how this shortens each statement.

Error Handling Statements

JScript 5.0 includes built-in error handling. This is done using the `try...catch` statement. It allows the developer to anticipate certain error messages, and provide a different code path to follow if that error occurs.

```
function ErrorHandler(x)
{
   try
   {
      try
      {
         if(x == 'OK')                     // Evalute argument
            throw "Value OK";              // Throw an error
         else
            throw "Value not OK";          // Throw a different error
      }
      catch(e)
      {                                    // Handle "x = OK" errors here
         if(e == "Value OK")               // Check for an error handled here
            return(e + " successfully handled.");     // Return error message
         else                              // Can't handle error here
            throw e;                       // Rethrow the error for next
      }                                    // error handler
   }
   catch(e)
   {                                       // Handle other errors here
      return(e + " handled elsewhere.");              // Return error message
   }
}

document.write(ErrorHandler('OK'));
document.write(ErrorHandler('BAD'));
```

The `throw` statement is used to generate error conditions that can then be handled by a `try...catch` block. The value that you throw can be any expression, including a string, Boolean or number.

Built-in Functions

JScript provides a number of built-in functions that can be accessed within code.

Function	Description
`escape(char)`	Returns a new string with all spaces, punctuation, accented characters and any non–ASCII characters encoded into the format `%XX`, where `XX` is their hexadecimal value
`eval(expression)`	Returns the result of evaluating the JScript `expression`
`isFinite(value)`	Returns a Boolean value of `true` if `value` is any value other than `NaN` (not a number), negative infinity, or positive infinity
`isNaN(value)`	Returns a Boolean value of `true` if `value` is not a legal number

Function	Description
`parseFloat(string)`	Converts `string` to a floating-point number
`parseInt(string, base)`	Converts `string` to an integer number with the base of `base`
`typeOf(object)`	Returns the data type of `object` as a string, such as `"boolean"`, `"function"`, etc
`unescape(char)`	Returns a string where all characters encoded with the `%XX` hexadecimal form are replaced by their ASCII character set equivalents

Built-in Objects

JScript provides a set of built-in objects that have their own sets of properties and methods and which can be accessed with JScript code.

ActiveXObject Object

The `ActiveXObject` object creates and returns a reference to an Automation object. To create a new `ActiveXObject` object, use:

```
// create an automation object referring to an Excel Spreadsheet
ExcelSheet = new ActiveXObject("Excel.Sheet");
```

Once you have created the object reference, you can interact with the object using its methods and properties.

Array Object

The `Array` object specifies a method of creating arrays and working with them. To create a new array, use:

```
cats = new Array();          // create an empty array
cats = new Array(10);        // create an array of 10 items

// or create and fill an array with values in one go:
cats = new Array("Boo Boo", "Purrcila", "Sam", "Lucky");
```

Property	Description
`length`	A read/write integer value specifying the number of elements in the array

Method	Description
`array1.concat(array2)`	Returns a new array consisting of the contents of two arrays
`join([string])`	Returns a string containing each element of the array, optionally separated with `string`.

Table Continued on Following Page

Method	Description
`reverse()`	Reverses the order of the array, without creating a new object.
`slice(start, [end])`	Returns a section of an array, starting at position `start` and going up to and including position `end`.
`sort([function])`	Sorts the array, optionally based upon the results of a function specified by `function`.
`toString()`	Returns the elements of an array converted to strings, concatenated and separated by commas.
`valueOf()`	Returns the elements of an array converted to strings, concatenated and separated by commas. Like `toString()`.

Early versions of JScript had no explicit array structure. However, JScript's object mechanisms allow for easy creation of arrays:

```
function MakeArray(n)
{
   this.length = n;
   for(var i = 1; i <= n; i++)
      this[i] = 0;
   return this;
}
```

With this function included in your script, you can create arrays with:

```
cats = new MakeArray(20);
```

You can then populate the array like this:

```
cats[0] = "Boo Boo";
cats[1] = "Purrcila";
cats[2] = "Sam";
cats[3] = "Lucky";
```

Boolean Object

The `Boolean` object is used to store simple yes/no, true/false values. To create a new Boolean object, use the syntax:

```
MyAnswer = new Boolean([value])
```

If *`value`* is `0`, `null`, omitted, or an empty string, the new Boolean object will have the value `false`. All other values, *including the string* `"false"`, create an object with the value `true`.

Method	Description
`toString()`	Returns the value of the Boolean as the string `true` or `false`
`valueOf()`	Returns the primitive numeric value of the object for conversion in calculations

Date Object

The `Date` object provides a method for working with dates and times inside of JScript. New instances of the `Date` object are invoked with:

```
newDateObject = new Date([dateInfo])
```

`dateInfo` is an optional specification for the date to set in the new object. If it is not specified, the current date and time are used. *`dateInfo`* can use any of the following formats:

`milliseconds` (since midnight GMT on January 1, 1970)
`year, month, day` (so `1997, 0, 27` is January 27, 1997)
`year, month, day, hours, minutes, seconds`
(so `1997, 8, 23, 08, 25, 30` is September 23 1997 at 08:25:30)

Times and dates are generally in **local time**, but the user can also specify Universally Coordinated Time (**UTC**, previously GMT).

Method	Description
`getDate()` `getUTCDate()`	Returns the day of the month as an integer between 1 and 31, using local time or UTC.
`getDay()` `getUTCDay()`	Returns the day of the week as an integer between 0 (Sunday) and 6 (Saturday), using local time or UTC.
`getFullYear()` `getUTCFullYear()`	Returns the year as an integer, using local time or UTC.
`getHours()` `getUTCHours()`	Returns the hours as an integer between 0 and 23, using local time or UTC.
`getMilliseconds()` `getUTCMilliseconds()`	Returns the milliseconds as an integer between 0 and 999, using local time or UTC.
`getMinutes()` `getUTCMinutes()`	Returns the minutes as an integer between 0 and 59, using local time or UTC.
`getMonth()` `getUTCMonth()`	Returns the month as an integer between 0 (January) and 11 (December), using local time or UTC.
`getSeconds()` `getUTCSeconds()`	Returns the seconds as an integer between 0 and 59, using local time or UTC.
`getTime()`	Returns the number of milliseconds between January 1, 1970 at 00:00:00 UTC and the current `Date` object as an integer.

Table Continued on Following Page

Method	Description
getTimeZoneOffset()	Returns the number of minutes between local time and UTC as an integer.
getVarDate()	Returns the date in VT_DATE format, which is used to interact with ActiveX objects.
getYear()	Returns the two-digit year as an integer.
parse(dateString)	Returns the number of milliseconds since Jan. 1, 1970 00:00:00 UTC in dateString.
setDate(dayValue) setUTCDate(dayValue)	Sets the day of the month, where dayValue is an integer between 1 and 31, using local time or UTC.
setFullYear(yearValue) setUTCFullYear(yearValue)	Sets the year, where yearValue indicates the 4-digit year, using local time or UTC.
setHours(hoursValue) setUTCHours(hoursValue)	Sets the hours, where hoursValue is an integer between 0 and 59, using local time or UTC.
setMilliSeconds(msValue) setUTCMilliSeconds(msValue)	Sets the milliseconds, where msValue is an integer between 0 and 999, using local time or UTC.
setMinutes(minutesValue) setUTCMinutes(minutesValue)	Sets the minutes, where minutesValue is an integer between 0 and 59, using local time or UTC.
setMonth(monthValue) setUTCMonth(monthValue)	Sets the month, where monthValue is an integer between 0 and 11, using local time or UTC.
setSeconds(secondsValue) setUTCSeconds(secondsValue)	Sets the seconds, where secondsValue is an integer between 0 and 59, using local time or UTC.
setTime(timeValue)	Sets the value of a Date object, where timeValue is an integer representing the number of milliseconds in a date string, since Jan. 1, 1970 00:00:00 GMT.
setYear(yearValue)	Sets the year, where yearValue is an integer (generally) greater than 1900.
toGMTString()	Converts a date to a string using GMT. Equivalent to toUTCString(), and included only for backwards compatibility.
toLocaleString()	Converts a date to a string using local time.
toUTCString()	Converts a date to a string using UTC.
UTC(year, month, day [,hrs][,min][,sec])	Returns the number of milliseconds in a date object, since Jan. 1, 1970 00:00:00 UTC.

Enumerator Object

The `Enumerator` object is used to enumerate, or step through, the items in a collection. The `Enumerator` object provides a way to access any member of a collection, and behaves similarly to the `For...Each` statement in VBScript.

```
newEnumeratorObj = new Enumerator(collection)
```

Method	Description
`atEnd()`	Returns a Boolean value indicating if the enumerator is at the end of the collection
`item()`	Returns the current item in the collection
`moveFirst()`	Resets the current item to the first item in the collection
`moveNext()`	Changes the current item to the next item in the collection

Error Object

The `Error` object contains information about run-time errors generated in JScript code. The scripting engine automatically generates this object. You can also create it yourself if you want to generate your own custom error states.

```
newErrorObj = new Error(number)
```

Property	Description
`description`	The descriptive string associated with a particular error
`number`	The number associated with a particular error

Function Object

The `Function` object provides a mechanism for compiling JScript code as a function. A new function is invoked with the syntax:

```
functionName = new Function(arg1, arg2, ..., functionCode)
```

where *`arg1`*, *`arg2`*, etc. are the argument names for the function object being created, and *`functionCode`* is a string containing the body of the function. This can be a series of JScript statements separated by semi-colons.

Property	Description
`arguments[]`	A reference to the `arguments` array that holds the arguments that were provided when the function was called
`caller`	Returns a reference to the function that invoked the current function
`prototype`	Provides a way for adding properties to a `Function` object

Method	Description
toString()	Returns a string value representation of the function
valueOf()	Returns the function

Arguments Object

The arguments object is a list (an array) of arguments in a function.

Property	Description
length	An integer specifying the number of arguments provided to the function when it was called

Math Object

Provides a set of properties and methods for working with mathematical constants and functions. Simply reference the Math object, then the method or property required:

```
MyArea = Math.PI * MyRadius * MyRadius;
MyResult = Math.floor(MyNumber);
```

Property	Description
E	e (the base of natural logarithms)
LN10	The value of the natural logarithm of 10
LN2	The value of the natural logarithm of 2
LOG10E	The value of the base 10 logarithm of E
LOG2E	The value of the base 2 logarithm of E
PI	The value of the constant π (pi)
SQRT1_2	The value of the square root of a half
SQRT2	The value of the square root of two

Method	Description
abs(number)	Returns the absolute value of number
acos(number)	Returns the arc cosine of number
asin(number)	Returns the arc sine of number
atan(number)	Returns the arc tangent of number
atan2(x, y)	Returns the angle of the polar coordinate of a point x, y from the x-axis

Method	Description
`ceil(number)`	Returns the next largest integer greater than `number` — it rounds up
`cos(number)`	Returns the cosine of `number`
`exp(number)`	Returns the value of `number` as the exponent of e, as in e^{number}
`floor(number)`	Returns the next smallest integer less than `number` — it rounds down
`log(number)`	Returns the natural logarithm of `number`
`max(num1, num2)`	Returns the greater of the two values `num1` and `num2`
`min(num1, num2)`	Returns the smaller of the two values `num1` and `num2`
`pow(num1, num2)`	Returns the value of `num1` to the power of `num2`
`random()`	Returns a random number between 0 and 1
`round(number)`	Returns the closest integer to `number` — it rounds up or down to the nearest whole number
`sin(number)`	Returns the sin of `number`
`sqrt(number)`	Returns the square root of `number`
`tan(number)`	Returns the tangent of `number`

Number Object

The `Number` object provides a set of properties that are useful when working with numbers:

```
newNumberObj = new Number(value)
```

Property	Description
`MAX_VALUE`	The maximum numeric value represented in JScript (~1.79E+308)
`MIN_VALUE`	The minimum numeric value represented in JScript (~2.22E-308)
`NaN`	A value meaning 'Not A Number'
`NEGATIVE_INFINITY`	A special value for negative infinity ("-Infinity")
`POSITIVE_INFINITY`	A special value for infinity ("Infinity")

Method	Description
`toString([radix_base])`	Returns the value of the number as a string to a radix (base) of 10, unless specified otherwise in `radix_base`
`valueOf()`	Returns the primitive numeric value of the object

RegularExpression Object

The `RegularExpression` object contains a regular expression. A regular expression is used to search strings for character patterns.

```
function RegExpDemo()
{
   var s = "AaBbCcDdEeFfGgHhIiJjKkLlMmNnOoPp"
   var r = new RegExp("g", "i");
   var a = r.exec(s);
   document.write(a);
   r.compile("g");
   var a = r.exec(s);
   document.write(a);
}
```

Property	Description
`lastIndex`	Character position at which to start the next match
`source`	Text of the regular expression

Method	Description
`compile()`	Converts the regular expression into an internal format for faster execution
`exec()`	Executes the search for a match in a particular string
`test()`	Returns a Boolean value indicating whether a pattern exists within a string

RegExp Object

The `RegExp` object stores information about regular expression pattern searches. It works in conjunction with the `RegularExpression` object. In the example below, even though the new method was called with the `RegExp` object as a parameter, a `RegularExpression` object was actually created:

```
function regExpDemo()
{
   var s;
   var re = new RegExp("d(b+)(d)","ig");
   var str = "cdbBdbsbdbdz";
   var arr = re.exec(str);
   s = "$1 contains: " + RegExp.$1 + "<BR>";
   s += "$2 contains: " + RegExp.$2 + "<BR>";
   s += "$3 contains: " + RegExp.$3;
   return(s);
}
```

Notice that when checking the properties for the `RegExp` object, we don't refer to an instance of that object. Rather the reference is made directly to the static `RegExp` object.

Property	Description
`$1...$9`	The 9 most recently found portions during pattern matching
`index`	Character position where the first successful match begins
`input`	String against which the regular expression is searched
`lastIndex`	Character position where the last successful match begins

String Object

The `String` object provides a set of methods for text manipulation. To create a new string object, the syntax is:

```
MyString = new String([value])
```

where *`value`* is the optional text to place in the string when it is created. If this is a number, it is converted into a string first.

Property	Description
`length`	An integer representing the number of characters in the string

Method	Description
`anchor("nameAttribute")`	Returns the original string surrounded by `<A>` and `</A>` anchor tags, with the `NAME` attribute set to `"nameAttribute"`
`big()`	Returns the original string enclosed in `<BIG>` and `</BIG>` tags
`blink()`	Returns the original string enclosed in `<BLINK>` and `</BLINK>` tags
`bold()`	Returns the original string enclosed in `<B>` and `</B>` tags
`charAt(index)`	Returns the single character at position `index` within the `String` object
`charCodeAt(index)`	Returns the Unicode encoding of the character at position `index`
`concat(string2)`	Returns a string containing `string2` added to the end of the original string

Table Continued on Following Page

Method	Description
fixed()	Returns the original string enclosed in <TT> and </TT> tags
fontcolor("color")	Returns the original string surrounded by <FONT> and </FONT> tags, with the COLOR attribute set to "color"
fontsize("size")	Returns the original string surrounded by <FONT> and </FONT> anchor tags, with the SIZE attribute set to "size"
fromCharCode(code1, ...code*n*)	Returns the string from a number of Unicode character values
indexOf(searchValue [,fromIndex])	Returns first occurrence of the string searchValue starting at index fromIndex
italics()	Returns the original string enclosed in <I> and </I> tags
lastIndexOf(searchValue [,fromIndex])	Returns the index of the last occurrence of the string searchValue, searching backwards from index fromIndex
link("hrefAttribute")	Returns the original string surrounded by <A> and </A> link tags, with the HREF attribute set to "hrefAttribute"
match(regExp)	Returns an array containing the results of a search using the regExp RegularExpression object
replace(regExp, replaceText)	Returns a string with text replaced using a regular expression
search(regExp)	Returns the position of the first sub-string match in a regular expression search
slice(start, [end])	Returns a section of a string starting at position start and ending at position end
small()	Returns the original string enclosed in <SMALL> and </SMALL> tags
split(separator)	Returns an array of strings created by separating the String object at every occurrence of separator
strike()	Returns the original string enclosed in <STRIKE> and </STRIKE> tags
sub()	Returns the original string enclosed in _{and} tags

Method	Description
`substr(start, [length])`	Returns a sub-string starting at position `start` and having a length of `length` characters
`substring(indexA, indexB)`	Returns the sub-string of the original `String` object from the character at `indexA` up to and including the one before the character at `indexB`
`sup()`	Returns the original string enclosed in `<SUP>` and `</SUP>` tags
`toLowerCase()`	Returns the original string with all the characters converted to lowercase
`toUpperCase()`	Returns the original string with all the characters converted to uppercase
`toString()`	Returns the value of the `String` object
`valueOf()`	Returns the string

VBArray Object

Provides access to an array created in VBScript. Since these arrays use a different memory structure than JScript arrays, it is necessary to use this object to access them. This object only provides read-only access.

```
<script language="VBScript">
   Dim arVBArray
   ' Populate this VBScript array...
</script>

<script language="JScript">
   function useVBArray()
   {
      var arJSArray = new VBArray(arVBArray);
      var arArray = arJSArray.toArray();
      // now arArray can be used like a JScript array
   }
</script>
```

Method	Description
`dimensions()`	Returns the number of dimensions in the `VBArray`
`getItem(dim1, dim2, ... dimn)`	Returns the item at the specified location
`lbound(dimension)`	Returns the lowest index value used at the dimension specified by `dimension`
`toArray()`	Returns a standard JScript array converted from the `VBArray` object
`ubound(dimension)`	Returns the highest index value used at the dimension specified by `dimension`

Reserved Words

The following are reserved words that can't be used for function, method, variable, or object names. Note that while some words in this list are not currently used as JScript keywords, they have been reserved for future use.

```
abstract    else         int         super
boolean     extends      interface   switch
break       false        long        synchronized
byte        final        native      this
case        finally      new         throw
catch       float        null        throws
char        for          package     transient
class       function     private     true
const       goto         protected   try
continue    if           public      typeof
default     implements   reset       var
delete      import       return      void
do          in           short       while
double      instanceof   static      with
```

For more information about JScript, visit Microsoft's JScript site at http://msdn.microsoft.com/scripting.

Index

Symbol

" (double-quote character), 81
"Hello World" script
HelloWorld.ws file, 22
programming example, 20
"Subscript out of range" error message, 57
"WSH is glue" scenario, 15
.cab files, 71
.doc files
loading, 50
.dot templates
defining, 288
.exe applications
releasing objects, 52
.frm files, 232
.ico files, 187
.js files, 26
activating from Windows shell, 27
adding to system's New menu, 281
context menu for, 27
.lnk files, 88
assigning as target paths of shortcuts, 90
.reg files, 15
configuring encoded scripts to run, 307
.tlb files, 115
.url extension, 88, 91
.vbs files, 26
activating from Windows shell, 27
adding to system's New menu, 281
context menu for, 27
.vbs modules
developing, 186
.ws files, 26
<comment> element, 118
<job> element, 112
<package> element, 112
<reference> element, 114
<resource> element, 118
<script> element, 115
activating from Windows shell, 27
benefits of, 106
combining VBScript and JScript in, 117
context menu for, 27
defined, 106
elements in, 109
including external files, 115, 116
multiple jobs in one file, 112
parsing, 34
referencing type libraries, 114
root elements in, 112
running, 107
run-time operations, 111
script blocks, 107
working with, 109
WSH 2.0 support for, 22
XML compliance, 110
XML features, 108, 109
.wsc files
embedding several components in, 204
syntax of, 204
testing, 208
.wsh files
settings stored in, 29
shortcuts, 29
.xls files
loading, 50
//? option, 24
//B option, 23, 25, 41
//D option, 24
//E:engine option, 24, 35
//H option, 23, 25
//I option, 23, 41
//Job:ID option, 24, 112
//logo option, 23
//nologo option, 23, 28
//S option, 23, 25, 44
//T:n option, 23, 44
//X option, 24

Index

+ operator, 111
<?job?> element, 111
<comment> element, 118
<component> element, 204
<event> element, 207, 211
<get> tags
in <property> elements, 206
<job> element, 109
multiple jobs in one file, 112
purpose of, 112
syntax, 112
<method> element, 207
<object> tag
purpose and syntax of, 113
<package> element, 109, 204
purpose and syntax of, 112
<parameter> tag, 207
<property> element, 206
<public> element, 204, 205
<put> tags
in <property> elements, 206
<reference> element
multiple jobs and, 115
syntax, 114
<registration> element, 204, 205
<resource> element, 118
<script> element, 195, 204, 208
including external files, 115, 116
mixing languages with, 117
specifying script execution, 116
syntax, 115

A

Abort button, 65, 66
about protocol, 83
about: pages
adding to registry, 84
Access database
for invoice preparation system, 283
Active Data Objects (ADO), 281
adding records to database with, 291
ADO 2.x object model, 284
creating ADO recordset objects, 285
for invoice preparation system, 284
Active Desktop, 90
system folder settings, 183
Active Directory Service Interfaces (ADSI), 15
ActiveX controls, 30
batch mode and, 25
ActiveXObject object, 48, 131
Add() method
Folder object, 158
Dictionary object, 164
AddPrinterConnection() method
WshNetwork object, 93, 94
AddToMenuNew.vbs script, 299
ADO recordset objects
creating, 285
creating instance of, 291
filling out, 291
opening directly, 285
ADSI (Active Directory Service Interfaces), 15
alignment
in text boxes, 225
Always On Top item, 68
Application property
WScript object, 38
application suites
scriptable, 14
application windows
style of, 80
applications
arranging together, 15
automating deployment of, 16
determining whether instance is running, 51
multi-layered, 16
non-Automation, 14
arguments. ***See also*** **command-line arguments**
in command line, 23
passing to encoded scripts, 309
passing to script files, 299
specifying in script files, 299
WshArguments collection object, 56
Arguments property
WScript object, 38, 87, 211
ASP pages
script block execution in, 107
assignment operator, 126
associative array, 164
asterisk (*)
displaying for input text, 224
asynchronous events, 55
AtEndOfLine property
TextStream object, 162
AtEndOfStream property
TextStream object, 162
attrib MS-DOS command
manipulating file attributes with, 185

Attributes property
Folder object, 153, 157, 158, 186
Automation interfaces, 13
Automation objects
defined, 30
internal collection of scriptable objects and, 36
returning references to, 46
Automation services, 113
Automation-compatible COM objects
producing reusable code with, 199
AvailableSpace property
Drive object, 151, 152

B

backing up
registry, 70
backslash character
delimiting nodes with, 72
batch (.bat) files, 7
MS-DOS, 9, 10
Windows, 10
uses of, 137
batch mode, 41
batch processing, 7
binary data
reading back from registry, 78
viewing in Registry Editor, 78
writing to registry, 78
binary files
for components, 251
support for, 169
bitmaps
opening from files, 50
bookmarks
adding, 288
defined, 288
for invoice preparation system, 290
in Word documents, 288
Browse component
defined, 252
using, 254
Browser_DownloadBegin(), 53
BuildPath() method
FileSystemObject object, 141
BuildVersion property
WScript object, 38
buttons
predefined combinations, 65
setting focus to, 68

C

callbacks, 129
Cancel button, 65, 66
catch blocks, 134
CDATA delimiters, 111, 116
CDO, 294
character data delimiters. *See* CDATA delimiters
class identifier. *See* CLSID
Class keyword, 123
Class_Initialize() subroutine, 124
Class_Terminate() subroutine, 125
classes
compatibility issues, 198
creating, 123
defined, 195
importing in VBScript files, 196, 197
importing with WSH 2.0, 125
in VBScript 5.0, 123
instantiating, 124
JScript, 198
requirements for, 182
support for events, 129
writing, 195
Click events, 261, 265
Close() method
TextStream object, 162
CLSID
defined, 30
generated by Windows Script Component Wizard, 203
getting from ProgID, 49
identifying COM objects by, 113
CLSID sub-node, 307
CLSIDFromProgID(), 49
CoCreateInstance(), 49
code reusability, 108, 181. *See also* reusable WSH code
collections
enumerating, 57, 103
Column property
TextStream object, 162
COM. *See* Component Object Model (COM)
COM modules
drag-and-drop handler, 299
COM objects
assigning local names to, 47
creating, 46, 49
demonstrations, 252

determining host executable for, 41
identifying by CLSID, 113
identifying by ProgID, 113
in Scripting Run-time Library, 137
management of, 46
object creation functions, 49
ProgID, 48
returning references to existing and new objects, 49
reusable WSH code and, 199
script-based, 200
COM servers
creating, 48
command line, 23
arguments in, 23
options, 23
passed to Run() method, 81
saving per user settings, 25
WshArguments object and, 299
command-line arguments, 38
addressing nth, 57
enumerating, 57
WshArguments collection object, 56, 58
commands
adding to Windows menus, 27
comments
in .ws files, 110
Common Controls
library, 268
CompareMode property
Dictionary object, 165
comparison operator, 126
components
binary files for, 251
demonstrations, 251
development of, 251
ComputerName property
WshNetwork object, 93
context menus
adding new items to, 75
copy command (MS-DOS), 143
Copy() method
Folder object, 157, 159
CopyFile() method
FileSystemObject object, 143, 144, 147
CopyFolder() method
FileSystemObject object, 145, 146, 156
CopyHere() method
Folder object, 171, 173
copying
aborting, 174
files, 173
files and folders, 143
Count, 97, 99, 102
Count property
collections, 56, 97, 99, 102, 158, 161, 165, 269
CreateFolder() method
FileSystemObject object, 146, 148, 158
CreateObject() method
VBScript, 48, 113, 122
WScript object, 39, 46, 55, 62, 113, 122
CreateShortcut() method
WshShell object, 62, 63, 88, 89
CreateTextFile() method
FileSystemObject object, 148, 157, 187
cscript.exe, 19, 33
associating encoded scripts with, 306
changing default host, 25
command line, 23
location of, 34
wscript.exe and, 20
CStr() function, 111
current user
locating folders for, 101
saving command line settings for, 25
custom folder icons
creating, 185
for system folders, 184
identifying for folders, 187
reusable WSH code for, 191

D

data source name (DSN), 282
data types
conversions, 71
supported by WSHShell object, 71
databases
for invoice preparation system, 282
opening ADO recordset directly, 285
DateCreated property
Folder object, 153, 158
DateDiff() function, 130
DateLastAccessed property
Folder object, 153, 158
DateLastModified property
Folder object, 153, 158
dates
entering in input boxes, 231
debug attribute, 111
debugging
.ws files, 111

default printer
getting, 96
setting, 95
Delete() method
Folder object, 157, 160
DeleteFile() method
FileSystemObject object, 149, 150
Description property
Error object, 132
WshShortcut object, 87
Desktop folder, 100
desktop.ini, 191
creating, 188
creating custom icon with, 185
DHTML events, 247
DHTML object model, 233, 237, 247
dialog boxes. *See also* message boxes
created by Echo() method, 21, 25
displaying, 21
Explorer-like view in, 257
HTML-based, 231, 233, 235, 285
in Win32, 232
modal, 259
modeless, 259
opening on specific folder, 255
predefined button combinations, 65
WSH limitations, 13
dialog template, 232
dialog.frm, 242, 245
DialogBox component, 235-245
Dictionary object, 138
creation of, 139
data structure, 165
methods, 164
performance of, 165
properties, 164
dir command, 166
DisconnectObject() method
WScript object, 39, 46, 55
disk quotas, 152
disk space
calculating, 152
Distributed COM (DCOM), 122
Document Type Definition (DTD), 108
DocumentComplete events, 53, 54
documents. *See also* Word documents
opening with Run() method, 82
double backslash (\\)
in JScript, 72
double slash (//)
prefixing options with, 23
double-quote character ("), 81
DownloadBegin event, 53, 55
drag-and-drop
passing arguments to script files with, 299
DropHandler shell extensions, 301
receiving folder name through, 301
Drive object, 138, 139
getting instances of, 151
properties, 151
Drive property
Folder object, 154, 158
DriveExists() method
FileSystemObject object, 150
DriveLetter property
Drive object, 151
drives
checking, 150
enumerating, 140
managing, 137
Drives collection, 138, 139, 151
DriveType property
Drive object, 151
DTD. *See* Document Type Definition
DWORD data
viewing in Registry Editor, 78
Dynamic HTML (DHTML), 281

E

Echo() method, 21, 38, 39
in cscript.exe, 21
in wscript.exe, 21
Popup () method vs., 64
suppressing message boxes created with, 25
syntax, 41
element names
in XML-based languages, 108
elements
in .ws files, 109
syntax, 109
encoded scripts. *See* script encoding
EnumNetworkDrives() method
WshNetwork object, 92, 94
EnumPrinterConnections() method
WshNetwork object, 93, 103
Environment property
WshShell object, 63
environment variables, 81, 96
Err object, 132, 147

error handling
.ws files, 111
in JScript, 121
Error object, 132
eval() function, 121, 126, 128, 194, 309
code reusablity and, 181
event handlers
naming, 53
event handling, 52
WScript.CreateObject() support for, 48
event sinks
creating, 47
defined, 30, 53
in .ws files, 113
Internet Explorer, 54
naming, 53
underscore (_) in name of, 53
events
ability to fire, 211
asynchronous, 55
for VBScript classes, 129
Excel workbooks
loading from specified file, 50
exception handling, 174
in JScript 5.0, 131
layers in, 132
executables, 19. *See also* wshom.ocx. *See also* wscript.exe. *See also* cscript.exe
Execute() function, 126, 128
ExecuteGlobal() function, 126, 195, 309
execution
predetermined maximum time for, 24
Exists() method
Dictionary object, 164
expandable strings, 77
ExpandEnvironmentStrings() method
WshShell object, 63, 77, 86
external files
including in .ws files, 115, 116
external programs
running with WshShell, 79

F

Favorites folder, 88, 100, 259
adding items to, 102
file attributes
adding column to Windows Explorer, 190
file extensions
hiding for known files, 189
file folders
special folders vs., 99
File Manager program, 190
File object, 138, 139
defined, 158
getting instances of, 151
methods, 159
properties, 158
file pointers, 163
file system objects
getting, 151
in SRL object model, 139
FileExists() method
FileSystemObject object, 89, 151, 275
files. *See also* Word documents. *See also* documents
browsing for, 252
changing attributes of, 160
checking, 150
copying, 143, 173
deleting, 149
in folders, enumerating, 209
loading objects from, 50
managing, 137
matching against patterns, 166, 168
moving, 147, 173
opening existing, 148
operations on, 159
renaming, from Windows Explorer, 189
selecting multiple, 255
writing to, 163
Files collection, 138, 139, 151
defined, 160
enumerating, 167
filtering, 165
properties, 160
Files property, 154
FileSystem property
Drive object, 152
FileSystemObject object, 128, 137, 138, 185, 187, 275
defined, 139
getting file system objects, 151
limitations of, 169
methods, 140, 143
properties, 139
Shell Automation objects vs., 176
filtering
Files collection, 165
FireEvent() function, 207, 211
flags
customizing message box appearance with, 65, 66

Folder object, 138, 139
defined, 153
Files collection and, 160
getting instances of, 151
properties, 153
Folder object (Shell Automation)
descriptive name, 171
enumerating contents of folder, 172
getting, 169
methods, 185
reading and writing file attributes with, 185
structure of, 171
folder options
Get/Set functions for, 188
Folder Options dialog box, 189
folder settings
modifying, 183
setting preferences programmatically, 183
FolderExists() method
FileSystemObject object, 89, 151
FolderItem object, 171, 172
for invoice preparation system, 292
FolderItems collection, 171, 173
FolderItemVerb object, 171
FolderItemVerbs collection, 171
folders
changing attributes of, 157
checking, 150
copying, 143, 145
creating, 148
deleting, 149
enumerating contents of, 172, 209
identifying, 170
identifying icon for, 187
managing, 137
moving, 147
opening with Run() method, 82
opening dialog box on specific folder, 254, 258
operations on, 156
pop-up descriptions of, 191
Properties window, 155
read-only, 186
switching on and off hidden style, 157
Folders collection, 138, 139, 151
properties, 157
Fonts folder, 100
frames
event handling, 53
FreeSpace property
Drive object, 152
FTP protocol, 83
FullName property
WScript object, 38, 41
WshShortcut object, 87, 88, 90, 91

G

GetAbsolutePathName() method
FileSystemObject object, 141
GetBaseName() method
FileSystemObject object, 141
GetDetailsOf() method
Folder object, 171, 173
GetDiskFreeSpace() function, 153
GetDrive() method
FileSystemObject object, 151
GetDriveName() method
FileSystemObject object, 141
GetExtensionName() method
FileSystemObject object, 141
GetFile() method
FileSystemObject object, 151, 158
GetFileName() method
FileSystemObject object, 142
GetFolder() method
FileSystemObject object, 151, 169
GetObject() function, 51, 268
GetObject() method
WScript object, 39, 46, 49, 50
GetParentFolderName() method
FileSystemObject object, 142, 146
getResource() function, 118
GetSpecialFolder() method
FileSystemObject object, 142
GetTempName() method
FileSystemObject object, 142
global functions, 195
global namespace.
ExecuteGlobal() function and, 127
global objects
creating, 113

H

hash tables, 165
helper objects, 96
help text
displayed in dialog boxes, 241, 247

hidden input
entering passwords as, 224
hives, 69. *See also* **root nodes**
HKEY_CLASSES_ROOT, 69, 298, 307
HKEY_CURRENT_CONFIG, 69
HKEY_CURRENT_USER, 69, 74
HKEY_DYN_DATA, 70
HKEY_LOCAL_MACHINE, 69
HKEY_USERS, 69
host executable, 33. *See also* **wscript.exe**
accessing, 34
adapting to, 41
functions of, 34
getting information about, 39
Hotkey property
WshShortcut object, 87
hovering
help text displayed in response to, 241, 247
HTML applications (HTAs), 234
HTML pages
accessing tags in, 241
as dialog templates, 285
referencing document object model, 288
HTML-based dialog boxes, 231, 233, 235
HTML-based messages
formatting on the fly, 84
sending to users, 83
http protocol, 83

I

IconLocation property
WshShortcut object, 87
icons. *See also* **customs icons**
0-based index of, 187
adding to Quick Launch tool bar, 90
IDispatch interface, 36
Ignore button, 65, 66
importing classes, 195, 196, 197
importing source code, 181, 182, 191, 193, 194
Include() function, 128, 191, 193, 194, 197, 309
Initialize event, 124
innerHTML property, 237
innerText property, 237
input focus
setting to a particular button, 68
InputBox component, 218-231
compatibility with WSH 1.0, 218
limitations of, 218, 219
InputBox() method
VBScript, 25
instanceof operator
JScript, 134
Interactive property
WScript object, 38, 41
turning off, 25
use of, 42
interface
defined, 30
outgoing, 30
Internet Explorer
determing folder containing cache, 74
event handling, 53
HTML applications (HTAs), 234
modal dialogs, 233
Internet Shortcuts, 91
interruptible operations, 262, 263
invoice preparation system, 281-295
InvokeVerb() method
FolderItem object, 292
IsDate() function
VBScript, 231
IsReady property
Drive object, 150, 152
IsRootFolder property
Folder object, 154
Item property
Dictionary object, 164
Files collection, 161
Folders collection, 158
WshArguments object, 56
WshCollection object, 102
WshEnvironment object, 97
WshSpecialFolders object, 99
Items() method
Dictionary object, 164
Folder object, 171, 172

J

JScript
ActiveXObject object, 48
assigning local names to COM objects with, 47
changing file attributes with, 160
code reusability in, 181
compatibility issues for classes, 198
data acquisition features, 220
long filenames, 81
message box customization in, 67
message boxes in, 21

mixing with VBScript, 22
providing template file in, 297
registering new file types, 298
releasing objects in, 52
reusable WSH code demonstration, 193
using WScript.CreateObject() with, 46
version 5.0, 120
Error object in, 132
exception handling in, 131
improvements in, 121
Internet Explorer 5 and, 105
new features, 131
release of, 120
remote automation in, 131
running encoded scripts, 305
using with other languages, 107
with VBScript in .ws files, 117
WSH compatibility, 11

K

Key property
Dictionary object, 165
keys. *see also* **registry**
defined, 70
deleting, 79
distinguishing from values, 72
registry structure and, 70
values for, 70
Keys() method
Dictionary object, 164
known file types
hiding extensions for, 189

L

length property
WshArguments object, 56
WshEnvironment object, 97
WshSpecialFolders object, 99
WshCollection object, 102
Line property
TextStream object, 162
lines (of text)
reading and writing, 161
local names
assigning to objects, 47
prefixes, 47
local namespace
Execute() function and, 127
long date format, 286
long filenames (LFNs), 58
Run() method and, 81
long integers
very large disks and, 153

M

mailto protocol, 83
sending e-mail invoices with, 293
MapNetworkDrive() method
WshNetwork object, 92, 93, 95
mapped drives
configuring, 190
displaying, 94
maximum text length
in input boxes, 224
menu items
adding to context menus, 75
message boxes
customizing appearance of, 66
display methods, 64
in JScript, 21
in VBScript, 21
keeping on top of all other windows, 68
setting input focus to a particular button, 68
suppressing, 25
timeout values for, 67
MessageBox() API function, 21, 64
Microsoft Data Access Components (MDAC), 49
Microsoft Office, 14
Microsoft Script Debugger, 260
Microsoft Script Encoder (MSE)
defined, 304
installing, 304
processing of encrypted files by, 304
Microsoft Visual Studio, 303
mkdir command (MS-DOS), 146
modal dialogs, 233, 259
creating, 259
HTML as template language for, 233
Internet Explorer, 233
modeless dialogs, 259
mouse hovering
help text displayed in response to, 241
Move() method
Folder object, 157
File object, 160
MoveFile() method
FileSystemObject object, 147

MoveFolder() method
FileSystemObject object, 147
MoveHere() method
Folder object, 172, 173
moving
files, 173
files and folders, 147
MS-DOS batch (.bat) files, 9, 10
limitations of, 10
uses of, 137
MS-DOS copy command, 143
MS-DOS mkdir command, 146
MSE. *See* **Microsoft Script Encoder (MSE)**
MsgBox() function, 20, 25, 42, 107, 259
VBScript wrapper for, 22
mshtml.dll, 234, 242
mshtml.tlb type library, 242
MyDocuments folder, 100

N

Name property
File object, 158
Folder object, 154
WScript object, 38
namespace extensions, 184
NameSpace() method
Shell object, 169, 170
NetHood folder, 100
network drives
enumerating, 103
establishing links to, 93
looping over all, 94
managing with WshNetwork object, 93
unmapping, 94
network printers
enumerating, 103
New menu (Windows Explorer)
adding .vbs and .js files to, 281
adding new items to, 297
creating scripts in, 296
registering new file type, 297
New operator
in VBScript 5.0, 123, 124
NewFolder folder, 145
NewFolder() method
Folder object, 172
No button, 65, 66
Notepad
creating shortcut to, 90
opening files in, 75, 82
Nothing, 52
Now() function
VBScript, 209
Number property
Error object (JScript), 132
Err object (VBScript), 147
numeric data
reading back from registry, 78
writing to registry, 78

O

object management, 38, 46
objects
assigning local names to, 47
creating, 46, 49
disconnecting, 55
existing, referencing, 51, 52
getting, 49
loading from files, 50
releasing, 52
returning references to existing and new objects, 49
setting reference to nothing or null, 52
OK button, 65, 66
OLE DB providers, 200
On Error, 147
On Error Resume Next, 132
Open dialog box, 253, 254
Open with MS-DOS Prompt, 27
OpenAsTextStream() method
File object, 160
OpenTextFile() method
FileSystemObject object, 148
operating system
detecting, 73
operations
interrupting, 262, 263
options
in command line, 23
outgoing interface
defined, 30
Outlook
sending e-mail invoices with, 293, 294

P

ParentFolder property
File object, 158
Folder object, 154, 171

ParseName() method
Folder object, 172
path names
manipulating, 143
methods for manipulating, 141
Path property
Drive object, 152
File object, 158
Folder object, 154
WScript object, 38
pattern property
RegExp object, 122
pixels
translating into twips, 244
Platform SDK, 234
popup messages
display methods, 64
Popup() method, 42, 63, 64
arguments, 64
Echo() method vs., 64
predefined button combinations, 65
return values, 66
timed-out message boxes, 67
undocumented features, 67
prefix names
assigning for event sinks, 52
for object local names, 47
Print command, 292
printers
getting default, 96
managing with WshNetwork, 94
removing links to, 95
setting default, 95
PrintHood folder, 101
Private keyword
VBScript, 124
reusable WSH code and, 191
Process component, 270
process ID
identifying running processes with, 273
processing instructions, 111
ProgID, 48, 131
defined, 30
getting CLSID from, 49
identifying COM objects by, 113
identifying which object's type library to be referenced with, 115
of COM server, 122
WSH objects, 61, 63
programmatic identifier. *See* **ProgID**
programs
determining registered document types for, 274
determining running processes, 267
determining version number for, 268
determining whether installed, 274
determining whether an application is running, 272
identifying multiple instances of, 273
Programs folder, 101
Properties dialog, 155
Property Get statements, 124
property page
WSH, 28
Property Set statements, 124
protocols
using from Windows Script Host, 82
Public keyword
VBScript, 124
reusable WSH code and, 191

Q

Quick Launch toolbar
adding icons to, 90
adding URL shortcuts to, 92
Quit() method
Word application, 52
WScript object, 39, 43

R

Range object
in Word documents, 290
Read() method
TextStream object, 161
read/write properties, 206, 237
readable properties, 206
ReadAll() method
TextStream object, 149, 161, 162
ReadLine() method
TextStream object, 161
read-only
attribute, 185
folders, 186
properties, 206
Recent folder, 101

recursive deletion, 79
referencing
type libraries, 114
REG_BINARY data type, 71, 74, 78
REG_DWORD data type, 71, 74, 78
REG_EXPAND data type, 77
REG_EXPAND_SZ data type, 71, 74, 77
REG_SZ data type, 71, 74, 77
RegDelete() method
WshShell object, 63, 71, 79
regedit.exe. *See* **Registry Editor**
RegExp object, 122
register() function, 205, 213
registered applications
opening objects from files in, 50
registered file types
adding, 297
determining for programs, 274
registry
accessing, 69
accessing user files, 74
adding about: pages to, 84
adjustments for encoded scripts, 305
backing up, 70
default printer name held in, 96
deleting from, 79
per-user command line settings, 25
programming with WSH, 71
reading from, 72
reading numeric data back from, 78
scripting engine selection and, 34
structure of, 69, 70
supported types, 71
writing to, 74, 75
Registry Checker, 71
Registry Editor, 69
determining if running, 272
removing user rights, 15
viewing numeric data in, 78
registry paths
defined, 72
detecting current operating sytem, 73
RegRead() method
WshShell object, 63, 71, 72, 73
regular expressions (RE), 122
validation with, 226, 227
RegWrite() method
WshShell object, 63, 71, 74, 79, 86
releasing objects, 52
remote automation
in JScript 5.0, 131
in VBScript 5.0, 122
Remote Data Service (RDS) component, 49
remote drives
unmapping, 94
remote printer
setting default, 95
Remove() method
WshEnvironment object, 97
Dictionary object, 164
RemoveAll() method
Dictionary object, 164
RemoveNetworkDrive() method
WshNetwork object, 92, 94
RemovePrinterConnection() method
WshNetwork object, 93, 95
renaming files
from Windows Explorer, 189
reserved characters
in .ws files, 111
resource (.rc) files, 232
Retry button, 65, 66
reusable WSH code
building, 186, 189
considerations, 191
defined, 182
goals of, 182
JScript demonstration, 193
Public/Private keywords and, 191
relative merits of techniques for, 198
system requirements for, 182
techniques, 182
through classes, 195
VBScript 5.0 demonstration, 192
WSH 1.0 demonstration, 196
WSH 2.0 demonstration, 197
root elements
in .ws files, 112
root nodes, 69
defined, 70
registry structure and, 70
roles of, 69
root object
instantiation of WScript, 35
of Shell Automation library, 169
RootFolder property
Drive object, 152
Run dialog box
launching scripts from, 299

Run() method
WshShell object, 44, 63, 79, 82
command line passed to, 81
long filenames and, 81
opening folders with, 82
parameters, 80
sending e-mail messages with, 83
synchronized execution with, 85
running processes
determining version number, 275
displaying list of, 267
generating report view of, 271
identifying, 273
modal window report of, 270
runtime
importing routines at, 128
run-time code evaluation
in VBScript 5.0, 121, 126
run-time errors
in JScript, 121

S

Save() method
WshShortcut object, 87
WshUrlShortcut object, 91
scanregw.exe, 71
Scheduled Tasks folder, 170
screnc.exe, 305
script blocks
execution of, 107
script code reusability
WSH limitations, 13
Script Control
downloading, 12
script encoding
arguments to encoded scripts, 309
configuring encoded scripts to run, 306
operation of, 305
purpose of, 304
registry adjustments for, 305
running encoded scripts, 305
script extensions
changing, 26
scripting engines and, 26
types of, 26
script management
WScript object functions, 38
Script property page, 28
scriptable objects collection
referencing, 35
script-based COM objects, 200
ScriptFullName property
WScript object, 39
scripting engines
applications for, 11
changing default host, 25
default, 33
Internet Explorer 5.0 and, 105
new versions, 120
script file extensions and, 26
selecting, 34
using multiple, 108
WSH compatibility, 11
scripting languages
mixing, 107, 108, 117
Scripting Run-time Library (SRL), 209
collections, 138
defined, 137
limitations of, 169
object model, 139
Scriptlets *see* **Windows Script Components**
script-level procedures, 186
ScriptName property
WScript object, 39
scripts
command line execution, 23
first executable line of, 43
management and execution from Windows, 13
pausing execution of, 119
running for predetermined time, 24
specifying timeouts for, 44
terminating, 43
valid, 43
scrobj.dll, 34, 200
scrrun.dll, 137
Send To popup menu, 102
creating shortcut to, 102
SendTo folder, 101
SerialNumber property
Drive object, 152
SetDefaultPrinter() method
WshNetwork object, 93, 95
settings files, 28
ShareName property
Drive object, 152
SHBrowseForFolder() API function, 259
Shell Automation objects, 62, 169
FileSystemObject vs., 176
Folder objects, 169
shell drag-and-drop, 301

shell extensions, 301
Shell facilities
for WSH scripts, 296
Shell Scriptable Objects, 62
shell32.dll, 276
shortcuts
.wsh files, 29
changing properties of, 90
creating, 88
creating in SendTo special folder, 102
Internet, 91
resolving, 89
URL, 91
uses of, 88
WshShortcut object, 86
ShortName property
Folder object, 154
File object, 158
ShortPath property
Folder object, 154
File object, 158
ShowHTMLDialog() API function, 234
showModalDialog() method
window object, 233, 234, 237, 240
ShowWindow() API function, 80
sinking events
assigning prefix names for, 52
WScript.CreateObject() method for, 212
Size property
Folder object, 154
File object, 158
Skip() method
TextStream object, 161, 163
SkipLine() method
TextStream object, 161, 163
slash (/)
keys identified with, 72
Sleep() method
WScript object, 39, 119
Sleep() SDK function, 119
SleepEx() API function, 120
spaces, in complex strings, 58
special folders, 99
application installation and, 99
enumerating, 101
types of, 99
user shell folders, 101
SpecialFolders property
WshShell object, 63, 88, 99
split() method, 162, 187, 256, 277
SQL
adding records to database with, 291
Start menu
adding items to, 102
StartMenu folder, 101
Startup folder, 101
SubFolders property
Folder object, 151, 154
suppressing
messages, 25
synchronized execution, 85
SysBckup folder, 71
system administration, 15
system folders
changing folder view properties, 183
custom icons for, 184
defined, 183
folder settings, 183
read-only attribute for, 185

T

target paths
of shortcults, assigning .lnk files as, 90
TargetPath property
WshShortcut object, 87, 88, 90
WshUrlShortcut object, 91
template files
copies created by shell, 297
documents sharing, 288
Templates folder, 101, 283, 290
temporary files
creating, 143
text alignment
in text boxes, 225
text files
opening existing, 148
opening with context menu items, 75
text length
maximum, in input boxes, 224
TextStream object, 138, 139
defined, 161
file pointers and, 163
limitations of, 162
methods, 161
opening existing text files, 148, 149
properties, 162
returning, 148
writing information to a file, 163
throw statement, 133
time slices, 119
Timeout property
WScript object, 39, 44

timeouts
expiration of, 66
setting, 24
specifying, 44
synchronized execution and, 85
values for message boxes, 67
tooltips, 184
topmost flag, 68
TotalSize property
Drive object, 152
toUpperCase() method
JScript, 223
try...catch blocks, 132, 133, 148, 174
twips, 244
type libraries
generating, 213
referencing, 114
Type property
Folder object, 154
File object, 158

U

underscore character (_)
in event sink names, 53, 54
unmapping network drives, 190
unregister() function, 205
URL protocols, 83
URL shortcuts, 91
user folders
accessing, 74
user interfaces
WSH limitations, 13
user shell folders
locating, 101
UserDomain property
WshNetwork object, 93
UserName property
WshNetwork object, 93
user-specific folders
in Windows NT, 101

V

validation
with regular expressions, 226, 227
validation code, 209
validity of scripts, 43
values
deleting, 79
distinguishing from keys, 72
for keys, 70
registry structure and, 70
use of backslash (\) in names, 72
Variant data type, 71
VBA IDE (Integrated Development Environment), 12
vbAbort, 66
vbAbortRetryIgnore, 65
vbCancel, 66
vbCritical, 66
vbCrLf, 218
vbExclamation, 66
vbIgnore, 66
vbInformation, 66
vbLongDate, 286
vbModal, 247
vbNo, 66
vbOK, 66
vbOKCancel, 65
vbOKOnly, 65
vbQuestion, 66
vbRetry, 66
vbRetryCancel, 65
VBScript
assigning names to COM objects in, 47
data acquisition features, 220
long filenames, 81
mixing with JScript, 22
providing template files in, 297
using WScript.CreateObject() with, 46
version 5.0, 120
classes, 123, 195
code reusability in, 181, 182
combining with JScript, 117
compatibility issues for classes, 198
Execute() function, 126, 128
ExecuteGlobal() function, 126, 128
general-purpose functions, 186
importing classes, 196, 197
importing routines at runtime, 128
Internet Explorer 5.0 and, 105
new features of, 121
New operator in, 123, 124
passing code among procedures, 128
regular expressions (RE), 122
remote automation in, 122
run-time code evaluation in, 126
support for events, 129
With statement in, 125
WSH compatibility, 11

vbSystemModal, 68
vbYes, 66
vbYesNo, 65
vbYesNoCancel, 65
version numbers
determining for installed files, 268
determining for running programs, 275
Version property
WScript object, 39
Visual Basic
DHTML events, 247
DialogBox component, 242
forms, 231, 232
referencing type libraries in, 114
twips, 244
Visual Basic 6 Object Browser, 42
Visual Basic for Applications (VBA), 11
file pattern matching, 166
VolumeName property
Drive object, 152

W

web sites
creating URL shortcuts to, 91
WebBrowser control, 244
Whiteboard component, 259
wildcards
folder operations with, 156
in CopyFile() method, 143
in source, 144
Win32 API functions
calling from withing scripts, 51
Win32 applications, 12
Win32 console applications, 20
Win32 SDK, 225
Windows 2000, 8, 75
custom folder icons in, 191
disk quotas, 152
returning list of running processes, 267
Windows 9x
custom folder icons in, 191
deleting from registry under, 79
folder settings, 183
Windows applications
Windows architecture and, 8
Windows Explorer
creating scripts in New menu, 296
details view of folders, 190
renaming files from, 189
Windows GUI
management and execution of WSH scripts from, 13
Windows NT, 15
deleting from registry under, 79
user-specific folders in, 101
Windows Script Component Wizard, 201
code generated by, 204, 205
Windows Script Components (WSCs), 106, 118, 200, 218
code reusability and, 181
creating, 200
defined, 181
generating a type library, 213
operation of, 200
requirements for, 182
writing with Windows Script Component Wizard, 201
Windows Script (.ws) files, 106. *See also* **.ws files**
Windows Script Host (WSH)
applications of, 13
availability of, 7
changing default host, 25
components, 33, 251
defined, 7, 8
executables, 19
facilities installed with, 27
features of, 13
history of, 9
limitations of, 13
modules, 19
need for, 8, 9
programming registry with, 71
property page, 28
purpose of, 10
scripting engine compatibility, 11
system adminstration, 15
uses of, 9, 12, 16
version 1.0
code reusability, 181
importing classes into VBScript files, 196
limitations of, 106
scripts, 106
specifying timeouts in, 44

version 2.0
code reusability, 182
importing classes into VBScript files, 197
importing classes with, 125
new features, 105
reusable code demonstration, 194
Windows Script support, 22
WSH 1.0 limitations and, 106
WSH object model features, 119
Windows Script Interfaces
defined, 11
initialization of, 34
Windows shell
activating script files from, 27
defined, 8
Windows system layer, 8
WindowStyle property
WshShortcut object, 87
WinMain() function, 81
With statement
in VBScript 5.0, 125
Word documents
bookmarks in, 288
creating dynamically, 282
creating programmatically, 289
printing, 293
Word object model
initializing, 289
WorkingDirectory property
WshShortcut object, 87
Write() method
TextStream object, 162
writeable properties, 206
WriteBlankLines() method
TextStream object, 162
WriteLine() method
TextStream object, 162, 260, 267
write-only properties, 206
WSC kit, 201
WScript object, 21, 37
creating, 49
defined, 35
event handling, 52
functions of, 38
getting information about, 39
initialization of, 35
methods, 39
object management functions, 46
properties, 38
wscript.exe, 19, 33. *See also* **host executable**
associating encoded scripts with, 306
changing default host, 25
command line, 23
cscript.exe and, 20
Echo() method in, 21
WSCs. *See* **Windows Script Components**
WSH. *See* **Windows Script Host**
WSH object model
implementation of, 61
purpose of, 61
structure of, 35
WSH 2.0 features, 119
WSH root object, 37
instantiation of, 34
WSH scripts
assigning a custom extension to, 35
changing script extension, 26
defined, 26
drag-and-drop handler for, 299
encoding, 304
execution of, 27
file extensions, 26
running, 56, 299
shell support for, 27, 296
sinking Internet Explorer events, 54
using ADO in, 281, 282, 284
using external data in, 299
WshArguments collection object, 37, 56, 58, 299
command line string and, 299
drag-and-drop handler and, 299
implementation of, 36
properties, 56
WshCollection object, 37, 96, 102
properties, 102
WshEnvironment object, 37, 96
enumerating variables in, 98
method, 97
options, 97
properties, 97
WshNetwork object, 35, 37, 92
internal restructuring of, 119
methods for managing network connections, 93
methods for managing printers, 94
ProgID of, 92
properties, 93
WshCollection object returned by, 102

wshom.ocx, 33
defined, 37, 61
objects made available by, 37
WshShell object, 35, 37, 62, 99
creating, 62
data type conversions, 71
methods, 63, 71
programming interface, 62
properties, 63
running external programs with, 79
WshShortcut object, 37, 61, 86
creating shortcuts with, 88
method, 87
properties, 87
resolving shortcuts and, 89
WshSpecialFolders object, 37, 82, 87, 96, 99
folders whose paths can be retrieved by, 100
navigating, 101
properties, 99
WshUrlShortcut object, 37, 91

X

XML
elements, 108, 109
processing instructions, 111
XML declaration, 110
XML entities, 111
XML files
.ws files as, 106, 108
XML tags
used in .ws files, 108, 109
XML-based languages
features of, 108

Y

Yes button, 65, 66